THE UNCERTAIN REASONER'S COMPANION

A MATHEMATICAL PERSPECTIVE

Cambridge Tracts in Theoretical Computer Science

Managing Editor Professor C.J. van Rijsbergen,
Department of Computing Science, University of Glasgow

Editorial Board

S. Abramsky, *Department of Computing Science, Imperial College of Science and Technology*
P.H. Aczel, *Department of Computer Science, University of Manchester*
J.W. de Bakker, *Centrum voor Wiskunde en Informatica, Amsterdam*
J.A. Goguen, *Programming Research Group, University of Oxford*
Y. Gurevich, *Department of Electrical Engineering and Computer Science, University of Michigan*
J.V. Tucker, *Department of Mathematics and Computer Science, University College of Swansea*

Titles in the series

1. G.Chaitin *Algorithmic Information Theory*
2. L.C.Paulson *Logic and Computation*
3. M.Spivey *Understanding Z*
4. G.Revesz *Lambda Calculus, Combinators and Functional Programming*
5. A.Ramsay *Formal Methods in Artificial Intelligence*
6. S.Vickers *Topology via Logic*
7. J-Y.Girard, Y.Lafont & P.Taylor *Proofs and Types*
8. J.Clifford *Formal Semantics & Pragmatics for Natural Language Processing*
9. M.Winslett *Updating Logical Databases*
10. K.McEvoy & J.V.Tucker (eds) *Theoretical Foundations of VLSI Design*
11. T.H.Tse *A Unifying Framework for Stuctured Analysis and Design Models*
12. G.Brewka *Nonmonotonic Reasoning*
14. S.G.Hoggar *Mathematics for Computer Graphics*
15. S.Dasgupta *Design Theory and Computer Science*
17. J.C.M.Baeten (ed) *Applications of Process Algebra*
18. J.C.M.Baeten & W. P.Weijland *Process Algebra*
21. D.A.Wolfram *The Clausal Theory of Types*
23. E.-R.Olderog *Nets, Terms and Formulas*
26. P.D.Mosses *Action Semantics*
27. W.H.Hesselink *Programs, Recursion and Unbounded Choice*
28. P.Padawitz *Deductive and Declarative Programming*
29. P.Gärdenfors (ed) *Belief Revision*
30. M.Anthony & N.Biggs *Computational Learning Theory*
31. T.F.Melham *Higher Order Logic and Hardware Verification*
32. R.L.Carpenter *The Logic of Typed Feature Structures*
33. E.G.Manes *Predicate Transformer Semantics*
34. F.Nielson & H.R.Nielson *Two Level Functional Languages*
35. L.Feijs & H.Jonkers *Formal Specification and Design*
36. S.Mauw & G.J.Veltink (eds) *Algebraic Specification of Communication Protocols*
37. V.Stavridou *Formal Methods in Circuit Design*

THE UNCERTAIN REASONER'S COMPANION
A MATHEMATICAL PERSPECTIVE

J.B. Paris

University of Manchester

CAMBRIDGE
UNIVERSITY PRESS

Published by the Press Syndicate of the University of Cambridge
The Pitt Building, Trumpington Street, Cambridge CB2 1RP
40 West 20th Street, New York, NY 10011-4211, USA
10 Stamford Road, Oakleigh, Melbourne 3166, Australia

© Cambridge University Press 1994

First published 1994

Printed in Great Britain at the University Press, Cambridge

Library of Congress cataloguing in publication data available

British Library cataloguing in publication data available

ISBN 0 521 46089 1 hardback

Contents

Introduction   ix

1 Motivation   1
  Example $\mathbb{E}$ 1
  Mathematical Formulation   4
  The Central Question   6
  Further Assumptions   7

2 Belief as Probability   10
  A Representation for Probability Functions   13
  A Reformulation of Question Q   14

3 Justifying Belief as Probability   17
  First Justification   17
  Second Justification   19
  Third Justification   24
  Criticism   33

4 Dempster–Shafer Belief   34
  An Equivalent Definition of DS-belief Functions   34
  First Justification   37
  Plausibility   38
  A Representation of DS-belief Functions   39
  Probability and DS-belief   39
  Conditional DS-belief   42
  Second Justification   48

5 Truth-functional Belief   52
  Justification for the choice of $F_\neg$ 54
  Justification for the choice of $F_\wedge$ 55
  Justification for the choice of $F_\vee$ 60
  Possibility Theory   62
  Conditional Possibility   65

6 Inference Processes   **66**

Inference Processes   68

Some Inference Processes based on Typicality   69

Some Inference Processes based on Information   76

Inference Processes for DS-belief Functions   79

Inference Processes for Truth-functional Belief   80

7 Principles of Uncertain Reasoning   **82**

Equivalence Principle   82

Principle of Irrelevant Information   87

Continuity   89

Open-mindedness Principle   95

Renaming Principle   95

Obstinacy Principle   99

Relativisation Principle 100

Principle of Independence 101

Atomicity Principle 102

Calibration 105

Discussion 108

8 Belief Revision   **112**

Bayesian Updating 114

Jeffrey's Updating 116

Minimum Cross Entropy Updating 118

Justifications for Minimum Cross Entropy Updating 120

9 Independence   **127**

An Example 128

Prospector Style Independence 129

Belief Networks 134

10 Computational Feasibility   **139**

Consistency 141

Calculation 148

Belief Networks and Complexity 155

11 Uncertain Reasoning in the Predicate Calculus   **160**

A Formalization 161

Belief as Probability 161

A Representation Theorem 164

The Completely Independent Solution 172

12 Principles of Predicate Uncertain Reasoning   **178**
     The Unary Case 183
     Carnap's Continuum of Inductive Methods 189
     First Justification 190
     Second Justification 194
     Solutions via Propositional Inference Processes 197

Glossary   **200**

Bibliography   **202**

Index   **207**

Introduction

This book developed out of lecture courses in Uncertain Reasoning given at the University of Manchester in 1989 and 1991 as part of the Master of Science degree in Mathematical Logic and is aimed at readers with some mathematical background who wish to understand the mathematical foundations of the subject. Thus the emphasis is on providing mathematical formulations, analyses and justifications of what I see as some of the major questions and assumptions underlying present day theories of Uncertain Reasoning whilst avoiding, as far as possible, lengthy philosophical discussions on the one hand and precise computer algorithms on the other. Much of the material presented appears already, in some form or other, in published papers, so that my main contribution is the assembling and presenting of it within a unified framework.

My hope is that by doing so I might encourage more 'mathematicians' to take an active interest in the subject whilst at the same time offering to those currently working on practical applications in the field easy access to some of the mathematics underlying their assumptions. In short it is the sort of book which I wish had been available to me when I first entered the area.

The subject of Uncertain Reasoning (also referred to as Approximate Reasoning and Reasoning under Uncertainty) dates back to Plato, if not beyond, but has seen an exponential expansion in the last decade with the drive towards intelligent computers, especially so called expert systems. In consequence it would be impractical to include any sort of complete bibliography in this short text. For that reason I have not even attempted it, preferring instead to quote mainly just those few papers containing original proofs of the results presented. Even so, I still run a risk, with such a voluminous literature, of failing to quote papers which contain similar, or even identical results, proved entirely independently, and indeed of omitting pertinent new material of which I was unaware. Anticipating this I herewith apologise to such authors for my omissions.

A second consequence of the current enormous activity in the area is that many of the topics discussed herein may well be discredited, or at least unfashionable, in ten, or even five, years time. Acknowledging this I can at least fall back on the defence, not available to many authors in the subject, that a theorem, at least, remains a theorem even if the original reason for proving it disappears, whilst a personal opinion has scientific value only as long as there remain people to hold it. (That is not to say that I have been entirely successful in avoiding subjectivity myself!)

Whilst this book is aimed at readers with some mathematical background I have attempted, as far as possible, to keep it self-contained and to assume as little prior knowledge of the reader as possible. In consequence I shall, on occasion, have to re-prove special cases of general results from mathematics. The advantage however to the reader in not having to be constantly consulting other textbooks seems to me to justify this approach. Thus provided the reader is familiar with the propositional and predicate calculus and elementary analysis and linear algebra he should have no difficulty with any of the chapters, with the possible exception of the section on Computational Complexity which will assume a knowledge of the basic notions in that area.

On a final point, the gender of the 'expert' throughout this text was decided by a toss of the coin and came out male. At the publisher's suggestion the medical patient was designated female. I am not sure this has done much to even things up!

Acknowledgements

I would like to thank Alena Vencovská for her enormous contribution to the material, research and preparation of this book. In fact she should really be a joint author.

I would also like to thank all those who, mostly unknowingly, provided material presented in this book and those who gave advice and opinions on earlier versions of this text, in particular George Wilmers, Ian Maung, Paul Courtney, Nic Wilson and Wilfrid Hodges. Finally I would like to express my appreciation to Julia Newbold and Francesca Moss for their skilful LaTeXing.

Chapter 1 ————————————————

Motivation

We shall structure this text around a particular question which seems to us to be central to the subject of uncertain reasoning. In order to introduce this question we shall first give a simple example where it arises naturally.

Example $\mathbb{E}$

Suppose that we are interested in constructing an expert system, say for diagnosing patients who turn up at a health centre. That is, we want to develop a computational device which, when given as input the presence, absence, severity of the various signs, symptoms, features etc. applying to the patient, outputs an acceptably accurate qualified diagnosis. Arguing that a doctor himself appears to be just such a device might lead us to be optimistic that this might be possible, provided that we can build enough knowledge and expertise into our expert system.

From discussions with a doctor we are led to understand that in the course of his work he has acquired a number of pieces of general knowledge which he considers relevant to this problem of diagnosis and these he freely relates to us. In this way we obtain a set, $\mathbb{K}_0$ say, of general knowledge statements such as:

Symptom D strongly suggests disease B
Symptom D is rather uncommon
A patient of type E cannot have disease B
About 50% of patients are of type E
Condition F is mainly found in patients of type E
etc. etc.

Having spent a sufficient length of time collecting $\mathbb{K}_0$ we might now feel that we can construct a reasonable expert system by simply reading the answers out of $\mathbb{K}_0$. For example if we were to input just

Patient complains of symptom D

the device would respond

Disease B strongly suggested

by directly using the corresponding ready made 'rule' in $\mathbb{K}_0$.

The trouble with this expert system is that it will only work if our input corresponds to the antecedent of a rule in $\mathbb{K}_0$, as in the above example. But what if instead we knew (just) that

Patient complains of symptom D and exhibits condition F

and we do not have a rule in $\mathbb{K}_0$ linking this antecedent directly to the diagnosis? The absence of any such rule might lead us to conclude that, despite the time already taken, $\mathbb{K}_0$ was still not a good representation of the doctor's knowledge, after all the doctor would not get stuck here, he would be able to pull out a suitable rule. So perhaps we should go back and directly ask the doctor for rules to cover all such eventualities.

However it should be clear that it is completely infeasible to do this since in the course of collecting $\mathbb{K}_0$, even for quite simple expert systems, the doctor has probably mentioned at least 40 signs, symptoms etc. so that asking the doctor for rules to cover all such combinations would require him to produce at least 2^{40}, around a million million, such rules.

Clearly then we had better come up with a method of producing such rules ourselves on the basis of what we do have, i.e. $\mathbb{K}_0$.

Furthermore we might well be optimistic that this is possible. After all the doctor surely cannot have all these rules already written down in his head, he must be generating them in some way from what he does know and hence, since he has endeavoured to embody in $\mathbb{K}_0$ what he believes to be relevant, $\mathbb{K}_0$ should surely suffice as a basis for us to generate, at least a reasonable approximation to, the rules the doctor would have given. The question is, how should we do it?

Similarly we might ask the same question not about unspecified rules but about unspecified base rates. For example the doctor can, apparently without much difficulty, say how likely he thinks it is for a patient to suffer from B and F. Arguing as above we might again feel that an approximation to this likelihood (we use such words here in a non-technical sense) should be derivable from $\mathbb{K}_0$. The question again is how?

Of course the reader might object to the above argument although whether or not one accepts it, the problem of constructing an expert system from $\mathbb{K}_0$ remains the same. However in the absence of such an argument there seems no reason, per se, why our endeavour should, or could, succeed.

The most natural way then to construct such an expert system in this situation would be to devise a system of inductive inference, or as we shall call it *uncertain reasoning*, which given the information $\mathbb{K}_0$ about the doctor would enable us to infer, or predict, the answers the doctor would give to further questions. In this text we would like to consider how this might be achieved. Indeed we would like to do rather more than that. For interesting and practically important as it may be to predict the human expert it is not our wish to limit ourselves to such a singular example of uncertain reasoning (although of course many of our ideas and stimuli will arise from considering ourselves). Rather we shall consider the more general problem of predicting the answers of an 'intelligent' agent, or expert (but not necessarily human) given only some fragment K of the agent's general knowledge. Thus we shall be interested in the *possibilities* for uncertain reasoning, arising out of making various mathematical assumptions, which might be considered reasonable for an 'intelligent' agent, although perhaps not holding for real human agents. (Hence the reader might find that this text makes more sense if expressions like 'doctor', 'agent', 'expert' are interpreted, as we intend, in this wider sense.) We shall pursue this interest by presenting some, popular, modes of uncertain reasoning which have been proposed for answering the sort of problem raised in example $\mathbb{E}$, and will concentrate in particular on the mathematical assumptions underlying them, and the justifications and consequences of these assumptions.

It is important here to emphasize that we are interested in the problem of predicting the expert's answers to questions. For in many such situations there are also notions of 'correct' answers. For example in $\mathbb{E}$ the actual proportion of patients suffering B and F at similar clinics in the past year could be taken as a 'correct' answer to the question of how likely it is that a patient will be suffering from B and F. Presumably the prediction of some such correct answers is the primary aim of expert-system builders. However, as we said, our target will be the expert's answer whether or not it agrees with 'the correct answer'.

One could, of course, question here why there should be any limit on the possibilities for uncertain reasoning, why any one mechanism, no matter how silly, would not be just as acceptable for generating answers given, say, $\mathbb{K}_0$ as in example $\mathbb{E}$, as any other. In reply to this, however, we observe that this would, for example, allow us to conclude from $\mathbb{K}_0$ that

Symptom D is a certain indicator of patient being of type E

However this conclusion appears inadmissible since it directly contradicts $\mathbb{K}_0$. Similarly the conclusion, based on the displayed first five statements in $\mathbb{K}_0$, that

Patients complaining of symptom D invariably have condition F

whilst not directly contradicting these first five statements would certainly seem to fly in the face of reasonableness or common sense. Thus requirements of consistency and common sense certainly seem to provide some sort of limits on the possibilities for uncertain reasoning.

Additional limits could also be argued for on other grounds. For example the knowledge statements $\mathbb{K}_0$ must, in some sense, be true for the doctor (i.e. he must be a model or semantics for $\mathbb{K}_0$) and so, presumably, his answers should also have this same property. Thus considerations as to the nature of this model can provide further limitations. For example we might impose requirements of practical feasibility, or accuracy, or ability to be formed by a learning strategy, on the model.

Before doing any of these things however we need to formulate the general problem suggested by example $\mathbb{E}$ in a mathematical setting.

Mathematical Formulation

Except for the last two chapters of this text we shall work within the following, limited, formulation of the problem. We shall assume that the general knowledge statements given by the expert (e.g. doctor in example $\mathbb{E}$) can be written in the form of a set of equations involving a belief function defined on sentences of a propositional language. This is best explained by an example. Consider the statement from example $\mathbb{E}$,

Symptom D is rather uncommon

We might express this as

$$Bel_0(D) = 0.01$$

where $Bel_0(X)$ stands for 'the doctor's belief that a random patient, or more concretely *the next patient through the door*, will have property X' and 0.01 is a number on the scale $[0,1]$ corresponding to 'rather uncommon' in this context, where $0 \equiv$ 'never', $1 \equiv$ 'always (or certain)' and $\frac{1}{2} \equiv$ 'no preference (or indifference)'.

Similarly the knowledge statement

Symptom D strongly suggests disease B

might be expressed as

$$Bel_0(B|D) = 0.9$$

where $Bel_0(X|Y)$ stands for the doctor's 'belief that the next patient through the door will have property X, given that he has property Y' and 0.9 corresponds to 'strongly suggested' on the same scale $[0,1]$.

More formally then, we are treating the signs, symptoms, diseases etc. such as B, D, E, F as propositional variables in some finite propositional language L and

$$Bel_0(\ ) : SL \longrightarrow [0,1]$$

$$Bel_0(\ |\ ) : SL \times SL \longrightarrow [0,1]$$

where SL are the sentences of L (formed by repeated application of the connectives $\vee$ (and), $\wedge$ (or), $\neg$ (not) to the propositional variables). We shall refer to $Bel_0(\ )$ as a *belief function* and $Bel_0(\ |\ )$ as a *conditional belief function*, and their values in $[0,1]$ as belief values. (Various other names are used in the literature, for example truth values, certainty factors, confidence coefficients.) We shall assume for the present that in this way then $\mathbb{K}_0$ of example $\mathbb{E}$ can be re-expressed as a finite set of identities over the reals, $\mathbb{R}$, involving $Bel_0(\theta)$ and further indentities involving $Bel_0(\phi \mid \psi)$ for some $\theta, \phi, \psi \in SL$.

A few comments are in order here. Firstly why are we justified in using real numbers in $[0, 1]$ to represent belief values? Well, in a sense, this does not *yet* need any justification because we could simply claim that 0.01, say, is just a code for 'rather uncommon' so that $Bel_0(D) = 0.01$ is just a coded version of '*Symptom D is rather uncommon*' and nothing has been lost. However this defence will not survive long since it is clear that our next step will be to apply arithmetic relations and operations to these numbers and hence, in effect, between their decoded versions. In particular the key use of this will be in the linear ordering so that, for example, it will be implicit that 0.01 ($\equiv$ rather uncommon) expresses less belief than 0.9 ($\equiv$ strongly suggested) which itself is less than 1 ($\equiv$ certain).

Indeed it may be that this assumption, that beliefs can be ordered like the reals in $[0, 1]$, may be sending us on the wrong path (what would that mean?) or at least unduly limiting the possibilities we spoke of earlier. However, in favour of this assumption it does seem that in practice the expert is able, when asked, to express his beliefs on this scale, whereas we see no more attractive setting for belief values. Indeed in the formalisation of our example $\mathbb{E}$ (and others like it) we shall assume that the figures given are the ones the doctor, or expert, would himself match with his verbal expressions of qualified belief.

A second objection here, perhaps, to this formalisation is that it is far from clear that the doctor's (or in general, expert's) beliefs are all of the same nature or quality; for certainly they might well arise from various origins. For example, whilst some of the doctor's beliefs might seem to result from some subconscious, personal, statistical data, it is surely the case that others have, at least partly, been influenced by reading books, by analogy, by symmetry, by personal prejudices etc. etc. (Indeed although use of the terms 'doctor' and 'expert' might suggest that they possess some sort of divine authority we wish to dispel here and now any misconception on this point. The term 'expert', or a synonym for it, will be used simply for the agent who provides the knowledge statements. We do not assume any objective truth for these statements.) Of course the fact that beliefs may come from various sources does not of itself imply that there are various different sorts of belief, just as iron is the same thing no matter where it is mined or how it is extracted, although it is certainly a point which we may well be forced to reconsider in the future. For this text however we shall try to simplify matters as much as possible by treating all beliefs as being of the same quality and nature.

The Central Question

Referring still to example $\mathbb{E}$, $\mathbb{K}_0$ has now been formalised as a finite set of identities of the forms

$$Bel_0(\theta) = a, \quad Bel_0(\phi \mid \psi) = b,$$

for some $\theta, \phi, \psi \in SL$. Here $Bel_0(\ )$ is the doctor's belief function, $Bel_0(\ \mid \ )$ his conditional belief function and these identities represent all we know about these functions. What we would like is to be able to predict the values of $Bel_0(\chi)$, $Bel_0(\chi \mid \eta)$ for some other $\chi, \eta \in SL$.

Rephrasing this slightly, let K_0 be the result of replacing the doctor's actual belief functions $Bel_0(\ )$, $Bel_0(\ \mid \ )$ throughout $\mathbb{K}_0$ by function variables $Bel(\ )$, $Bel(\ \mid \ )$ standing for a belief function and a conditional belief function respectively. Then our problem can be expressed as: what values to give to $Bel(\chi)$, $Bel(\chi \mid \eta)$ on the basis of the set of constraints K_0, for $\chi, \eta \in SL$? Notice that $Bel(\ ) = Bel_0(\ )$, $Bel(\ \mid \ ) = Bel_0(\ \mid \ )$ is a solution of K_0 and that this sums up all we know about $Bel_0(\ )$ and $Bel_0(\ \mid \ )$. This question is a special case of the main question around which this book will be centred, viz.

Q *Suppose K is a finite consistent set of linear constraints over $\mathbb{R}$,*

$$\sum_{j=1}^{r} a_{ji} Bel(\theta_j) = b_i \qquad i = 1, ..., m,$$

$$\sum_{j=1}^{r'} a'_{ji} Bel(\theta_j \mid \phi_i) = b'_i \qquad i = 1, ..., m',$$

for some $\theta_j, \phi_i \in SL$. Then on the basis of K what value should be given to $Bel(\theta)$, $Bel(\theta \mid \phi)$ for $\theta, \phi \in SL$?

Here L is a finite language for the propositional calculus and $Bel(\ )$, $Bel(\ \mid \ )$ are function variables standing, respectively, for a belief function and a conditional belief function, that is functions from SL into $[0, 1]$ and from $SL \times SL$ into $[0, 1]$. (Of course in the rest of this text we shall often blur this distinction between a variable standing for a function and an actual function, for example using Bel in both roles.)

Several points about this question Q require explanation. Firstly *consistent* here means that, with whatever additional conditions currently apply to $Bel(\ )$, $Bel(\ \mid \ )$, there is a solution satisfying these conditions and the equations in K.

Secondly we have generalised K beyond the form (assumed) of K_0 in example $\mathbb{E}$ by allowing linear constraints rather than the simple identities that, in practice, arise naturally. As we shall see shortly however, further conditions which we shall consider imposing on $Bel(\ )$, $Bel(\ \mid \ )$, will naturally give rise to such generalised constraints, so that mathematically it is more elegant to start with this general form. (It is true of course that this might complicate the derivation of the 'answers' $Bel(\theta)$, $Bel(\theta \mid \phi)$ we might propose, and indeed many practical procedures do limit themselves to the former, simpler, K.) Obviously our K could be generalised still further by allowing polynomial, rather than just linear, constraints; indeed the reader might have felt that our original natural language knowledge statements in example $\mathbb{E}$ could conceivably have yielded such constraints. However this introduces some significant new difficulties, as we shall see in Chapter 9, so on the basis that we already have problems enough, we shall resist the temptation. Other possible generalisations here would be to allow inequalities and/or constraints mixing conditional and unconditional beliefs. However these seem rather unnatural to us so we shall stick for the present with the above question Q.

Finally, and most importantly, in question Q the word 'should' is not intended to suggest necessity but rather invites a search for justifications.

Further Assumptions

Unfortunately as things stand it would be very exceptional if the set K of constraints in question Q determined $Bel(\theta)$ or $Bel(\theta \mid \phi)$ without any further assumptions. Thus we need, in general, to invoke some additional assumptions and considerations. Ideally these should have some sort of justification in terms of the context although this ideal is in practice sometimes flouted for the sake of producing a working device.

As a first step assumptions frequently involve properties of $Bel(\ )$ and $Bel(\mid)$ beyond simply that they are functions from SL, $SL \times SL$ into $[0, 1]$ respectively. Some particularly popular ones which we shall consider in this text are:

(a) **$Bel(\ )$ is a probability function.** That is, for $\theta, \phi \in SL$,

$(P1)$ if $\models \theta$ (*i.e.* θ is a tautology) then $Bel(\theta) = 1$,

$(P2)$ if $\models \neg(\theta \wedge \phi)$ (*i.e.* θ and ϕ are exclusive)
       then $Bel(\theta \vee \phi) = Bel(\theta) + Bel(\phi)$,

and $Bel(\mid)$ is the corresponding conditional probability, that is,

$$Bel(\theta \mid \phi) = \frac{Bel(\theta \wedge \phi)}{Bel(\phi)} \quad \text{for} \quad Bel(\phi) \neq 0.$$

Thus $(P1)$ says that tautologies get belief value 1 whilst $(P2)$ says that if θ and ϕ cannot both be satisfied at the same time then the belief value of $\theta \vee \phi$ is the sum of the belief value of θ and the belief value of ϕ.

(b) **$Bel(\ )$ is a Dempster–Shafer belief function.** That is, for

$\theta, \phi, \theta_1, ..., \theta_n \in SL,$

(DS1) if $\models \theta$ then $Bel(\theta) = 1,\ Bel(\neg\theta) = 0,$

(DS2) if $\models (\theta \leftrightarrow \phi)$ (i.e. θ and ϕ are logically equivalent, written $\theta \equiv \phi$)
then $Bel(\theta) = Bel(\phi),$

(DS3) $Bel(\bigvee_{i=1}^{n} \theta_i) \geq \sum_{\emptyset \neq S \subseteq \{1,...,n\}} (-1)^{|S|-1} Bel(\bigwedge_{i \in S} \theta_i),$

and

$$Bel(\theta \mid \phi) = \frac{Bel(\theta \vee \neg\phi) - Bel(\neg\phi)}{1 - Bel(\neg\phi)} \quad \text{for} \quad Bel(\neg\phi) \neq 1.$$

(Here $\mid S \mid$ is the cardinality of the set S.)

Thus (DS1) says that tautologies get Dempster–Shafer belief 1 and their negations belief 0. (DS2) says that logically equivalent sentences get the same belief and
hence, with (DS1), that contradictions get belief 0. We shall leave any explanation
of (DS3) and conditional Dempster–Shafer belief until Chapter 4.

(c) **Bel( ) and Bel(|) are truth–functional.** That is, there are functions

$$F_\wedge, F_\vee, F_| : [0,1]^2 \longrightarrow [0,1] \quad \text{and} \quad F_\neg : [0,1] \longrightarrow [0,1]$$

such that, for $\theta, \phi \in SL,$

$$Bel(\theta \wedge \phi) = F_\wedge(Bel(\theta), Bel(\phi)),$$

$$Bel(\theta \vee \phi) = F_\vee(Bel(\theta), Bel(\phi)),$$

$$Bel(\neg\theta) = F_\neg(Bel(\theta)),$$

$$Bel(\theta \mid \phi) = F_|(Bel(\theta), Bel(\phi)).$$

A particular example of such functions (which is frequently referred to as fuzzy logic)
is

$$F_\wedge(x, y) = \min(x, y), \quad F_\vee(x, y) = \max(x, y),$$

$$F_\neg(x) = 1 - x, \qquad F_|(x, y) = \min(1, 1 - y + x).$$

In the next four chapters we shall consider justifications and consequences of each
of these three assumptions in turn.

It will later be clear in (a),(b) that if, in the definition of conditional belief, the
denominator is zero then so is the numerator. Hence for (a) and (b) the conditional
constraints in K in question Q can be replaced by equivalent unconditional linear

constraints provided we take as vacuous conditional constraints in cases (a) and (b) when the denominator is zero.

Thus, whilst working under assumptions (a) or (b) we may assume that the set K of constraints in Q has the simpler form

$$\sum_{j=1}^{r} a_{ji} Bel(\theta_j) = b_i \quad i = 1, ..., m,$$

and restrict ourselves to the problem of assigning a value to $Bel(\theta)$.

Throughout this text L, L', etc. stand for *finite* propositional languages unless otherwise stated. Unless otherwise indicated we shall assume that $L = \{p_1, ..., p_n\}$ throughout.

Chapter 2

Belief as Probability

In this chapter we shall prove some simple properties of probability functions and consider some consequences of the assumption that Bel satisfies $(P1\text{--}2)$ for the question Q.

Throughout the chapter we assume that $Bel : SL \to [0, 1]$ satisfies$(P1\text{--}2)$, that is, for $\theta, \phi \in SL$,

(P1)   If $\models \theta$ then $Bel(\theta) = 1$,

(P2)   If $\models \neg(\theta \wedge \phi)$ then $Bel(\theta \vee \phi) = Bel(\theta) + Bel(\phi)$.

Notice that if V is a (two-valued) valuation on L in the usual sense of the propositional calculus then V satisfies $(P1\text{--}2)$ and hence is a probability function. In this sense belief as probability extends the classical two-valued semantics.

Proposition 2.1 *For* $\theta, \phi, \theta_1, \theta_2, ..., \theta_n \in SL$

(a) $Bel(\neg\theta) = 1 - Bel(\theta)$.

(b) If $\models \theta$ then $Bel(\neg\theta) = 0$.

(c) If $\theta \models \phi$ then $Bel(\theta) \leq Bel(\phi)$ and if $\models (\theta \leftrightarrow \phi)$ then $Bel(\theta) = Bel(\phi)$.

(d) $Bel(\theta \vee \phi) = Bel(\theta) + Bel(\phi) - Bel(\theta \wedge \phi)$.

More generally,

$$Bel\left(\bigvee_{i=1}^{n} \theta_i\right) = \sum_{\emptyset \neq S \subseteq \{1,...,n\}} (-1)^{|S|-1} Bel\left(\bigwedge_{i \in S} \theta_i\right).$$

Proof (a) follows directly from$(P1\text{--}2)$ since $\models \theta \vee \neg\theta$ and $\models \neg(\theta \wedge \neg\theta)$.

(b) now follows from $(P1)$ and (a).

(c) If $\theta \models \phi$ then $\models \neg(\theta \wedge \neg\phi)$ so, by $(P2)$,

$$1 \geq Bel(\theta \vee \neg\phi) = Bel(\theta) + Bel(\neg\phi) = Bel(\theta) + 1 - Bel(\phi)$$

by (a), and (c) follows. The second part now follows since if $\models (\theta \leftrightarrow \phi)$ then $\theta \models \phi$ and $\phi \models \theta$.

(d) By (c), $Bel(\theta \vee \phi) = Bel((\theta \wedge \neg\phi) \vee \phi)$, since $\models (\theta \vee \phi) \leftrightarrow ((\theta \wedge \neg\phi) \vee \phi)$. By (P2), this equals $Bel(\theta \wedge \neg\phi) + Bel(\phi)$. Also, by (c) and (P2) respectively, $Bel(\theta) = Bel((\theta \wedge \neg\phi) \vee (\theta \wedge \phi)) = Bel(\theta \wedge \neg\phi) + Bel(\theta \wedge \phi)$. Removing $Bel(\theta \wedge \neg\phi)$ gives the result.

The generalization is proved by induction on $n \geq 2$. Assume the result for $n-1$. Then, using (c) freely and collecting summands which do/do not contain $(\theta_{n-1} \vee \theta_n)$ as a conjunct,

$$Bel\left(\bigvee_{i=1}^{n} \theta_i\right) = Bel\left(\bigvee_{i=1}^{n-2} \theta_i \vee (\theta_{n-1} \vee \theta_n)\right) =$$

$$\sum_{\emptyset \neq S \subseteq \{1,\dots,n-2\}} (-1)^{|S|-1} Bel\left(\bigwedge_{i \in S} \theta_i\right) + \sum_{S \subseteq \{1,\dots,n-2\}} (-1)^{|S|} Bel\left((\theta_{n-1} \vee \theta_n) \wedge \bigwedge_{i \in S} \theta_i\right).$$

Now since

$$\models ((\theta_{n-1} \vee \theta_n) \wedge \bigwedge_{i \in S} \theta_i) \leftrightarrow (\theta_{n-1} \wedge \bigwedge_{i \in S} \theta_i) \vee (\theta_n \wedge \bigwedge_{i \in S} \theta_i)$$

we can replace $Bel((\theta_{n-1} \vee \theta_n) \wedge \bigwedge_{i \in S} \theta_i)$ in this last expression by

$$Bel(\theta_{n-1} \wedge \bigwedge_{i \in S} \theta_i) + Bel(\theta_n \wedge \bigwedge_{i \in S} \theta_i) - Bel(\theta_{n-1} \wedge \theta_n \wedge \bigwedge_{i \in S} \theta_i)$$

and sorting out terms now gives the required right hand side in (d). □

Given a probability function Bel on SL it is completely standard to extend it (partially) to a conditional probability function as well by setting

$$Bel(\theta|\phi) = \frac{Bel(\theta \wedge \phi)}{Bel(\phi)}$$

whenever $Bel(\phi) \neq 0$, whilst leaving open this value when $Bel(\phi) = 0$. We shall adopt this convention henceforth. Notice that by (c) above, as $\theta \wedge \phi \models \phi$, $Bel(\theta \wedge \phi) \leq Bel(\phi)$ so for $Bel(\phi) \neq 0$, $0 \leq Bel(\theta \mid \phi) \leq 1$.

Furthermore since $Bel(\theta \wedge \phi) \leq Bel(\phi)$, if $Bel(\phi) = 0$ then $Bel(\theta \wedge \phi) = 0$ so that the requirement $Bel(\theta \mid \phi) = \dfrac{Bel(\theta \wedge \phi)}{Bel(\phi)}$ for $Bel(\phi) \neq 0$ is equivalent to $Bel(\phi) \cdot Bel(\theta \mid \phi) = Bel(\theta \wedge \phi)$ (whether or not $Bel(\phi) = 0$).

Proposition 2.2 *Fix $\phi \in SL$ such that $Bel(\phi) \neq 0$. Then, as a function of $\theta \in SL$, $Bel(\theta|\phi)$ is a probability function, $Bel(\phi|\phi) = 1$; if $Bel(\eta|\phi) \neq 0$ then $Bel(\eta \wedge \phi) \neq 0$ and for the corresponding conditional probability function for $Bel(\theta|\phi)$,*

$$\frac{Bel(\theta \wedge \eta|\phi)}{Bel(\eta|\phi)} = Bel(\theta|\eta \wedge \phi).$$

Proof If $\models \theta$ then $\models (\theta \wedge \phi) \leftrightarrow \phi$ so using (c) of 2.1

$$Bel(\theta|\phi) = \frac{Bel(\theta \wedge \phi)}{Bel(\phi)} = \frac{Bel(\phi)}{Bel(\phi)} = 1$$

giving (P1). If $\models \neg(\theta \wedge \psi)$ then $\models \neg((\theta \wedge \phi) \wedge (\psi \wedge \phi))$ so

$$Bel(\theta \vee \psi|\phi) = \frac{Bel((\theta \vee \psi) \wedge \phi)}{Bel(\phi)} = \frac{Bel((\theta \wedge \phi) \vee (\psi \wedge \phi))}{Bel(\phi)}$$

$$= \frac{Bel(\theta \wedge \phi) + Bel(\psi \wedge \phi)}{Bel(\phi)} = Bel(\theta|\phi) + Bel(\psi|\phi)$$

The rest of the proposition follows easily by substituting in the definition. $\square$

Notice that by the identity in proposition 2.2 and proposition 2.1(c) the result of successively conditioning on $\phi_1, \phi_2, \ldots, \phi_k$ is the same as conditioning, once, on $\bigwedge_{i=1}^{k} \phi_i$ and hence is independent of the order of $\phi_1, \phi_2, \ldots, \phi_k$.

Henceforth we shall make free use of propositions 2.1 and 2.2 and (P1–2) without explicit mention.

The following theorem, due to Suppes [66], generalises proposition 2.1(c).

Theorem 2.3 *For $\phi, \theta_1, \ldots, \theta_n \in SL$, if $\theta_1, \ldots, \theta_n \models \phi$ then*

$$Bel(\phi) \geq 1 - \sum_{i=1}^{n} Bel(\neg\theta_i) = \sum_{i=1}^{n} Bel(\theta_i) - (n-1),$$

and furthermore this bound cannot be improved.

Proof The proof is by induction on n. For $n = 1$ the result is true by proposition 2.1(c). Assume the result for $n - 1$. Then $\theta_1, \ldots, \theta_n \models \phi$ implies that $\theta_1, \ldots, \theta_{n-1} \models \neg\theta_n \vee \phi$ so, by inductive hypothesis,

$$Bel(\neg\theta_n \vee \phi) \geq 1 - \sum_{i=1}^{n-1} Bel(\neg\theta_i).$$

By proposition 2.1(d)

$$Bel(\neg\theta_n \vee \phi) = Bel(\phi) + Bel(\neg\theta_n) - Bel(\theta_n \wedge \phi) \leq Bel(\phi) + Bel(\neg\theta_n),$$

and from this the result follows. To see that, in general, this bound cannot be improved, take $\theta_1, \ldots, \theta_n, \phi$ to be tautologies. $\square$

A Representation for Probability Functions

Taking L to be our 'default' language $\{p_1, p_2, ..., p_n\}$ let $\alpha_1, ..., \alpha_J$, where $J = 2^n$, run through the *atoms* of L, that is all conjunctions of the form

$$p_1^{\epsilon_1} \wedge p_2^{\epsilon_2} \wedge ... \wedge p_n^{\epsilon_n}$$

where $\epsilon_1, ..., \epsilon_n \in \{0, 1\}$ and $p^1 = p$, $p^0 = \neg p$.

Then, by the disjunctive normal form theorem, for any $\phi \in SL$ there is a unique set

$$S_\phi \subseteq \{\alpha_1, ..., \alpha_J\}$$

such that

$$\models \phi \leftrightarrow \bigvee S_\phi$$

(where we take $\bigvee \emptyset = p_1 \wedge \neg p_1$, $\bigwedge \emptyset = p_1 \vee \neg p_1$ by convention).

It is easy to see that

$$S_\phi = \{\alpha_i | \alpha_i \models \phi\},$$

$$\models (\phi \leftrightarrow \theta) \iff S_\phi = S_\theta,$$

$$\models (\phi \to \theta) \iff S_\phi \subseteq S_\theta,$$

$$S_{\theta \wedge \phi} = S_\theta \cap S_\phi,$$

$$S_{\theta \vee \phi} = S_\theta \cup S_\phi,$$

$$S_{\neg \phi} = At^L - S_\phi,$$

where $At^L = \{\alpha_i | i = 1, ..., J\}$. Now since $\models \neg(\alpha_i \wedge \alpha_j)$ for $i \neq j$, repeated use of (P2) gives

$$Bel(\phi) = Bel(\bigvee S_\phi) = \sum_{\alpha_i \in S_\phi} Bel(\alpha_i) \quad \text{(even if } S = \emptyset\text{)}.$$

Also, since $\models \bigvee_{i=1}^{J} \alpha_i$, $1 = \sum_{i=1}^{J} Bel(\alpha_i)$ and of course the $Bel(\alpha_i) \geq 0$.

From this it follows that Bel is completely determined by its values on the atoms α_i, i.e. by the vector

$$\langle Bel(\alpha_1), ..., Bel(\alpha_J) \rangle \in \mathbb{D}^L \text{ where } \mathbb{D}^L = \{\vec{x} \in \mathbb{R}^J | \vec{x} \geq 0, \sum_{i=1}^{J} x_i = 1\}.$$

Conversely given $\vec{a} \in \mathbb{D}^L$ define a function $Bel' : SL \to [0, 1]$ by

$$Bel'(\phi) = \sum_{\alpha_i \in S_\phi} a_i.$$

Then for $\models \phi$, $S_\phi = \{\alpha_1, ..., \alpha_J\}$ and $Bel'(\phi) = \sum_{i=1}^J a_i = 1$. Also if $\models \neg(\theta \wedge \phi)$ then $S_{\theta \wedge \phi} = S_\theta \cap S_\phi = \emptyset$ so $S_{\theta \vee \phi}$ is the disjoint union of S_θ and S_ϕ and

$$Bel'(\theta \vee \phi) = \sum_{\alpha_i \in S_\theta \cup S_\phi} a_i = \sum_{\alpha_i \in S_\theta} a_i + \sum_{\alpha_i \in S_\phi} a_i = Bel'(\theta) + Bel'(\phi).$$

Finally $Bel'(\alpha_i) = a_i$ since $S_{\alpha_i} = \{\alpha_i\}$, so

$$\vec{a} = \langle Bel'(\alpha_1), ..., Bel'(\alpha_J) \rangle.$$

Summing up, what we have demonstrated here is that each probability function Bel (on SL) is determined by the point $\langle Bel(\alpha_1), ..., Bel(\alpha_J) \rangle \in \mathbb{D}^L$ and conversely every point $\vec{a} \in \mathbb{D}^L$ determines a unique probability function Bel satisfying

$$\langle Bel(\alpha_1), ..., Bel(\alpha_J) \rangle = \vec{a}.$$

This 1–1 correspondence between probability functions on L and points in $\mathbb{D}^L$ will be very useful in what follows. Indeed we shall frequently identify these notions, referring to a point in $\mathbb{D}^L$ as a probability function and conversely to a probability function as a point in $\mathbb{D}^L$.

Throughout this book α, α_i etc. will stand for atoms of L unless otherwise indicated.

A Reformulation of Question Q

Let K be as in the version of Q given at the end of Chapter 1, say K is the set of constraints

$$\sum_{j=1}^r c_{ji} Bel(\theta_j) = b_i \quad i = 1, ..., m$$

consistent with $(P1$–$2)$, i.e. having a solution satisfying also $(P1$–$2)$.

Now replace each $Bel(\theta_j)$ in K by $\sum_{\alpha_i \in S_{\theta_j}} Bel(\alpha_i)$ and, in matrix notation, let

$$\langle Bel(\alpha_1), ..., Bel(\alpha_J) \rangle A_K = \vec{b}_K$$

be the resulting set of equations together with the equation

$$\sum_{i=1}^J Bel(\alpha_i) = 1.$$

Then if Bel is a probability function satisfying K, the point $\langle Bel(\alpha_1), ..., Bel(\alpha_J) \rangle$ from $\mathbb{D}^L$ satisfies

$$\vec{x} A_K = \vec{b}_K, \quad \vec{x} \geq 0.$$

Conversely if $\vec{a} \in \mathbb{R}^J$ satisfies these equalities and inequalities, then $\vec{a} \in \mathbb{D}^L$ and the corresponding probability function Bel such that $Bel(\alpha_i) = a_i$, $i = 1, ..., J$ satisfies K.

Summing up then, the natural correspondence between probability functions and points in $\mathbb{D}^L$ gives a correspondence between solutions of K satisfying (P1–2) and points in

$$V^L(K) = \{\vec{x} \in \mathbb{R}^J | \; \vec{x} A_K = \vec{b}_K, \; \vec{x} \ge 0\} \subseteq \mathbb{D}^L.$$

The problem posed by Q, namely what value should we give to $Bel(\theta)$, for Bel satisfying K and (P1–2), now becomes, what value should we give to $\sum_{\alpha_i \in S_\theta} x_i$, given that $\vec{x} A_K = \vec{b}_K$, $\vec{x} \ge 0$. Of course in this reformulated version the connection with uncertain reasoning seems to have been 'abstracted away'. Nevertheless it will often be useful to consider the reformulated version in what follows.

Notice that the matrix A_K, as presented here, has size $J \times (m+1)$ where m is the original number of equations in K. In practice it is almost always the case that m is much less than J $(= 2^n)$ so the system

$$\vec{x} A_K = \vec{b}_K, \quad \vec{x} \ge 0$$

rarely permits solving uniquely for $\vec{x}$ or indeed for $\sum_{\alpha_i \in S_\theta} x_i$, so that further assumptions beyond just (P1–2) are needed in order to answer question Q. We shall consider some such assumptions in Chapter 6. For the present however we give a simple example, using the above representation.

Example
The quintessential example of our question Q is when

$$K = \{Bel(q) = b, \; Bel(p|q) = a\}, \quad b > 0, \quad L = \{p, q\},$$

and we wish to give a value to $Bel(p)$. We consider this problem, and also the problem of assigning a value to $Bel(\neg p)$, under the assumptions (P1–2).

In this case $Bel(p|q) = a$ reduces to $Bel(p \wedge q) = aBel(q) = ab$ (using the other constraint). The atoms of L are $p \wedge q$, $p \wedge \neg q$, $\neg p \wedge q$, $\neg p \wedge \neg q$ $(= \alpha_1, \alpha_2, \alpha_3, \alpha_4$ – in that order, say) and expanding the constraints in terms of the $Bel(\alpha_i)$ gives

$$Bel(p \wedge q) = ab,$$

$$Bel(q) = Bel((p \wedge q) \vee (\neg p \wedge q)) = Bel(p \wedge q) + Bel(\neg p \wedge q) = b,$$

whilst also

$$Bel(p \wedge q) + Bel(p \wedge \neg q) + Bel(\neg p \wedge q) + Bel(\neg p \wedge \neg q) = 1.$$

Hence setting $x_i = Bel(\alpha_i)$ there is a 1–1 correspondence between probability functions (on SL) satisfying K and $\langle x_1, x_2, x_3, x_4 \rangle$ satisfying

$$\langle x_1, x_2, x_3, x_4 \rangle \begin{pmatrix} 1 & 1 & 1 \\ 1 & 0 & 0 \\ 1 & 0 & 1 \\ 1 & 0 & 0 \end{pmatrix} = \langle 1, ab, b \rangle, \quad x_1, x_2, x_3, x_4 \geq 0.$$

The minimum value of $x_1 + x_2$ over these $\langle x_1, x_2, x_3, x_4 \rangle$ (equivalently the minimum possible value of $Bel(p \wedge q) + Bel(p \wedge \neg q) = Bel(p)$ for Bel a probability function satisfying K) is ab (when $x_1 = ab$, $x_2 = 0$, $x_3 = b(1-a)$, $x_4 = 1-b$). Arguing in this way we see that for a probability function Bel satisfying K, the range of consistent values for $Bel(p)$ is

$$1 - b + ab \geq Bel(p) \geq ab,$$

and for $Bel(\neg p)$

$$1 - ab \geq Bel(\neg p) \geq b(1-a).$$

Chapter 3

Justifying Belief as Probability

In this chapter we shall present three arguments supporting the assumption that belief functions should be identified with probability functions, that is satisfy (P1–2), and that conditional belief should be identified with conditional probability (when defined).

First Justification

Returning yet again to our example $\mathbb{E}$ consider attempting to give a meaning to the doctor's statement that

Symptom D is rather uncommon

which, with the doctor's assent, has been formalised as

$$Bel_0(D) = 0.01.$$

We might argue as follows: The doctor was not born with his knowledge, the simplest explanation of where it came from is from the, presumably considerable, set M of patients x he has previously seen. Given this model of his knowledge as simply this set M the obvious explanation of his statement that symptom D is rather uncommon is that rather a small proportion of patients in M have complained of D and indeed, further, that the figure 0.01 represents an estimate of this proportion. In other words, ideally, $Bel_0(D)$ is to be identified with

$$\frac{|\{x \in M \mid x \text{ has } D\}|}{|M|}.$$

More generally $Bel_0(\theta)$ is to be identified with

$$\frac{|\{x \in M \mid x \text{ has } \theta\}|}{|M|}$$

for $\theta \in SL$, and by an exactly similar argument $Bel_0(\theta|\phi)$ is to be identified with

$$\frac{|\{x \in M \mid x \text{ has } \theta \text{ and } x \text{ has } \phi\}|}{\{x \in M \mid x \text{ has } \phi\}|}.$$

Then with this simple model of the doctor's knowledge, commonly referred to as the *urn model*, and its relationship to his knowledge statements, Bel_0 does indeed come out to be a probability function and $Bel_0(\ |\ )$ the corresponding conditional probability. To see this notice that for each $x \in M$ we can define a valuation V_x on the language L by

$\qquad V_x(p) = 1$ (i.e. true)   if x has p,
$\qquad V_x(p) = 0$ (i.e. false)   if x does not have p,

for $p \in L$ (i.e. p a propositional variable of L). Then for $\theta \in SL$, $x \in M$,

$$V_x(\theta) = 1 \iff x \text{ has } \theta$$

so

$$\{x \in M \mid x \text{ has } \theta\} = \{x \in M \mid V_x(\theta) = 1\}.$$

Now if $\models \theta$ then $V(\theta) = 1$ for any valuation V so $\{x \in M \mid V_x(\theta) = 1\} = M$ and $Bel_0(\theta) = 1$, giving (P1). Also if $\models \neg(\theta \wedge \phi)$ then for no valuation V does $V(\theta) = V(\phi) = 1$ hold (otherwise $V(\theta \wedge \phi) = 1$) and so, since

$$V(\theta \vee \phi) = 1 \iff V(\theta) = 1 \text{ or } V(\phi) = 1,$$

$\{x \in M \mid V_x(\theta \vee \phi) = 1\}$ is the union of the disjoint sets $\{x \in M \mid V_x(\theta) = 1\}$ and $\{x \in M \mid V_x(\phi) = 1\}$ from which (P2) follows easily.

An obvious criticism of this model is that it is not clear how it is supposed to model beliefs obtained indirectly, such as from books or theoretical considerations. Furthermore the model also assumes that, in this case, the doctor has complete knowledge of all the previous patients $x \in M$ which would, in practice, be quite unrealistic. In reality the doctor could never hope to have more than partial, uncertain knowledge of his past patients.

A much more serious criticism however is that even in, for example, a very specialized medical field there would be so many signs, symptoms etc. that almost every patient would present a hitherto unseen combination. Hence if the doctor attempted to determine his belief that a patient had a particular disease by looking at the proportion of previous patients exhibiting the same combination of signs and symptoms who also had this disease then he would almost always land up with the indeterminate 0/0.

A final shortcoming of this model is that it seems inapplicable in many situations in which we form beliefs, such as who will win the next Derby.

On the other hand, in situations in which it is appropriate, the urn model provides both a simple explanation of how the expert's beliefs could have arisen from his experience and a justification for the properties assumed of his belief function (i.e. being a probability function). Clearly for any assumptions about what properties belief should have the existence of such a model, explaining how such a belief function arises from the expert's experiences, is highly desirable – some might even say necessary. Unfortunately for many proposed notions of belief (such as those we shall encounter in Chapter 5) there is as yet no such satisfactory model. Instead the asserted properties of belief tend to be explained by appealing to our beliefs about beliefs.

The model we presented above could be viewed as a special case, albeit a rather natural one, of a 'possible worlds' interpretation of belief. That is we suppose that the 'real world' is one of the worlds in a non-empty set $\mathcal{W}$ of possible worlds w and that for $X \subseteq \mathcal{W}, \mu(X) \in [0,1]$ is the measure of our belief that the real world is in X. (By a *possible world* here we simply understand an object w for which some relation $w \models \theta$ is defined for $\theta \in SL$ so as to satisfy the usual inductive definition of truth. Note that we do not assume that if

$$w_1 \models \theta \Leftrightarrow w_2 \models \theta$$

for all $\theta \in SL$, then $w_1 = w_2$.) More precisely we assume of the function μ that it is defined on all subsets of $\mathcal{W}$, that $\mu(\mathcal{W}) = 1$ and $\mu(\emptyset) = 0$ and that for all $X, Y \subseteq \mathcal{W}$ with $X \cap Y = \emptyset$,

$$\mu(X \cup Y) = \mu(X) + \mu(Y),$$

i.e. μ is finitely additive.

In this context then we might imagine that an expression like $Bel(\phi) = c$ stands for

$$\mu\{w \in \mathcal{W} \mid w \models \phi\} = c.$$

For example in the above model $\mathcal{W} = M$, for $x \in M$,

$$x \models \phi \Leftrightarrow V_x(\phi) = 1$$

and for $X \subseteq M$,

$$\mu(X) = \frac{\mid X \mid}{\mid M \mid}.$$

With this interpretation it is easy to check that *Bel* is a probability function. Conversely if *Bel* is a probability function then it is generated by such a possible worlds approach, namely the possible worlds are the atoms α_i, $\alpha_i \models \phi$ has its usual meaning (i.e. equivalent to $\alpha_i \in S_\phi$) and $\mu(X) = Bel\,(\bigvee X)$, since in this case

$$Bel\,(\phi) = Bel\,(\bigvee S_\phi) = \mu(S_\phi) = \mu\{\alpha_i \mid \alpha_i \models \phi\}$$

as required.

Second Justification

A second justification for belief as probability emerges from some early work of Ramsey, de Finetti, Kemeny and Shimony (see [61], [19], [20], [37], [65]). The idea is to identify an expert's belief $Bel(\theta)$ in $\theta \in SL$ with his willingness to bet on θ being true in the real world, that is on $V(\theta) = 1$ where $V : L \rightarrow \{0, 1\}$ is the valuation which represents the true (but possibly unknown) state of the world.

To be precise suppose that $0 \leq p \leq 1$ and that the expert is required to make a choice, for stake $S > 0$, between

(i) gaining $S(1 - p)$ if $V(\theta) = 1$ whilst losing Sp if $V(\theta) = 0$,

(ii) losing $S(1 - p)$ if $V(\theta) = 1$ whilst gaining Sp if $V(\theta) = 0$.

Clearly if $p = 0$ he could not do better than to choose (i) whilst if $p = 1$ he could not do better than to choose (ii).

Furthermore if $0 \leq p' < p \leq 1$ then it would be irrational of the expert (i.e. against his best interests) to choose (i) for p and (ii) for p'. For suppose he was to make such choices. Then he stands to gain strictly more by choosing (i) at p' than he did by choosing it at p (since he would gain $S(1 - p') > S(1 - p)$ if successful and lose $Sp' < Sp$ if not). However he picked (ii) at p' so, rationally, he must believe that he stands to gain at least as much by picking (ii) at p' as (i) at p'-and hence strictly more than (i) at p. But then, as above, since $p > p'$ he stands to gain more by picking (ii) at p than he did by picking (ii) at p' and hence by picking (i) at p. But this contradicts the rationality of his choice of (i) at p.

From this it follows that if β is the least upper bound of the set of $p \in [0, 1]$ for which the expert prefers (i) then for any $0 \leq p < \beta$ he prefers (assuming as we do that he is rational) (i) at p and for any $\beta < p \leq 1$ he prefers (ii) at p.

Thus β could be said to measure the expert's willingness to bet on θ, since if $0 \leq p < \beta$ he prefers a bet which pays him if θ is true whilst if $\beta < p \leq 1$ he prefers a bet which pays him if θ is false. Identifying belief with willingness to bet then leads to identifying $Bel(\theta)$ with β.

Now suppose that $Bel(\theta)$ is defined in this way for all $\theta \in SL$. Then it could be said that these values are rational or *fair* if it is not possible for an opponent to arrange a Dutch Book against him, that is arrange a finite set of bets (for various stakes) each of which the expert would agree to but whose combined effect would be to cause him certain loss no matter what V is.

To make this notion of fairness mathematically precise notice that if $p < Bel(\theta)$ then, as above, the expert would choose (i) and would stand to gain

$$S(1 - p)V(\theta) - Sp(1 - V(\theta)) = S(V(\theta) - p),$$

where negative gain equals loss. Similarly if $Bel(\theta) < p$ then he would choose (ii) and would stand to gain

$$Sp(1 - V(\theta)) - S(1 - p)V(\theta) = -S(V(\theta) - p).$$

With this observation we can define fairness (for $Bel : SL \longrightarrow [0,1]$ as usual) to mean that there do not exist $S_i, T_j > 0$, $\theta_i, \phi_j \in SL$, $p_i < Bel(\theta_i)$, $Bel(\phi_j) < q_j$ for $i = 1, ..., n$, $j = 1, ..., m$ such that for all valuations V

$$\sum_{i=1}^{n} S_i(V(\theta_i) - p_i) - \sum_{j=1}^{m} T_j(V(\phi_j) - q_j) < 0.$$

Theorem 3.1 *If the values $Bel(\theta)$ for $\theta \in SL$ are fair then Bel satisfies (P1–2) and hence is a probability function.*

Proof To show $(P1)$ suppose that $\models \theta$ but that $Bel(\theta) < 1$, say $Bel(\theta) < q < 1$. Then since $V(\theta) = 1$ for all valuations V,

$$-1(V(\theta) - q) < 0$$

for all valuations V, contradicting fairness.

To show $(P2)$ suppose that $\models \neg(\phi \wedge \theta)$ but

$$Bel(\theta \vee \phi) \neq Bel(\theta) + Bel(\phi),$$

say $Bel(\theta \vee \phi) > Bel(\theta) + Bel(\phi)$. Pick $Bel(\theta \vee \phi) > p > q_1 + q_2$ where $q_1 > Bel(\theta), q_2 > Bel(\phi)$. Then since

$$V(\theta \vee \phi) = V(\theta) + V(\phi)$$

for all valuations V,

$$1(V(\theta \vee \phi) - p) - 1(V(\theta) - q_1) - 1(V(\phi) - q_2) = q_1 + q_2 - p < 0,$$

contradicting fairness. A similar argument shows that

$$Bel(\theta \vee \phi) \not< Bel(\theta) + Bel(\phi)$$

and hence $(P2)$ follows. □

In a similar fashion we could argue for identifying the expert's conditional belief, $Bel(\theta|\phi)$, with his willingness to bet on θ on condition that ϕ holds. (If ϕ does not hold then the bet is null and void.) Again, as above, if $p < Bel(\chi \mid \eta)$ then the expert would choose (i) and stand to gain

$$V(\eta)S(V(\chi) - p),$$

whilst if $p > Bel(\chi|\eta)$ he would choose (ii) and stand to gain

$$-V(\eta)S(V(\chi) - p).$$

Generalising the above definition then we define the values $Bel(\theta)$, $Bel(\theta|\phi)$, for $\theta, \phi \in SL$, to be fair if there do not exist $S_i, T_j, R_{i'}, U_{j'} > 0$, θ_i, ϕ_j, $\chi_{i'}$, $\eta_{i'}$, $\psi_{j'}$, $\lambda_{j'} \in SL$, $p_i < Bel(\theta_i)$, $q_j > Bel(\phi_j)$, $r_{i'} < Bel(\chi_{i'} \mid \eta_{i'})$, $u_{j'} > Bel(\psi_{j'} \mid \lambda_{j'})$ etc. such that for all valuations V,

$$\sum_{i=1}^{n} S_i(V(\theta_i) \; - \; p_i) - \sum_{j=1}^{m} T_j(V(\phi_j) - q_j) \; +$$

$$+ \; \sum_{i'=1}^{n'} R_{i'} V(\eta_{i'})(V(\chi_{i'}) - r_{i'}) - \sum_{j'=1}^{m'} U_{j'} V(\lambda_{j'})(V(\psi_{j'}) - u_{j'}) \; < \; 0.$$

Theorem 3.2 *If the values $Bel(\theta), Bel(\theta|\phi), \theta, \phi \in SL$ are fair then Bel is a probability function and*

$$Bel(\theta \mid \phi)Bel(\phi) = Bel(\theta \wedge \phi).$$

Proof We already have $(P1\text{--}2)$ from theorem 3.1. To complete the proof suppose, on the contrary, that

$$Bel(\theta \mid \phi)Bel(\phi) < Bel(\theta \wedge \phi).$$

If $Bel(\theta \mid \phi) < Bel(\theta \wedge \phi)$ then for $Bel(\theta \mid \phi) < p < r < Bel(\theta \wedge \phi)$,

$$(V(\theta \wedge \phi) - r) - V(\phi)(V(\theta) - p) = -r + V(\phi)p \le p - r < 0$$

for any valuation V, since $V(\theta \wedge \phi) = V(\theta)V(\phi)$, contradicting fairness. Hence $Bel(\phi) \ne 1$. Also $Bel(\theta|\phi) < 1$ since by proposition 2.1, $Bel(\theta \wedge \phi) \le Bel(\phi)$. Thus we can pick

$$p > Bel(\theta \mid \phi), \quad q > Bel(\phi), \quad r < Bel(\theta \wedge \phi)$$

such that $pq < r$. But then for any valuation V,

$$(V(\theta \wedge \phi) - r) - p(V(\phi) - q)) - V(\phi)(V(\theta) - p) = pq - r < 0$$

contradicting fairness.

A similar proof shows that the assumption

$$Bel(\theta \wedge \phi) < Bel(\theta \mid \phi)Bel(\phi)$$

also contradicts fairness and the required identity follows. □

To sum up then identifying belief with willingness to bet and imposing requirements of rationality forces Bel to be a probability function.

At this point it is natural to ask if the requirement of fairness does not put some additional conditions on Bel beyond simply being a probability function with the standard derived conditional probability. The following theorem shows that it does not.

Theorem 3.3 *Suppose that Bel* $: SL \longrightarrow [0,1]$ *satisfies (P1–2) and that for all* $\theta, \phi \in SL$ $Bel(\theta \mid \phi)$ *is defined and satisfies* $Bel(\theta \mid \phi)Bel(\phi) = Bel(\theta \wedge \phi)$. *Then the fairness condition is satisfied.*

Proof Suppose on the contrary that fairness fails. Then, referring back to the notation used in the definition of fairness, the inequality still holds if p_i is replaced by $Bel(\theta_i)$ etc. (Indeed this gives us an equivalent definition of fairness.) Combining the first and second and the third and fourth sums then we obtain an inequality

$$\sum_{\chi} G_\chi(V(\chi) - Bel(\chi)) + \sum_{\theta, \phi} H_{\theta, \phi} V(\phi)(V(\theta) - Bel(\theta \mid \phi)) < 0$$

which holds for all valuations V.

Now let α_i be an atom such that $Bel(\alpha_i) > 0$ and let V be the valuation such that $V(\alpha_i) = 1$, so $V(\alpha_j) = 0$ for $j \neq i$. Then for this valuation we obtain

$$\sum_{\alpha_i \in S_\chi} G_\chi - \sum_{\chi} G_\chi Bel(\chi) + \sum_{\substack{\alpha_i \in S_\phi \\ \alpha_i \in S_\theta}} H_{\theta, \phi} - \sum_{\substack{\theta \\ \alpha_i \in S_\phi}} H_{\theta, \phi} Bel(\theta \mid \phi) < 0.$$

Multiplying each such inequality by $Bel(\alpha_i)$ and summing over those α_i for which $Bel(\alpha_i) > 0$ gives

$$\sum_{\substack{Bel(\alpha_i) > 0}} \sum_{\alpha_i \in S_\chi} G_\chi Bel(\alpha_i) - \left(\sum_{\chi} G_\chi Bel(\chi) \right) \cdot \left(\sum_{\substack{Bel(\alpha_i) > 0}} Bel(\alpha_i) \right)$$

$$+ \sum_{\substack{Bel(\alpha_i) > 0}} \left(\sum_{\substack{\alpha_i \in S_\phi \\ \alpha_i \in S_\theta}} H_{\theta, \phi} Bel(\alpha_i) \right) - \sum_{\phi, \theta} H_{\theta, \phi} Bel(\theta \mid \phi) \left(\sum_{\substack{\alpha_i \in S_\phi \\ Bel(\alpha_i) > 0}} Bel(\alpha_i) \right) < 0.$$

But the first two expressions are clearly both equal to

$$\sum_{\chi} G_\chi Bel(\chi),$$

whilst the last two are both equal to

$$\sum_{\theta, \phi} H_{\theta, \phi} Bel(\theta \wedge \phi),$$

hence giving the required contradiction. (To see this for the final expression notice that the sum

$$\sum_{\substack{\alpha_i \in S_\phi \\ Bel(\alpha_i) > 0}} Bel(\alpha_i)$$

equals $Bel(\phi)$ whether or not it is empty, and $Bel(\theta \mid \phi) \cdot Bel(\phi) = Bel(\theta \wedge \phi)$.) $\square$

Third Justification

A third justification for belief as probability (or at least a scaled version of probability) appeared in a paper by R.T. Cox in the American Journal of Physics in 1946 [9]. Cox's proof is not, perhaps, as rigorous as some pedants might prefer and when an attempt is made to fill in all the details some of the attractiveness of the original is lost. Nevertheless his results certainly provide a valuable contribution to our understanding of the nature of belief.

We state here a rigorous version of Cox's main theorem which has aspects which are both stronger and weaker than the original. Slightly stronger versions still can be proved but the increased complications do not seem to justify doing so.

Just for the statement and proof of this theorem we shall assume that L is infinite (or alternatively that L, although finite, is variable).

Theorem 3.4 (Cox's theorem) *Suppose that whenever $\psi \in SL$ is consistent (i.e. non-contradictory) we can give a conditional belief $Bel(\theta \mid \psi) \in [0,1]$ to θ given ψ. Suppose further that for $\phi \wedge \psi$ consistent, $\theta, \phi, \psi \in SL$ etc.*

(Co1) If $\models (\theta \leftrightarrow \theta')$, $\models (\psi \leftrightarrow \psi')$ then $Bel(\theta \mid \psi) = Bel(\theta' \mid \psi')$.

(Co2) If $\models (\psi \to \theta)$ then $Bel(\theta \mid \psi) = 1$ and $Bel(\neg \theta \mid \psi) = 0$.

(Co3) $Bel(\theta \wedge \phi \mid \psi) = F(Bel(\theta \mid \phi \wedge \psi), Bel(\phi \mid \psi))$ for some continuous function $F : [0,1]^2 \longrightarrow [0,1]$ which is strictly increasing (in both coordinates) on $(0,1]^2$.

(Co4) $Bel(\neg \theta \mid \psi) = S(Bel(\theta \mid \psi))$ for some decreasing function $S : [0,1] \longrightarrow [0,1]$.

(Co5) For any $0 \le \alpha, \beta, \gamma \le 1$ and $\epsilon > 0$ there are $\theta_1, \theta_2, \theta_3, \theta_4 \in SL$ with $\theta_1 \wedge \theta_2 \wedge \theta_3$ consistent such that each of

$$| \, Bel(\theta_4 \mid \theta_1 \wedge \theta_2 \wedge \theta_3) - \alpha \, |, \ | \, Bel(\theta_3 \mid \theta_1 \wedge \theta_2) - \beta \, |, \ | \, Bel(\theta_2 \mid \theta_1) - \gamma \, |$$

is less than ϵ.

Then there is a continuous, strictly increasing, surjective function $g : [0,1] \to [0,1]$ such that $gBel(\theta \mid T)$ (where T is any tautology) satisfies (P1–2) and

$$g \, Bel(\theta \mid \psi) \cdot g \, Bel(\psi \mid T) = g \, Bel(\theta \wedge \psi \mid T),$$

i.e. $gBel(\theta \mid \psi)$ agrees with the conditional probability resulting from the probability function $gBel(\mid T)$ provided $gBel(\psi \mid T) \ne 0$.

Aside In his original, (Co3) and (Co4) were Cox's main assumptions. Cox justifies (Co3) by the example of a runner (of whom we assume ψ) and argues that our belief that he can run to a distant place (ϕ) and return (θ) should only be a function of our belief that he will get there, $(Bel(\phi \mid \psi))$ and, having got there, that he will return $(Bel(\theta \mid \phi \wedge \psi))$. $(Co4)$ is justified by the argument that as one's belief in θ given ψ increases from 0 to 1 so one's belief in $\neg\theta$ given ψ decreases from 1 to 0.

The assumption that $Bel(\theta \mid \phi)$ is defined whenever ϕ is consistent can be dropped in this theorem provided we strengthen $(Co1)$, $(Co3)$, $(Co4)$ to assert that the existence of the right hand side of the equation implies the existence of the left hand side, and we strengthen $(Co2)$, $(Co5)$ to asserting that these conditional beliefs exist. The proof is essentially the same as the one we are about to give except that in our conclusion we need to assume that the relevant belief values are defined.

Cox appears to neglect what we perceive as a need for $(Co5)$, as does J. Aczel in a rather similar result in [1]. The importance of $(Co5)$ will become clear during the proof of the theorem.

Cox's theorem will be proved via a series of lemmas. Since only one of these, lemma 3.7, will be needed in later chapters the casual reader might be forgiven for skipping the rather involved proof and jumping straight to the easier material beyond.

In the lemmas which now follow we shall assume $(Co1$–$5)$.

Lemma 3.5 *For* $x, y, z \in [0, 1]$,

$$F(F(x, y), z) = F(x, F(y, z)).$$

That is, as a binary operation, F is associative.

Proof For $\theta_1 \wedge \theta_2 \wedge \theta_3$ consistent,

$$
\begin{aligned}
Bel(\theta_4 \wedge \theta_3 \wedge \theta_2 \mid \theta_1) &= F(Bel(\theta_4 \wedge \theta_3 \mid \theta_1 \wedge \theta_2), Bel(\theta_2 \mid \theta_1)) \text{ by } (Co1), (Co3) \\
&= F(F(Bel(\theta_4 \mid \theta_1 \wedge \theta_2 \wedge \theta_3), Bel(\theta_3 \mid \theta_1 \wedge \theta_2)), Bel(\theta_2 \mid \theta_1)) \\
&\quad \text{by } (Co3).
\end{aligned}
$$

Also

$$
\begin{aligned}
Bel(\theta_4 \wedge \theta_3 \wedge \theta_2 \mid \theta_1) &= F(Bel(\theta_4 \mid \theta_1 \wedge \theta_2 \wedge \theta_3), Bel(\theta_3 \wedge \theta_2 \mid \theta_1)) \\
&= F(Bel(\theta_4 \mid \theta_1 \wedge \theta_2 \wedge \theta_3), F(Bel(\theta_3 \mid \theta_1 \wedge \theta_2), Bel(\theta_2 \mid \theta_1))).
\end{aligned}
$$

Putting $x = Bel(\theta_4 \mid \theta_1 \wedge \theta_2 \wedge \theta_3)$, $y = Bel(\theta_3 \mid \theta_1 \wedge \theta_2)$, $z = Bel(\theta_2 \mid \theta_1)$ gives $F(F(x, y), z) = F(z, F(y, z))$. By $(Co5)$ the set of points $\langle x, y, z \rangle \in [0, 1]^3$ for which this holds is dense in $[0, 1]^3$ and, since a continuous function is determined by its value on any dense set of points, the continuity of F ensures that this identity holds everywhere on $[0, 1]^3$. $\qquad\square$

Notice the critical use here of $(Co5)$ and continuity to argue from a result about certain numbers of the form $Bel(\theta \mid \chi)$ to general, independent, variables in $[0, 1]$.

Lemma 3.6 *For $x, y \in [0, 1]$*

$$F(x, 1) = F(1, x) = x, \quad F(x, y) \le x, y, \quad F(0, x) = F(x, 0) = 0.$$

Proof For $\theta \wedge \psi$ consistent,

$$
\begin{aligned}
Bel(\theta \mid \psi) \ &= \ Bel(\theta \wedge \theta \mid \psi) \ \text{by } (Co1) \\
&= \ F(Bel(\theta \mid \theta \wedge \psi), Bel(\theta \mid \psi)) = F(1, Bel(\theta \mid \psi)) \ \text{by } (Co2).
\end{aligned}
$$

Hence by continuity of F and $(Co5)$, $x = F(1, x)$ holds for all $x \in [0, 1]$. Similarly $x = F(x, 1)$ by using

$$
\begin{aligned}
Bel(\theta \mid \psi) \ &= \ Bel(\theta \wedge (\theta \vee \neg\theta) \mid \psi) \\
&= \ F(Bel(\theta \mid \psi \wedge (\theta \vee \neg\theta)), Bel(\theta \vee \neg\theta \mid \psi)) \\
&= \ F(Bel(\theta \mid \psi), 1) \ \text{by } (Co1), (Co2).
\end{aligned}
$$

Hence by monotonicity of F, $F(x, y) \le F(x, 1) = x$, $F(x, y) \le F(1, y) = y$ (using continuity for $x = 0$ or $y = 0$) and the last identities are now immediate.   □

Lemma 3.7 *The structure $([0, 1], F, <)$ is isomorphic to $([0, 1], \times, <)$, where $\times$ denotes the usual multiplication, i.e. there is a 1–1 onto function $g : [0, 1] \longrightarrow [0, 1]$ such that for all $x, y, \in [0, 1]$,*

$$
\begin{aligned}
x < y \quad &\Leftrightarrow \quad g(x) < g(y) \\
g F(x, y) \ &= \ g(x) g(y)
\end{aligned}
$$

Proof For notational simplicity we shall write $x \cdot y$ for $F(x, y)$ and $\dot{x}^n$ for $x \cdot x \cdot \ldots \cdot x$ n times. By associativity of F this is unambiguous. Fix $0 < \alpha < 1$.

Since $\dot{1}^m = 1 > \alpha > 0 = \dot{0}^m$ by continuity and (strict) monotonicity $(Co3)$ there is a unique β such that $\dot{\beta}^m = \alpha$ for $0 < m \in \mathbb{N}$ (= the set of natural numbers). Denote by $\dot{\alpha}^{\frac{n}{m}}$ the number $\dot{\beta}^n$. Then if $\dot{\delta}^{rm} = \alpha$ then $\dot{\delta}^{rm} = \dot{\beta}^m$ so by monotonicity $\beta = \dot{\delta}^r$.

Hence $\dot{\alpha}^{\frac{n}{m}} = \dot{\beta}^n = \dot{\delta}^{rn} = \dot{\alpha}^{\frac{rn}{rm}}$. Using this cancellation 'rule' we see that

$$\dot{\alpha}^{\frac{n}{m}} \cdot \dot{\alpha}^{\frac{r}{s}} = \dot{\alpha}^{\frac{ns}{ms}} \cdot \dot{\alpha}^{\frac{mr}{ms}} = \dot{\alpha}^{(\frac{ns+mr}{ms})} = \dot{\alpha}^{(\frac{n}{m} + \frac{r}{s})}$$

and also if $\frac{n}{m} < \frac{r}{s}$ then $\dot{\alpha}^{\frac{r}{s}} = \dot{\alpha}^{\frac{n}{m}} \cdot \dot{\alpha}^{(\frac{r}{s} - \frac{n}{m})} < \dot{\alpha}^{\frac{n}{m}}$ by lemma 3.6 and monotonicity of F on $(0, 1]^2$, since $0 < \dot{\alpha}^{\frac{r}{s} - \frac{n}{m}} < 1$.

Now notice that the sequence $\dot{\alpha}^n$ is decreasing so $\lim_{n \to \infty} \dot{\alpha}^n = \gamma$ for some $\gamma \ge 0$. If $0 < \gamma$ then, since $\gamma < \alpha < 1$, $\gamma < \dot{\gamma}^{\frac{1}{2}}$ so $\dot{\alpha}^n < \dot{\gamma}^{\frac{1}{2}}$ for some n. But then $\dot{\alpha}^{2n} < \gamma$, contradiction. Hence $\gamma = 0$. Similarly the sequence $\dot{\alpha}^{\frac{1}{n}}$ is increasing with limit 1.

Now given $0 < \beta < 1$ let

$$r = \sup\{\frac{p}{q} \mid \dot{\alpha}^{\frac{p}{q}} \geq \beta\} \in \mathbb{R},$$

where $p, q \in \mathbb{N}$, $q \neq 0$. Notice that this set is non-empty since $\dot{\alpha}^{\frac{1}{2^n}} > \beta$ for some n. We claim that

$$\inf\{\dot{\alpha}^{\frac{p}{q}} \mid \frac{p}{q} < r\} = \inf\{\dot{\alpha}^{\frac{p}{q}} \mid \frac{p}{q} \leq r\} = \beta$$

$$= \sup\{\dot{\alpha}^{\frac{p}{q}} \mid \frac{p}{q} \geq r\} = \sup\{\dot{\alpha}^{\frac{p}{q}} \mid \frac{p}{q} > r\} \qquad (3.1)$$

For suppose not. Then there are γ_1, γ_2 such that

$$\inf\{\dot{\alpha}^{\frac{p}{q}} \mid \frac{p}{q} < r\} > \gamma_1 > \gamma_2 > \sup\{\dot{\alpha}^{\frac{p}{q}} \mid \frac{p}{q} > r\}.$$

Pick m such that $\gamma_2 < \dot{\alpha}^{\frac{1}{m}} \cdot \gamma_1$, which must be possible since $\lim_{n \to \infty} \dot{\alpha}^{\frac{1}{2^n}} = 1$ and $\gamma_2 < \gamma_1 = 1 \cdot \gamma_1$. Now pick $\frac{p}{q} > r > \frac{p}{q} - \frac{1}{m}$.

Then $\dot{\alpha}^{\frac{p}{q}} < \gamma_2 < \dot{\alpha}^{\frac{1}{m}} \cdot \gamma_1 < \dot{\alpha}^{\frac{1}{m}} \cdot \dot{\alpha}^{(\frac{p}{q} - \frac{1}{m})} = \dot{\alpha}^{\frac{p}{q}}$, contradiction.

Thus we have shown that for each $\beta \in (0, 1)$ there is a unique $r \in (0, \infty)$ such that (3.1) holds, and conversely given $r \in (0, \infty)$ we can find $\beta \in (0, 1)$ such that (3.1) holds, so we can unambiguously write $\dot{\alpha}^r$ for β. Furthermore by the result for rational r already proved, $\dot{\alpha}^{r_1} \cdot \dot{\alpha}^{r_2} = \dot{\alpha}^{(r_1 + r_2)}$. It is now clear that if we define $g : [0, 1] \longrightarrow [0, 1]$ by $g(0) = 0$, $g(1) = 1$, $g(\dot{\alpha}^r) = (\frac{1}{2})^r$ for $r \in (0, \infty)$ then g is the required isomorphism. $\qquad \square$

Remark In order to prove this lemma we have only used that F is associative and continuous on $[0, 1]^2$, strictly increasing on $(0, 1]^2$ and for all $x \in [0, 1]$, $F(x, 1) = F(1, x) = x$. We shall later have occasion to use this lemma in a different context in which these conditions hold.

Notice that in the proof of the lemma 3.7 we have a free choice of $\alpha \in (0, 1)$. Notice also that since g is a strictly order-preserving function from $[0, 1]$ onto $[0, 1]$ it must be continuous since if $\gamma_n \in [0, 1]$, $\lim_{n \to \infty} \gamma_n = \gamma$ and, say, $\beta = \liminf_{n \to \infty} g(\gamma_n) < g(\gamma)$ then $g(\gamma_n) < \beta + \frac{g(\gamma) - \beta}{2} < g(\gamma)$ for arbitrarily large n so $\gamma_n < g^{-1}(\beta + \frac{g(\gamma) - \beta}{2}) < \gamma$ for all such n, contradiction.

We now derive some properties of S. Towards this end let

$$B = \{Bel(\theta \mid \psi) \mid \theta, \psi \in SL \text{ and } \psi \text{ consistent}\}.$$

Then $0, 1 \in B$ and by $(Co5)$ B is dense in $[0, 1]$.

Lemma 3.8 $S(0) = 1$, S is onto $[0, 1]$, *strictly decreasing, continuous and S^2 is the identity.*

Proof By $(Co2)$ $S(0) = S(Bel(\theta \wedge \neg\theta \mid \theta \vee \neg\theta)) = Bel(\neg(\theta \wedge \neg\theta) \mid \theta \vee \neg\theta) = 1$.

To show the remaining parts we first show that S^2 is the identity on B. This follows since for $\theta, \psi \in SL$, ψ consistent,

$$S^2(Bel(\theta \mid \psi)) = S(Bel(\neg\theta \mid \psi)) = Bel(\neg\neg\theta \mid \psi) = Bel(\theta \mid \psi)$$

by $(Co4)$.

To show that S is onto $[0,1]$ suppose $\gamma \in [0,1]$ and let

$$\tau = \sup\{\beta \mid S(\beta) \geq \gamma\} = \inf\{\beta \mid S(\beta) < \gamma\}.$$

Then $S(\tau) = \gamma$. For if not, say $S(\tau) < \gamma$, then for some $\beta \in B$, $\gamma > \beta > S(\tau)$. Then since $\beta = S^2(\beta) > S(\tau)$, $S(\beta) < \tau$ so, by definition of τ, $\gamma \leq S^2(\beta) = \beta$, contradiction.

To show that S is strictly decreasing suppose on the contrary that $\gamma < \delta$ but $S(\gamma) = S(\delta)$. Pick $\beta, \tau \in B$ such that $\gamma < \beta < \tau < \delta$. Then $S(\gamma) = S(\beta) = S(\tau) = S(\delta)$ so $\beta = S^2(\beta) = S^2(\tau) = \tau$, contradiction. As in the above remark it now follows that S is continuous and hence S^2, being the identity on the dense set B, must be the identity on $[0,1]$. $\square$

Remark If we assume that given any $0 < \beta, \gamma \leq 1$ we can find θ_3 and consistent $\theta_1 \wedge \theta_2$ such that $Bel(\theta_2 \mid \theta_1) = \beta$, $Bel(\theta_3 \mid \theta_1 \wedge \theta_2) = \gamma$ then it is no longer necessary to assume that S is decreasing, it can be derived. To see this suppose $\delta < \beta$. By continuity of F and lemma 3.6, $\delta = F(\gamma, \beta)$ for some $\gamma < 1$. Let $\theta_1, \theta_2, \theta_3$ be as above (clearly they also exist if $\gamma = 0$). Then

$$\delta = Bel(\theta_2 \wedge \theta_3 \mid \theta_1)$$

and

$$
\begin{aligned}
S(\beta) &= Bel(\neg\theta_2 \mid \theta_1) \\
&= Bel((\neg\theta_2 \vee \neg\theta_3) \wedge (\neg\theta_2 \vee \theta_3) \mid \theta_1) \\
&= F(Bel(\neg\theta_2 \vee \theta_3 \mid \theta_1 \wedge (\neg\theta_2 \vee \neg\theta_3)), Bel(\neg\theta_2 \vee \neg\theta_3 \mid \theta_1)),
\end{aligned}
$$

so, since F is increasing and $S(\delta) = Bel(\neg\theta_2 \vee \neg\theta_3 \mid \theta_1)$, by lemma 3.6, $S(\beta) \leq S(\delta)$.

Since S is continuous and $S(0) > 0$, $S(1) < 1$ we can pick $0 < \nu < 1$ such that $S(\nu) = \nu$. Let g be as in lemma 3.7 with $\alpha = \nu$. If we now define

$$
\begin{aligned}
Bel'(\theta \mid \psi) &= g\,Bel(\theta \mid \psi), \\
F'(x,y) &= gF(g^{-1}(x), g^{-1}(y)) = xy \text{ by lemma 3.7,} \\
S'(x) &= gSg^{-1}(x),
\end{aligned}
$$

then $(Co1\text{--}5)$ hold with Bel', F', S' in place of Bel, F, S. We shall prove Cox's theorem for this g. Without loss of generality and to simplify the notation we may assume $Bel = Bel'$, $S = S'$, $F = F' = $ multiplication on $[0, 1]$. Notice that now $S(\frac{1}{2}) = \frac{1}{2}$.

To simplify matters further we shall often henceforth write $1 \dot{-} x$ for $S(x)$. Notice that $x = S^2(x) = 1 \dot{-}(1 \dot{-}x)$.

For $0 \leq u \leq v \leq 1$ set $v \dot{-} u = v(1 \dot{-} \frac{u}{v})$ ($= 0$ if $v = 0$). Notice that $v \dot{-} u$ is increasing in v and decreasing in u. Our aim now is to show that $v \dot{-} u = v - u$. We shall first derive an important identity, involving S, which appears in Cox's original proof.

Lemma 3.9 *For $0 < x \leq y < 1$,*

$$yS\left(\frac{x}{y}\right) = S(x)S\left(\frac{S(y)}{S(x)}\right).$$

Proof First consider the case when $y = Bel(\theta \mid \psi)$, $\frac{x}{y} = Bel(\phi \mid \theta \wedge \psi)$ with $\theta \wedge \psi$ consistent. Then, since F is now multiplication, $x = Bel(\theta \wedge \phi \mid \psi)$ and $\psi \wedge \neg(\theta \wedge \phi)$ must be consistent since $S(x) > 0$. Hence

$$yS\left(\frac{x}{y}\right) = Bel(\neg\phi \mid \theta \wedge \psi)Bel(\theta \mid \psi) = Bel(\theta \wedge \neg\phi \mid \psi)$$

whilst

$$S(y) = Bel(\neg\theta \mid \psi) = Bel((\neg\theta \vee \neg\phi) \wedge (\neg\theta \vee \phi) \mid \psi)$$
$$S(x) = Bel(\neg\theta \vee \neg\phi \mid \psi)$$

so, as above,

$$S(x)S\left(\frac{S(y)}{S(x)}\right) = S(x) \cdot S(Bel(\neg\theta \vee \phi \mid \psi \wedge (\neg\theta \vee \neg\phi)))$$
$$= S(x) \cdot Bel(\theta \wedge \neg\phi \mid \psi \wedge (\neg\theta \vee \neg\phi))$$
$$\dot{=} Bel((\theta \wedge \neg\phi) \wedge (\neg\theta \vee \neg\phi) \mid \psi)$$
$$= Bel(\theta \wedge \neg\phi \mid \psi).$$

The result now follows by $(Co5)$ and continuity of S. $\qquad \square$

Lemma 3.10 *For $u, v, w \in [0, 1]$ if $u \leq v$ and $w \leq v \dot{-} u$ then $w \leq v$ and $u \leq v \dot{-} w$ and $(v \dot{-} u) \dot{-} w = (v \dot{-} w) \dot{-} u$.*

Proof If $w \leq v \dot{-} u$ then $w \leq v(1 \dot{-} \frac{u}{v}) \leq v$ and $\frac{w}{v} \leq (1 \dot{-} \frac{u}{v})$ for $v \neq 0$ so taking S of both sides gives $\frac{u}{v} \leq 1\dot{-}\frac{w}{v}$ as required. Finally

$$(v\dot{-}u)\dot{-}w = v(1\dot{-}\frac{u}{v})\left(1\dot{-}\frac{w}{v(1\dot{-}\frac{u}{v})}\right)$$

$$(v\dot{-}w)\dot{-}u = v(1\dot{-}\frac{w}{v})\left(1\dot{-}\frac{u}{v(1\dot{-}\frac{w}{v})}\right).$$

Putting $y = 1\dot{-}\frac{u}{v}, x = \frac{w}{v}$ these become $vyS(\frac{x}{y})$ and $vS(x)S\left(\frac{S(y)}{S(x)}\right)$ which are equal by lemma 3.9 for $u, w > 0$. The cases for $u = 0$, $w = 0$ follow by inspection.   □

Lemma 3.11 For $0 \leq u \leq z \leq 1$, $z\dot{-}u \leq z$ and $z\dot{-}(z\dot{-}u) = u$.

Proof $z\dot{-}u = z(1\dot{-}\frac{u}{z}) \leq z$. Also

$$z\dot{-}(z\dot{-}u) = z\dot{-}z(1\dot{-}\frac{u}{z}) = z(1\dot{-}(1\dot{-}\frac{u}{z})) = z.\frac{u}{z} = u.$$

□

Now for $u, v \in [0, 1]$ and $u \leq 1\dot{-}v$ define

$$u\dot{+}v = 1\dot{-}((1\dot{-}u)\dot{-}v).$$

We now derive a string of (expected) properties of $\dot{+}$.

Lemma 3.12 Let $u, v, w \in [0, 1]$ and $u \leq 1\dot{-}v$. Then

(i) $v \leq 1\dot{-}u$.

(ii) $u\dot{+}v = v\dot{+}u$.

(iii) $(u\dot{+}v) \geq u, v$.

(iv) $(u\dot{+}v)\dot{-}u = v$.

(v) For $u \leq w$, $(w\dot{-}u)\dot{+}u = w$.

(vi) For $w \leq 1\dot{-}(u\dot{+}v)$, $w \leq 1\dot{-}v$ and $u \leq 1\dot{-}(v\dot{+}w)$ and $u\dot{+}(v\dot{+}w) = (u\dot{+}v)\dot{+}w$.

(vii) $wu \leq 1\dot{-}wv$ and $w(u\dot{+}v) = wu\dot{+}wv$.

Proof (i) is immediate since S is decreasing, and (ii) follows by (i) and lemma 3.10. For (iii) notice that $1\dot{-}u \geq (1\dot{-}u)\dot{-}v$ so that applying S to both sides gives the result. To show (iv) we have

$$
\begin{aligned}
(u\dot{+}v)\dot{-}u &= (1\dot{-}((1\dot{-}u)\dot{-}v))\dot{-}u \\
&= (1\dot{-}u)\dot{-}((1\dot{-}u)\dot{-}v) \quad \text{by lemma 3.10,} \\
&= v \quad \text{by lemma 3.11.}
\end{aligned}
$$

For (v),

$$
\begin{aligned}
(w\dot{-}u)\dot{+}u &= u\dot{+}(w\dot{-}u) = 1\dot{-}((1\dot{-}u)\dot{-}(w\dot{-}u)) \\
&= 1\dot{-}((1\dot{-}u)\dot{-}((1\dot{-}(1\dot{-}w))\dot{-}u)) \\
&= 1\dot{-}((1\dot{-}u)\dot{-}((1\dot{-}u)\dot{-}(1\dot{-}w))) \quad \text{by lemma 3.10,} \\
&= 1\dot{-}(1\dot{-}w) = w \quad \text{by lemma 3.11.}
\end{aligned}
$$

To show (vi) notice that if $w \leq 1\dot{-}(u\dot{+}v)$ then

$$1\dot{-}w \geq u\dot{+}v \geq v.$$

Hence $w \leq 1\dot{-}v$. Also $(1\dot{-}w)\dot{-}v \geq (u\dot{+}v)\dot{-}v = u$ which gives $u \leq 1\dot{-}(w\dot{+}v)$. Finally then

$$
\begin{aligned}
u\dot{+}(v\dot{+}w) &= 1\dot{-}((1\dot{-}u)\dot{-}(1\dot{-}((1\dot{-}v)\dot{-}w))) \\
&= 1\dot{-}((1\dot{-}(1\dot{-}((1\dot{-}v)\dot{-}w)))\dot{-}u) \\
&= 1\dot{-}(((1\dot{-}v)\dot{-}w)\dot{-}u)
\end{aligned}
$$

and by lemma 3.10 the u, v, w can be permuted to give the answer. To show (vii), $wu \leq u \leq 1\dot{-}v \leq 1\dot{-}wv$ since $wv \leq v$. Also

$$
\begin{aligned}
wu &= w((u\dot{+}v)\dot{-}v) = w(u\dot{+}v)\left(1\dot{-}\tfrac{v}{u\dot{+}v}\right) \\
&= w(u\dot{+}v)\left(1\dot{-}\tfrac{wv}{w(u\dot{+}v)}\right) \quad (=0 \text{ if } w = 0) \\
&= w(u\dot{+}v)\dot{-}wv,
\end{aligned}
$$

and the result follows by adding wv to both sides. $\quad\square$

We shall now show that $\dot{+}$ and $+$ are the same thing, first in some special cases and then in general.

Lemma 3.13 *For $n > 0$,* $\frac{1}{2^n}\dot{+}\frac{1}{2^n} = \frac{1}{2^{n-1}}$.

Proof $\frac{1}{2}\dot{+}\frac{1}{2} = 1\dot{-}((1\dot{-}\tfrac{1}{2})\dot{-}\tfrac{1}{2}) = 1\dot{-}(\tfrac{1}{2}\dot{-}\tfrac{1}{2}) = 1$. For $n > 1$ we can straightforwardly use induction and lemma 3.12(vii). $\quad\square$

For $m \leq 2^n$ let $\dot{m}\left(\frac{1}{2^n}\right)$ stand for $\frac{1}{2^n}\dot{+}\frac{1}{2^n}\dot{+}...\dot{+}\frac{1}{2^n}$ m times. Since $2^n\left(\frac{1}{2^n}\right) = 1$, by lemma 3.12 the additions here are easily seen to be well defined.

Lemma 3.14 *For $n, m > 0$ and $m < 2^n$ we have* $\dot{m}\left(\frac{1}{2^n}\right) = \frac{m}{2^n}$.

Proof Suppose $\dot{m}\left(\frac{1}{2^n}\right) < \frac{m}{2^n}$ (the other case is similar), say,

$$\dot{m}\left(\frac{1}{2^n}\right) < \frac{1}{2^{\frac{p}{q}}} < \frac{m}{2^n} \text{ with } p, q \in \mathbb{N},\ q > 0.$$

Then by lemma 3.12 (vii),

$$\left(\dot{m}\left(\frac{1}{2^n}\right)\right)^q = \dot{m}^q\left(\frac{1}{2^{nq}}\right) < \frac{1}{2^p} < \frac{m^q}{2^{nq}}.$$

But since $m^q > 2^{nq-p}$,

$$\dot{m}^q\left(\frac{1}{2^{nq}}\right) > \dot{2}^{nq-p}\left(\frac{1}{2^{nq}}\right) = \frac{2^{nq-p}}{2^{nq}} = \frac{1}{2^p}$$

by lemma 3.13, giving the required contradiction. □

Lemma 3.15 *For* $0 \le x \le y \le 1,\ y\dot{-}x = y - x.$

Proof By lemma 3.12 (iv) and lemma 3.14 this is true for x, y of the form $\frac{m}{2^n}$ $(n, m > 0,\ m < 2^n)$ and hence by continuity for all x, y. □

Corollary 3.16 *For* $x, y \in [0, 1]$ *with* $x \le 1\dot{-}y,\ x\dot{+}y = x + y.$

Proof Immediate from the definition of $\dot{+}$ and lemma 3.15. □

We are ready to complete the proof of Cox's theorem.

Proof of theorem 3.4

That $Bel(\theta \mid T) = 1$ for $\models \theta$ is clear from $(Co2)$. If $\models \neg(\theta \wedge \phi)$ then either $\theta \vee \phi$ is contradictory, in which case each of $Bel(\theta \vee \phi \mid T),\ Bel(\theta \mid T),\ Bel(\phi \mid T)$ is zero, or else

$$Bel(\theta \vee \phi \mid T) - Bel(\theta \mid T) = Bel(\theta \vee \phi \mid T) - Bel((\theta \vee \phi) \wedge \neg\phi \mid T)$$

by $(Co1)$ since $\models \theta \leftrightarrow ((\theta \vee \phi) \wedge \neg\phi)$,

$$\begin{aligned}
&= && Bel(\theta \vee \phi \mid T) - Bel(\neg\phi \mid \theta \vee \phi)Bel(\theta \vee \phi \mid T) \\
& && \text{since } F \text{ is multiplication,} \\
&= && Bel(\theta \vee \phi \mid T)Bel(\phi \mid \theta \vee \phi) \text{ by lemma 3.15} \\
&= && Bel(\phi \wedge (\theta \vee \phi) \mid T) = Bel(\phi \mid T) \text{ by } (Co1).
\end{aligned}$$

Either way we obtain $(P2)$ for Bel.

Finally since F is multiplication, if $Bel(\psi \mid T) \ne 0$ then ψ is consistent and by $(Co3)$, $Bel(\theta \wedge \psi \mid T) = Bel(\theta \mid \psi)Bel(\psi \mid T)$ as required. □

Criticism

Despite these arguments for belief as probability, or scaled probability, the unpleasant fact is that if, as in example $\mathbb{E}$, one does elicit such knowledge and belief values from the expert then the set K very often turns out to be (seriously) inconsistent with belief as (scaled) probability and indeed with the other interpretations given in the next chapters. (On this point see [68] and also, for contrary views, [28], [51].)

We shall later see some further criticisms of belief as probability in Chapter 10. For the present however we can at least say that the results of this chapter have provided strong arguments in favour of belief as probability being the ideal.

Chapter 4 ———————

Dempster–Shafer Belief

In this chapter we shall give two arguments in support of belief functions being identified (under certain conditions) with Dempster–Shafer (DS) belief functions, originally introduced by Dempster in [11], and will relate them to probability functions. First however we shall develop a little of their theory. A much fuller account of these functions may be found in Shafer's seminal treatise [63]. Our framework may appear slightly more restrictive than that used by Shafer, but the differences are, in fact, inconsequential.

An Equivalent Definition of DS-belief Functions

The definition of DS-belief Functions given in Chapter 1 was chosen there because it required no additional notation and because it was easy to see a relationship with belief as probability. However an alternative, equivalent, definition which we now give is, in practice, easier to work with and more transparent.

Alternative definition: Bel: $SL \longrightarrow [0,1]$ is a Dempster–Shafer belief function if there is a function $m : \overline{SL} \longrightarrow [0,1]$ such that

$$\sum_{\overline{\theta} \in \overline{SL}} m(\overline{\theta}) = 1, \quad m(\mathbf{0}) = 0$$

and for all $\phi \in SL$,

$$Bel\,(\phi) = \sum_{\overline{\theta} \le \overline{\phi}} m(\overline{\theta}).$$

Here $\overline{SL}$ is the Lindenbaum algebra of L, that is $\overline{SL} = \{\overline{\theta} \mid \theta \in SL\}$ where $\overline{\theta} = \{\phi \in SL \mid \theta \equiv \phi\}$ and $\equiv$ is the equivalence relation $\models (\theta \leftrightarrow \phi)$, with the (well defined) operations, constants and relations

$$\overline{\theta} \wedge \overline{\phi} = \overline{(\theta \wedge \phi)}, \quad \overline{\theta} \vee \overline{\phi} = \overline{(\theta \vee \phi)}, \quad \neg\overline{\theta} = \overline{(\neg\theta)},$$

$$\mathbf{1} = \overline{\theta \vee \neg\theta}, \quad \mathbf{0} = \overline{\theta \wedge \neg\theta},$$

$$\overline{\theta} \le \overline{\phi} \iff \models (\theta \to \phi) \iff \overline{\theta} \wedge \overline{\phi} = \overline{\theta}.$$

It is useful to observe that $\overline{\theta} \mapsto S_\theta$ is an isomorphism of this algebra with the field of all subsets of At^L.

The function m in this definition is called a basic probability assignment, bpa, for Bel. Notice that according to this definition belief in ϕ is a sum of 'basic chunks of belief', $m(\overline{\theta})$, in the $\overline{\theta} \leq \overline{\phi}$, equivalently in the S_θ for $S_\theta \subseteq S_\phi$. In this sense then $m(\overline{\theta})$ is the belief in θ beyond that in any ψ with $\overline{\psi} < \overline{\theta}$.

The equivalence of these definitions follows from the next two results due to Shafer.

Theorem 4.1 *Let Bel^m be the DS-belief function defined via the bpa m as in the above definition. Then Bel^m satisfies (DS1–3).*

Proof $(DS1)$ and $(DS2)$ are immediate since if $\models (\theta \leftrightarrow \phi)$ then $\overline{\theta} = \overline{\phi}$ and if $\models \theta$ then $\overline{\theta} = 1, \overline{\neg\theta} = \mathbf{0}$ so $\overline{\phi} \leq \overline{\theta}$ for all $\overline{\phi}$ and

$$Bel^m(\theta) = \sum_{\overline{\phi}} m(\overline{\phi}) = 1, \quad Bel^m(\neg\theta) = \sum_{\overline{\phi} \leq \mathbf{0}} m(\overline{\phi}) = m(\mathbf{0}) = 0.$$

It only remains to prove $(DS3)$. Using the notation of $(DS3)$,

$$\sum_{\emptyset \neq S} (-1)^{|S|-1} Bel^m(\bigwedge_{i \in S} \theta_i) = \sum_{\emptyset \neq S} (-1)^{|S|-1} \sum_{\overline{\psi} \leq \bigwedge_{i \in S} \theta_i} m(\overline{\psi})$$

$$= \sum_{I(\overline{\psi}) \neq \emptyset} m(\overline{\psi}) \sum_{\emptyset \neq S \subseteq I(\overline{\psi})} (-1)^{|S|-1} \quad \text{where } I(\overline{\psi}) = \{i \mid \overline{\psi} \leq \overline{\theta_i}\}$$

$$= \sum_{I(\overline{\psi}) \neq \emptyset} m(\overline{\psi}) = \sum_{\substack{\overline{\psi} \leq \overline{\theta_i} \\ \text{for some } i}} m(\overline{\psi}) \leq \sum_{\overline{\psi} \leq \bigvee_i \theta_i} m(\overline{\psi}) = Bel^m(\bigvee_i \theta_i),$$

as required, since for a finite set $X \neq \emptyset$,

$$\sum_{Y \subseteq X} (-1)^{|Y|-1} = \text{Number of odd cardinality subsets of } X$$

$$- \text{Number of even cardinality subsets of } X$$

$$= 0 \quad \text{by induction on } |X|,$$

so

$$\sum_{\substack{\emptyset \neq S \\ S \subseteq I(\overline{\psi})}} (-1)^{|S|-1} = 0 - (-1)^{|\emptyset|-1} = 1 \quad \text{for } I(\overline{\psi}) \neq \emptyset.$$

$\square$

Theorem 4.2 *If Bel satisfies* (DS1–3) *then there is a unique bpa m such that* $Bel = Bel^m$, *where* Bel^m *is defined from m as in the above definition.*

Proof Set $m(0) = 0$ and for $\emptyset \neq R = \{\alpha_{j_1}, ..., \alpha_{j_q}\} \subseteq \{\alpha_1, ..., \alpha_J\}$ set

$$m(\overline{\bigvee R}) = \sum_{S \subseteq R} (-1)^{|R-S|} Bel(\bigvee S).$$

We first show that $m(\overline{\bigvee R}) \geq 0$. This is clear if $|R| \leq 1$. Otherwise

$$m(\overline{\bigvee R}) = Bel(\bigvee R) + \sum_{S \subset R} (-1)^{|R-S|} Bel(\theta_{i_1} \wedge ... \wedge \theta_{i_k}),$$

by (DS2), where $R - S = \{\alpha_{j_{i_1}}, ..., \alpha_{j_{i_k}}\}$ and $\theta_{i_r} = \alpha_{j_1} \vee \alpha_{j_2} \vee ... \vee \alpha_{j_{i_r-1}} \vee \alpha_{j_{i_r+1}} \vee ... \vee \alpha_{j_q}$. This further equals

$$Bel(\bigvee_{i=1}^{q} \theta_i) + \sum_{\emptyset \neq T \subseteq \{1,...,q\}} (-1)^T Bel (\bigwedge_{i \in T} \theta_i) \geq 0 \ by \ (DS3).$$

Hence, since $\overline{\phi} = \overline{\bigvee S_\phi}$, $m(\overline{\phi}) \geq 0$ for all $\overline{\phi} \in \overline{SL}$. Also

$$\sum_{\overline{\theta} \leq \overline{\phi}} m(\overline{\theta}) = \sum_{R \subseteq S_\phi} m(\overline{\bigvee R})$$

$$= \sum_{R \subseteq S_\phi} \sum_{S \subseteq R} (-1)^{|R-S|} Bel(\bigvee S)$$

$$= \sum_{S} Bel(\bigvee S) \sum_{S \subseteq R \subseteq S_\phi} (-1)^{|R-S|} = Bel(\bigvee S_\phi) = Bel(\phi)$$

by (DS2) since, as above, the sum $\displaystyle\sum_{S \subseteq R \subseteq S_\phi} (-1)^{|R-S|}$ is zero if $S \subset S_\phi$. Hence also

$$\sum_{\overline{\theta}} m(\overline{\theta}) = \sum_{\overline{\theta} \leq \overline{\phi \vee \neg \phi}} m(\overline{\theta}) = Bel(\phi \vee \neg \phi) = 1,$$

so m is a bpa and $Bel = Bel^m$. Finally m is the unique bpa for Bel since if m, m' are distinct bpa's then there must be a smallest set $R \subseteq \{\alpha_1, ..., \alpha_J\}$ for which $m(\overline{\bigvee R}) \neq m'(\overline{\bigvee R})$ and so $Bel^m(\bigvee R) \neq Bel^{m'}(\bigvee R)$ □

We now give a justification (or explanation) of Dempster–Shafer belief. A second justification will be given later when we have developed a little more notation and familiarity.

First Justification

Consider the following situation. Suppose an agent knows he will be receiving a message of the form 'θ is true' for some $\theta \in SL$, θ consistent. For example the message might arise from some experiment. Let $p(\bar{\theta})$ be the, possibly subjective, probability that the message will be that 'θ is true' (or a sentence logically equivalent to θ, which the agent would take to be just as good). Then $\sum_{\bar{\theta}} p(\bar{\theta}) = 1$, $p(\bar{\theta}) \geq 0$, $p(\mathbf{0}) = 0$ and for $\phi \in SL$,

Probability agent will learn ϕ is true	$=$	Probability he will receive a message 'θ is true' with θ logically implying ϕ
	$=$	$\sum_{\bar{\theta} \leq \bar{\phi}} p(\bar{\theta}).$

Thus, according to the definition above, identifying belief in ϕ with the probability of *learning* the truth of ϕ gives belief as a DS-belief function and at the same time provides an explanation of the bpa. From the point of view of belief as probability a DS-belief function is measuring the belief that one will *learn* the truth of a sentence θ rather than just the truth of θ.

Whether or not that is what an expert means when he gives figures such as those in our example $\mathbb{E}$ is perhaps debatable, although the above example shows how sets of constraints K might arise in which Dempster–Shafer belief was appropriate.

A second criticism one might raise against this justification is that, whilst learning the truth of a sentence logically equivalent to θ might *theoretically* be just as good as learning θ, the *practical* problem of deciding (in general) whether such a logical equivalence holds is, assuming $P \neq NP$, infeasible. (A similar criticism can be raised at various other points in this book.)

A particular example of this situation occurs by considering a refinement of the urn model used to justify belief as probability in the previous chapter. Recall that, in the case of a doctor diagnosing patients, the idea was that the doctor's belief in θ, $Bel(\theta)$, is identified with

$$\frac{|\{x \in M \mid x \text{ has } \theta\}|}{|M|}$$

where M is the set of patients x he has previously seen. Here it was assumed that the doctor has complete knowledge of each previous patient x, that is that x having θ is the same as the doctor knowing that x has θ.

However, this is clearly unrealistic: in practice the knowledge, ϕ_x, the doctor has about x would not necessarily be complete, i.e. ϕ_x would not necessarily be an atom. Nevertheless if we now proceed as before to define Bel_0 by

$$Bel_0(\theta) \;=\; \frac{|\{x \in M \mid \text{The doctor knows } x \text{ has } \theta\}|}{|M|}$$

$$=\; \frac{|\{x \in M \mid \phi_x \models \theta\}|}{|M|},$$

then it is easy to check that Bel_0 is a DS-belief function with bpa

$$m(\overline{\theta}) = \frac{|\{x \in M \mid \overline{\phi_x} = \overline{\theta}\}|}{|M|}.$$

Again it seems questionable whether the figures given by the doctor in our example $\mathbb{E}$ could be interpreted in this way. However this clearly provides an argument that DS-belief is a possibility for an intelligent agent.

Plausibility

Directly from $(DS3)$ we see that for Bel a DS-belief function and $\theta, \phi \in SL$,

$$Bel(\theta \vee \phi) \geq Bel(\theta) + \mathrm{Bel}(\phi) - \mathrm{Bel}(\theta \wedge \phi).$$

In particular for $\phi = \neg\theta$,

$$1 = Bel(\theta \vee \neg\theta) \geq Bel(\theta) + \mathrm{Bel}(\neg\theta) \quad \text{since} \quad Bel(\theta \wedge \neg\theta) = 0$$

so $Bel(\theta) \leq 1 - Bel(\neg\theta)$.

The difference $1 - (Bel(\theta) + Bel(\neg\theta))$ could be thought of as the unassigned, or uncommitted, belief between θ and $\neg\theta$, a large value here corresponding to ignorance of θ and $\neg\theta$. In particular complete ignorance of θ and $\neg\theta$ would correspond to $Bel(\theta) = Bel(\neg\theta) = 0$, as opposed to $Bel(\theta) = Bel(\neg\theta) = \frac{1}{2}$ for belief as probability. In this way then DS-belief functions could be said to have the ability to distinguish between genuine uncertainty and simple ignorance.

The plausibility of θ, $Pl(\theta)$, is defined by

$$Pl(\theta) = 1 - Bel(\neg\theta)$$

and could be thought of as unassigned belief which could all go to θ. Notice that $Bel(\theta) \leq 1 - Bel(\neg\theta) = Pl(\theta)$ and in terms of the bpa m for Bel,

$$Pl(\theta) = 1 - Bel(\neg\theta) = \sum_{\phi} m(\overline{\phi}) - \sum_{\phi \leq \neg\theta} m(\overline{\phi}) = \sum_{0 < \phi \wedge \theta} m(\overline{\phi}).$$

(Many other perceived facets of belief can similarly be captured by DS-belief functions but they will not be relevant here.)

A Representation of DS-belief Functions

Let $\bar{\theta}_i, i = 1, ..., r$ enumerate the non-zero elements of $\overline{SL}$ (so $r = 2^{2^n} - 1$ for our 'default' language $L = \{p_1, ..., p_n\}$). Then the above theorem 4.2 shows that any DS-belief function Bel on SL can be uniquely specified by the vector

$$\langle m(\bar{\theta}_1), ..., m(\bar{\theta}_r)\rangle$$

where m is the (unique) bpa of Bel. Furthermore, of course, the $m(\bar{\theta}_i) \geq 0$ and $\sum_i m(\bar{\theta}_i) = 1$.

Conversely given a vector $\langle x_1, ..., x_r\rangle$ with $x_i \geq 0$, $\sum_i x_i = 1$ we can define a bpa m by $m(\bar{\theta}_i) = x_i$, $m(0) = 0$ and hence a DS-belief function corresponding to this vector.

To sum up then there is a 1–1 correspondence between DS-belief functions on SL and points in

$$\{\langle x_1, ..., x_r\rangle \mid \sum x_i = 1, x_i \geq 0\}.$$

This is exactly similar to the situation for probability functions except that now the vector is of length $2^{2^n} - 1$ rather than 2^n.

Again, exactly as for belief as probability, we can identify DS-belief functions satisfying K (as given at the close of Chapter 1) with points $\langle x_1, ..., x_r\rangle \in \mathbb{R}^r$ satisfying

$$\vec{x}D_k = \vec{e_k}, \quad \vec{x} \geq 0$$

for some matrix D_k and vector $\vec{e_k}$ (obtained by replacing each $Bel(\theta_j)$ by $\sum_{\phi \leq \theta_j} m(\bar{\phi})$ throughout K and adding in also $\sum_{\phi} m(\bar{\phi}) = 1$). However, the now double exponential length of $\vec{x}$ makes using this form of the question Q somewhat more complicated in practice.

Probability and DS-belief

Using the first definition of DS-belief functions it is clear that any probability function is also a DS-belief function since, by proposition 2.1 and $(P1)$, $(DS1$–$3)$ hold, with equality, for any probability function. The converse is false however. To see this notice that if the bpa m gives a probability function Bel then

$$1 = \sum_{i=1}^{J} Bel(\alpha_i) = \sum_{i=1}^{J} \sum_{\bar{\phi} \leq \bar{\alpha}_i} m(\bar{\phi}) = \sum_{i=1}^{J}(m(\mathbf{0}) + m(\bar{\alpha}_i)) = \sum_{i=1}^{J} m(\bar{\alpha}_i),$$

and conversely if $\sum_{i=1}^{J} m(\overline{\alpha_i}) = 1$ then for $\overline{\phi} \notin \{\overline{\alpha_i} \mid i = 1, ..., J\}$, $m(\overline{\phi}) = 0$, since $\sum_{\overline{\phi}} m(\overline{\phi}) = 1$ and $m(\overline{\phi}) \geq 0$, so

$$Bel(\theta) = \sum_{\overline{\phi} \leq \overline{\theta}} m(\overline{\phi}) = \sum_{\overline{\alpha_i} \leq \overline{\theta}} m(\overline{\alpha_i}) = \sum_{\alpha_i \in S_\theta} Bel(\alpha_i),$$

from which it is clear from Chapter 1 that Bel is a probability function. Thus a DS-belief function is a probability function just if $\sum_{i=1}^{J} m(\overline{\alpha_i}) = 1$ and hence to produce a DS-belief function which is not a probability function it is enough to choose the bpa m such that $m(\overline{\phi}) > 0$ for some $\overline{\phi} \notin \{\overline{\alpha_i} \mid i = 1, ..., J\}$.

A second equivalent to a DS-belief function Bel being a probability function is that

$$Bel(\theta) + Bel(\neg\theta) = 1, \quad i.e. \quad Bel(\theta) = Pl(\theta), \quad \text{for all } \theta \in SL.$$

For clearly this condition holds if Bel is a probability function. Conversely if Bel is not a probability function suppose $m(\overline{\phi}) > 0$ where $\overline{\phi} \notin \{\overline{\alpha_i} \mid i = 1, ..., J\}$ and m is the bpa of Bel. Then for $\alpha_j \in S_\phi$ ($\neq \emptyset$ since $m(\overline{\phi}) > 0$) there are no non-zero common terms in the sums

$$\sum_{\overline{\theta} \leq \overline{\alpha_j}} m(\overline{\theta}), \quad \sum_{\overline{\theta} \leq \neg\overline{\alpha_j}} m(\overline{\theta})$$

and neither sum contains $m(\overline{\phi})$, since $\overline{\alpha_j} < \overline{\phi}$, so

$$Bel(\alpha_j) + Bel(\neg\alpha_j) < \sum_{\overline{\theta}} m(\overline{\theta}) = 1.$$

Another connection between probability and DS-belief is provided by the following theorem due to Dempster [11] and Kyburg [41] which shows that DS-belief functions can be viewed as *sets* of probability functions. Alternatively this theorem can be viewed as showing to what extent a DS-belief function can be 'refined' into a probability function.

In the following theorem let Bel be a DS-belief function on SL and let
$$W(Bel) = \{w \mid \ w \text{ is a probability function on } SL \text{ and}$$
$$w(\theta) \geq Bel(\theta) \text{ for all } \theta \in SL\}.$$

Theorem 4.3   (i) *If Bel is a probability function then* $W(Bel) = \{Bel\}$.

(ii) *For each* $\theta \in SL$ *there is* $w \in W(Bel)$ *such that* $w(\theta) = Bel(\theta)$.

(iii) *For each* $\theta \in SL$ *and* $w \in W(Bel)$, $w(\theta) \leq 1 - Bel(\neg\theta) = Pl(\theta)$.

(iv) For each $\theta \in SL$ there is $w \in W(Bel)$ such that $w(\theta) = 1 - Bel(\neg\theta) = Pl(\theta)$.

Proof For (iii) notice that if $w(\theta) > 1 - Bel(\neg\theta)$ then

$$Bel(\neg\theta) > 1 - w(\theta) = w(\neg\theta)$$

contradicting $w \in W(Bel)$.

For (i) notice that if Bel is a probability function then $Bel \in W(Bel)$ and if $w \in W(Bel)$ and $w \neq Bel$ then $w(\theta) > Bel(\theta)$ for some θ so

$$w(\neg\theta) = 1 - w(\theta) < 1 - Bel(\theta) = Bel(\neg\theta)$$

contradicting $w \in W(Bel)$.

Part (iv) follows from (ii) since if $w(\neg\theta) = Bel(\neg\theta)$ with $w \in W(Bel)$ then $w(\theta) = 1 - w(\neg\theta) = 1 - Bel(\neg\theta)$.

So it only remains to prove (ii). Given $\theta \in SL$ let m be the bpa of Bel. For each $\overline{\psi} > \mathbf{0}$ pick an atom $\beta_{\overline{\psi}} \in S_{\psi}$ such that if $S_{\psi \wedge \neg\theta} \neq \emptyset$ then $\beta_{\overline{\psi}} \in S_{\psi \wedge \neg\theta} \subseteq S_{\psi}$. Now define, for each atom α, $w(\alpha) = \displaystyle\sum_{\beta_{\overline{\psi}} = \alpha} m(\overline{\psi}) \geq 0$. Clearly each $m(\overline{\psi})$ is associated with exactly one atom α so

$$\sum_{\alpha} w(\alpha) = \sum_{\overline{\psi}} m(\overline{\psi}) = 1$$

and hence w extends to a probability function by defining

$$w(\theta) = \sum_{\alpha \in S_\theta} w(\alpha) \ \ for \ \theta \in SL.$$

For any $\overline{\phi}$,

$$
\begin{aligned}
Bel(\phi) \ &= \ \sum_{\overline{\psi} \leq \overline{\phi}} m(\overline{\psi}) = \sum_{\alpha \in S_\phi} \sum_{\substack{\overline{\psi} \leq \overline{\phi} \\ \beta_{\overline{\psi}} = \alpha}} m(\overline{\psi}) \leq \sum_{\alpha \in S_\phi} \sum_{\beta_{\overline{\psi}} = \alpha} m(\overline{\psi}) = \sum_{\alpha \in S_\phi} w(\alpha) \\
&= \ w(\phi)
\end{aligned}
$$

so $w \in W(Bel)$. Finally in the case $\phi = \theta$, if $\beta_{\overline{\psi}} = \alpha \in S_\phi$ it must be the case that, by choice of $\beta_{\overline{\psi}}$, $S_{\psi \wedge \neg\theta} = \emptyset$, i.e. $\overline{\psi} \leq \overline{\theta}$, so that in the above expression equality holds and $Bel(\theta) = w(\theta)$. $\qquad\square$

This result is attractive in the sense that it identifies a DS-belief function Bel with the (consistent) *set* of inequality constraints

$$w(\theta) \geq Bel(\theta) \quad \text{for} \quad \theta \in SL,$$

on a probability function w. Unfortunately not all such (consistent) sets of constraints correspond to DS-belief functions.

To see this consider, for $L = \{p, q\}$, the set of inequality constraints

$$w(\alpha_i) \geq 0, \; w(\alpha_i \vee \alpha_j) \geq \frac{1}{3}, \; w(\alpha_i \vee \alpha_j \vee \alpha_k) \geq \frac{2}{3}, \; w(\alpha_1 \vee \alpha_2 \vee \alpha_3 \vee \alpha_4) \geq 1$$

for distinct $i, j, k \in \{1, ..., 4\}$. For each of these lower bounds there is a probability function satisfying the constraints and assuming that lower bound. So if Bel was a DS-belief function such that $W(Bel)$ was exactly the set of (probability function) solutions to these constraints we should have, by theorem 4.3 (ii), that

$$Bel(\alpha_i) = 0, \quad Bel(\alpha_i \vee \alpha_j) = \frac{1}{3}, \quad Bel(\alpha_i \vee \alpha_j \vee \alpha_k) = \frac{2}{3}$$

for distinct $i, j, k \in \{1, ..., 4\}$. But for the bpa, m, of Bel this forces $m(\overline{\alpha_i}) = 0$, $m(\overline{\alpha_i \vee \alpha_j}) = \frac{1}{3}$ so

$$\frac{2}{3} = Bel(\alpha_1 \vee \alpha_2 \vee \alpha_3) \geq m(\overline{\alpha_1 \vee \alpha_2}) + m(\overline{\alpha_1 \vee \alpha_3}) + m(\overline{\alpha_2 \vee \alpha_3}) = 1,$$

contradiction.

Conditional DS-belief

Amongst the several possible alternatives which have been suggested the (currently) most popular way to define a conditional DS-belief function from a DS-belief function Bel is to set

$$Bel(\theta \mid \phi) = \frac{Bel(\theta \vee \neg\phi) - Bel(\neg\phi)}{1 - Bel(\neg\phi)} \quad \text{whenever } Bel(\neg\phi) \neq 1.$$

This rather unlikely looking formula arises as follows. According to Shafer if m_1, m_2 are bpa's for DS-belief functions corresponding to 'independent' sources of belief then they may be combined using *Dempster's rule of combination* to give a bpa

$$m_1 \oplus m_2(\overline{\psi}) = \frac{\displaystyle\sum_{\overline{\lambda} \wedge \overline{\tau} = \overline{\psi}} m_1(\overline{\lambda}) m_2(\overline{\tau})}{1 - \displaystyle\sum_{\overline{\lambda} \wedge \overline{\tau} = \mathbf{0}} m_1(\overline{\lambda}) m_2(\overline{\tau})} \quad \text{for} \quad \overline{\psi} > \mathbf{0}$$

which is well defined provided the denominator is non-zero. That this is indeed a bpa in this case follows by noticing that

$$1 = \sum_{\overline{\lambda}} m_1(\overline{\lambda}) \cdot \sum_{\overline{\tau}} m_2(\overline{\tau}) = \sum_{\overline{\psi}} \sum_{\overline{\lambda} \wedge \overline{\tau} = \overline{\psi}} m_1(\overline{\lambda}) m_2(\overline{\tau}).$$

If the denominator is zero it must be the case that whenever $m_1(\overline{\lambda}), m_2(\overline{\tau}) > 0$ then $\overline{\lambda} \wedge \overline{\tau} = \mathbf{0}$. In this case then $Bel_1(\theta) = 1 = Bel_2(\phi)$, where $\overline{\theta} = \bigvee_{m_1(\overline{\lambda}) > 0} \overline{\lambda}$, $\overline{\phi} = \bigvee_{m_2(\overline{\tau}) > 0} \overline{\tau}$, and θ, ϕ contradict each other. Clearly in this circumstance it seems unreasonable to expect to be able to combine Bel_1 and Bel_2.

Now suppose that m is the bpa of Bel and we wish to condition on ϕ. In this context it seems reasonable to represent the 'evidence' that ϕ holds by the DS-belief function with bpa m' defined by $m'(\overline{\phi}) = 1$, $m'(\overline{\lambda}) = 0$ for $\overline{\lambda} \neq \overline{\phi}$ (obviously we cannot do this if ϕ is contradictory, i.e. $\overline{\phi} = \mathbf{0}$) and to take Bel conditioned on ϕ to be the DS-belief function with bpa $m \oplus m'$. This gives

$$Bel(\theta \mid \phi) = \sum_{\overline{\psi} \leq \overline{\theta}} m \oplus m'(\overline{\psi}) = k \sum_{0 < \overline{\psi} \leq \overline{\theta}} \sum_{\overline{\lambda} \wedge \overline{\phi} = \overline{\psi}} m(\overline{\lambda})$$

where $k = (1 - \sum_{\overline{\lambda} \wedge \overline{\phi} = \mathbf{0}} m(\overline{\lambda}))^{-1} = (1 - Bel(\neg\phi))^{-1}$.

Hence

$$Bel(\theta \mid \phi) = k \sum_{\mathbf{0} < \overline{\lambda} \wedge \overline{\phi} \leq \overline{\theta}} m(\overline{\lambda}) = k \left(\sum_{\overline{\lambda} \leq \overline{\theta} \vee \neg\phi} m(\overline{\lambda}) - \sum_{\overline{\lambda} \leq \neg\phi} m(\overline{\lambda}) \right)$$

$$= \frac{Bel(\theta \vee \neg\phi) - Bel(\neg\phi)}{1 - Bel(\neg\phi)},$$

provided the denominator is non-zero, i.e. provided Bel does not give belief 1 to $\neg\phi$.

Notice that for the corresponding plausibilities we obtain the expression

$$Pl(\theta \mid \phi) = 1 - Bel(\neg\theta \mid \phi) = 1 - \frac{Bel(\neg\theta \vee \neg\phi) - Bel(\neg\phi)}{1 - Bel(\neg\phi)}$$

$$= \frac{1 - Bel(\neg\theta \vee \neg\phi)}{1 - Bel(\neg\phi)} = \frac{Pl(\theta \wedge \phi)}{Pl(\phi)}$$

which is exactly similar to that for conditional probability.

In connection with the justification for reducing the set of constraints K in question Q (at the close of Chapter 1) to involve simply unconditional belief, notice that if $1 - Bel(\neg\phi) = 0$ then also $Bel(\theta \vee \neg\phi) - Bel(\neg\phi) = 0$ for a DS-belief function Bel, so that, as for probability, the unconditional form of the constraint formed by multiplying through by the denominator of the $Bel(\theta_i \mid \phi)$ will be trivially satisfied.

Returning briefly to Dempster's rule of combination, as indicated above this rule is intended to allow the combination of 'independent' evidences and indeed plays a central role in the theory of DS-belief. Unfortunately the version of 'independence' required to make this rule compatible with our earlier justification of DS-belief functions is still a matter of contention, even if we generalise our justification to allow the possibility that the message 'θ is true' might be incorrect and now take $Bel(\theta)$ to be the probability of the agent being led to conclude, on the basis of the message, that θ is true.

In view of the representation given in theorem 4.3 of a DS-belief function Bel as the set of probability functions $W(Bel)$, it would seem natural to define the derived conditional DS-belief, $Bel(\theta||\phi)$ (so denoted to distinguish it from the previous function), by

$$Bel(\theta||\phi) = \inf\{w(\theta|\phi)|\ w \in W(Bel)\}.$$

Notice that provided $Bel(\phi) > 0$ this is well defined since $w(\phi) \geq Bel(\phi)$ for $w \in W$. What is much less obvious is that if $Bel(\phi) > 0$ then $Bel(\theta||\phi)$, as a function of $\theta \in SL$, is also DS-belief function. This surprising result is due to Fagin and Halpern [14] and (independently) Jaffray, see [14].

Before we give a proof of this, notice that if $w \in W(Bel)$ and $Bel(\phi) > 0$ then

$$Bel(\theta \wedge \phi) \leq w(\theta \wedge \phi),$$

$$w(\neg\theta \wedge \phi) \leq Pl(\neg\theta \wedge \phi),$$

by theorem 4.3, and

$$Bel(\theta \wedge \phi) + Pl(\neg\theta \wedge \phi) > 0$$

since if m is the bpa of Bel then

$$0 < Bel(\phi) = \sum_{\overline{\psi} \leq \overline{\phi}} m(\overline{\psi}) = \sum_{\overline{\psi} \leq \overline{\theta \wedge \phi}} m(\overline{\psi}) + \sum_{\substack{\overline{\psi} \leq \overline{\phi} \\ 0 < \overline{\psi} \wedge \neg\theta}} m(\overline{\psi})$$

$$\leq \sum_{\overline{\psi} \leq \overline{\theta \wedge \phi}} m(\overline{\psi}) + \sum_{0 < \overline{\psi} \wedge \neg\theta \wedge \phi} m(\overline{\psi}) = Bel(\theta \wedge \phi) + Pl(\neg\theta \wedge \phi).$$

Hence

$$
\begin{aligned}
w(\theta|\phi) &= \frac{w(\theta \wedge \phi)}{w(\theta \wedge \phi) + w(\neg\theta \wedge \phi)} \\
&\geq \frac{w(\theta \wedge \phi)}{w(\theta \wedge \phi) + Pl(\neg\theta \wedge \phi)} \\
&\geq \frac{Bel(\theta \wedge \phi)}{Bel(\theta \wedge \phi) + Pl(\neg\theta \wedge \phi)}.
\end{aligned}
$$

Furthermore this lower bound is attained since by adapting the proof of theorem 4.3(ii) so that $\beta_{\overline{\psi}} \in S_{\psi \wedge \neg\theta \wedge \phi}$ if possible, otherwise $\beta_{\overline{\psi}} \in S_{\psi \wedge (\neg\theta \vee \neg\phi)}$ if possible, we can produce $w \in W(Bel)$ such that

$$w(\theta \vee \neg\phi) = Bel(\theta \vee \neg\phi),$$

$$w(\theta \wedge \phi) = Bel(\theta \wedge \phi).$$

Hence

$$w(\theta|\phi) = \frac{w(\theta \wedge \phi)}{w(\theta \wedge \phi) + 1 - w(\theta \vee \neg\phi)} = \frac{Bel(\theta \wedge \phi)}{Bel(\theta \wedge \phi) + Pl(\neg\theta \wedge \phi)}$$

as required.

It now follows that provided $Bel(\phi) > 0$,

$$Bel(\theta||\phi) = \frac{Bel(\theta \wedge \phi)}{Bel(\theta \wedge \phi) + Pl(\neg\theta \wedge \phi)} \tag{4.1}$$

Theorem 4.4 *Let Bel be a DS-belief function on SL with $Bel(\phi) > 0$. Then $Bel(\theta||\phi)$, as a function of $\theta \in SL$, is a DS-belief function on SL.*

Proof $(DS1)$ and $(DS2)$ are straightforward to check. To show $(DS3)$ let m be the bpa for Bel and let

$$\{\overline{\theta}_1, \ldots, \overline{\theta}_t\} = \{\overline{\eta} \in \overline{SL}|m(\overline{\eta}) > 0, \overline{\eta} \leq \overline{\phi}\},$$

$$\{\overline{\phi}_1, \ldots, \overline{\phi}_s\} = \{\overline{\eta} \in \overline{SL}|m(\overline{\eta}) > 0, \overline{\eta} \not\leq \overline{\phi}, \mathbf{0} < \overline{\eta} \wedge \overline{\phi}\}.$$

Then by using (4.1) above,

$$Bel(\theta||\phi) = \frac{\sum_{\overline{\theta}_j \leq \overline{\theta} \wedge \overline{\phi}} m(\overline{\theta}_j)}{\sum_{\overline{\theta}_j \leq \overline{\theta} \wedge \overline{\phi}} m(\overline{\theta}_j) + \sum_{\mathbf{0} < \overline{\theta}_j \wedge \neg\overline{\theta} \wedge \overline{\phi}} m(\overline{\theta}_j) + \sum_{\mathbf{0} < \overline{\phi}_j \wedge \neg\overline{\theta} \wedge \overline{\phi}} m(\overline{\phi}_j)}$$

$$= \frac{\sum_{\overline{\theta}_j \leq \overline{\theta} \wedge \overline{\phi}} m(\overline{\theta}_j)}{D - \sum_{\overline{\phi}_j \wedge \overline{\phi} \leq \overline{\theta}} m(\overline{\phi}_j)}$$

where $D = \sum_{j=1}^{t} m(\overline{\theta}_j) + \sum_{j=1}^{s} m(\overline{\phi}_j)$.

Hence to show $(DS3)$, i.e.

$$Bel\left(\bigvee_{i=1}^{m} \psi_i \,\middle|\middle|\, \phi\right) \geq \sum_{\emptyset \neq I \subseteq \{\psi_1, \ldots, \psi_m\}} (-1)^{|I|-1} Bel\left(\bigwedge I \,\middle|\middle|\, \phi\right),$$

we must show that

$$\frac{\sum_{\overline{\theta}_j \leq \overline{\phi} \wedge \overline{\bigvee \psi_i}} m(\overline{\theta}_j)}{D - \sum_{\overline{\phi}_j \wedge \overline{\phi} \leq \overline{\bigvee \psi_i}} m(\overline{\phi}_j)} \geq \sum_{\emptyset \neq I \subseteq \{\psi_1, \ldots, \psi_m\}} (-1)^{|I|-1} \frac{\sum_{\overline{\theta}_j \leq \overline{\phi} \wedge \overline{\bigwedge I}} m(\overline{\theta}_j)}{D - \sum_{\overline{\phi}_j \wedge \overline{\phi} \leq \overline{\bigwedge I}} m(\overline{\phi}_j)}. \tag{4.2}$$

Let $\bar{\theta}_j \leq \bar{\phi} \wedge \bigvee \bar{\psi}_i$ and, without loss of generality, suppose that $\psi_1, \ldots, \psi_k$ are those ψ_i such that $\bar{\theta}_j \leq \bar{\phi} \wedge \bar{\psi}_i$. Then by isolating the terms in (4.2) in which $m(\bar{\theta}_j)$ occurs it is clearly enough to show that

$$\frac{1}{D - \sum_{\bar{\phi}_j \wedge \bar{\phi} \leq \bigvee \bar{\psi}_i} m(\bar{\phi}_j)} \geq \sum_{\emptyset \neq I \subseteq R} (-1)^{|I|-1} \frac{1}{D - \sum_{\bar{\phi}_j \wedge \bar{\phi} \leq \bigwedge I} m(\bar{\phi}_j)} \tag{4.3}$$

where $R = \{\psi_1, \ldots, \psi_k\}$.

In order to show (4.3) we now appeal to a rather technical lemma.

Lemma 4.5 *Let $S, C_1, \ldots, C_k$ be sets of strictly positive reals. Then*

$$\sum_{I \subseteq \{C_1, \ldots, C_k\}} (-1)^{|I|} (x - \sum \{y \in S | y \in \bigcap I\})^{-m} \geq 0$$

whenever $m > 0$ and $x > \sum_{y \in S} y$.

Proof. The proof is by induction on $|S|$ (for all $C_1, \ldots, C_k$ and $m > 0$). For $|S| = 0$, i.e. $S = \emptyset$, the expression becomes

$$\sum_{I \subseteq \{C_1, \ldots, C_k\}} (-1)^{|I|} x^{-m}$$

which, as we have already seen, is x^{-m} if $k = 0$ and zero otherwise. Either way it is non-negative, as required.

Now let $|S| = n > 0$ and assume the result for $n - 1$. Let $a \in S$ and without loss of generality let $C_1, \ldots, C_r$ be those C_i such that $a \in C_i$. Then

$$\sum_{I \subseteq \{C_1, \ldots, C_k\}} (-1)^{|I|} (x - \sum \{y \in S | y \in \bigcap I\})^{-m}$$

$$= \sum_{I \subseteq \{C_1, \ldots, C_r\}} \cdots + \sum_{\substack{I \subseteq \{C_1, \ldots, C_k\} \\ I \not\subseteq \{C_1, \ldots, C_r\}}} \cdots$$

$$= \sum_{I \subseteq \{C_1, \ldots, C_r\}} (-1)^{|I|} ((x - a) - \sum \{y \in S' | y \in \bigcap I\})^{-m}$$

$$+ \sum_{\substack{I \subseteq \{C_1, \ldots, C_k\} \\ I \not\subseteq \{C_1, \ldots, C_r\}}} (-1)^{|I|} (x - \sum \{y \in S' | y \in \bigcap I\})^{-m}$$

where $S' = S - \{a\}$. This further equals

$$\sum_{I \subseteq \{C_1, \ldots, C_r\}} (-1)^{|I|} ((x - a) - \sum \{y \in S' | y \in \bigcap I\})^{-m}$$

$$- \sum_{I \subseteq \{C_1,\ldots,C_r\}} (-1)^{|I|} (x - \sum \{y \in S' | y \in \bigcap I\})^{-m}$$

$$+ \sum_{I \subseteq \{C_1,\ldots,C_k\}} (-1)^{|I|} (x - \sum \{y \in S' | y \in \bigcap I\})^{-m}.$$

By inductive hypothesis the last of these three terms is non-negative. To show that the sum of the first two is also non-negative it suffices to show that

$$\sum_{I \subseteq \{C_1,\ldots,C_r\}} (-1)^{|I|} (x - \sum \{y \in S' | y \in \bigcap I\})^{-m}$$

is decreasing (in x) for $x > \sum_{y \in S'} y$. But this follows since by using the inductive hypothesis again (for $m + 1$) its derivative with respect to x can be seen to be non-positive. $\qquad\square$

Returning to the proof of (4.2) suppose for the moment that the numbers $m(\overline{\phi_i})$ are all distinct. Then putting

$$S = \{m(\overline{\phi_j}) | \; \overline{\phi_j} \wedge \overline{\phi} \le \bigvee_{i=1}^{m} \overline{\psi_i}\},$$

$$C_i = \{m(\overline{\phi_j}) | \; \overline{\phi_j} \wedge \overline{\phi} \le \overline{\psi_i}\},$$

and $m = 1$, $x = D$ in the lemma and noticing that the left hand side of (4.3) can be written as

$$(-1)^{|I|} (D - \sum \{y \in S | y \in \bigcap I\})^{-1}$$

for $I = \emptyset$, we see that the theorem follows directly from the lemma. Clearly the result generalises to non-distinct $m(\overline{\phi_i})$, for example by perturbing these values slightly and letting the perturbation go to zero. (The reason for not directly proving the required generalisation of the lemma in this case is the rather obfuscating notation which would need to be introduced.) $\qquad\square$

It is easy to see that $Bel(\theta|\phi)$, $Bel(\theta||\phi)$ as defined above are different, even assuming $Bel(\phi) > 0$. For example if $L = \{p_1, p_2\}$, $\theta = p_1$, $\phi = p_2$ and the bpa m of Bel is given by $m(\overline{p_1}) = 1 - \delta$, $m(\overline{p_2}) = \delta > 0$ then $Bel(\phi) = \delta > 0$, $Bel(\theta||\phi) = 0$ but $Bel(\theta|\phi) = 1 - \delta$. For Bel a probability function both agree with the standard conditional probability whilst in general $Bel(\theta|\phi) \ge Bel(\theta||\phi)$ and $Pl(\theta||\phi) \ge Pl(\theta|\phi)$. To see this notice, that by expressing both sides in terms of the bpa m of Bel,

$$Bel(\theta \wedge \phi) + Pl(\neg\theta \wedge \phi) \le Pl(\phi),$$

so, provided $Bel(\phi) > 0$,

$$
\begin{aligned}
Bel(\theta|\phi) &= 1 - Pl(\neg\theta|\phi) = 1 - \frac{Pl(\neg\theta \wedge \phi)}{Pl(\phi)} \\
&\geq 1 - \frac{Pl(\neg\theta \wedge \phi)}{Bel(\theta \wedge \phi) + Pl(\neg\theta \wedge \phi)} = Bel(\theta||\phi).
\end{aligned}
$$

Whilst the conditional belief $Bel(\theta||\phi)$ has a certain naturalness, it suffers from the (apparent) shortcoming that repeated conditionings do not commute. That is, even when well defined, conditioning with respect to ϕ_1, ϕ_2, in that order, is not necessarily the same as conditioning with respect to ϕ_2, ϕ_1, in that order, and hence not necessarily the same as the single conditioning on $\phi_1 \wedge \phi_2$. (This occurs for example in the case $L = \{p_1, p_2\}$, $\theta = p_1 \wedge p_2$, $\phi_1 = p_1$, $\phi_2 = p_1 \vee p_2$ with Bel given by $m(p_1 \wedge p_2) = m(p_1 \wedge \neg p_2) = \frac{1}{4}, m(\neg p_1) = \frac{1}{2}$.) These three values are however always equal for $Bel(\theta|\phi)$, as can be readily checked.

For a further discussion on the relative suitability of $Bel(\theta|\phi)$, $Bel(\theta||\phi)$ for capturing the notion of conditional belief in the context of Dempster–Shafer belief see [11]. Notice that since the denominator in $Bel(\theta||\phi)$ involves θ, linear constraints involving $Bel(\theta_1||\phi), \ldots, Bel(\theta_m||\phi)$ cannot in general be simplified to linear constraints in the unconditional belief function, unlike the other notions we have considered in this book.

We now turn to a second justification, or explanation, of DS-belief functions.

Second Justification

In a similar fashion to the 'possible worlds' justification of belief as probability suppose we had a set $\mathcal{W}$ of possible worlds and a measure μ defined on a set $\mathcal{S}$ of subsets of $\mathcal{W}$ (rather than on all subsets of $\mathcal{W}$) with the properties:

(i) $\mathcal{W} \in \mathcal{S}$, $\emptyset \in \mathcal{S}$, $\mu(\mathcal{W}) = 1$, $\mu(\emptyset) = 0$.

(ii) If $X, Y \in \mathcal{S}$ then $X \cup Y$, $\mathcal{W} - X \in \mathcal{S}$ (so also $X \cap Y \in \mathcal{S}$).

(iii) If $X, Y \in \mathcal{S}$ and $X \cap Y = \emptyset$ then $\mu(X \cup Y) = \mu(X) + \mu(Y)$.

(That is, μ is a finitely additive measure on the field of sets $\mathcal{S}$.) Then for any $Z \subseteq \mathcal{W}$ (not necessarily in $\mathcal{S}$) we may define the *inner measure*, $\mu_*(Z)$, by

$$
\mu_*(Z) = sup\{\mu(X) \mid X \in \mathcal{S} \text{ and } X \subseteq Z\}
$$

and define, by analogy with the possible worlds interpretation of belief as probability,

$$
Bel(\theta) = \mu_*\{w \in \mathcal{W} \mid w \models \theta\}.
$$

The next two theorems, which appear in a paper, [17], of Fagin and Halpern, show that not only is *Bel* defined in this way a DS-belief function but, further, that any DS-belief function has such a possible worlds interpretation.

Theorem 4.6 *Bel defined as above is a DS-belief function.*

Proof We use the first definition of DS-belief functions. Conditions $(DS1\text{--}2)$ are immediate. To show $(DS3)$ let $\epsilon > 0$, $\theta_1, ..., \theta_n \in$ SL and for each $\overline{\psi} \in \overline{SL}$ pick $Z_{\overline{\psi}} \in \mathcal{S}$ such that

$$Z_{\overline{\psi}} \subseteq \{w \in W \mid w \models \psi\}$$

and

$$\mu(Z_{\overline{\psi}}) \leq \mu_*\{w \in W \mid w \models \psi\} \leq \mu(Z_{\overline{\psi}}) + \epsilon \tag{4.4}$$

We may assume that for $\overline{\phi} \leq \overline{\psi}$, $Z_{\overline{\phi}} \subseteq Z_{\overline{\psi}}$, otherwise replace $Z_{\overline{\psi}}$ by $\bigcup_{\overline{\phi} \leq \overline{\psi}} Z_{\overline{\phi}}$, this only tightens (4.4). Then

$$Bel(\bigvee_{i=1}^{n} \theta_i) \;=\; \mu_*\{w \in W \mid w \models \bigvee_{i=1}^{n} \theta_i\} \geq \mu(Z_{\overline{\theta}_1} \cup ... \cup Z_{\overline{\theta}_n})$$

$$= \sum_{\emptyset \neq S \subseteq \{1,...,n\}} (-1)^{|S|-1} \mu(\bigcap_{i \in S} Z_{\overline{\theta}_i})$$

(this is proved as in proposition 2.1(d)))

$$\geq \sum_{\emptyset \neq S \subseteq \{1,...,n\}} (-1)^{|S|-1} \mu_*\{w \in W \mid w \models \bigwedge_{i \in S} \theta_i\} - 2^n \epsilon$$

since

$$Z_{\overline{\bigwedge_{i \in S} \theta_i}} \subseteq \bigcap_{i \in S} Z_{\overline{\theta}_i} \subseteq \{w \in W \mid w \models \bigwedge_{i \in S} \theta_i\},$$

so

$$\mu\left(Z_{\overline{\bigwedge_{i \in S} \theta_i}}\right) \leq \mu\left(\bigcap_{i \in S} Z_{\overline{\theta}_i}\right) \leq \mu_*\{w \in W \mid w \models \bigwedge_{i \in S} \theta_i\} \leq \mu(\bigcap_{i \in S} Z_{\overline{\theta}_i}) + \epsilon.$$

$(DS3)$ now follows since

$$\mu_*\{w \in W \mid w \models \bigwedge_{i \in S} \theta_i\} = Bel(\bigwedge_{i \in S} \theta_i)$$

and $\epsilon > 0$ was arbitrary. $\qquad\square$

An origin for $(DS3)$ is now clear; it is simply a reformulated version of an inequality which always holds for inner measures.

Theorem 4.7 *If Bel is a DS-belief function then there are $W, \mathcal{S}, \mu$ as above such that for all $\theta \in SL$,*

$$Bel(\theta) = \mu_*\{w \in W \mid w \models \theta\}.$$

Proof Let $\mathcal{W} = \{\langle \alpha, Y \rangle \mid \alpha \in Y \subseteq At^L\}$ where, as usual, $At^L = \{\alpha_1, ..., \alpha_J\}$ is the set of atoms of SL. For $\emptyset \neq Y \subseteq At^L$ let

$$R_Y = \{\langle \alpha, Y \rangle \mid \alpha \in Y\}.$$

Notice that the R_Y are pairwise disjoint, with union $\mathcal{W}$. Let $\mathcal{S}$ consist of all subsets of $\mathcal{W}$ of the form

$$R_{Y_1} \cup R_{Y_2} \cup ... \cup R_{Y_q} \quad (Y_i \text{ distinct})$$

and define $\mu(R_{Y_1} \cup R_{Y_2} \cup ... \cup R_{Y_q}) = \sum_{i=1}^{q} m(\bigvee Y_i)$, where m is the bpa of Bel. It is straightforward to check that $\mathcal{S}, \mu$ satisfy (i)–(iii) above.

For $\langle \alpha, Y \rangle \in \mathcal{W}$ we define, for $\theta \in SL$,

$$\langle \alpha, Y \rangle \models \theta \quad \Leftrightarrow \quad \alpha \models \theta \text{ (in the usual sense)}.$$

Then

$$\mu_*\{\langle \alpha, Y \rangle \in \mathcal{W} \mid \langle \alpha, Y \rangle \models \theta\} \;=\; \mu_*\{\langle \alpha, Y \rangle \in \mathcal{W} \mid \alpha \models \theta\}$$

$$=\; \mu_*\{\langle \alpha, Y \rangle \in \mathcal{W} \mid \alpha \in S_\theta\}.$$

Clearly $R_X \subseteq \{\langle \alpha, Y \rangle \in \mathcal{W} \mid \langle \alpha, Y \rangle \models \theta\}$ for $\emptyset \neq X \subseteq S_\theta$ and, conversely, if $R_X \subseteq \{\langle \alpha, Y \rangle \in \mathcal{W} \mid \langle \alpha, Y \rangle \models \theta\}$ then $\langle \beta, X \rangle \models \theta$ must hold for each $\beta \in X$ so $X \subseteq S_\theta$. Hence $\bigcup_{\emptyset \neq X \subseteq S_\theta} R_X$ is the largest set in $\mathcal{S}$ which is a subset of $\{\langle \alpha, Y \rangle \in \mathcal{W} \mid \langle \alpha, Y \rangle \models \theta\}$ so

$$\mu_*\{\langle \alpha, Y \rangle \in \mathcal{W} \mid \langle \alpha, Y \rangle \models \theta\} = \mu(\bigcup_{\emptyset \neq X \subseteq S_\theta} R_X) = \sum_{\emptyset \neq X \subseteq S_\theta} m(\bigvee X) = Bel(\theta)$$

as required.   □

Remark Notice that if $\mu_*\{w \in \mathcal{W} \mid w \models \theta\} = Bel(\theta)$ with μ, etc. as above then

$$Pl(\theta) = 1 - Bel(\neg\theta) \;=\; 1 - \sup\{\mu(Z) \mid Z \in \mathcal{S} \text{ and } Z \subseteq X\}$$

$$\text{where } X = \{w \in \mathcal{W} \mid w \models \neg\theta\}$$

$$=\; 1 - \sup\{\mu(\mathcal{W} - Z) \mid Z \in \mathcal{S} \text{ and } \mathcal{W} - Z \subseteq X\}$$

$$=\; \inf\{1 - \mu(\mathcal{W} - Z) \mid Z \in \mathcal{S} \text{ and } \mathcal{W} - X \subseteq Z\}$$

$$=\; \inf\{\mu(Z) \mid Z \in \mathcal{S} \text{ and } \{w \in \mathcal{W} \mid w \models \theta\} \subseteq Z\}$$

$$=\; \mu^*\{w \in \mathcal{W} \mid w \models \theta\}$$

where μ^* is the *outer measure* on $\mathcal{W}$ derived from μ.

An Example Recall the simple example of question Q already considered in Chapter 2, namely, given

$$K = \{Bel(q) = b, \ Bel(p \mid q) = a\} \quad (b > 0)$$

what value should be assigned to $Bel(p)$? to $Bel(\neg p)$?

In this case if we further assume that Bel is a DS-belief function, i.e. satisfies $(DS1$–$3)$, and conditional belief is defined as above then the constraints become

$$\{Bel(q) = b, \ Bel(p \vee \neg q) - Bel(\neg q) = a(1 - Bel(\neg q))\}.$$

As indicated earlier we can re-express these in terms of the $m(\bar{\theta})$, $\bar{\theta} \in \overline{SL}$ and hence find the consistent ranges. However even for $L = \{p, q\}$ this involves $2^{2^2} - 1 = 15$ unknowns. Carrying out the calculation yields (maximal) ranges for $Bel(p), Bel(\neg p)$ of

$$1 + ab - b \geq Bel(p) \geq \max(0, a + b - 1),$$

$$1 - ab \geq Bel(\neg p) \geq 0.$$

A similar investigation using the conditional belief $Bel(p \| q)$ yields ranges

$$1 + ab - b \geq Bel(p) \geq ab,$$

$$1 - ab \geq Bel(\neg p) \geq 0.$$

Chapter 5

Truth-functional Belief

In this chapter we shall consider the assumption that $Bel(\ )$, $Bel(\ |\ )$ are truth-functional, in other words that there are functions $F_\wedge$, $F_\vee$, $F_| : [0,1]^2 \to [0,1]$ and $F_\neg : [0,1] \to [0,1]$ such that $Bel(\ )$, $Bel(\ |\ )$ satisfy

$$Bel(\theta \wedge \phi) = F_\wedge(Bel(\theta), Bel(\phi)),$$

$$Bel(\theta \vee \phi) = F_\vee(Bel(\theta), Bel(\phi)),$$

$$Bel(\neg\theta) = F_\neg(Bel(\theta)),$$

$$Bel(\theta|\phi) = F_|(Bel(\theta), Bel(\phi)).$$

With such a choice of $F_\wedge$, $F_\vee$ etc., $Bel(\theta)$ and $Bel(\theta|\phi)$ are determined by the values of the $Bel(p)$, $p \in L$ so that the only free part of Bel is the choice of values it gives to the propositional variables. This is exactly similar to the situation in the classical (two-valued) propositional calculus where a valuation $V : L \to \{0,1\}$ extends uniquely to $V : SL \to \{0,1\}$. For this reason we shall call $Bel : SL \to [0,1]$ satisfying the above conditions a 'valuation over the logic given by $F_\wedge$, $F_\vee$, $F_|$, $F_\neg$'. (Throughout this book we take $F_\to$ and $F_\leftrightarrow$ to be defined from $F_\wedge$, $F_\vee$, $F_\neg$ in the standard way. This suffices for us here although of course a rather wider-ranging investigation might well call for introducing $F_\to$, $F_\leftrightarrow$, and maybe other connectives, independently.)

A particular example of such a logic, which is often referred to as fuzzy logic, is when

$$(\mathbf{F_1}) \quad \begin{aligned} F_\wedge(x,y) &= \min(x,y) \\ F_\vee(x,y) &= \max(x,y) \\ F_\neg(x) &= 1 - x \\ F_|(x,y) &= \min(1, 1 - y + x) \end{aligned}$$

Two further examples are

$(\textbf{F}_2)$ $F_\wedge(x,y) = xy$

$F_\vee(x,y) = x + y - xy$

$F_\neg(x) = 1 - x$

$F_|(x,y) = \begin{cases} \frac{x}{y} & \text{if } x < y \\ 1 & \text{otherwise} \end{cases}$

$(\textbf{F}_3)$ $F_\wedge(x,y) = \max(0, x + y - 1)$

$F_\vee(x,y) = \min(1, x + y)$

$F_\neg(x) = 1 - x$

$F_|(x,y) = \min(1, 1 - y + x)$

Notice that in each of these examples $F_\wedge$ and $F_\vee$ are related in the 'standard', classical, way:

$$F_\vee(x,y) = F_\neg(F_\wedge(F_\neg(x), F_\neg(y)))$$
$$F_\wedge(x,y) = F_\neg(F_\vee(F_\neg(x), F_\neg(y))).$$

We should point out here that these are just a sample (although relevant for our later discussion) of the possible choices which have been proposed in the literature.

For each of these possibilities we could ask questions about completeness, compactness, expressibility etc., but if we were to do that, this book (if it ever ended) would seem to miss our main target of considering the assumptions underlying uncertain reasoning at the present time. So rather than do this we shall simply concentrate on the two fundamental questions of justifying, firstly, belief as truth-functional, and secondly, given that, the choices to make for $F_\wedge$, $F_\vee$, $F_\neg$, $F_|$.

Concerning the assumption that belief is truth-functional we are, regrettably, unaware of any satisfactory justification for this, except possibly on pragmatic grounds.

At the same time a satisfactory explanation of what such 'fuzzy' truth values mean seems to be lacking. For example, in this area statements such as 'my belief that someone of height 178 cm is tall is 0.6' are often quoted as assertions of fuzzy belief, but how should the figure of 0.6 be understood? One explanation is that it represents my estimate of the proportion of the population who would agree that someone of height 178 cm is tall. However, this corresponds to the first justification in Chapter 3 which gave belief as probability, and, as we shall shortly see, provides no justification for truth-functional belief.

It is true that making this assumption means (clearly) that for $\theta \in SL$, $Bel(\theta)$ can be expressed as a function of the $Bel(p)$ for p a propositional variable appearing in θ and this may *appear* to simplify the situation (although results in Chapter 10 will argue against this being true in general). However, this scarcely seems to warrant the status of a justification.

On the other hand it seems rather easy to criticize the assumption that belief is truth-functional on the grounds that, for example, it forces $Bel(\theta \wedge \phi)$ to be a fixed function, $F_\wedge$, of $Bel(\theta)$, $Bel(\phi)$ no matter what the relationship between θ and ϕ is. So for example, if $Bel(p) = Bel(\neg p) > 0$ then

$$Bel(p \wedge p) = F_\wedge(Bel(p), Bel(p)) = F_\wedge(Bel(p), Bel(\neg p)) = Bel(p \wedge \neg p)$$

so $Bel(p \wedge p) = Bel(p \wedge \neg p)$. However in almost any such real example this conclusion seems paradoxical.

Referring back now to just $\mathbf{F_1}$, $\mathbf{F_2}$, $\mathbf{F_3}$ notice that for $x, y \in \{0, 1\}$ each of $F_\wedge$, $F_\vee$, $F_\neg$ agrees with the corresponding function in the classical propositional calculus. Hence if $Bel(p) \in \{0, 1\}$ for all $p \in L$ then, for $\theta \in SL$,

$$Bel(\theta) = V(\theta)$$

where V is the valuation on L agreeing with Bel on L, for each of $\mathbf{F_1}$, $\mathbf{F_2}$, $\mathbf{F_3}$. This observation, that $\mathbf{F_1}$, $\mathbf{F_2}$, $\mathbf{F_3}$ extend the classical propositional calculus, provides a tiny argument in their favour. In fact it is easy to check that this same result holds for probability functions (but not for DS-belief functions since there it is consistent to have $Bel(\theta \vee \phi) = 1$, $Bel(\theta) = Bel(\phi) = 0$). In general however probability functions are not truth-functional as the following two probability functions which agree on p, q but not on $p \wedge q$ show:

$p \wedge q$	$p \wedge \neg q$	$\neg p \wedge q$	$\neg p \wedge \neg q$
$\frac{1}{4}$	$\frac{1}{4}$	$\frac{1}{4}$	$\frac{1}{4}$

$p \wedge q$	$p \wedge \neg q$	$\neg p \wedge q$	$\neg p \wedge \neg q$
$\frac{1}{2}$	0	0	$\frac{1}{2}$

Having summarily considered the justification for belief being truth-functional we now accept this point and consider justifying particular choices of $F_\wedge$, $F_\vee$, $F_\neg$, $F_|$.

The general rationale here, say for a particular choice of $F_\wedge$, is to write down certain properties we feel $F_\wedge$ should possess, and then show that this in fact restricts the choice of $F_\wedge$ to one's personal favourite. Of course this often results in having to require $F_\wedge$ to possess rather unintuitive properties. Nevertheless there are several arguments along these lines which seem worthy of mention.

We first consider $F_\neg$. To simplify the notation we shall write $\neg$ in place of $F_\neg$ and $\wedge$ in place of $F_\wedge$ etc. Thus $\neg$ is standing both for a connective and a function from $[0,1]$ to $[0,1]$.

Justification for the choice of $F_\neg$

The function $\neg$ might, intuitively, be argued to have the following properties:

(N1) $\qquad\qquad\qquad\qquad \neg 0 = 1, \quad \neg 1 = 0.$

(N2) $\qquad\qquad\qquad\qquad \neg$ is decreasing.

(N3) $\qquad\qquad\qquad\qquad \neg\neg x = x$ for $x \in [0, 1]$.

Thus $(N1)$ says that the negation of a certainly false statement should be certainly true and vice-versa, $(N2)$ says that as belief in a statement increases belief in its negation decreases.

Assuming $(N1\text{--}3)$ we conclude, by $(N3)$, that $\neg$ is 1–1 onto $[0,1]$ since for $x, y \in [0, 1]$, $x = \neg(\neg x)$ and

$$\neg x = \neg y \Rightarrow \neg\neg x = \neg\neg y \Rightarrow x = y$$

Hence by $(N2)$ and the remark following lemma 3.7 $\neg$ must be strictly decreasing and continuous. The following theorem is due to Trillas [67].

Theorem 5.1 *If $\neg$ satisfies $(N1\text{--}3)$ then $([0, 1], \neg, <)$ is isomorphic to $([0, 1], 1 - x, <)$ (and conversely, since $\neg x = 1 - x$ satisfies $(N1\text{--}3)$).*

Proof First notice that since $\neg 0 > 0$ and $\neg 1 < 1$, the continuity of $\neg$ ensures the existence of $0 < c < 1$ such that $\neg c = c$. Define, for $0 \leq x \leq 1$,

$$f(x) = \begin{cases} \frac{x}{2c} & \text{if } x \leq c, \\[2mm] 1 - \frac{\neg x}{2c} & \text{if } x \geq c. \end{cases}$$

Then $f(0) = 0$, $f(1) = 1$, $f(c) = \frac{1}{2}$ (either way!) and it is easy to check that f is strictly increasing and continuous, hence onto. Finally for $x \leq c$, $\neg x \geq \neg c = c$ so

$$f(\neg x) = 1 - \frac{\neg\neg x}{2c} = 1 - \frac{x}{2c} = 1 - f(x)$$

as required, and similarly for $x \geq c$. Hence f is the required isomorphism. $\qquad\square$

Notice that this f is not unique; for example the above proof also works with $2(\frac{x}{2c})^2$ in place of $\frac{x}{2c}$ etc.

Justification for the choice of $F_\wedge$

The function $\wedge : [0, 1]^2 \rightarrow [0, 1]$ might intuitively be argued to satisfy the following:

$(C1)$ $0 \wedge 1 = 1 \wedge 0 = 0$, $1 \wedge 1 = 1$.

$(C2)$ $\wedge$ is continuous.

$(C3)$ $\wedge$ is increasing (not necessarily strictly) in each coordinate.

$(C4)$ $x \wedge (y \wedge z) = (x \wedge y) \wedge z$ for $x, y, z \in [0, 1]$.

(A function satisfying $(C1\text{--}4)$ is also known as a T-norm.)

$(C1)$ might be justified on the grounds that for the categorical truth values $0, 1$ $\wedge$ should act like classical conjunction. $(C2)$ is justified on the grounds that small changes in one's beliefs in θ and ϕ should only cause small changes in one's belief in $\theta \wedge \phi$. (*C3*) is justified on the grounds that increasing one's belief in θ (or ϕ) should not decrease one's belief in $\theta \wedge \phi$. Finally (*C4*) could be defended on the grounds that in natural language we do not differentiate between $\theta \wedge (\phi \wedge \psi)$ and $(\theta \wedge \phi) \wedge \psi$. (A similar argument to justify $\wedge$ being commutative seems open to question, see for example [62], although in fact, as we shall see later, commutativity follows from (*C1*–4).) In view of (*C4*) we can unambiguously drop parentheses from multiple application of $\wedge$.

Notice that $F_\wedge$ in $\mathbf{F_1}$, $\mathbf{F_2}$, $\mathbf{F_3}$ satisfy (*C1*–4). Indeed if $\wedge$ satisfies (*C1*–4) then it must be a 'hybrid' of the $F_\wedge$ in $\mathbf{F_1}$–$\mathbf{F_3}$ as the subsequent discussion will show.

Assume that $\wedge$ satisfies (*C1*–4). We first show that (*C1*) can be strengthened to

$$x \wedge 0 = 0 \wedge x = 0, \quad x \wedge 1 = 1 \wedge x = x \;\; for \;\; 0 \leq x \leq 1.$$

The first of these identities follows directly from (*C1*), (*C3*). For the second notice that by (*C1*), for $0 \leq a \leq 1$,

$$0 = 0 \wedge 1 \leq a \leq 1 \wedge 1 = 1$$

so by continuity, (*C3*) and the intermediate value theorem, $a = t \wedge 1$ for some $0 \leq t \leq 1$. Then

$$a \wedge 1 = t \wedge 1 \wedge 1 = t \wedge 1 = a$$

by (*C1*),(*C4*). The identity $1 \wedge a = a$ follows similarly.

Using these identities and (*C3*) we now have that $x \wedge y \leq 1 \wedge y = y$ (and similarly $x \wedge y \leq x$). We shall use these identities frequently and without further reference in what follows.

Now suppose $b \wedge b = b$. Then for $a \geq b \geq c$, $b = b \wedge 1 \geq c \geq b \wedge 0 = 0$ so by continuity $c = b \wedge t$ for some t and hence $c \geq a \wedge c = a \wedge b \wedge t \geq b \wedge b \wedge t = b \wedge t = c$. We conclude that for $a \geq b \geq c$ and $b \wedge b = b$,

$$a \wedge c = c = \min(a, c) \quad (= c \wedge a \text{ similarly})$$

In particular we have the following theorem, due to Fu & Fung [22] and Bellman & Giertz [2].

Theorem 5.2 *If in addition to (C1–4) $\wedge$ also satisfies $x \wedge x = x$ for all x then $\wedge = \min$ (as in $\mathbf{F_1}$).* $\square$

Notice that the result gives that $\wedge$ is commutative. Indeed we shall shortly see that this follows just from (*C1*–4).

Now suppose $d \neq d \wedge d$. Then, since $0 \wedge 0 = 0 < d < 1 = 1 \wedge 1$, by continuity there exists a largest $a < d$ and least $b > d$ such that $a \wedge a = a$, $b \wedge b = b$. Notice that for $x, y \in [a, b]$, $x \wedge y \in [a, b]$ since $a = a \wedge a \leq x \wedge y \leq b \wedge b = b$.

Theorem 5.3 ($[a, b], \wedge, <$) *is isomorphic either to* ($[0, 1], \times, <$) *(as in* F_2*) or to* ($[0, 1], \max(0, x + y - 1), <$) *(as in* F_3*). The latter holds just if for some $a < c < b$, $c \wedge c = a$.*

Proof First suppose that for no $a < c < b$ do we have $c \wedge c = a$. We shall show that $\wedge$ is strictly increasing on $(a, b]^2$. To see this suppose $a < c \le b$, $a \le x < y \le b$ but $c \wedge x = c \wedge y$. Since, by the above argument,

$$y \wedge a = \min(a, y) = a \le x < y = \min(b, y) = y \wedge b$$

there exists $a \le t < b$ such that $x = y \wedge t$. Hence

$$c \wedge x \wedge t = c \wedge y \wedge t = c \wedge x.$$

Let $s \ge a$ be minimal such that $c \wedge x \wedge s = c \wedge x$. Then $s < b$ (since $t < b$) and $a < s$, otherwise $s = a$ and

$$c \wedge y = c \wedge x = c \wedge x \wedge a = \min(c \wedge x, a) = a,$$

so for $u = \min(c, y) > a$,

$$a = c \wedge y \ge u \wedge u \ge a \wedge a = a, \quad \text{i.e. } u \wedge u = a,$$

contradiction. Hence $a < s < b$. But $c \wedge x \wedge s \wedge s = c \wedge x \wedge s = c \wedge x$ and $a \le s \wedge s \le s$ so by minimality of s, $s \wedge s = s$, contradiction. We have shown that $\wedge$ is strictly increasing on $(a, b]^2$ whilst by earlier results $x \wedge a = a \wedge x = a$, $x \wedge b = b \wedge x = x$ for $x \in [a, b]$.

Now we have all the required conditions of lemma 3.7, which was used to prove F is isomorphic to multiplication in Cox's theorem, and it follows exactly similarly that

$$([a, b], \wedge, <) \cong ([0, 1], \times, <).$$

Now suppose that $c \wedge c = a$ for some $a < c < b$. Let $a < \alpha < b$ be maximal such that $\alpha \wedge \alpha = a$. We now proceed in a similar fashion to the first case. We first show, by a similar proof, that if $a \le x < y \le b$, $a \le c \le b$ and $c \wedge y > a$ then $c \wedge x < c \wedge y$. For if $c \wedge x = c \wedge y$ let $s \ge a$ be minimal such that $c \wedge x \wedge s = c \wedge x$. Then, as before, $s = s \wedge s$ so $s = a$ and

$$a = c \wedge x \wedge s = c \wedge x = c \wedge y,$$

contradiction.

Now proceed as in the proof of lemma 3.7 to define $\dot{\alpha}^{\frac{m}{n}} = \dot{\gamma}^m$ where $\dot{\gamma}^n = \alpha$. Then by similar arguments,

(i) $\dot{\alpha}^{\frac{km}{kn}} = \dot{\alpha}^{\frac{m}{n}}$,

(ii) $\dot{\alpha}^{\frac{m}{n}} \wedge \dot{\alpha}^{\frac{p}{q}} = \dot{\alpha}^{\frac{mq+np}{nq}}$,

(iii) $\dot{\alpha}^{\frac{m}{n}} < \dot{\alpha}^{\frac{p}{q}}$ for $\frac{p}{q} < 2, \frac{m}{n}$,

(iv) $\dot{\alpha}^{\frac{m}{n}} = a$ for $\frac{m}{n} \geq 2$,

(v) $\lim\limits_{n \to \infty} \dot{\alpha}^{\frac{1}{n}} = b$,

etc. and hence

$$g : ([a, b], \wedge, <) \cong ([0, 2], \min(2, x + y), >)$$

where $g(\dot{\alpha}^r) = r$ ($g(a) = 2$, $g(b) = 0$). The result now follows by noticing that this latter structure is isomorphic to $([0, 1], \max(0, x + y - 1), <)$ via the isomorphism $h(x) = 1 - \frac{x}{2}$.

Summing up then we see that $\wedge$ satisfying $(C1\text{--}4)$ looks like a union of intervals $[a, b]$ with only, possibly, end points in common such that on each of these $\wedge$ acts like the $\wedge$ in one of $\mathbf{F_1}$, $\mathbf{F_2}$, $\mathbf{F_3}$ whereas across such intervals it looks like min.

Notice that if we assume that we also have $\neg$ satisfying $(N1\text{--}3)$ and

$(N4)$ $x \wedge \neg x = 0$ for all $x \in [0, 1]$

(a consistent assumption since $(N1\text{--}4)$, $(C1\text{--}4)$ hold in $\mathbf{F_3}$) then there can be no $0 < b < 1$ such that $b \wedge b = b$, for otherwise we should have

$$0 = b \wedge \neg b = \min(b, \neg b) > 0.$$

Hence $([0, 1], \wedge, <)$ must be isomorphic to one of $\mathbf{F_2}$, $\mathbf{F_3}$ (restricted to $F_\wedge$, $<$) and since the first of these satisfies $x, y > 0 \Rightarrow x \wedge y > 0$ we conclude that $([0, 1], \wedge, <)$ must be isomorphic to $([0, 1], \max(0, x + y - 1), <)$. In contrast to this, theorem 5.2 provides an attractive argument for $a \wedge b = \min(a, b)$.

Another argument for this latter choice (within the context of question Q) has been given by Kreinovich et al. in [39], [40] and goes as follows. Consider again our example $\mathbb{E}$. Initially the expert used expressions like 'rather uncommon', 'good indicator' etc. With the agreement of the expert these were then converted into numbers. Now it seems unlikely that this same expert, but on a different occasion, would use *exactly* the same numbers even though he gave essentialy the same natural language statements K. Nevertheless we might argue that one set of such numbers is just a re-scaled version of any other and that if expression X gets a higher number than Y (i.e. X is deemed to denote stronger belief than Y) in one numbering, then it will in any other, although the individual numbers may change. In other words any two numberings should preserve the order. Now presumably 1 is always identified with certainty and 0 with impossibility so such a rescaling between numberings would be an order-preserving function g from $[0,1]$, 1–1 onto $[0,1]$ satisfying $g(0) = 0$, $g(1) = 1$.

Simply at the level of the initial knowledge K the assumption that the numbers are only codes for words, and only the order is relevant, causes no difficulties. However suppose having 'numbered' K we use some uncertain reasoning to conclude $Bel(\theta) = c$. Then this c is a function of the initial numbers assigned to, or coding, expressions, and it would seem highly undesirable if the decoded version of c was different for compatible initial codings.

Thus Kreinovich et al. argue: if one numbering, $\mathcal{N}$, for K gave $Bel(p) = a$, $Bel(q) = b$ and a second compatible numbering $\mathcal{M}$ gave $Bel(p) = g(a)$, $Bel(q) = g(b)$, where g is the rescaling between $\mathcal{N}$ and $\mathcal{M}$, and our uncertain reasoning gave

$$Bel(p \wedge q) = \alpha(a, b)$$

in the first case and

$$Bel(p \wedge q) = \alpha(g(a), g(b))$$

in the second case then we should have

$$g(\alpha(a, b)) = \alpha(g(a), g(b)).$$

Now in the context of belief being truth-functional and $F_\wedge$ satisfying $(C1\text{--}4)$ this amounts to

$$g(a \wedge b) = g(a) \wedge g(b) \quad \text{for any rescaling } g \tag{5.1}$$

Now suppose $a \wedge b$ was not an element of $\{a, b, 0, 1\}$. Then clearly there is a rescaling g which fixes $a, b, 0, 1$ whilst moving $a \wedge b$ so that the identity 5.1 fails. Thus it must be the case that $a \wedge b \in \{a, b, 0, 1\}$. Without loss of generality suppose $0 < a \le b$ so the only possibilities for $a \wedge b$ are $a, 0$. If $a \wedge b = 0$ then $a \wedge a = 0$ so let c be maximal such that $c \wedge c = 0$. Then for $d > c$, $d \wedge d = d$ (because the only choices for $d \wedge d$ are d and 0) so, by continuity $c = \lim_{d \searrow c} d \wedge d = c \wedge c = 0$, contradiction. Hence $a \wedge b = a = \min(a, b) \ (= b \wedge a$ similarly$)$.

Attractive as this argument might initially appear, if we apply it to negation we obtain that

$$g(\neg x) = \neg g(x)$$

so the only possibilities for $\neg x$ are $0, 1, x$ none of which is consistent with $(N1\text{--}3)$. If we drop $(N3)$ then

$$\neg x = \begin{cases} 1 & \text{for } x < 1, \\ 0 & \text{for } x = 1, \end{cases} \qquad \neg x = \begin{cases} 0 & \text{for } x > 0, \\ 1 & \text{for } x = 0, \end{cases}$$

are the only possibilities and indeed these have been proposed in the literature.

One way to correct such anomalies (if that is what they are) would be to put additional requirements on the notion of a rescaling with the aim of enlarging the possibilities for $F_\wedge$, $F_\neg$. A difficulty here however seems to be finding convincing additional, 'natural', requirements on the rescaling.

Justification for the choice of $F_\vee$

The natural requirements on $\vee$ are:

(D1) $0 \vee 0 = 0, \quad 1 \vee 0 = 1.$

(D2) $\vee$ is continuous.

(D3) $\vee$ is increasing (not necessarily strictly) in each coordinate.

(D4) $x \vee (y \vee z) = (x \vee y) \vee z$ for all $x, y, z \in [0, 1]$.

(A function satisfying (D1–4) is also called a T-conorm.)

Results on disjunction follow directly from results on conjunction (and conversely) by noticing that if $\vee$ satisfies (D1–4) then

$$x \wedge y = 1 - (1 - x) \vee (1 - y)$$

satisfies (C1–4) and conversely if $\wedge$ satisfies (C1–4) then

$$x \vee y = 1 - (1 - x) \wedge (1 - y)$$

satisfies (D1–4).

In particular from the results on conjunction we obtain that if $x = x \vee x$ for all x then, assuming (D1–4), $x \vee y = y \vee x = \max(x, y)$. Also any $\vee$ satisfying (D1–4) 'looks like' a union of intervals [a,b] with only end points, possibly, in common, on which $\vee$ acts, up to order isomorphism, like $x + y - xy$ or like $\min(1, x + y)$ (on [0,1]) and acts like $\max(x, y)$ across intervals. Finally the rescaling considerations of Kreinovich et al. give again $x \vee y = \max(x, y)$.

Notice also that we again get commutativity for free.

Remarks We shall not consider in such detail justifications for the choice of $F_|$ because in this case it seems far less clear what axioms should hold for this function. For example by considering $Bel(\theta | \theta \wedge \phi)$ it seems reasonable to suppose (assuming (C1–3)) that $F_|(x, y) = 1$ if $x \geq y$. However, assuming (N1–3) this would give that for any $\theta \in SL$, $Bel(\theta | \neg \theta) = 1$ or $Bel(\neg \theta | \theta) = 1$ which, somehow, seems too difficult to entertain in this context.

One argument that has been suggested for the choice of $F_|$ is that it should satisfy, for $x, y, z \in [0, 1]$,

$$x \leq F_|(y, z) \Leftrightarrow x \wedge z \leq y.$$

It is easy to check that this holds for $\mathbf{F_2}$ and $\mathbf{F_3}$ but not $\mathbf{F_1}$. If instead we try to *define $F_|$ for $\mathbf{F_1}$ to satisfy this* we would obtain

$$\begin{aligned} x \leq F_|(y, z) \quad &\Leftrightarrow \quad \min(x, z) \leq y \\ &\Leftrightarrow \quad z \leq y \text{ or } (x \leq y \text{ and } y < z), \end{aligned}$$

giving

$$F_|(y, z) = \begin{cases} 1 & \text{if } z \le y, \\ y & \text{otherwise.} \end{cases}$$

However neither this function nor $F_|$ of $\mathbf{F_2}$ is continuous. Indeed in the presence of $(C1\text{-}4)$, $\mathbf{F_1}$ defined in this way will be discontinuous at $\langle b, b \rangle$ whenever $0 < b < 1$ and $b \wedge b = b$.

In view of theorems 5.2 and 5.3 this gives the following theorem.

Theorem 5.4 *If $\wedge$ satisfies $(C1\text{-}4)$ and $F_|$ is continuous and satisfies for $x, y, z \in [0, 1]$*

$$x \wedge z \le y \Leftrightarrow x \le F_|(y, z)$$

then $([0, 1], \wedge, F_|, <)$ is isomorphic to $([0, 1], \max(0, x + y - 1), \min(1, 1 - y + x), <)$, i.e. $\mathbf{F_3}$ restricted to $F_\wedge$, $F_|$. □

If we drop $F_|$ from our considerations then the earlier arguments we gave seem, to us, to marginally favour $\mathbf{F_1}$ over $\mathbf{F_2}$, $\mathbf{F_3}$. There is furthermore another sense in which $\mathbf{F_1}$ scores best. For suppose we have $\wedge$, $\neg$ satisfying $(C1\text{-}4)$, $(N1\text{-}3)$ respectively. Then if $([0, 1], \wedge, <)$ is isomorphic to $([0, 1], \min(x, y), <)$ then $\wedge$ must already be min. and the isomorphism of $([0, 1], \neg, <)$ with $([0, 1], 1 - x, <)$ will extend to an isomorphism of $([0, 1], \wedge, \neg, <)$ with $([0, 1], \min(x, y), 1 - x, <)$. However, in the cases of $\mathbf{F_2}$, $\mathbf{F_3}$, whilst there may be isomorphisms of $([0, 1], \wedge, <)$ with the respective $([0, 1], F_\wedge, <)$ of $\mathbf{F_2}$, $\mathbf{F_3}$ and similarly for negation, there may not be an isomorphism which achieves both simultaneously (even with $(N4)$ for $\mathbf{F_3}$).

To see this for $\mathbf{F_2}$ consider the case when (already) $x \wedge y = xy$, whilst $\neg$ satisfies $(N1\text{-}3)$ and $\neg\frac{1}{2} = \frac{1}{2}$, $\neg\frac{1}{4} = \frac{2}{3}$ (which is clearly consistent). If such an isomorphism existed it would have to satisfy

$$f(\frac{1}{4}) = f(\frac{1}{2}) \cdot f(\frac{1}{2}) = \frac{1}{2} \cdot \frac{1}{2} = \frac{1}{4} \text{ (since } f(\neg\frac{1}{2}) = 1 - f(\frac{1}{2})),$$

$$f(\frac{2}{3}) = f(\neg\frac{1}{4}) = 1 - f(\frac{1}{4}) = \frac{3}{4},$$

$$\frac{1}{2} = f(\frac{1}{2}) = f(\frac{2}{3}) \cdot f(\frac{3}{4}) = \frac{3}{4} \cdot f(\frac{3}{4}),$$

so $f(\frac{3}{4}) = \frac{2}{3}$ and f is not increasing.

A similar argument with $x \wedge y = \max(0, x + y - 1)$, $\neg x = (1 - \sqrt{x})^2$ (so $\neg\frac{1}{4} = \frac{1}{4}$) works for $\mathbf{F_3}$ (with $(N4)$) by observing that $f(\frac{1}{2}) > f(\frac{1}{4}) = \frac{1}{2}$, whilst $f(\frac{1}{2}) \wedge f(\frac{1}{2}) = f(0) = 0$.

An Example

Recall the example of question Q already considered in Chapters 2 and 4, namely, given

$$K = \{Bel(q) = b, \ Bel(p|q) = a\} \quad (b > 0)$$

what value should be given to $Bel(p)$? to $Bel(\neg p)$? Taking the case of $\mathbf{F_1}$ (or $\mathbf{F_3}$) we see that K is equivalent to

$$Bel(q) = b, \quad \min(1, 1 - Bel(q) + Bel(p)) = a$$

These are only consistent (i.e. have a solution) if $a + b - 1 \geq 0$. If $a = 1$ the bounds on $Bel(p)$ are

$$1 \geq Bel(p) \geq b,$$

whilst if $a < 1$ we can solve for

$$Bel(p) = a + b - 1.$$

Notice that this latter value is lower (strictly if $b < 1$) than the lower bound of ab obtained in Chapter 1 (with belief as probability) since

$$ab - (a + b - 1) = (1 - a)(1 - b) \geq 0.$$

Similarly, assuming $a + b - 1 \geq 0$, the range of values for $Bel(\neg p)$ is

$$1 - b \geq Bel(\neg p) \geq 0 \quad \text{if } a = 1,$$
$$Bel(\neg p) = 2 - a - b \quad \text{if } a < 1,$$

and this latter figure is greater (strictly if $b < 1$) than the upper bound on $Bel(\neg p)$ obtained in Chapter 1.

At this point it is convenient to consider a (currently) popular, partially truth-functional interpretation of belief.

Possibility Theory

A belief function $Bel : SL \rightarrow [0, 1]$ is a *possibility function* if it satisfies, for all $\theta, \phi \in SL$

(Po1)	If $\models \theta$ then $Bel(\theta) = 1$ and $Bel(\neg \theta) = 0$.
(Po2)	If $\models (\theta \leftrightarrow \phi)$ then $Bel(\theta) = Bel(\phi)$.
(Po3)	$Bel(\theta \vee \phi) = \max(Bel(\theta), Bel(\phi))$.

We can think of $Bel(\theta)$ as the possibility of θ being true. Thus for example it seems reasonable to give value 1 to the *possibility* that a certain coin will land heads although one might only give it (subjective) *probability* $\frac{1}{2}$. In this sense then a possibility measure is measuring yet another aspect of belief. Again, as with DS-belief functions, it is questionable whether the figures in our initial example $\mathbb{E}$ could be interpreted in this way. Nevertheless possibility functions seem to be being investigated with an eye to their use in uncertain reasoning so we shall briefly review them here.

We first remark that there is a dual notion here. We say that *Bel* is a *necessity function* on SL if it satisfies, for θ, $\phi \in SL$

(i)   If $\models \theta$ then $Bel(\theta) = 1$ and $Bel(\neg\theta) = 0$.

(ii)   If $\models (\theta \leftrightarrow \phi)$ then $Bel(\theta) = Bel(\phi)$.

(iii) $Bel(\theta \wedge \phi) = \min(Bel(\theta), Bel(\phi))$.

It is easy to check that if *Bel* is a possibility function then $1 - Bel(\neg\theta)$ is a necessity function and conversely if *Bel* is a necessity function then $1 - Bel(\neg\theta)$ is a possibility function. Hence it is enough to limit our attention to possibility.

Let *Bel* be a possibility function. Then for $\theta \in SL$, θ consistent, by $(Po2\text{--}3)$

$$Bel(\theta) = Bel(\bigvee S_\theta) = \max\{Bel(\alpha_i) \mid \alpha_i \in S_\theta\}.$$

In particular for θ a tautology $(Po1)$ gives

$$1 = \max\{Bel(\alpha_i) \mid 1 \leq i \leq J\}.$$

Thus we see

$$\langle Bel(\alpha_1), ..., Bel(\alpha_J) \rangle \in C^L = \{\langle x_1, ..., x_J \rangle \in \mathbb{R}^J \mid x_i \geq 0, \ max(x_i) = 1\}.$$

Conversely given $\langle a_1, ..., a_J \rangle \in C^L$ we can define

$$Bel(\theta) = \max\{a_i \mid \alpha_i \in S_\theta\} \quad (= 0 \text{ if } S_\theta = \emptyset),$$

and it is easy to check that *Bel* is a possibility function. In particular then a possibility function is, as for a probability function, uniquely determined by its values on the atoms.

We now show that possibility functions are special cases of DS-plausibility functions. (For historical background see Klir and Folger [38].)

Let m be a bpa. We say that m (or its corresponding belief or plausibility function) is *consonant* if it satisfies that whenever $m(\bar\phi)$, $m(\bar\theta) > 0$ then either $\bar\theta \leq \bar\phi$ or $\bar\phi \leq \bar\theta$.

Theorem 5.5 *If m is a consonant bpa then its plausibility function, Pl, is a possibility function. Conversely given a possibility function Bel there is a (unique) consonant bpa for which Bel = Pl.*

Proof Given m let $\bar\theta_1, ..., \bar\theta_r$ enumerate $\{\bar\theta \mid m(\bar\theta) > 0\}$. (Such $\bar\theta$ are called *focal elements* of m.) By consonance we may assume $\bar\theta_1 < \bar\theta_2 < ... < \bar\theta_r$. Now for $\theta \in SL$

$$Pl(\theta) \quad = 1 - Bel(\neg\theta)$$

$$= \textstyle\sum_{\bar\psi} m(\bar\psi) - \sum_{\bar\psi \leq \neg\theta} m(\bar\psi)$$

$$= \textstyle\sum_{\bar\psi \wedge \bar\theta > 0} m(\bar\psi)$$

$$= \textstyle\sum_{j=t}^{r} m(\bar\theta_j) \quad \text{where } t \text{ is minimal such that } \bar\theta \wedge \bar\theta_t > 0,$$
$$\text{since if } \bar\theta_i \wedge \bar\theta > 0 \text{ and } i < j \leq r \text{ then } \bar\theta_j \wedge \bar\theta > 0 \quad \dots \quad (*)$$

$$= \textstyle\sum_{j=t}^{r} m(\bar\theta_j) \quad \text{where } t \text{ is minimal such that } \bar\alpha \wedge \bar\theta_t > 0$$
$$\text{for some } \alpha \in S_\theta \quad (\text{even if } S_\theta = \emptyset)$$

$$= max \; \{Pl(\alpha) \mid \alpha \in S_\theta\}, \text{ by using the characterisation at } (*).$$

Also if $\alpha \in S_{\theta_1}$, then $Pl(\alpha) = \sum_{i=1}^{r} m(\bar\theta_i) = 1$ so $\langle Pl(\alpha_1), ..., Pl(\alpha_J)\rangle \in C^L$ and, as above, Pl is a possibility function.

Conversely given a possibility function Bel let the distinct values of the $Bel(\alpha)$, $\alpha \in At^L$, be $\beta_1, ..., \beta_r$ in decreasing order and define a bpa m by

$$m(\bar\theta_1) = \beta_1 - \beta_2, \; m(\bar\theta_2) = \beta_2 - \beta_3, \; ..., \; m(\bar\theta_r) = \beta_r - \beta_{r+1}$$

where $\beta_{r+1} = 0$ and $\theta_i = \bigvee\{\alpha \mid Bel(\alpha) \geq \beta_i\}$, and $m(\bar\psi) = 0$ otherwise. Then m is a bpa since the $\bar\theta_i$ are distinct and

$$\sum_{\bar\psi} m(\bar\psi) = \sum_{i=1}^{r} m(\bar\theta_i) = \sum_{i=1}^{r}(\beta_i - \beta_{i+1}) = \beta_1 - \beta_{r+1} = \beta_1 = 1,$$

since $Bel(\alpha) = 1$ for some atom.

Clearly the $\bar\theta_i$ are consonant and so, as above, the corresponding plausibility function Pl^m is a possibility function. Furthermore for any atom α,

$$Pl^m(\alpha) \quad = \textstyle\sum_{i=t}^{r} m(\bar\theta_i) \quad \text{where } t \text{ is minimal such that } \alpha \in S_{\theta_t}$$
$$= \beta_t,$$

and since α is in S_{θ_t} but not in $S_{\theta_{t-1}}$ it must be the case that $Bel(\alpha) = \beta_t$ also. Hence Pl^m, Bel agree on atoms and hence agree everywhere. Clearly m is unique here since different m would produce different DS-belief functions, hence different plausibility functions.   □

Notice that every consonant bpa yields a DS-belief function which is a necessity function and conversely every necessity function can arise in this way. Notice also that if the bpa m is not consonant then its plausibility function cannot be a possibility function, by the uniqueness of its bpa (theorem 4.2).

Theorem 5.5 provides an interesting connection between DS-belief and possibility. Unfortunately however Dempster's rule of combination does not preserve consonance as may easily be checked by considering $m_1 \oplus m_2$ where m_1, m_2 are the consonant bpas for $L = \{p_1, p_2\}$ given by $m_1(\overline{p_1}) = m_1(\overline{p_1 \vee \neg p_2}) = \frac{1}{2}$, $m_2(\overline{\neg p_1}) = m_2(\overline{\neg p_1 \vee p_2}) = \frac{1}{2}$.

Conditional Possibility

In view of the above characterisation of possibility as consonant plausibility it might seem natural to define conditional possibility in terms of the corresponding conditional plausibility given in Chapter 4. That is, given a plausibility function Pl^m with consonant bpa m, we define

$$Pl^m(\theta|\phi) = \frac{Pl^m(\theta \wedge \phi)}{Pl^m(\phi)} \quad \text{for } Pl^m(\phi) > 0.$$

It is straightforward to see that this conditional plausibility is a possibility function (or equivalently that its bpa is consonant). Considering again our example of

$$K = \{Bel(q) = b, \ Bel(p|q) = a\}$$

with $b > 0$, $L = \{p, q\}$, if we take the above definition with Bel a possibility function we obtain the equivalent constraints

$$Bel(p \wedge q) = ab,$$

$$\max(Bel(p \wedge q), Bel(\neg p \wedge q)) = b,$$

$$\max(Bel(p \wedge q), Bel(p \wedge \neg q), Bel(\neg p \wedge q), Bel(\neg p \wedge \neg q)) = 1.$$

This gives range $ab \le Bel(p) \le 1$ for $Bel(p)$ and ranges for $Bel(\neg p)$ of

$$b \le Bel(\neg p) \le 1 \quad if \ a < 1,$$

$$0 \le Bel(\neg p) \le 1 \quad if \ a = 1.$$

Chapter 6

Inference Processes

In this and the following three chapters we shall assume, unless otherwise stated, that Bel is a probability function and $L = \{p_1, ..., p_n\}$. Thus, as we saw in Chapter 2, the problem of giving a value to $Bel(\theta)$ given consistent K is equivalent to giving a value to

$$\sum_{\alpha_i \in S_\theta} x_i$$

when $\vec{x} A_K = \vec{b}_K$, $x_i \geq 0$ (equivalently $\vec{x} \in V^L(K)$).

In general $V^L(K)$ will be infinite and there will be a range of possible values for $\sum_{\alpha_i \in S_\theta} x_i$. Notice however that the possible range is a closed interval. This is an immediate consequence of the following proposition.

Proposition 6.1 *(i) $V^L(K)$ is closed, i.e. if $\vec{a}(i) \in V^L(K)$ for $i \in \mathbb{N}$ and $\vec{a}(i) \to \vec{a}$ as $i \to \infty$ then $\vec{a} \in V^L(K)$. Indeed $V^L(K)$ is compact since it is also bounded.*

(ii) $V^L(K)$ is convex, i.e. if $\vec{a}, \vec{b} \in V^L(K)$ then every point on the straight line segment between $\vec{a}$ and $\vec{b}$ is in $V^L(K)$, equivalently $\lambda \vec{a} + (1 - \lambda)\vec{b} \in V^L(K)$ for $0 \leq \lambda \leq 1$.

Indeed rather more is true, $V^L(K)$ is an affine subset of $\mathbb{D}^L$, i.e. if $\vec{a}, \vec{b} \in V^L(K)$ then every point of the form $\lambda \vec{a} + (1 - \lambda)\vec{b}$, for $\lambda \in \mathbb{R}$ which is in $\mathbb{D}^L$ is in $V^L(K)$. $\qquad\qquad \square$.

We omit the proof of this proposition since it follows easily from the definition of $V^L(K)$ as $\{\vec{x} \in \mathbb{R}^J | \vec{x} A_k = \vec{b}_k, \vec{x} \geq 0\}$.

The fact that there may be many possible values for $\sum_{\alpha_i \in S_\theta} x_i$ for $\vec{x} \in V^L(K)$ means that we must seek further rational criteria for limiting this choice and providing answers to question Q.

As indicated in Chapter 1 one such source of criteria is common sense considerations and indeed that will be the main guiding light in this chapter. (The criterion of consistency has already been implicitly applied in the sense that we are asking for a choice of a value from $\{ \sum_{\alpha_i \in S_\theta} x_i \mid \vec{x} \in V^L(K) \}$ rather than simply $\{ \sum_{\alpha_i \in S_\theta} x_i \mid \vec{x} \in \mathbb{D}^L \}$.)

In view of the central role of 'common sense considerations' will play it seems that one might first, briefly, question why they are relevant at all in the context of question Q (as derived from situations such as example $\mathbb{E}$). One such justification is, we believe, based on the common (but usually implicit) assumption that the elicited knowledge K is not simply a shadow or description of the expert's knowledge but that, provided we have spent sufficient time collecting it,

K is (essentially) all the expert's relevant knowledge.

That is, that the expert's knowledge *is* simply such a set of statements which given sufficient effort we can elicit. We shall refer to this as the Watts Assumption.

If we make this assumption then our task of giving a value to $Bel(\theta)$ given K is exactly the task that the expert himself carries out. Furthermore, since we might feel that his answer should be commonsensical, applying common sense considerations to our assignment should still keep us within the realm of viable uncertain reasoning processes. (Despite its importance we shall avoid any philosophical or mathematical discussion of what we mean by common sense, or *why* we expect the expert's assignments to be commonsensical. Instead we hope the reader shares our view of what does or does not constitute common sense.) Of course even if we do not make the Watts Assumption we might feel it is unreasonable to violate common sense without strong reasons for so doing.

As an example of the sort of common sense considerations we have in mind consider the following example. Suppose that (under Watts Assumption) the expert actually knows nothing, i.e. $K = \emptyset$, where $L = \{p_1, p_2\}$, and he is asked to give a value to $Bel(p_1 \vee p_2)$. In this case any value between 0 and 1 is consistent with K (and Bel a probability function). However he might argue that since he knows nothing about p_1, p_2 each of the atoms (possible worlds!)

$$p_1 \wedge p_2, \quad p_1 \wedge \neg p_2, \quad \neg p_1 \wedge p_2, \quad \neg p_1 \wedge \neg p_2 \quad (= \alpha_1, \alpha_2, \alpha_3, \alpha_4)$$

has, for him, equal status. Therefore since there are no grounds to distinguish them it would seem common sense to assign them all the same belief, i.e. $\frac{1}{4}$ since we must have

$$Bel(p_1 \wedge p_2) + Bel(p_1 \wedge \neg p_2) + Bel(\neg p_1 \wedge p_2) + Bel(\neg p_1 \wedge \neg p_2) = 1.$$

Hence, since

$$\models (p_1 \vee p_2) \leftrightarrow ((p_1 \wedge p_2) \vee (p_1 \wedge \neg p_2) \vee (\neg p_1 \wedge p_2)), \quad \text{i.e. } S_{p_1 \vee p_2} = \{\alpha_1, \alpha_2, \alpha_3\},$$

so

$$Bel(p_1 \vee p_2) = Bel(p_1 \wedge p_2) + Bel(p_1 \wedge \neg p_2) + Bel(\neg p_1 \wedge p_2) = \frac{3}{4}.$$

As this example shows then there are principles of uncertain reasoning, based on common sense, which enable us to go beyond the assumption that *Bel* is a probability function and whose application may enable us to give an answer to question Q, or at least further restrict the possibilities. (As indicated earlier such common sense principles are not the only sort of considerations which might apply.)

It is our intention in the next chapter to investigate some such principles. However before we can do that we need to set up some apparatus in which to formulate them.

Inference Processes

Recalling again our original example $\mathbb{E}$ it would have seemed irrational or inconsistent (in the natural language sense) if on one instance the expert asserted that

Disease B and condition F are never found together

and then, in a separate instance that

Patients with condition F and disease B

but not exhibiting condition D are not uncommon

despite the fact that both these answers are separately consistent with $\mathbb{K}_0$.

From this example we see that, in the more general context of question Q, consistency requires that not only should the expert's answers to various questions be separately consistent with K but furthermore they themselves should all be consistent with each other. That is, if having given K as his knowledge the expert would assign value β_θ to $Bel(\theta)$ for $\theta \in SL$ then

$$K + \{Bel(\theta) = \beta_\theta \mid \theta \in SL\}$$

should be consistent, i.e. there should be a probability function simultaneously satisfying all these. But clearly there could only be one such function since all its values are specified, indeed just its values on the $\alpha_1, ..., \alpha_J$ would be enough.

If we make the Watts Assumption then, essentially, in assigning beliefs given K the expert is – or should be, if he values consistency – *picking* a probability function *Bel* to satisfy K, equivalently, picking a point in $V^L(K)$. A belief assignment process which satisfies this extended notion of consistency shall be called an *inference process*.

Precisely, let CL be the set of all finite consistent sets of linear constraints

$$\left\{ \sum_{j=1}^{r} a_{ji} Bel(\theta_j) = b_i \;\middle|\; i = 1, \ldots, m \right\}$$

where the $\theta_j \in SL$ and the $b_i, a_{ji} \in \mathbb{R}$.

Definition *An inference process on L is a function N such that for $K \in CL$, $N(K)$ is a probability function, Bel, on SL satisfying K.*

That is N *picks* a solution to K or equivalently N picks a point in $V^L(K)$.

Our main reason for introducing inference processes is that by invoking the Watts Assumption and thinking of intelligent agents as inference processes acting on knowledge bases many common sense principles of uncertain reasoning can be formulated in terms of them. In turn we can argue that the values $N(K)(\theta)$ given by inference processes N satisfying such principles provide justified answers to our question Q. In what follows we shall consider some specific inference processes which have been proposed in the literature.

The general sorts of justification for these inference processes appear to fall under two, or maybe three, headings. In the first (as typified by the forthcoming CM^L, CM^L_∞), the point $N(K) \in V^L(K)$ is chosen to be as typical or average or as representative of the points in $V^L(K)$ as possible. Alternatively these may be justified by assuming that K is actually a set of accurate knowledge statements about a *real* probability function P (i.e. $Bel = P$ satisfies K) and $N(K)$ is a statistical estimate of P. Thus, for example, in example $\mathbb{E}$ we could interpret K_0 as referring to the (assumed) real world (joint) probability distribution of the signs, symptoms, features applying to the patients turning up at the health centre. Indeed this interpretation of K and Q is very widespread in situations such as $\mathbb{E}$ and a great deal has been written concerning the estimation, or calculation of P. (See, for example, [58] or [26].)

In this book however we shall not assume the existence of such a function P and in consequence our coverage will, with the exception of some topics in Chapter 9, be mainly disjoint from that of books such as the above. Our main reason for avoiding the path of assuming the existence of P is that it is far from clear in many examples of uncertain reasoning that P exists or, even assuming that it does exist, that K actually refers to this function. Nevertheless we do certainly draw on many ideas and suggestions originating within statistics (such as the inference processes mentioned above) although we would seek to judge them on their standing as logical, rather than statistical, methods of inference.

Returning to the question of justification for inference processes, as well as the rationale of choosing $N(K)$ to be a typical point in $V^L(K)$ another commonly seen suggestion is to choose $N(K)$ to be that point in $V^L(K)$ which 'contains as little information beyond K as possible'. We shall consider two inference processes of this sort, MD^L and ME^L.

Some Inference Processes based on Typicality

The *centre of mass inference process* for L, CM^L, is defined by

$$CM^L(K) = \quad \text{that point } \langle x_1, ..., x_J \rangle$$
$$\text{which is the centre of mass of } V^L(K),$$

assuming uniform density, i.e.

$$CM^L(K)(\alpha_i) = \frac{\int_{V^L(K)} x_i dV}{\int_{V^L(K)} dV}$$

where the integrals are taken over the relative dimension of $V^L(K)$ (this makes sense for closed convex bounded sets such as $V^L(K)$) using the same basis.

Hence

$$CM^L(K)(\theta) = \frac{\int_{V^L(K)} (\sum_{\alpha_i \in S_\theta} x_i) dV}{\int_{V^L(K)} dV}.$$

Intuitively it is clear that since $V^L(K)$ is convex its centre of mass must be in $V^L(K)$. (Notice this could have been false if we had allowed non-linear constraints – this poses problems for generalising in this way.) Indeed we can give a simple proof of this since if

$$\sum a_j Bel(\theta_j) = b$$

is in K then

$$
\begin{aligned}
\sum a_j CM^L(K)(\theta_j) &= \frac{\int_{V^L(K)} \sum a_j (\sum_{\alpha_i \in S_{\theta_j}} x_i) dV}{\int_{V^L(K)} dV} \\
&= \frac{\int_{V^L(K)} b \, dV}{\int_{V^L(K)} dV} \quad (\text{since } \sum a_j \sum_{\alpha_i \in S_{\theta_j}} x_i = b \text{ on } V^L(K)) \quad = b
\end{aligned}
$$

so $CM^L(K)$ satisfies this equation.

CM^L may be, in part, justified by the so called *principle of indifference* (or Laplace's principle) by which we mean that given some facts all the possible worlds consistent with the facts should be viewed as equally likely. In this case then each point in $V^L(K)$ should be given equal weight and the choice of the centre of mass (with uniform density) just corresponds to picking the 'balance point' or the average or most representative of the points in $V^L(K)$. In a sense then this is a mathematical formulation of what we appear to mean by 'weighing up the evidence'.

It is interesting to note that we end up with exactly the same value for $Bel(\theta)$ given K here if instead we had set $Bel(\theta)$ to be that $\beta \in [0, 1]$ for which the expected square difference between $Bel(\theta)$ and β, i.e.

$$\int_{V^L(K)} (\beta - \sum_{\alpha_i \in S_\theta} x_i)^2 dV,$$

is minimal. This follows since the derivative of this integral with respect to β is

$$2\int_{V^L(K)} (\beta - \sum_{\alpha_i \in S_\theta} x_i) dV$$

which equals zero for

$$\beta = \frac{\int_{V^L(K)} \sum_{\alpha_i \in S_\theta} x_i dV}{\int_{V^L(K)} dV}.$$

(If we replace square here by any other positive integer power of the modulus we do not obtain an inference process since the values need not all be consistent with each other and K.)

Whilst this principle of indifference can be made rigorous in the case of a finite number of possible worlds (see the renaming principle in the next chapter, indeed we have already invoked it earlier in this form to justify $N(\emptyset)(p_1 \vee p_2) = \frac{3}{4}$) we are here applying it in the case of an infinite number of possible worlds, i.e. the points in $V^L(K)$, and in this case the accurate use of the principle (if such there always is) can be far from intuitively obvious as the celebrated case of Bertrand's paradox indicates. This paradox runs as follows.

A stick is randomly thrown so that the line determined by the stick intersects the unit circle, as below. Question: what is the expected value of d?

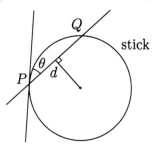

1st answer. By rotating the picture if necessary we may assume the stick is parallel to the x-axis and $d \geq 0$. So by indifference each value between 0 and 1 is equally likely and the average is $\frac{1}{2}$.

2nd answer. By indifference any value of θ between 0 and $\frac{\pi}{2}$ is equally likely so the expected value of d is

$$\frac{2}{\pi} \int_0^{\frac{\pi}{2}} \cos \theta \; d\theta = \frac{2}{\pi}.$$

3rd answer. Having rotated the picture so that P is in some fixed position any length $y \in [0, 2]$ for PQ is, by indifference, equally likely, so the expected value of d is

$$\frac{1}{2} \int_0^2 \sqrt{1 - \frac{y^2}{4}} \; dy = \frac{\pi}{4}.$$

The fact that applying the same principle in three different ways, each of which appears at first sight quite reasonable, can produce three different answers is at the very least a severe hazard warning on the cavalier use of this princple. In fact as Jaynes points out in [33] (which also contains a nice biography on the paradox) there are invariances implicit in the statement of the problem, such as the size of the circle, which can be employed to show the 1st answer to be correct.

Indeed if we 'relativise' the situation and imagine that it is the circle that is thrown onto the line (or equivalently onto a floor covered in parallel lines one diameter width apart) then the principle of indifference seems to unreservedly argue for this 1st answer.

This deeper analysis then has, it seems, resolved this paradox and reprieved the principle of indifference. However, as Jaynes points out, we have no reason to suppose that in cases of conflict we will always be able to distinguish which uses of the principle are correct and which fallacious. The moral appears to be that the principle should only be used with caution and should preferably be justified by additional arguments based on invariance – such as those presented in [33].

Whilst CM^L may initially seem rather intuitive it has several undesirable features. For consider the following example of the Brandeis dice problem (appearing in [50]). Suppose we are told that a certain die, with just three sides, numbered 1,2,3, has an expected score when thrown of 2, exactly as it would if it was fair. What belief should we give to the next throw of the die landing 3?

Letting $L = \{p_1, p_2\}$ where p_1 stands for 'will land 1' p_2 stands for 'will land 2' (so $\neg p_1 \wedge \neg p_2$ stands for 'will land 3') the knowledge K consists of

$$Bel(p_1 \wedge p_2) = 0,$$

$$Bel(p_1) = Bel(\neg p_1 \wedge \neg p_2),$$

since an expected score of 2 just means that 1 and 3 are equally likely, together of course with

$$Bel(p_1 \wedge p_2) + Bel(p_1 \wedge \neg p_2) + Bel(\neg p_1 \wedge p_2) + Bel(\neg p_1 \wedge \neg p_2) = 1.$$

Letting

$$Bel(p_1 \wedge p_2) = x_1, \quad Bel(p_1 \wedge \neg p_2) = x_2, \quad Bel(\neg p_1 \wedge p_2) = x_3, \quad Bel(\neg p_1 \wedge \neg p_2) = x_4$$

we obtain

$$x_1 + x_2 = x_4,$$

$$x_1 = 0,$$

$$x_1 + x_2 + x_3 + x_4 = 1,$$

$$x_1, x_2, x_3, x_4 \geq 0,$$

i.e.

$$V^L(K) = \{\langle x_1, x_2, x_3, x_4 \rangle \mid \vec{x} \geq 0, x_1 = 0, x_2 = x_4, x_3 = 1 - 2x_4\}.$$

Hence

$$CM^L(K)(\neg p_1 \wedge \neg p_2) = \frac{\int_{x_4=0}^{\frac{1}{2}} x_4 dx_4}{\int_{x_4=0}^{\frac{1}{2}} dx_4} = \frac{1}{4}$$

thus

$$\text{Belief die will land } 3 \;=\; \frac{1}{4}$$

and

$$CM^L(K)(p_2) = CM^L(K)(\neg p_1 \wedge p_2) = 1 - 2(\frac{1}{4}) = \frac{1}{2},$$

i.e.

$$\text{Belief die will land } 2 \;=\; \frac{1}{2}.$$

Thus, paradoxically one may feel, although everything we know is consistent with the die being fair, applying this inference process would lead to the belief that it will land 2 being twice that of it landing 3 (or 1).

A second criticism of CM^L is that if we view this process also as a function of the finite language L then it is not *language invariant*.

Definition *Suppose we have a family of inference processes N^L, one for each finite language L. Then this family is said to be* language invariant *if whenever $L_1 \subseteq L_2$ (so $SL_1 \subseteq SL_2$ and $CL_1 \subseteq CL_2$) and $K \in CL_1$ then $N^{L_2}(K)$ agrees with $N^{L_1}(K)$ on SL_1.*

The CM^L are not language invariant: adding additional propositional variables to the language will in general alter the belief given to θ on the basis of K even though the new variables do not explicitly appear in θ or K. For example suppose in the Brandeis dice problem above we had included some other propositional variable p_3 in the language standing for, say, 'it will rain tomorrow'. Then in that case we would have obtained $CM^L(\neg p_1 \wedge \neg p_2) = \frac{3}{10}$, a slight increase in our belief that a 3 will be thrown although the state of the weather, one might feel, should have no effect upon the answer. Clearly this is a most undesirable feature of the centre of mass family of inference processes. One way to correct this variability as the size of the overlying language changes, as the next theorem shows, is to consider the limiting inference process we obtain by saturating the context with new propositional variables. (An alternative, which we shall not consider here, is to use a family of marginalizing Dirichlet priors in place of the uniform distribution, see [43].)

Theorem 6.2 *Let $K \in CL$, $\theta \in SL$. Then*

$$\lim_{\substack{L \subseteq L' \\ |L'| \to \infty}} CM^{L'}(K)(\theta) \;\text{ exists and equals } CM_\infty^L(K)(\theta)$$

where CM_∞^L is the limit centre of mass *inference process for L which on argument K picks that $\vec{x} \in V^L(K)$ at which the function $\sum_{i \notin I^L(K)} \log(x_i)$ is maximal, where*

$$I^L(K) = \{i \mid \forall \vec{y} \in V^L(K), y_i = 0\} \quad (\text{so} \quad x_i = 0 \text{ for } i \in I^L(K)).$$

$\square$

We shall not give a proof of this result since it seems rather peripheral to our main theme. A proof may be found in the paper [56] by A. Vencovská and the author.

In this theorem it does make sense to talk of the maximum value of the function

$$\sum_{i \notin I^L(K)} \log(x_i)$$

for $\vec{x} \in V^L(K)$. For it might have been feared that possibly for every $\vec{x} \in V^L(K)$ some x_i, with $i \notin I^L(K)$, would be zero and hence $\sum_{i \notin I^L(K)} \log(x_i)$ would only take the value $-\infty$ on $V^L(K)$. However there must be a point $\vec{a} \in V^L(K)$ such that $a_i \neq 0$ for all $i \notin I^L(K)$. To see this notice that for each $i \notin I^L(K)$ there is some $\vec{b}^i \in V^L(K)$ with $b_i^i > 0$. By convexity then

$$\frac{\sum_{i \notin I^L(K)} \vec{b}^i}{J - |I^L(K)|} \in V^L(K)$$

and this is such an $\vec{a}$.

In a similar vein notice that $\sum_{i \notin I^L(K)} \log(x_i)$ has a unique maximal point since this function is concave on $0 < x_i$, $i \notin I^L(K)$.

In the Brandeis dice problem CM_∞^L gives the expected (?) belief of $\frac{1}{3}$ of the die landing 3. Furthermore CM_∞^L is language invariant as we now show.

Proposition 6.3 CM_∞^L *is language invariant.*

Proof It suffices to show that $CM_\infty^L(K)(\alpha_i) = CM_\infty^{L'}(K)(\alpha_i)$ where $L = \{p_1, ..., p_n\}$, $L' = L \cap \{p_{n+1}\}$, $K \in CL$ and, as usual, $At^L = \{\alpha_1, ..., \alpha_J\}$. Let $\beta_{2j-1} = \alpha_j \wedge p_{n+1}$, $\beta_{2j} = \alpha_j \wedge \neg p_{n+1}$ so the β_k for $k = 1, ..., 2J$ are the atoms of L'. Now notice that by the way $V^L(K)$ is formed,

$$\langle x_1, ..., x_{2J} \rangle \in V^{L'}(K) \Leftrightarrow \langle x_1 + x_2, x_3 + x_4, ..., x_{2J-1} + x_{2J} \rangle \in V^L(K).$$

So $I^{L'}(K) = \{2j - 1, 2j \mid j \in I^L(K)\}$. To simplify the notation let us suppose that $I^L(K) = \emptyset$ and let

$$\begin{aligned} CM_\infty^L(K) &= \langle \tau_1, \tau_2, ..., \tau_J \rangle \in V^L(K), \\ CM_\infty^{L'}(K) &= \langle \rho_1, \rho_2, ..., \rho_{2J} \rangle \in V^{L'}(K). \end{aligned}$$

Then by definition,

$$\sum_{j=1}^{J} \log(\tau_j) \;\geq\; \sum_{j=1}^{J} \log(\rho_{2j-1} + \rho_{2j})$$

$$\text{since} \quad \langle \rho_1 + \rho_2, ..., \rho_{2J-1} + \rho_{2J} \rangle \in V^L(K),$$

$$= \; J\log(2) + \frac{1}{2}\sum_{j=1}^{J} 2\log\left(\frac{\rho_{2j-1} + \rho_{2j}}{2}\right)$$

$$\geq \; J\log(2) + \frac{1}{2}\sum_{j=1}^{J} (\log(\rho_{2j-1}) + \log(\rho_{2j}))$$

$$\text{since} \quad \log(x) \text{ is concave,}$$

$$\geq \; J\log(2) + \frac{1}{2}\sum_{j=1}^{J} 2\log(\frac{\tau_j}{2})$$

$$\text{since} \quad \langle \tfrac{\tau_1}{2}, \tfrac{\tau_1}{2}, \tfrac{\tau_2}{2}, \tfrac{\tau_2}{2}, ..., \tfrac{\tau_J}{2}, \tfrac{\tau_J}{2} \rangle \in V^{L'}(K)$$

$$= \; \sum_{j=1}^{J} \log(\tau_j).$$

Hence by the uniqueness of the maximum points

$$\frac{\rho_{2j-1} + \rho_{2j}}{2} = \rho_{2j-1} = \rho_{2j} = \frac{\tau_j}{2},$$

and the result follows since

$$CM_\infty^L(K)(\alpha_i) \;=\; \tau_i = \rho_{2i-1} + \rho_{2i} = CM_\infty^{L'}(K)(\beta_{2i-1}) + CM_\infty^{L'}(K)(\beta_{2i})$$

$$= \; CM_\infty^{L'}(K)(\alpha_i). \qquad \square$$

For inference processes such as CM_∞^L which are language invariant we shall, without danger of confusion, occasionally drop the superscript L.

Finally under this heading we mention the *barycentre inference process* [60] which on argument $K \in CL$ picks that $\vec{x} \in V^L(K)$ for which

$$\sup\{d(\vec{x}, \vec{y}) \mid \vec{y} \in V^L(K)\}$$

is minimal, where d is some (reasonable) metric on $\mathbb{R}^J$.

Again, as for the centre of mass, this could be viewed as attempting to choose a most representative point from all the equally likely points in $V^L(K)$. Alternatively we could view it as aiming to choose a point which minimises the worst error that could be made, assuming the existence of a true, target, probability function P in $V^L(K)$.

Some Inference Processes based on Information

The *minimum distance inference process*, MD^L, is defined by

$$MD^L(K) \;=\; \text{the nearest (usual metric) point in } V^L(K) \text{ to } \langle \tfrac{1}{J}, ..., \tfrac{1}{J}\rangle \in \mathbb{R}^J$$

$$=\; \text{that } \vec{x} \in V^L(K) \text{ for which } \sum_{i=1}^{J}(x_i - \tfrac{1}{J})^2 \text{ is minimal.}$$

Notice that for $\vec{x} \in V^L(K)$,

$$\sum_{i=1}^{J}(x_i - \frac{1}{J})^2 = \sum_{i=1}^{J}x_i^2 - \frac{2}{J}\sum_{i=1}^{J}x_i + \sum_{i=1}^{J}\frac{1}{J^2} = \sum_{i=1}^{J}x_i^2 - \frac{1}{J}$$

since $\sum_{i=1}^{J} x_i = 1$, so also

$$MD^L(K) = \text{that } \vec{x} \in V^L(K) \text{ for which } \sum_{i=1}^{J}x_i^2 \text{ is minimal.}$$

That this point is unique follows since $\sum x_i^2$ is convex.

A justification for picking this point is that since the point $\langle \tfrac{1}{J}, \tfrac{1}{J}, ..., \tfrac{1}{J}\rangle$ represents the least informative belief function (in that it gives no preferences amongst the atoms, or possible worlds) then in order to pick the least informative point in $V^L(K)$, equivalently the point that contains as little information beyond K as possible, we should pick that point in $V^L(K)$ closest to the point representing total ignorance, that is $\langle \tfrac{1}{J}, \tfrac{1}{J}, ..., \tfrac{1}{J}\rangle$. (Of course this still leaves open the question of why the usual, Euclidean, metric is chosen.)

MD^L is language invariant, a fact that can be proved straightforwardly by adapting the proof of proposition 6.3. The same is true of the next inference process we introduce.

The *maximum entropy inference process* ME^L, is defined by

$$ME^L(K) \;=\; \text{that } \vec{x} \in V^L(K) \text{ for which the entropy, i.e. Shannon measure}$$
$$\text{of uncertainty, } -\sum_{i=1}^{J} x_i \log(x_i), \text{ is maximal.}$$

(Here $x \log(x) = 0$ when $x = 0$.) Notice this point is unique by the convexity of $\sum x_i \log(x_i)$.

In this process then we choose the point which has the greatest measure of uncertainty, or equivalently the least information, according to Shannon's measure. Again then we are picking that point in $V^L(K)$ which goes as little beyond the information given by the constraints K as possible.

This particular measure was justified by Shannon in his book with Weaver [64] as follows. Suppose we know that exactly one of the events $A_1, ..., A_K$ holds and we initially believe that the probability of A_i holding is x_i where the $x_j \geq 0$ and $\sum_{j=1}^{k} x_j = 1$. Let $H(\vec{x})$ be the measure of our uncertainty. Then

$$H : \bigcup_{k \geq 1} D_k \longrightarrow [0, \infty),$$

where

$$D_k = \{\langle x_1, ..., x_k \rangle \in \mathbb{R}^k \mid \vec{x} \geq 0 \text{ and } \sum x_j = 1\},$$

should have the following properties:

(a) For each $k > 0, H \restriction D_k$ (H restricted to D_k) is continuous.

(b) For $0 < n < m$, $H(\frac{1}{n}, ..., \frac{1}{n}) < H(\frac{1}{m}, ..., \frac{1}{m})$.

(c) If $\sum_{j=1}^{m_i} y_{ij} = 1$ and $y_{ij} \geq 0$ for $i = 1, ..., k$ and $\vec{x} \in D_k$ then

$$H(x_1 y_{11}, x_1 y_{12}, ..., x_1 y_{1m_1}, x_2 y_{21}, ..., x_i y_{ij}, ...)$$
$$= H(\vec{x}) + \sum_{i=1}^{k} x_i H(y_{i1}, ..., y_{im_i}).$$

Of these (a) could be justified on the usual grounds that small changes in $\vec{x} \in D_k$ should only result in changes in $H(\vec{x})$ of the same order. Condition (b) is justified if we think of uncertainty as the information we expect to gain when we see which of the events A_i hold, since learning which of n equally probable events holds is less informative than learning which of m, $m > n$, such events holds. Condition (c) is justified similarly by considering that learning which of the events corresponding to $x_i y_{ij}$ holds is equivalent to first learning the event for x_i and then learning the event for y_{ij}. To see that (a)–(c) determine H to be the entropy (at least up to a positive scalar multiple) assume (a)–(c) and let $A(n) = H(\frac{1}{n}, ..., \frac{1}{n})$. Then by (c),

$$A(k^m) = A(k) + A(k^{m-1}) = mA(k).$$

Now given $\epsilon > 0$ let $\frac{1}{m} < \epsilon$ and $\frac{n}{m} \leq \frac{\log(k)}{\log(2)} < \frac{n+1}{m}$. Then $2^n \leq k^m < 2^{n+1}$ so by (b),

$$nA(2) = A(2^n) \leq A(k^m) = mA(k) < (n+1)A(2)$$

and

$$\frac{n}{m} \leq \frac{A(k)}{A(2)} < \frac{n+1}{m} < \frac{n}{m} + \epsilon$$

Hence $| \frac{\log(k)}{\log(2)} - \frac{A(k)}{A(2)} | < 2\epsilon$ and so, since $\epsilon > 0$ was arbitrary, $A(k) = \frac{A(2)}{\log(2)} \cdot \log(k) = c \log(k)$ say, where $c > 0$ by (b).

Now let $0 \leq \frac{n_i}{n} \in \mathbb{Q}$, $\sum_{i=1}^{m} \frac{n_i}{n} = 1$. Then

$$A(n) = H(\underbrace{\frac{1}{n}, ..., \frac{1}{n}}_{n_1}, \underbrace{\frac{1}{n}, ..., \frac{1}{n}}_{n_2}, ...) = H(\frac{n_1}{n}, ..., \frac{n_m}{n}) + \sum_{i=1}^{m} \frac{n_i}{n} A(n_i)$$

so

$$H(\frac{n_1}{n}, ..., \frac{n_m}{n}) = c\log(n) - \sum_{i=1}^{m} \frac{cn_i}{n} \log n_i = -\sum_{i=1}^{m} \frac{cn_i}{n} \log(\frac{n_i}{n})$$

and by the denseness of the rationals and (a)

$$H(x_1, ..., x_m) = -\sum_{i=1}^{m} cx_i \log(x_i)$$

for $\vec{x} \in D_m$ as required.

A second justification for the maximum entropy inference process originates with some early work of Boltzmann in atomic physics and, in the context of question Q, arises by reconsidering our first justification of belief as probability in Chapter 3. Recall that in that example we considered interpreting the expert's statement $\mathrm{Bel}(\theta) = \alpha$ as

$$|\{x \in M \mid x \text{ satisfies } \theta\}| = \alpha \mid M \mid$$

where M is the considerable set of, in this case, patients previously seen by the expert, say $M = \{x_1, ..., x_N\}$. Now suppose that we had elicited knowledge K,

$$K = \left\{ \sum_{j=1}^{r} a_{ji} \mathrm{Bel}(\theta_j) = b_i \mid i = 1, ..., m \right\},$$

from this expert. Then this interpretation would lead us to conclude that

$$\sum_{j=1}^{r} a_{ji} |\{x \in M \mid x \text{ satisfies } \theta_j\}| = b_i |M| \quad for \ i = 1, ..., m.$$

However, for this to hold would, in general, put very strong constraints on the (natural) number N $(= |M|)$ whilst we might reasonably feel that, for the most part, one patient more or less was irrelevant. Thus it seems more reasonable to conclude that

$$\sum_{j=1}^{r} a_{ji} \mid \{x \in M \mid x \text{ satisfies } \theta_j\}| \approx b_i |M| \qquad (6.1)$$

holds for $i = 1, ..., m$ where $\approx$ is some sensible relation of 'approximately equals'.

Having done this we might now argue as follows: All we know about M is that 6.1 holds and, according to this interpretation, what we would like to know, as in question Q, is a good approximation to

$$\frac{|\{x \in M \mid x \text{ satisfies } \theta\}|}{|M|}. \tag{6.2}$$

Now suppose that we consider all possible M of size N (i.e. all possible choices of $V_{x_1}, V_{x_2}, ..., V_{x_N}$) which satisfy (6.1). Then for N sufficiently large, almost all the corresponding values of (6.2) are clustered around one point – and that point is $ME^L(K)(\theta)$. Precisely:

Theorem 6.4 *Let $K \in CL$ be as above. Then there is a fixed constant $c_K > 0$ such that for any $\delta > 0$ there exists N_0 and $\epsilon > 0$ such that for any $\theta \in SL$ and $N \geq N_0$ and $\approx$ satisfying*

$$y_1 \approx y_2 \Rightarrow |y_1 - y_2| \leq \epsilon N \quad \text{and} \quad | y_1 - y_2 | \leq c_K \Rightarrow y_1 \approx y_2,$$

for $y_1, y_2 \in [0, N]$, the proportion of the M's of size N satisfying (6.1) for which

$$\left| \frac{|\{x \in M \mid x \text{ satisfies } \theta\}|}{|M|} - ME^L(K)(\theta) \right| < \delta$$

is at least $1 - \delta$.   □

In particular then if we knew only that M satisfied (6.1) and believed N to be large then it would seem reasonable to suppose that our expert was amongst the overwhelming majority for whom the above inequality holds and hence that $ME^L(K)(\theta)$ was a good approximation to the value $Bel(\theta)$ which our expert would give to θ. (To be fair, the value of N_0 in this theorem would in practice tend to be so large that it is doubtful that our expert could ever hope to see that many patients. Nevertheless the result provides an argument for the maximum entropy inference process in an 'ideal world'.)

The full proof of theorem 6.4 is rather long and technical so, with apologies, we shall omit it and refer the interested reader to [57] where an (inessentialy simpler) version of theorem 6.4 is proved in detail.

In the next chapter we shall describe yet another justification for the maximum entropy inference process. (We say 'yet another' here because there is quite an industry of providing justifications for the use of Maximum Entropy in various contexts.)

We finally remark that since ME^L, MD^L are language invariant, we can abbreviate them to ME, MD respectively.

Inference Processes for DS-belief Functions

The processes defined above for probability functions can also be defined for DS-belief functions, since the set of points $\vec{x} \in \mathbb{R}^{2^{2^n}-1}$ corresponding to bpa's whose DS-belief function satisfies K is again closed and convex, although their justification may well not carry over. For example in the case of DS-belief functions it is the vacuous bpa m given by $m(1) = 1$, $m(\overline{\theta}) = 0$ otherwise, which corresponds to total ignorance, not the bpa with constant value $(2^{2^n} - 1)^{-1}$. This raises the new possibility of defining inference processes for DS-belief functions which aim to pick the solution to K which maximises the ignorance, or as it is usually referred to, the *nonspecificity*.

As an example if, say, $K = \{Bel(p_1 \vee p_2) = \frac{1}{2}\}$ then the bpa m for which $m(\overline{p_2 \vee p_1}) = \frac{1}{2}$, $m(1) = \frac{1}{2}$, $m(\overline{p_2}) = 0$ otherwise (so $Bel^m(p_1 \vee p_2) = \frac{1}{2}$) is less specific than the bpa m with $m(\overline{p_1}) = \frac{1}{3}$, $m(\overline{\theta}) = \frac{1}{6}, m(1) = \frac{1}{2}$ (which also gives $Bel^m(p_1 \vee p_2) = \frac{1}{2}$) in that the former tells us nothing about the distribution of the belief in $p_1 \vee p_2$.

Typically measures, $U(m)$, of nonspecificity of the form

$$U(m) = \sum_{\psi} m(\overline{\psi}) f(|\, S_\psi \,|)$$

have been proposed in the literature, where $f : \mathbb{N} \longrightarrow [0, \infty)$ is strictly increasing, see [38]. (Notice that $U(m)$ is minimal, with value $f(1)$, when m is a probability function and maximal when m is the vacuous bpa, i.e. $m(1) = 1$.)

Unfortunately such measures cannot, in general, determine a unique solution for a set K of linear constraints on Bel since, for example, the constraints

$$\sum_{\psi} m(\overline{\psi}) f(|\, S_\psi \,|) = f(2),$$

$$\sum_{\psi} m(\overline{\psi}) = 1, \qquad L = \{p_1, p_2\}$$

can, by theorem 4.2, be expressed as linear constraints in Bel and yet clearly have many solutions all with the same nonspecificity. Indeed for the, currently popular choice of $f(x) = \log(x)$ there is not even a unique solution for the simple case of $K = \{Bel(p_1) = \frac{1}{2}, \ Bel(p_2) = \frac{1}{2}\}$, as can easily be checked.

For a recent survey see [52].

Inference Processes for Truth-functional Belief

A serious difficulty with attempting to define inference processes for truth-functional belief is that the set of solutions to a set K of linear constraints is not in general connected, let alone convex. For example the constraints

$$\{Bel(p_1 \wedge p_2) = \frac{1}{4}, \ Bel(p_1 \vee p_2) = \frac{3}{4}\}$$

have exactly two solutions in $\mathbb{F}_1$, either $Bel(p_1) = \frac{1}{4}$, $Bel(p_2) = \frac{3}{4}$ or $Bel(p_1) = \frac{3}{4}$, $Bel(p_2) = \frac{1}{4}$. In this case then it is very difficult to see how to make a rational choice of a preferred single answer. An alternative would be to drop the requirement that the answer in question Q be consistent with both K and the other answers, although we shall not pursue that line further in this text.

For belief as possibility however there is a rather natural inference process based on picking the most non-specific, or least informative solution, in the restricted case of K of the form

$$a_i Bel(\theta_i) = b_i Bel(\phi_i) + c_i, \qquad i = 1, ..., m,$$

where the $a_i, b_i, c_i \geq 0$, since, by results of I. Maung in [45], the set of possibility function solutions is closed under (coordinatewise) sup and this clearly yields the unique most non-specific solution of K.

Chapter 7

Principles of Uncertain Reasoning

In the previous chapter we introduced a selection of the more popular inference processes which have been proposed. This raises the question of why to prefer one such process over any other. In this chapter we shall consider this question by presenting a number of properties, or as we shall call them, principles, which it might be deemed desirable that an inference process, N, should satisfy.

For the most part these principles could be said to be based on common sense or rationality or 'consistency' in the natural language sense of the word. A justification for assuming that adherence to common sense is a desirable property of an inference process comes from the Watts Assumption given in Chapter 5. For if K genuinely does represent all the expert's knowledge then any conclusion the expert draws from K should be the result of applying what, by consensus, we consider correct reasoning, i.e. of common sense.

So our plan now is to present a list of such principles. We shall limit ourselves to the case where *Bel* is a probability function, although the same criteria could be applied to inference processes for DS-belief functions, possibility functions etc. In what follows N stands for an inference process for L. Here L is to be thought of as variable. If we wish to consider a principle for a particular language L we shall insert 'for L'.

Equivalence Principle

If $K_1, K_2 \in CL$ are equivalent in the sense that $V^L(K_1) = V^L(K_2)$ then $N(K_1) = N(K_2)$.

That is, if K_1, K_2 put exactly the same constraints on a probability function *Bel* (in that *Bel* satisfies one iff it satisfies the other) then the principle asserts that $N(K_1), N(K_2)$ should be equal. The principle implies then that N is a function of the convex sets $V^L(K)$ rather than the $K \in CL$ from which they are derived.

This principle may be justified directly from the Watts Assumption by arguing that it is implicit in that assumption that the knowledge *is* the constraints it puts on *Bel* rather than the particular way in which the constraints are expressed.

One might perhaps question at this point if there is not another, perhaps more reasonable, notion of K_1, K_2 being equivalent, namely that every constraint in K_2 can be derived from K_1, together with the assumption that *Bel* is a probability function, by some simple algebraic or syntactic manipulations, and conversely. After all it could be that despite $V^L(K_1), V^L(K_2)$ being equal the expert had no elementary way of seeing this, whilst equivalence in the second sense would be saying that there is a uniform, elementary *demonstration* that every solution of K_1 is a solution of K_2, and conversely.

Fortunately this second notion is equivalent to the first as our next theorem will show.

In order to present this result clearly we shall introduce a sequent calculus $\mathbb{I}$ for manipulating sets of constraints in CL. Just as in the propositional calculus $\mathbb{I}$ will have axioms, rules of proof and proofs, the intention being that for $K_1, K_2 \in CL$ the sequent $K_1 \mid K_2$ will be derivable in $\mathbb{I}$ just if $V^L(K_1) \subseteq V^L(K_2)$, whilst at the same time the axioms and rules of proof are elementary and syntactic.

A precise description of $\mathbb{I}$ is as follows, where, in line with common abuse of notation, we write K, ξ or $K + \xi$ for $K \cup \{\xi\}$ etc.

Logical Axioms: $K \mid K$

Logical Rules:

$$\frac{K_1 \mid K_2, \; K_1 \mid K_3}{K_1 \mid K_2, K_3} \qquad \frac{K_1 \mid K_2}{K_1 \mid K_3} \; for \; K_3 \subseteq K_2$$

Arithmetic Axioms: $K \mid Bel(\theta) - Bel(\theta) = 0$

Arithmetic Rules:

$$\frac{K_1 \mid K_2, \; \displaystyle\sum_{j=1}^{r} a_j Bel(\theta_j) = b, \; \displaystyle\sum_{j=1}^{r} a'_j Bel(\theta_j) = b'}{K_1 \mid K_2, \; \displaystyle\sum_{j=1}^{r}(\alpha a_j + \beta a'_j) Bel(\theta_j) = (\alpha b + \beta b')}$$

$$\frac{K_1 \mid K_2, \; \displaystyle\sum_{j=1}^{r} a_j Bel(\theta_j) = b}{K_1 \mid K_2, \; \displaystyle\sum_{j=1}^{r} a_{\sigma(j)}, Bel(\theta_{\sigma(j)}) = b}$$

where σ is a permutation of $1, ..., r$

$$\frac{K_1 \mid K_2, \ \sum_{j=1}^{r} a_j Bel(\theta_j) = b}{K_1 \mid K_2, \ \sum_{j=1}^{r-1} a_j Bel(\theta_j) = b}$$

when $a_r = 0$. (The double line indicates that this rule goes both ways.)

Probability Axioms: $K \mid \xi$ whenever ξ is one of

$$Bel(\bigwedge_{i=1}^{s} \theta_i) - Bel(\bigwedge_{i=1}^{s} \theta_{\sigma(i)}) = 0$$

where σ is a permutation of $1, ..., s$,

$$Bel(\theta \wedge (\phi \vee \chi)) - Bel(\theta \wedge \phi \wedge \neg \chi) - Bel(\theta \wedge \chi) = 0,$$

$$Bel(\theta \wedge \neg(\phi \vee \chi)) - Bel(\theta \wedge \neg \phi \wedge \neg \chi) = 0,$$

$$Bel(\theta \wedge \neg(\phi \wedge \chi)) - Bel(\theta \wedge (\neg \phi \vee \neg \chi)) = 0,$$

$$Bel(\theta \wedge \neg \neg \phi) - Bel(\theta \wedge \phi) = 0,$$

$$Bel(\theta) - Bel(\theta \wedge (\phi \vee \neg \phi)) = 0,$$

$$Bel(\phi \wedge \neg \phi) = 0,$$

$$Bel(\phi \vee \neg \phi) = 1.$$

Probability Rule:

$$\frac{K \mid \sum_{j=1}^{r} a_j Bel(\theta_j) = 0}{K \mid Bel(\theta_i) = 0}$$

whenever $1 \leq i \leq r$ and $a_j > 0$ for $j = 1, ..., r$.

The following theorem which appears in [54] is closely related to a special case of results of Fagin, Halpern and Megiddo in [15].

Theorem 7.1 *For $K, K' \in CL$, $V^L(K) \subseteq V^L(K')$ if and only if the sequent $K \mid K'$ is derivable in $\mathbb{I}$, written $K \vdash_{\mathbb{I}} K'$.*

Before proving this theorem we shall derive two lemmas from linear algebra. In these lemmas A is a $J \times m$ matrix.

Lemma 7.2 *Suppose that $\vec{x}A = \vec{b}$ has a solution $\vec{y} \geq 0$ but that for any solution $\vec{x} \geq 0$, $x_1 = 0$. Then there is $\vec{a} \geq 0$ such that $a_1 > 0$ and $\vec{x}\vec{a}^T = 0$ whenever $\vec{x}A = \vec{b}$ (having removed the condition $\vec{x} \geq 0$).*

Proof Without loss of generality suppose that $x_1, ..., x_r$ are those coordinates x_i such that whenever $\vec{x}A = \vec{b}$, $\vec{x} \geq 0$ then $x_i = 0$. Let $\vec{u} \geq 0$, $\vec{u}A = \vec{b}$ and $u_i > 0$ for $i = r + 1, ..., J$. Notice that such a $\vec{u}$ exists since for any $r < i \leq J$ we can pick

$$\vec{u}^{(i)} \geq 0, \ \vec{u}^{(i)}A = \vec{b}, \ u_i^{(i)} > 0 \text{ so } \vec{u} = \sum_{i=1+1}^{J} \frac{\vec{u}^{(i)}}{J - r} \text{ suffices. Perforce } u_i = 0 \text{ for}$$

$1 \leq i \leq r$. Then $\{\vec{v} - \vec{u} \mid \vec{v}A = \vec{b}\} = \{\vec{z} \mid \vec{z}A = \vec{0}\}$ is a subspace of $\mathbb{R}^J$. Hence

$$W = \{\langle z_1, ..., z_r \rangle \mid \exists \vec{v}, \ \vec{v}A = \vec{b} \ \& \ z_i = v_i - u_i (= v_i) \ for \ 1 \leq i \leq r\}$$

is a subspace of $\mathbb{R}^r$. Also $\vec{0}$ is the only positive vector in W. For suppose that $\langle z_1, ..., z_r \rangle \in W$ with $\langle z_1, ..., z_r \rangle \geq 0$ and, say, $z_1 > 0$. Let $\vec{v}$ be such that $\vec{v}A = \vec{b}$, $\langle z_1, ..., z_r \rangle = \langle v_1, ..., v_r \rangle$. Then for $\epsilon > 0$ small enough $\epsilon \vec{v} + (1 - \epsilon)\vec{u} \geq 0$ and $(\epsilon \vec{v} + (1 - \epsilon)\vec{u})A = \vec{b}$ whilst the first coordinate of this vector is greater than zero, contradiction.

Hence, since $\vec{0}$ is the only positive vector in W, by Gordon's theorem (see for example [47]) there is a strictly positive vector, $\vec{a} \in \mathbb{R}^r$, normal to W, i.e. $\vec{a}^T \vec{w} = 0$ for all $\vec{w} \in W$. It follows that if $\vec{x}A = \vec{b}$ then $\langle x_1, ..., x_r \rangle \in W$ and $\sum_{i=1}^{J} a_i x_i = 0$ as required, where $a_i = 0$ for $r < i \leq J$. □

Lemma 7.3 *Suppose that whenever $\vec{x}A = \vec{b}$, $\vec{x} \geq \vec{0}$ then $\sum_{i=1}^{J} c_i x_i = d$. Then also $\sum_{i=1}^{J} c_i x_i = d$, whenever $\vec{x}A = \vec{b}$ and $x_{i_j} = 0$ for $j = 1, ..., s$, where $i_1, ..., i_s$ are those m such that for all $\vec{x} \geq \vec{0}$ satisfying $\vec{x}A = \vec{b}$, $x_m = 0$. (So in the case $A = A_k$, $\{i_1, ..., i_s\} = I^L(K)$.)*

Proof Let $\vec{u} \geq \vec{0}$ be such that $\vec{u}A = \vec{b}$ and $u_m > 0$ for $m \notin \{i_1, ..., i_s\}$. So $\sum_{i=1}^{J} c_i u_i = d$. Now suppose $\vec{x}A = \vec{b}$, $x_{i_j} = 0$ for $j = 1, ..., s$. Then for sufficiently small $\epsilon > 0$, $(\epsilon \vec{x} + (1 - \epsilon)\vec{u})A = \vec{b}$ and $(\epsilon \vec{x} + (1 - \epsilon)\vec{u}) \geq \vec{0}$ so

$$\sum_{i=1}^{J} c_i(\epsilon x_i + (1 - \epsilon)u_i) = d.$$

Hence

$$\sum_{i=1}^{J} \epsilon c_i x_i = d - (1 - \epsilon) \sum_{i=1}^{J} c_i u_i = \epsilon d$$

so

$$\sum_{i=1}^{J} c_i x_i = d$$

as required.   □

Proof of theorem 7.1 By considering each axiom and rule in turn it is straight-forward to show, by induction on the length of the proof, that if $K \vdash_{\mathrm{I}} K'$ then $V^L(K) \subseteq V^L(K')$.

To show the converse suppose $V^L(K) \subseteq V^L(K')$. Then starting with the axiom $K \mid K$ we can systematically use the probability and arithmetic axioms and the arithmetic and logical rules to derive

$$K \mid \langle Bel(\alpha_1), ..., Bel(\alpha_J) \rangle A_K = \vec{b}_K \tag{7.1}$$

Now suppose that $(\sum c_i Bel(\theta_i) = d)$ is one of the constraints in K' and that

$$\sum_{i=1}^{J} e_i Bel(\alpha_i) = d$$

is the result of replacing each such $Bel(\theta_i)$ in this constraint by $\sum_{\alpha_j \in S_{\theta_i}} Bel(\alpha_j)$ and collecting terms. Then, by noticing that we can reverse the sort of procedure which led from $K \mid K$ to (7.1) we see that to show $K \vdash_{\mathrm{I}} K'$ it is sufficient to show that we can derive $K \mid (\sum_{i=1}^{J} e_i Bel(\alpha_i) = d)$ from (7.1).

Now if $x_{j_0} = 0$ for all $\vec{x} \in V^L(K)$ then, by lemma 7.2, there is $\vec{a} \geq 0$ such that $a_{j_0} > 0$ and $\vec{x}\vec{a}^T = 0$ whenever $\vec{x}A_K = \vec{b}_K$. By the standard reduction of a set of simultaneous linear equations to row echelon form we see that by taking linear combinations we can obtain from $\vec{x}A_K = \vec{b}_K$ a system of equations

$$\langle x_{i_1}, ..., x_{i_p} \rangle - (\langle x_{i_{p+1}}, ..., x_{i_J} \rangle D + \langle g_1, ..., g_p \rangle) = \vec{0}, \tag{7.2}$$

where $i_1, ..., i_J$ is a permutation of $1, ..., J$, having exactly the same solutions. Hence

$$(\langle x_{i_{p+1}}, ..., x_{i_J} \rangle D + \langle g_1, ..., g_p \rangle) \langle a_{i_1}, ..., a_{i_p} \rangle^T + \sum_{j=p+1}^{J} x_{i_j} a_{i_j} \tag{7.3}$$

must be identically zero. This is only possible if all the coefficients of the x_{i_j}, $j = p + 1, ..., J$, are zero. Hence (7.3) is derivable from the identities $x_{i_j} - x_{i_j} = 0$ for $j = p + 1, ..., J,$. Multiplying the left hand side of (7.2) by $\langle a_{i_1}, ..., a_{i_p} \rangle^T$ and adding this to (7.3) gives $\vec{x}\vec{a}^T = 0$.

From this it follows that by using the logical and arithmetical rules and axioms we can obtain

$$K \mid \langle Bel(\alpha_1), ..., Bel(\alpha_J) \rangle \vec{a}^T = 0$$

from (7.1) and hence, by the probability rule,

$$K \mid Bel(\alpha_{j_0}) = 0.$$

Hence by the logical rules we can obtain

$$K \mid \langle Bel(\alpha_1), ..., Bel(\alpha_J) \rangle A_K = \vec{b}_K, \ Bel(\alpha_j) = 0 \text{ for } j \in I^L(K),$$

where

$$I^L(K) = \{ j \mid \forall \vec{x} \in V^L(K), \ x_j = 0 \}.$$

Using lemma 7.3 and the above method we can now derive

$$K \mid \sum_{i=1}^{J} e_i Bel(\alpha_i) = d$$

as required. □

By retaining K on the right as well as the left of the sequents we see that the proof of this theorem may be viewed as a justification of the equivalence principle since it shows that if K_1, K_2 are equivalent then $K_1 + K_2$ can be derived from either of K_1 or K_2 via a series of steps each of which transparently preserves the nature of the constraints. Thus it would seem irrational if any one such step caused an expert to alter his beliefs. Arguing like this along these (possibly very lengthy) derivations would yield the conclusions $N(K_1) = N(K_1 + K_2)$, $N(K_2) = N(K_1 + K_2)$ and hence that $N(K_1) = N(K_2)$.

Since all of the processes $CM^L, CM^L_\infty, MD^L, ME^L$ are defined in terms of $V^L(K)$ they all satisfy the principle of equivalence. Henceforth in this chapter when presenting other principles we shall assume that N satisfies the principle of equivalence.

Principle of Irrelevant Information

Suppose that $K_1, K_2 \in CL$, $\theta \in SL$ but that no propositional variable appearing in θ or in any sentence in K_1 also appears in a sentence in K_2. Then

$$N(K_1 + K_2)(\theta) = N(K_1)(\theta).$$

The justification for this principle is that the knowledge provided by K_2 is irrelevant to K_1 and θ since it concerns a completely separate set of propositional variables (i.e. features) and hence the belief given to θ on the basis of $K_1 + K_2$ should be the same as on the basis of K_1 alone.

We note here that for such separate $K_1, K_2 \in CL$, $K_1 + K_2$ is consistent, and hence in CL. To see this suppose that Bel_1, Bel_2 are probability functions on SL satisfying K_1, K_2 respectively, and suppose that $K_1 \in CL_1$, $K_2 \in CL_2$ where $L_1 \cup L_2 = L$, $L_1 \cap L_2 = \emptyset$. Let $\alpha_1^1, ..., \alpha_{J_1}^1$ and $\alpha_1^2, ..., \alpha_{J_2}^2$ be the atoms of L_1, L_2 respectively so that (up to logical equivalence) the atoms of L are $\alpha_i^1 \wedge \alpha_j^2$ for $i = 1, ..., J_1$, $j = 1, ..., J_2$. Define a probability function Bel on SL by

$$Bel(\alpha_i^1 \wedge \alpha_j^2) = Bel_1(\alpha_i^1) Bel_2(\alpha_j^2).$$

Then Bel agrees with Bel_1 on SL_1, since

$$Bel(\alpha_i^1) = \sum_{j=1}^{J_2} Bel(\alpha_i^1 \wedge \alpha_j^2) = Bel_1(\alpha_i^1) \sum_{j=1}^{J_2} Bel_2(\alpha_j^2) = Bel_1(\alpha_i^1),$$

and with Bel_2 on SL_2, so Bel satisfies both K_1 and K_2.

Theorem 7.4 *The maximum entropy inference process, ME, satisfies the principle of irrelevant information.*

Proof Let K_1, K_2, θ etc. be as in the above discussion and let $\vec{\rho} = ME^{L_1}(K_1)$, $\vec{\tau} = ME^{L_2}(K_2)$. By the above discussion it is enough to show that

$$\rho_i \tau_j = ME^L(K_1 + K_2)(\alpha_i^1 \wedge \alpha_j^2).$$

Let $\nu_{ij} = ME^L(K_1 + K_2)(\alpha_i^1 \wedge \alpha_j^2)$ and $\nu_{i.} = \sum_{j=1}^{J_2} \nu_{ij}$, $\nu_{.j} = \sum_{i=1}^{J_1} \nu_{ij}$. Then since $\langle \nu_{1.}, \nu_{2.}, ..., \nu_{J_1.} \rangle \in V^{L_1}(K_1)$ and $\langle \nu_{.1}, \nu_{.2}, ..., \nu_{.J_2} \rangle \in V^{L_2}(K_2)$,

$$- \sum_i \nu_{i.} \log(\nu_{i.}) \leq - \sum_i \rho_i \log(\rho_i), \tag{7.4}$$

and

$$- \sum_j \nu_{.j} \log(\nu_{.j}) \leq - \sum_j \tau_j \log(\tau_j). \tag{7.5}$$

Also since $Bel(\alpha_i^1 \wedge \alpha_j^2) = \rho_i \tau_j$ satisfies $K_1 + K_2$,

$$- \sum_{i,j} \rho_i \tau_j \log(\rho_i \tau_j) \leq - \sum_{i,j} \nu_{ij} \log(\nu_{ij}). \tag{7.6}$$

Using (7.4), (7.5) the sum of the first two terms in the identity

$$- \sum_{i,j} \nu_{ij} \log(\nu_{ij}) = - \sum_i \nu_{i.} \log(\nu_{i.}) - \sum_j \nu_{.j} \log(\nu_{.j})$$
$$- \sum_{i,j} \nu_{i.} \nu_{.j} \left[\frac{\nu_{ij}}{\nu_{i.} \nu_{.j}} \log \left(\frac{\nu_{ij}}{\nu_{i.} \nu_{.j}} \right) \right]$$

is at most

$$-\sum_i \rho_i \log(\rho_i) - \sum_j \tau_j \log(\tau_j) = -\sum_{i,j} \rho_i \tau_j \log(\rho_i \tau_j)$$

whilst, by the concavity of $-x\log(x)$ on $[0,1]$, the third term is bounded above by

$$-\left(\sum_{i,j} \nu_i.\nu_{.j} \frac{\nu_{ij}}{\nu_i.\nu_{.j}}\right) \log\left(\sum_{i,j} \nu_i.\nu_{.j} \frac{\nu_{ij}}{\nu_i.\nu_{.j}}\right) = 0,$$

since $\sum_{i,j} \nu_{ij} = 1$. Hence equality holds in (7.6) and $\nu_{ij} = \rho_i \tau_j$ follows by the uniqueness of the point of maximum entropy in $V^L(K_1 + K_2)$. $\quad\square$

We remark that none of CM^L, MD^L, CM^L_∞ satisfy this principle. This is clear for CM^L since, by taking $K_2 = \{Bel(\beta) = 1\}$ for β an atom of L_2, we see that this principle would imply $CM^L(K_1) = CM^L(K_1 + K_2) = CM^{L_1}(K_1)$ (by definition of CM) and hence language invariance would hold.

Continuity

The essence of this principle, or desideratum, is that, for $\theta \in SL$, a microscopic change in the knowledge K should not cause a macroscopic change in the value $N(K)(\theta)$ of the belief assigned to θ on the basis of K. The justification for this is that it is unreasonable to expect that the knowledge K of the expert is not subject to minor chance fluctuations even if he receives no new knowledge. Nevertheless it would seem inconsistent, in the natural language sense, if this caused appreciable changes in his beliefs (and the subsequent commitments they engender). Thus common sense, or at least our common understanding of the function of belief as condoning actions, requires that the values $N(K)(\theta)$ display a certain robustness in the face of minor fluctuations in the knowledge K.

In formulating this principle however we are faced with the problem of finding a metric on CL which captures the idea that nearness in the metric corresponds to nearness in knowledge content. An immediate response might well be to use some standard metric on the matrices $\begin{pmatrix} \vec{b}_K \\ A_K \end{pmatrix}$,

for example

$$\| A - B \| = \max | a_{ji} - b_{ji} |$$

where $A = (a_{ji})$, $B = (b_{ji})$. Indeed this appears on the face of it to be just what is required since it would seem that a 'minor fluctuation' of K would correspond exactly to a minor fluctuation in the coefficients a_{ji}, b_i appearing in K and hence to a matrix close to A_K in this metric.

Unfortunately this metric does not capture the idea of distance between knowledge contents as the following example shows. Suppose $L = \{p\}$ and

$$K = \{0 \cdot Bel(p) = 0\}, \quad K_\epsilon = \{\epsilon Bel(p) = 0\},$$

$$K'_\epsilon = \{\epsilon Bel(\neg p) = 0\}, \quad K''_\epsilon = \{\epsilon Bel(p) - \epsilon Bel(\neg p) = 0\}$$

Then

$$\begin{pmatrix} \vec{0} \\ A_{K_\epsilon} \end{pmatrix}, \begin{pmatrix} \vec{0} \\ A_{K'_\epsilon} \end{pmatrix}, \begin{pmatrix} \vec{0} \\ A_{K''_\epsilon} \end{pmatrix} \longrightarrow \begin{pmatrix} \vec{0} \\ A_K \end{pmatrix} \quad as \ \epsilon \to 0$$

in the above metric. However it is clear that in terms of the knowledge they express, $K_\epsilon, K'_\epsilon, K''_\epsilon$, for $\epsilon > 0$, are about as distant from each other as one could imagine. Of course one could argue that this is a rather transparent and unnatural example. However there are much more subtle (and natural) examples, as the following, due to Courtney [8], shows.

Suppose a certain disease d has a symptom s and possible complication c (so $L = \{d, s, c\}$). A Medical expert gives the following as his knowledge about their relationships:

1. $Bel(d \wedge s) = 0.75 Bel(s)$ 4. $Bel(d \wedge \neg s) = 0.25 Bel(\neg s)$

2. $Bel(\neg c \wedge d \wedge s) = 0.15 Bel(s)$ 5. $Bel(\neg c \wedge d \wedge \neg s) = 0.6 Bel(d \wedge \neg s)$

3. $Bel(c \wedge d \wedge s) = 0.8 Bel(d \wedge s)$ 6. $Bel(c \wedge d \wedge \neg s) = 0.1 Bel(\neg s)$

These are certainly consistent, for example take

$$Bel(s) = 1, \ Bel(c \wedge d \wedge s) = 0.6,$$
$$Bel(\neg c \wedge d \wedge s) = 0.15, \ Bel(c \wedge \neg d \wedge s) = 0.25$$

and all the other atoms zero.

However, since the equations $4, 5, 6$ force

$$Bel(d \wedge \neg s) \ = \ Bel(c \wedge d \wedge \neg s) + Bel(\neg c \wedge d \wedge \neg s)$$

$$= \ (0.6 + \tfrac{0.1}{0.25}) Bel(d \wedge \neg s),$$

any change in one coefficient in $4, 5, 6$ forces $Bel(d \wedge \neg s) = Bel(\neg s) = 0$. Similarly any change in any one coefficient in $1, 2, 3$ forces $Bel(s) = 0$.

The conclusion that such examples force upon us is that closeness of $\begin{pmatrix} \vec{b}_K \\ A_K \end{pmatrix}$,

$\begin{pmatrix} \vec{b}_{K'} \\ A_{K'} \end{pmatrix}$ (in the above metric) does not correspond to closeness of knowledge content (although it must be admited that it is questionable whether or not the above intuitions about the commonsensicality of continuity were not in fact based on closeness in the former sense!). What is required here is a metric which better corresponds to distance between knowledge contents. One natural criterion for K, K' to be close to each other is that every solution, *Bel*, to K is close to a solution to K' and vice-versa. When expressed in terms of the convex sets $V^L(K)$ this is just the well known Blaschke metric, $\triangle$, defined, for convex subsets C, D of $\mathbb{D}^L$, by

$$\triangle(C, D) = \inf\{\delta \mid \forall \vec{x} \in C \; \exists \vec{y} \in D, \; |\vec{x} - \vec{y}| \leq \delta \; \& \; \forall \vec{y} \in D \; \exists \vec{x} \in C, \; |\vec{x} - \vec{y}| \leq \delta\}$$

where $\mid \vec{x} - \vec{y} \mid$ is the usual Euclidean distance between the points $\vec{x}$ and $\vec{y}$. (See Eggleston [13] for further details of this metric and its induced topology.)

We can now state the continuity requirement on an inference process N as the requirement that N, as a function of the convex sets $V^L(K)$, is continuous with respect to this Blaschke metric, i.e.

$$\text{If } \theta \in SL, \quad K, K_i \in CL \text{ for } i \in \mathbb{N} \text{ and } \lim_{i \to \infty} \triangle(V^L(K), V^L(K_i)) = 0$$

$$\text{then } \lim_{i \to \infty} N(K_i)(\theta) = N(K)(\theta).$$

Notice that it is enough here to restrict θ to being an atom. The following theorem, due to I. Maung [45], shows that ME, CM_∞, MD are continuous.

Theorem 7.5 *If the process N on L satisfies*

$$N(K) = \text{ that } \vec{x} \in V^L(K) \text{ at which } F(\vec{x}) \text{ is maximal,}$$

for some (strictly) concave function $F : \mathbb{D}^L \longrightarrow \mathbb{R}$, then N is continuous.

Proof Since F is concave, F is uniformly continuous on $\mathbb{D}^L$. Given $K \in CL$ and $\epsilon > 0$ let

$$\nu = \inf\{F(N(K)) - F(\vec{x}) \mid \vec{x} \in V^L(K) \; \& \; |\vec{x} - N(K)| \geq \frac{\epsilon}{2}\}$$

Notice that $\nu > 0$, since if not then by the continuity of F and compactness of $V^L(K)$ there would be $\vec{z} \in V^L(K)$ with $F(\vec{z}) = F(N(K))$ and $\mid \vec{z} - N(K) \mid \geq \frac{\epsilon}{2}$. But then the value of F at $\frac{1}{2}(\vec{z} + N(K)) \in V^L(K)$ would exceed $F(N(K))$, contradiction.

By the uniform continuity of F let δ be such that for $\vec{x}, \vec{y} \in \mathbb{D}^L$, $\mid \vec{x} - \vec{y} \mid < \delta$ implies $\mid F(\vec{x}) - F(\vec{y}) \mid < \min\left(\frac{\nu}{2}, \frac{\epsilon}{2}\right)$. Now suppose $\triangle(V^L(K), V^L(K')) < \delta$. Pick $\vec{x} \in V^L(K), \vec{y} \in V^L(K')$ such that

$$\mid \vec{x} - N(K') \mid < \delta \text{ and } \mid \vec{y} - N(K) \mid < \delta.$$

Then

$$F(N(K')) \;\; < \;\; F(\vec{x}) + \frac{\nu}{2} \;\; \leq \;\; F(N(K)) + \frac{\nu}{2},$$

$$F(N(K)) \;\; < \;\; F(\vec{y}) + \frac{\nu}{2} \;\; \leq \;\; F(N(K')) + \frac{\nu}{2},$$

so

$$| F(\vec{x}) - F(N(K)) | < \nu.$$

Hence $| \vec{x} - N(K) | < \frac{\epsilon}{2}$, by definition of ν, so $| N(K) - N(K') | < \frac{\epsilon}{2} + \delta < \epsilon$ as required.   □

The inference process CM^L does not satisfy continuity for this metric. For example for $L = \{p, q\}$ and K_ϵ ($\epsilon \geq 0$) being

$$(1 - \epsilon) Bel(\neg p \wedge q) + Bel(\neg p \wedge \neg q) = 1 - \epsilon,$$

$$(1 - \epsilon) Bel(p) - \epsilon Bel(\neg p \wedge \neg q) = 0,$$

it is the case that $CM^L(K_0)(\neg p \wedge q) = \frac{1}{2}$ whilst $CM^L(K_\epsilon)(\neg p \wedge q) = \frac{1}{3}$ for $\epsilon > 0$ despite the fact that $V^L(K_\epsilon)$ tends to $V^L(K_0)$ in the Blaschke topology as ϵ tends to zero. The reason for this discontinuity here is that for $\epsilon > 0$, $V^L(K_\epsilon) \subseteq \mathbb{D}^L$ is an isosceles triangle with base on $x_3 = 0$ and apex on $x_3 = 1$ so its centre of mass satisfies $x_3 = \frac{1}{3}$. As ϵ tends to zero however the sides fold together yielding in the limit a line with centre of mass satisfying $x_3 = \frac{1}{2}$.

Returning again to the earlier, flawed, idea that continuity of an inference process N at K should mean that if

$$\left\| \begin{pmatrix} \vec{b}_K \\ A_K \end{pmatrix} - \begin{pmatrix} \vec{b}_{K'} \\ A_{K'} \end{pmatrix} \right\|$$

is small then $N(K)$ is close to $N(K')$, it is now natural to ask under what conditions

$$\left\| \begin{pmatrix} \vec{b}_K \\ A_K \end{pmatrix} - \begin{pmatrix} \vec{b}_{K'} \\ A_{K'} \end{pmatrix} \right\|$$

being small forces $V^L(K), V^L(K')$ to be close in the Blaschke topology.

In fact there are two situations in which this can fail. The first is when $I^L(K) \neq I^L(K')$, the second when $\hat{A}_K, \hat{A}_{K'}$ have different ranks, where $\hat{A}_K$ is the result of deleting the ith row from A_K for each $i \in I^L(K)$. Indeed these are the reasons continuity fails in the first example given above. We now show a result (due to Courtney [8]) that if these situations do not occur then closeness of the coefficients in K' to those in K does indeed force $V^L(K), V^L(K')$ to be close in the Blaschke sense.

Theorem 7.6 *Let $K \in CL$ and $\epsilon > 0$. Then there is $\delta > 0$ such that if $K' \in CL$, $A_{K'}$ has the same number of rows as A_K and*

(i) Rank $(\hat{A}_K) = Rank(\hat{A}_{K'})$,

(ii) $I^L(K) = I^L(K')$,

(iii) $\left\| \begin{pmatrix} \vec{b}_K \\ A_K \end{pmatrix} - \begin{pmatrix} \vec{b}_{K'} \\ A_{K'} \end{pmatrix} \right\| < \delta,$

then $\triangle(V^L(K), V^L(K')) < \epsilon.$

Proof Fix K, ϵ and to simplify the notation write A for $A_K, \vec{b}$ for $\vec{b}_K$ etc., and assume that $I^L(K) = \{r+1, r+2, ..., J\}$, and that

$$\hat{A} = \begin{pmatrix} A_1 & A_2 \\ A_3 & A_4 \end{pmatrix}$$

where A_1 is non-singular and every column of $\begin{pmatrix} A_2 \\ A_4 \end{pmatrix}$ is a linear combination of

columns from $\begin{pmatrix} A_1 \\ A_3 \end{pmatrix}$, say $\begin{pmatrix} A_1 \\ A_3 \end{pmatrix} Q = \begin{pmatrix} A_2 \\ A_4 \end{pmatrix}$ so $A_1 Q = A_2$, $A_3 Q = A_4$.

Let $\hat{A}' = \begin{pmatrix} A'_1 & A'_2 \\ A'_3 & A'_4 \end{pmatrix}$ be close to $\hat{A}$ (in the $\|\,.\,\|$ metric). Then, since

$Det(A_1) \neq 0$, $Det(A'_1) \neq 0$ and $(A'_1)^{-1}$ is close to $(A_1)^{-1}$. (Recall that K is fixed throughout.) Hence

$$\begin{pmatrix} A_1^{-1} & Q \\ 0 & -I \end{pmatrix} \text{ is close to } \begin{pmatrix} (A'_1)^{-1} & (A'_1)^{-1}A'_2 \\ 0 & -I \end{pmatrix}$$

and pre-multiplying these by $\hat{A}, \hat{A}'$ respectively gives

$$\begin{pmatrix} I & 0 \\ A_3 A_1^{-1} & 0 \end{pmatrix}, \begin{pmatrix} I & 0 \\ A'_3(A'_1)^{-1} & C \end{pmatrix}$$

for some C which, we see by (i), must also be zero.

To sum up then we have now simplified the problem to the case where

$$\hat{A} = \begin{pmatrix} I \\ B \end{pmatrix}, \quad \hat{A}' = \begin{pmatrix} I \\ B' \end{pmatrix}.$$

We first show that for $\left\| \begin{pmatrix} \vec{b} \\ A \end{pmatrix} - \begin{pmatrix} \vec{b}' \\ A' \end{pmatrix} \right\|$ sufficiently small, every element $\vec{x} \in$

$V^L(K')$ is within ϵ of an element of $V^L(K)$. For suppose this fails. Then we can pick $A'_n, \vec{b}'_n$ and $\vec{x}_n \geq 0$ such that

$$\left\| \begin{pmatrix} \vec{b} \\ A \end{pmatrix} - \begin{pmatrix} \vec{b}_n \\ A_n \end{pmatrix} \right\| \longrightarrow 0 \qquad \text{as } n \to \infty,$$

$\vec{x}_n A_n = \vec{b}_n$ but $|\vec{x}_n - \vec{y}| \geq \epsilon$ for all $\vec{y} \in V^L(K)$. But then the $\vec{x}_n$ have a subsequence with limit point $\vec{x}$ and clearly $\vec{x}A = \vec{b}, \vec{x} \geq 0$ whilst $|\vec{x} - \vec{y}| \geq \epsilon$ for all $\vec{y} \in V^L(K)$, a contradiction.

To complete the proof we need to show that for $\left\| \begin{pmatrix} \vec{b} \\ A \end{pmatrix} - \begin{pmatrix} \vec{b}' \\ A' \end{pmatrix} \right\|$ sufficiently small, every $\vec{x} \in V^L(K)$ is within ϵ of an element of $V^L(K')$. To show this first fix $\vec{u} \in V^L(K)$ such that $u_i > 0$ for $i = 1, ..., r$, and now let $\vec{x} \in V^L(K)$. Then for $\vec{y} = \vec{x} + \frac{\epsilon}{4}(\vec{u} - \vec{x})$,

$$|\vec{x} - \vec{y}| \leq \frac{\epsilon}{2}, \quad \vec{y}A = \vec{b} \quad \text{and} \quad y_i \geq \frac{\epsilon}{4}u_i > 0 \quad \text{for} \quad i = 1, ..., r.$$

($y_i = 0$ of course for $r + 1 \leq i \leq J$.) Let $\hat{A}$ be $r \times m$ and recall that we are assuming $\hat{A} = \begin{pmatrix} I \\ B \end{pmatrix}$ etc. Let

$$\vec{z} = \langle \vec{b}' - \langle y_{m+1}, y_{m+2}, ..., y_r \rangle B', \ y_{m+1}, y_{m+2}, ..., y_J \rangle$$

Then, for $\begin{pmatrix} \vec{b}' \\ A' \end{pmatrix}$ sufficiently close to $\begin{pmatrix} \vec{b} \\ A \end{pmatrix}$, $|\vec{z} - \vec{y}| < \frac{\epsilon}{4} \min\{u_j \mid 1 \leq j \leq r\}$ since $\vec{b}' - \langle y_{m+1}, ..., y_r \rangle B'$ is close to

$$\vec{b} - \langle y_{m+1}, ..., y_r \rangle B = \vec{b} - \langle y_1, ..., y_r \rangle \begin{pmatrix} I \\ B \end{pmatrix} + \langle y_1, ..., y_m \rangle = \langle y_1, ..., y_m \rangle.$$

Hence $|\vec{z} - \vec{x}| < \epsilon$. Also $\vec{z} \geq 0$, since $z_i = 0$ for $i > r$ whilst for $i \leq r$,

$$z_i > y_i - \frac{\epsilon}{4} \min\{u_j \mid 1 \leq j \leq J\} \geq y_i - \frac{\epsilon}{4}u_i \geq 0,$$

and $\langle z_1, ..., z_r \rangle \begin{pmatrix} I \\ B' \end{pmatrix} = \vec{b}'$ so $\vec{z} \in V^L(K')$, completing the proof. $\qquad \square$

We finally remark, omitting the proof, that if $K, K_n \in CL$ are such that

$$\left\| \begin{pmatrix} \vec{b}_K \\ A_K \end{pmatrix} - \begin{pmatrix} \vec{b}_{K_n} \\ A_{K_n} \end{pmatrix} \right\| \longrightarrow 0 \text{ as } n \to \infty$$

and $Rank(\hat{A}_K) = Rank(\hat{A}_{K_n})$, $I^L(K) = I^L(K_n)$ for all n then $\lim_{n \to \infty} CM^L(K_n) = CM^L(K)$, so CM^L is continuous in this weaker sense. Nevertheless in this text we shall take continuity for an inference process to mean continuity for the Blaschke topology.

Open-mindedness Principle

If $K \in CL$, $\theta \in SL$ and $K + Bel(\theta) \neq 0$ is consistent then $N(K)(\theta) \neq 0$.

The justification for this principle is that if it is consistent with K that θ is possible (i.e. $Bel(\theta) \neq 0$) then the inference process N should not dismiss, or classify, θ as impossible since this would amount to introducing assumptions beyond those in K. This principle highlights the very special nature of categorical beliefs (i.e. with values $0, 1$) as compared with beliefs in the range $(0, 1)$. (A explanation of this, perhaps, is that beliefs in the range $(0, 1)$ are perceived as having no absolute meaning.)

It is easy to convince oneself by a geometric argument that MD^L does not satisfy this principle whilst CM^L does. ME^L and CM_∞^L also satisfy this principle, essentially because the derivatives of $-x\log(x)$ and $\log(x)$ tend to infinity as x tends to zero. To see this for the case of ME^L suppose $ME^L(K) = \vec{p}$ and $ME^L(K)(\theta) = 0$ whilst there is $\vec{a} \in V^L(K)$ with $a_j > 0$ for some $\alpha_j \in S_\theta$. Then for ϵ small $\vec{p} + \epsilon(\vec{a} - \vec{p}) \in V^L(K)$ and by choice of $\vec{p}$,

$$
\begin{aligned}
0 \ &< \ -\sum_i p_i \log(p_i) + \sum_i (p_i + \epsilon(a_i - p_i)) \log(p_i + \epsilon(a_i - p_i)) \\
&= \ \epsilon \sum_i (a_i - p_i)[1 + \log(p_i + \lambda\epsilon(a_i - p_i))]
\end{aligned}
$$

for some $0 < \lambda < 1$, by the mean value theorem.

Now if $p_i > 0$ or $a_i = 0$ the ith term inside this sum is bounded in modulus by C_i for some constant $C_i > 0$. However if $p_i = 0, a_i > 0$ (as indeed happens for at least one i) then this ith term is negative and less than $D_i \log(\epsilon)$ for some constant $D_i > 0$. Clearly as ϵ tends downwards to zero such terms dominate the C_i and the sum becomes negative, giving the required contradiction.

A similar argument works for CM_∞^L.

Renaming Principle

Suppose $K_1, K_2 \in CL$,

$$
\begin{aligned}
K_1 \ &= \ \{\sum_{j=1}^J a_{ji} Bel(\gamma_j) = b_i \mid i = 1, ..., m\}, \\
K_2 \ &= \ \{\sum_{j=1}^J a_{ji} Bel(\delta_j) = b_i \mid i = 1, ..., m\},
\end{aligned}
$$

where $\gamma_1, ..., \gamma_J, \delta_1, ..., \delta_J$ are permutations of $\alpha_1, ..., \alpha_J$. Then

$$
N(K_1)(\gamma_j) = N(K_2)(\delta_j).
$$

The justification for this principle is that the atoms of SL all share the same status of being simply possible worlds and so the particular ordering $\alpha_1, ..., \alpha_J$ of these atoms which we choose should not be significant. In a sense this principle can be viewed as a restricted version of the principle of indifference. Unlike this latter principle, however, renaming carries no risk as we shall shortly see.

Whilst this principle is comparatively easy to accept in this form (which is why we presented it thus) it gains much more strength when used in conjunction with language invariance.

Theorem 7.7 *Suppose*

$$K_1 = \{\sum_{j=1}^{r} c_{ji} Bel(\theta_j) = b_i \mid i = 1, ..., m\} \in CL_1,$$

$$K_2 = \{\sum_{j=1}^{r} c_{ji} Bel(\phi_j) = b_i \mid i = 1, ..., m\} \in CL_2$$

and $\sigma : \overline{SL}_1 \cong \overline{SL}_2$ is such that $\sigma(\overline{\theta}_j) = \overline{\phi}_j$ for $j = 1, ..., r$ and $\sigma(\overline{\theta}) = \overline{\phi}$. Then for an inference process N satisfying language invariance and the principle of renaming,

$$N(K_1)(\theta) = N(K_2)(\phi).$$

Proof Such a σ is uniquely determined by its action on the $\{\overline{\alpha} \mid \alpha \in At^{L_1}\}$ which it maps 1–1 onto the $\{\overline{\beta} \mid \beta \in At^{L_2}\}$, say $\sigma(\overline{\alpha}) = \overline{\tau(\alpha)}$ for $\alpha \in At^{L_1}$. From this it follows that for suitable orderings of their atoms K_1, K_2 yield the same equivalent sets of linear equations when written out in terms of $Bel(\alpha), Bel(\beta)$ respectively, say

$$K_1 = \{\sum_{j=1}^{J} a_{ji} Bel(\alpha_j) = b_i \mid i = 1, ..., m\},$$

$$K_2 = \{\sum_{j=1}^{J} a_{ji} Bel(\tau(\alpha_j)) = b_i \mid i = 1, ..., m\}$$

where $At^{L_1} = \{\alpha_1, ..., \alpha_J\}$, and furthermore, since $\sigma(\overline{\theta}) = \overline{\phi}$, if $\theta \equiv \alpha_{i_1} \vee ... \vee \alpha_{i_t}$ then $\phi \equiv \tau(\alpha_{i_1}) \vee ... \vee \tau(\alpha_{i_t})$.

If $L_1 \cap L_2 = \emptyset$ we may take the atoms of $L_1 \cup L_2$ to be $\{\alpha \wedge \tau(\alpha') \mid \alpha, \alpha' \in At^L\}$

and, as elements of $C(L_1 \cup L_2)$,

$$K_1 = \{\sum_{j=1}^{J} a_{ji} \left(\sum_{k=1}^{J} Bel(\alpha_j \wedge \tau(\alpha_k)) \right) = b_i \mid i = 1, ..., m\},$$

$$K_2 = \{\sum_{j=1}^{J} a_{ji} \left(\sum_{k=1}^{J} Bel(\alpha_k \wedge \tau(\alpha_j)) \right) = b_i \mid i = 1, ..., m\}.$$

With respect to the permutation λ of $At^{L_1 \cup L_2}$ given by

$$\lambda(\alpha_j \wedge \tau(\alpha_k)) = \alpha_k \wedge \tau(\alpha_j),$$

K_1 and K_2 satisfy the hypotheses of the renaming principle so, by renaming,

$$N^{L_1 \cup L_2}(K_1)(\alpha_j \wedge \tau(\alpha_k)) = N^{L_1 \cup L_2}(K_2)(\alpha_k \wedge \tau(\alpha_j)).$$

Summing both sides over k gives

$$N^{L_1 \cup L_2}(K_1)(\alpha_j) = N^{L_1 \cup L_2}(K_2)(\tau(\alpha_j)).$$

Therefore, by language invariance,

$$N^{L_1}(K_1)(\alpha_j) = N^{L_2}(K_2)(\tau(\alpha_j))$$

and hence $N^{L_1}(K_1)(\theta) = N^{L_2}(K_2)(\phi)$, as required.

If $L_1 \cap L_2 \neq \emptyset$ let $\overline{SL}_3$ be an isomorphic copy of $\overline{SL}_1$, with $L_1 \cap L_3 = L_2 \cap L_3 = \emptyset$ and K_3 the corresponding copy of K_1. Now apply the result already proved twice, once between K_1 and K_3 and then between K_3 and K_2. □

Notice that in the special case when we have a 1–1 onto map η from L_1 to L_2 and we extend η to SL_1, CL_1 etc. in the obvious way and $\eta(K_1) = K_2, \eta(\theta) = \phi$ the theorem shows that for N satisfying language invariance and renaming,

$$N(K_1)(\theta) = N(K_2)(\phi).$$

In this case the conclusion seems so especially reasonable that it deserves the title *weak renaming principle*.

We can reformulate the renaming principle in terms of the convex sets $V^L(K)$ as follows. For σ a permutation of $1, ..., J$ extend σ to $\mathbb{R}^J$ by

$$\sigma\langle x_1, ..., x_J\rangle = \langle x_{\sigma(1)}, ..., x_{\sigma(J)}\rangle.$$

Then N satisfying the renaming principle is equivalent to N satisfying

$$\sigma N(V^L(K)) = N(\sigma V^L(K))$$

for $K \in CL$, σ a permutation of $1, ..., J$ – here we are directly treating N as a choice function on the sets $V^L(K)$.

To see this, notice that if

$$K = \{ \sum_{j=1}^{J} a_{ji} Bel(\alpha_j) = b_i \mid i = 1, ..., m \},$$

$$K' = \{ \sum_{j=1}^{J} a_{ji} Bel(\alpha_{\sigma^{-1}(j)}) = b_i \mid i = 1, ..., m \},$$

then $V^L(K') = \sigma V^L(K)$, since $\langle x_1, ..., x_J \rangle$ satisfies K iff $\langle y_1, ..., y_J \rangle$ satisfies K' where $y_{\sigma^{-1}(j)} = x_j$, or equivalently $y_j = x_{\sigma(j)}$ for $j = 1, ..., J$, and renaming asserts that

$$N(V^L(K'))(\alpha_{\sigma^{-1}(j)}) = N(V^L(K))(\alpha_j),$$

from which the result follows.

The renaming principle holds for the inference processes CM^L, CM_∞^L, MD^L, ME^L since they are all easily seen to have this latter property that $\sigma N(V^L(K)) = N(\sigma V^L(K))$. This is simply because these processes do give all the variables x_i (i.e. atoms in $Bel(\alpha_i)$) equal status. Nevertheless this principle seems not beyond criticism. Certainly it is hard to object to it in the case where $\gamma_1, ..., \gamma_J$ is just the result of transposing all occurences of two propositional variables p_s, p_t in the atoms $\delta_1, ..., \delta_J$ (i.e. $p_1^{\epsilon_1} \wedge ... \wedge p_s^{\epsilon_s} \wedge ... \wedge p_t^{\epsilon_t} \wedge ... \wedge p_n^{\epsilon_n}$ would become $p_1^{\epsilon_1} \wedge ... \wedge p_s^{\epsilon_t} \wedge ... \wedge p_t^{\epsilon_s} \wedge ... \wedge p_n^{\epsilon_n}$) or of transposing $p_s, \neg p_s$ (i.e $p_1^{\epsilon_1} \wedge ... \wedge p_s^{\epsilon_s} \wedge ... \wedge p_n^{\epsilon_n}$ would become $p_1^{\epsilon_1} \wedge ... \wedge p_s^{1-\epsilon_s} \wedge ... \wedge p_n^{\epsilon_n}$) since these look like genuine 'renamings'. However arbitrary permutations are perhaps rather stretching the notion of renaming. For example for $L = \{p_1, p_2, p_3\}$, the constraint $Bel(p_1 \wedge p_2) = b$ (equivalently $Bel(p_1 \wedge p_2 \wedge p_3) + Bel(p_1 \wedge p_2 \wedge \neg p_3) = b$) could be 'renamed' as $Bel(\neg p_1 \wedge p_2 \wedge p_3) + Bel(p_1 \wedge \neg p_2 \wedge p_3) = b$ and in this case one might feel that renaming has changed the content of the constraint. (For an interesting discussion on this point see Miller [49].) If an inference process N satisfies renaming then it also satisfies the following 'principle of indifference'.

If $K = \{Bel(\theta) = 1\}$ where $\theta \in SL$ then $N^L(K)(\alpha_i) = |S_\theta|^{-1}$ for $\alpha_i \in S_\theta$ (and is necessarily zero otherwise).

In other words all worlds consistent with K get equal belief, or probability.

To see this, notice that K is equivalent to the single constraint

$$\sum_{\alpha_i \in S_\theta} Bel(\alpha_i) = 1.$$

Now if $\alpha_k, \alpha_j \in S_\theta$ and we consider the permutation of the atoms which simply transposes α_k, α_j then K will not alter, so by the renaming principle

$$N^L(K)(\alpha_k) = N^L(K)(\alpha_j).$$

The result now follows since $N^L(K)$ must satisfy K, i.e.

$$\sum_{\alpha_i \in S_\theta} N^L(K)(\alpha_i) = 1.$$

We shall refer to this as the *weak principle of indifference* to distinguish it from the suspect principle of indifference considered in the previous chapter.

Notice that the set of constraints

$$Bel(\theta_i) = 1, \ i = 1, ..., m \qquad Bel(\phi_j) = 0, \ j = 1, ..., q$$

is equivalent to the single constraint

$$Bel(\bigwedge_{i=1}^{m} \theta_i \wedge \bigwedge_{j=1}^{q} \neg\phi_j) = 1$$

so that the above principle can be applied whenever our constraint set K consists solely of constraints of this form.

Obstinacy Principle

Suppose $K_1, K_2 \in CL$ and $N(K_1)$ satisfies K_2. Then $N(K_1 + K_2) = N(K_1)$.

The justification for this principle is that since $N(K_1)$ satisfies K_2, K_2 would (according to the inference process N) be believed on the basis of K_1, so adding to K_2 to K_1 provides no more information, or alternatively gives no grounds for changing beliefs.

It is easy to convince oneself with a geometric argument that except in the case $|L| = 1$, CM^L does not satisfy obstinacy. However ME^L, CM^L_∞, MD^L all do satisfy this principle. Indeed this is a consequence of the general fact that if an inference process N^L can be specified as

$$N^L(K) = \text{the unique maximum point } \vec{x} \in V^L(K) \text{ of } F^L$$

where F^L is a function from $\mathbb{D}^L$ into a linearly ordered set, then N^L is obstinate (for L). This follows since if $\vec{x}$ is the maximum point of F^L in $V^L(K_1)$ and $\vec{x} \in V^L(K_2)$ then $\vec{x} \in V^L(K_1) \cap V^L(K_2) = V^L(K_1 + K_2)$ and, because $V^L(K_1 + K_2) \subseteq V^L(K_1)$, $\vec{x}$ must also be the maximum point of F^L on this set.

From this example it might be hoped that every obstinate inference could be represented in this way for some such F^L. Unfortunately however examples of obstinate inference processes can be found which are not of this form.

Relativisation Principle

Suppose $K_1, K_2 \in CL$, $0 < c < 1$ and

$$K_1 \;=\; \{Bel(\phi) = c\} + \left\{ \sum_{j=1}^{r} a_{ji} Bel(\theta_i \mid \phi) = b_i \mid \; i = 1, ..., m \right\},$$

$$K_2 \;=\; K_1 + \left\{ \sum_{j=1}^{q} e_{ji} Bel(\psi_i \mid \neg\phi) = f_i \mid \; i = 1, ..., s \right\}.$$

Then for $\theta \in SL$, $N(K_1)(\theta \mid \phi) = N(K_2)(\theta \mid \phi)$.

Here conditional beliefs are to be interpreted, of course, as conditional probabilities. The justification for this principle is that K_1, K_2 both give the same belief to ϕ and, given ϕ, they both express exactly the same knowledge (constraints) – since given ϕ the additional knowledge in K_2 becomes vacuous. Hence the conditional belief given to θ given ϕ by N on the basis of K_1 should be the same as that given on the basis of K_2.

This principle fails for CM^L, CM_∞^L, MD^L but holds for ME^L as we now show.

Theorem 7.8 ME^L *satisfies the relativisation principle.*

Proof Let K_1, K_2 be as above and let

$$K_2' = K_1' = \{Bel(\phi) = 1\} \; + \; \left\{ \sum_{j=1}^{r} a_{ji} Bel(\theta_i \wedge \phi) = b_i \mid \; i = 1, ..., m \right\}$$

$$K_1'' = \{Bel(\neg\phi) = 1\}$$

$$K_2'' = \{Bel(\neg\phi) = 1\} \; + \; \left\{ \sum_{j=1}^{q} e_{ji} Bel(\psi_i \wedge \neg\phi) = f_i \mid \; i = 1, ..., s \right\}$$

and to simplify the notation suppose that $S_\phi = \{\alpha_1, ..., \alpha_h\}$. It follows from proposition 2.2 that K_2', K_2'' are consistent since K_2 is. Let

$$\vec{\rho} = ME(K_2'), \quad \vec{\tau} = ME(K_2''), \quad \vec{\nu} = ME(K_2),$$

so $\sum_{j=1}^{h} \nu_j = c$ and $\tau_1 = ... = \tau_h = \rho_{h+1} = ... = \rho_J = 0$. Also

$$c\vec{\rho} + (1-c)\vec{\tau} \in V^L(K_2), \quad \left\langle \frac{\nu_1}{c}, ..., \frac{\nu_h}{c}, 0, ..., 0 \right\rangle \in V^L(K_2'),$$

$$\left\langle 0, ..., 0, \frac{\nu_{h+1}}{1-c}, ..., \frac{\nu_J}{1-c} \right\rangle \in V^L(K_2'').$$

Putting $E(\vec{x}) = -\sum_{j=1}^{J} x_i \log x_i$, we have, by the choice of $\vec{\rho}, \vec{\tau}, \vec{\nu}$,

$$
\begin{aligned}
E(\vec{\nu}) \quad &= \quad cE(\tfrac{\nu_1}{c}, ..., \tfrac{\nu_h}{c}, 0, ..., 0) + (1-c)E(0, ..., 0, \tfrac{\nu_{h+1}}{1-c}, ..., \tfrac{\nu_J}{1-c}) \\
&\quad -c\log c - (1-c)\log(1-c) \\
&\leq \quad cE(\vec{\rho}) + (1-c)E(\vec{\tau}) - c\log c - (1-c)\log(1-c) \\
&= \quad E(c\vec{\rho} + (1-c)\vec{\tau}) \leq E(\vec{\nu}).
\end{aligned}
$$

Hence $\vec{\nu} = c\vec{\rho} + (1-c)\vec{\tau}$. Thus $\nu_i = \rho_i c$ for $i = 1, ..., h$. Clearly a similar argument with K_1 also gives $ME(K_1)(\alpha_i) = \rho_i c$ for $i = 1, ..., h$. Thus

$$ME(K_1)(\alpha_i) = ME(K_2)(\alpha_i) \quad \text{for } \alpha_i \in S_\phi,$$

so $ME(K_1)(\theta \wedge \phi) = ME(K_2)(\theta \wedge \phi)$ for $\theta \in SL$, and the result follows. $\quad\square$

Principle of Independence

In the special case of $L = \{p_1, p_2, p_3\}$ *and*

$$K = \{Bel(p_1) = a, \ Bel(p_2 \mid p_1) = b, \ Bel(p_3 \mid p_1) = c\} \quad (a > 0),$$

$N^L(K)(p_2 \wedge p_3 \mid p_1) = bc.$

Again here conditional beliefs are identified with conditional probabilities. The justification for this principle is that since beliefs are probabilities and in K there is no material connection between p_2 and p_3 given p_1, so p_2, p_3 should be treated as statistically independent given p_1, i.e.

$$Bel(p_2 \wedge p_3 \mid p_1) = Bel(p_2 \mid p_1) \cdot Bel(p_3 \mid p_1),$$

which yields the conclusion of the principle. (Of course, that statistical independence exactly captures one's intuitive idea of independence might perhaps not be universally accepted. We shall return to this point in a later chapter.)

As can easily be checked, ME^L satisfies this principle, whilst CM^L, CM_∞^L, MD^L do not, yielding for this K in the case $a = 1, b = c = \frac{1}{n}$, $n > 3$, the answers $\frac{1}{2n}$, $\frac{1}{8}(\frac{8}{n} - 3 + \sqrt{9 + \frac{32}{n^2} - \frac{32}{n}})$, 0 respectively. Interestingly however in the case

$K = \{Bel(p_1) = a, Bel(p_2 \mid p_1) = b\}$ we find $ME(K)(p_2) = ab + \frac{1}{2}(1 - a)$, not the expected (?) answer b.

In as much as the principles introduced so far could be said to principles of common sense or rationality they clearly provide an argument in favour of ME^L, the maximum entropy inference process, as against CM^L, CM^L_∞, MD^L, since ME^L is the only one of these processes to satisfy all these principles. In fact they provide an argument favouring ME^L over any other inference process, as the following result due to the author and Vencovská [55] shows.

Theorem 7.9 *ME is the only inference process satisfying continuity and the principles of equivalence, irrelevant information, open-mindedness, renaming, obstinacy, relativisation and independence.*

Since common sense, or rationality, was used to justify belief as probability one could claim that ME is the only inference process consistent with common sense. We should be aware however that in coming to this conclusion we have made the assumption that the knowledge statements K themselves constitute the knowledge. Without this assumption the very relevance of common sense principles is questionable.

In view of the lengthy proof of 7.9 we shall, sadly, be forced to omit it from this modest volume. We refer the reader to [55].

We now go on to consider the two other principles, or at least desiderata.

Atomicity Principle

Let $\theta \in SL_2$ be neither a contradiction nor a tautology, $K \in CL_1$, $\phi \in SL_1$, $L_1 \cap L_2 = \emptyset$, $L_1, L_2 \subseteq L$. Let ϕ^θ etc. be the result of replacing a particular propositional variable $p \in L_1$ everywhere in ϕ by θ. Then $N^L(K)(\phi) = N^L(K^\theta)(\phi^\theta)$.

This principle might be justified by arguing that in practice the things we denote by propositional variables are determined not by some intrinsic property that they possess but simply because we choose to stop the depth of our analysis at this point. Presumably this reflects our belief that analysing them more deeply would not cause our answers to alter and the principle simply asserts this.

Unfortunately this likely-looking principle is inconsistent with belief as probability! To see that suppose $K = \emptyset$, $L = \{p, p_2, p_3\}$. Taking $\phi = p$ and, in turn, $\theta = (p_2 \wedge p_3)$, $(p_2 \wedge \neg p_3)$, p_2, $\neg p_2$ we see that $N^L(\emptyset)$ would have to give each of these the same value and this, combined with $N^L(\emptyset)(p_2) + N^L(\emptyset)(\neg p_2) = 1$, gives a contradiction.

Nevertheless this principle is consistent, and indeed is satisfied by ME, if we add the requirement that $(Bel(p) = a) \in K$ for some a (although it is hard to see that the intuition, which previously appeared to justify an untenable principle, is in any way altered by this insertion).

Theorem 7.10 *Suppose θ, K etc. are as in the statement of the atomicity principle and $(Bel(p) = a) \in K$. Then $ME^L(K)(\phi) = ME^L(K^\theta)(\phi^\theta)$.*

Proof Let α_i^1, $i = 1, ..., J_1$ be the atoms of $L_1 - \{p\}$, α_i^2, $i = 1, ..., J_2$ the atoms of L_2 and let $L_3 = L_2 \cup (L_1 - \{p\})$. Without loss of generality assume that

$$\models \theta \leftrightarrow \bigvee_{k=1}^{q} \alpha_k^2$$

and let $ME^{L_1}(K)(p \wedge \alpha_i^1) = \rho_i$, $ME^{L_1}(K)(\neg p \wedge \alpha_i^1) = \tau_i$, $ME^{L_3}(K^\theta)(\alpha_j^2 \wedge \alpha_i^1) = \nu_{ij}$. By considering K and K^θ, written out in terms of Bel of atoms of L_1, L_3 respectively, we see that wherever $Bel(p \wedge \alpha_i^1)$ $(Bel(\neg p \wedge \alpha_i^1))$ appears in K then

$$\sum_{j=1}^{q} Bel(\alpha_j^2 \wedge \alpha_i^1) \quad \left(\sum_{j=q+1}^{J_2} Bel(\alpha_j^2 \wedge \alpha_i^1) \right) \text{ appears in } K^\theta. \text{ Hence}$$

$$Bel(\alpha_j^2 \wedge \alpha_i^1) = \begin{cases} \frac{\rho_i}{q} & \text{if } j \leq q \\ \\ \frac{\tau_i}{J_2 - q} & \text{if } j > q \end{cases}$$

satisfies K^θ and

$$Bel(p \wedge \alpha_i^1) = \sum_{j=1}^{q} \nu_{ij},$$

$$Bel(\neg p \wedge \alpha_i^1) = \sum_{j=q+1}^{J_2} \nu_{ij},$$

satisfies K.

Also, by transposing atoms $\alpha_j^2 \wedge \alpha_i^1$, $\alpha_k^2 \wedge \alpha_i^1$ for $j, k \leq q$ or $j, k > q$, we see that by the renaming principle (which ME satisfies) $\nu_{ij} = \nu_{ik}$ for $j, k \leq q$ or $j, k > q$, so $\sum_{j=1}^{q} \nu_{ij} = q\nu_{i1}$ and $\sum_{j=q+1}^{J_2} \nu_{ij} = (J_2 - q)\nu_{iJ_2}$. (Notice that since θ is neither a tautology nor contradictory, $1 \leq q < J_2$.)

Hence, by definition of $\bar{\nu}$,

$$-\sum_{i=1}^{J_1} \left[\sum_{j=1}^{q} \frac{\rho_i}{q} \log\left(\frac{\rho_i}{q}\right) + \sum_{j=q+1}^{J_2} \frac{\tau_i}{J_2 - q} \log\left(\frac{\tau_i}{J_2 - q}\right) \right] \leq -\sum_{i=1}^{J_1}\sum_{j=1}^{J_2} \nu_{ij} \log(\nu_{ij})$$

$$= -\sum_{i=1}^{J_1} [q\nu_{i1} \log(\nu_{i1}) + (J_2 - q)\nu_{iJ_2} \log(\nu_{iJ_2})] .$$

Since $(Bel(p) = a) \in K$ we have

$$\sum_{i=1}^{J_1} \rho_i = a = \sum_{i=1}^{J_1} q\nu_{i1},$$

$$\sum_{i=1}^{J_1} \tau_i = (1-a) = \sum_{i=1}^{J_1} (J_2 - q)\nu_{iJ_2}.$$

Hence subtracting $a\log(q) + (1-a)\log(J_2 - q)$ from both sides of the above inequality gives

$$-\sum_{i=1}^{J_1} [\rho_i \log(\rho_i) + \tau_i \log(\tau_i)] \le -\sum_{i=1}^{J_1} [q\nu_{i1} \log(q\nu_{i1}) + (J_2 - q)\nu_{iJ_2} \log((J_2 - q)\nu_{iJ_2})]$$

which, by choice of $\vec{\rho}, \vec{\tau}$, gives $\rho_i = q\nu_{i1}$, $\tau_i = (J_2 - q)\nu_{iJ_2}$.

Finally if

$$\models \left[\phi \leftrightarrow \bigvee_{i \in R} (p \wedge \alpha_i^1) \vee \bigvee_{i \in S} (\neg p \wedge \alpha_i^1) \right]$$

then

$$\models \left[\phi^\theta \leftrightarrow \bigvee_{i \in R} (\theta \wedge \alpha_i^1) \vee \bigvee_{i \in S} (\neg \theta \wedge \alpha_i^1) \right]$$

so

$$\models \left[\phi^\theta \leftrightarrow \bigvee_{\substack{i \in R \\ j \le q}} (\alpha_j^2 \wedge \alpha_i^1) \vee \bigvee_{\substack{i \in S \\ q < j}} (\alpha_j^2 \wedge \alpha_i^1) \right]$$

Hence

$$
\begin{aligned}
ME^L(K^\theta)(\phi^\theta) &= ME^{L_3}(K^\theta)(\phi^\theta) \\[2mm]
&= \sum_{\substack{i \in R \\ j \le q}} \nu_{ij} + \sum_{\substack{i \in S \\ q < j}} \nu_{ij} \\[2mm]
&= \sum_{i \in R} q\nu_{i1} + \sum_{i \in S} (J_2 - q)\nu_{iJ_2} \\[2mm]
&= \sum_{i \in R} \rho_i + \sum_{i \in S} \tau_i \\[2mm]
&= ME^{L_1}(K)(\phi) = ME^L(K)(\phi)
\end{aligned}
$$

as required.   □

The principles we have introduced so far were motivated by considerations of common sense or rationality. However there are certainly other sources which might inspire principles or at least desiderata. One such source is considerations of computational feasibility and we shall consider this in chapter 9.

Another is the requirement of accuracy. After all in practice accuracy is the main priority – all the common sense in the world is of no value if it produces woefully incorrect answers. This, of course, raises the question of what 'correct' means, or could mean, in the context of uncertain reasoning, especially as regards the relationship of the knowledge statements K to the real world. Interesting as this question is however we shall resist the temptation to discuss it and, for this volume at least, we shall content ourselves with considering one, rather strong, notion of correctness, namely, that of being *calibrated*.

Calibration

Let $K \in CL$. Then we shall say that a solution Bel_0 to K is *calibrated* if for each $\theta \in SL$ and $w \in V^L(K)$,

$$Bel_0(\theta) = \frac{1}{q} \sum_{i=1}^{q} w(\theta_i)$$

where $\{\overline{\theta}_1, ..., \overline{\theta}_q\} = \{\overline{\phi} \mid Bel_0(\phi) = Bel_0(\theta)\}$, or equivalently,

$$\{S_{\theta_1}, ..., S_{\theta_q}\} = \{R \subseteq \{\alpha_1, ..., \alpha_J\} \mid Bel_0(\bigvee R) = Bel_0(\theta)\}.$$

This version of calibration was introduced by Lehner [44] (there called expected calibration) developing ideas of Horwich [32]. To see a relationship between calibration and the, presumably, desirable property of accuracy consider the following example. An expert maintains that some particular outcome is almost certain to occur but in the event it does not occur. Well, he could be excused, after all he did not actually assert that the outcome was certain so he was acknowledging that there was an outside chance that the outcome might fail to materialise. (For example he might, quite reasonably, inform anyone who asked that their lottery ticket was almost certainly not going to win. Nevertheless we would not expect all his answers to be vindicated since *someone* is going to win.) But now suppose that this happened repeatedly, that the expert claimed a particular outcome was almost certain but, in the event, it did not occur. In that case we would start to seriously doubt the accuracy of the expert's beliefs, indeed, more importantly from the point of view of this text, the expert himself should have doubts about his beliefs.

Assuming then that the expert has well-thought-out beliefs which he is not inclined to change, his beliefs should be such that, in his view, they do not seriously risk him committing a high proportion of (distinct) errors. To take a slightly more precise example, suppose the expert answers a large questionnaire concerning his beliefs in certain statements. Then of those statements about which he expresses belief b we might expect that, in the event, a proportion b, or thereabouts, of them would in fact turn out to be true. Certainly a proportion here differing significantly from b should cause the expert to re-examine his beliefs and the mechanism by which he arrived at them.

Now suppose that the expert has given a constraint set K and we make the Watts Assumption that K *is* exactly his knowledge and hence that his further beliefs are made on the basis of 'knowledge' K alone. Then in inferring beliefs from K the expert would, presumably, not wish to risk being inaccurate in the above sense. Indeed if this was his top priority, he might prefer not to seek higher principles on which to base his particular choice of a belief function satisfying K but rather, if possible, to assign beliefs in such a way that he runs no risk of consistently erring in this fashion no matter which choice of belief function is 'correct'. That is, in asserting K, he is asserting that, in his opinion, the correct answer satisfies K, but rather than go further and make a definite, and possibly inaccurate, choice of 'correct', he prefers to assign beliefs in such a way that he runs no risk of consistently erring in the above fashion.

Formally then, if $\theta_1, ..., \theta_q$ are exactly the distinct outcomes to which the expert gives belief b on the basis of some general knowledge K then he should ideally prefer that for any probability function w satisfying K the expected proportion of $\theta_1, ..., \theta_q$ which occur, according to w, is b, i.e.

$$b = \frac{1}{q}\sum_{i=1}^{q}w(\theta_i).$$

Identifying 'distinct outcomes' here with a maximal set of inequivalent outcomes then provides the justification for choosing, if possible, a calibrated solution.

Unfortunately calibrated solutions do not always exist for $K \in CL$ although, as we shall see, if a calibrated solution does exist then it is unique.

Our aim now is to give a characterisation of the calibrated solution, when it exists, due to Lehner [44], and then to connect calibration with two principles mentioned earlier.

The following theorem and discussion is due to Lehner [44].

Theorem 7.11 *Let $K \in CL$ and $Bel_0 \in V^L(K)$. Then Bel_0 is calibrated iff Bel_0 is calibrated with respect to atoms, that is, for $1 \leq i \leq J$ and $w \in V^L(K)$,*

$$Bel_0(\alpha_i) = \frac{1}{|T_i|}\sum_{\alpha_j \in T_i} w(\alpha_j)$$

where $T_i = \{\alpha_j \mid Bel_0(\alpha_i) = Bel_0(\alpha_j)\}$.

Proof We first make some general observations about a solution Bel_0 of K. To simplify the notation suppose that $Bel_0(\alpha_1) < Bel_0(\alpha_2) < ... < Bel_0(\alpha_s)$ are all the distinct values Bel_0 takes on the atoms and let

$$T_i = \{\alpha_j \mid Bel_0(\alpha_i) = Bel_0(\alpha_j)\} \text{ for } 1 \leq i \leq s$$

so $T_1, T_2, ..., T_s$ is a partition of the set of atoms. For $\theta \in SL$ let Y_θ be the set of those integer vectors $\langle n_1, ..., n_s \rangle$ such that

$$Bel_0(\theta) = \sum_{i=1}^{s}n_i Bel_0(\alpha_i)$$

and $0 \le n_i \le |T_i|$ for $i = 1, ..., s$. Then since for $\phi \in SL$,

$$Bel_0(\phi) = \sum_{\alpha \in S_\phi} Bel_0(\alpha) = \sum_{i=1}^{s} \sum_{\alpha \in S_\phi \cap T_i} Bel_0(\alpha) = \sum_{i=1}^{s} |S_\phi \cap T_i| Bel(\alpha_i),$$

we see that

$$Bel_0(\phi) = Bel_0(\theta) \Leftrightarrow \langle |S_\phi \cap T_1|, ..., |S_\phi \cap T_s| \rangle \in Y_\theta.$$

Furthermore since $\phi_1 \equiv \phi_2$ just if $S_{\phi_1} = S_{\phi_2}$,

$$\{R \subseteq \{\alpha_1, ..., \alpha_J\} \mid Bel_0(\bigvee R) = Bel_0(\theta)\}$$

$$= \{R \subseteq \{\alpha_1, ..., \alpha_J\} \mid \langle |R \cap T_1|, ..., |R \cap T_s| \rangle \in Y_\theta\}.$$

Also for a particular $\langle n_1, ..., n_s \rangle \in Y_\theta$ and $\alpha \in T_i$, where $1 \le i \le s$, there are

$$\binom{|T_1|}{n_1} ... \binom{|T_s|}{n_s} \frac{n_i}{|T_i|}$$

$R \subseteq \{\alpha_1, ..., \alpha_J\}$ for which $\alpha \in R$ and $\langle |R \cap T_1|, ..., |R \cap T_s| \rangle = \vec{n}$, so for $w \in V^L(K)$ and summing over $R \subseteq \{\alpha_1, ..., \alpha_J\}$ for which $Bel_0(\theta) = Bel_0(\bigvee R)$,

$$\sum_{R} w(\bigvee R) = \sum_{\vec{n} \in Y_\theta} \sum_{i=1}^{s} \sum_{\alpha \in T_i} \binom{|T_1|}{n_1} ... \binom{|T_s|}{n_s} \frac{n_i}{|T_i|} w(\alpha). \qquad (7.7)$$

Now suppose Bel_0 is calibrated with respect to atoms. Then the right hand side of (7.7) equals

$$\sum_{\vec{n} \in Y_\theta} \sum_{i=1}^{s} \binom{|T_1|}{n_1} ... \binom{|T_s|}{n_s} \frac{n_i}{|T_i|} |T_i| Bel_0(\alpha_i)$$

$$= \sum_{\vec{n} \in Y_\theta} \binom{|T_1|}{n_1} ... \binom{|T_s|}{n_s} Bel_0(\theta), \quad \text{by definition of } Y_\theta,$$

$$= Bel_0(\theta) \mid \{R \subseteq \{\alpha_1, ..., \alpha_J\} \mid \langle |R \cap T_1|, ..., |R \cap T_s| \rangle \in Y_\theta\} \mid,$$

as required.

Conversely suppose that Bel_0 is calibrated and $1 \le j \le s$ and we already have established calibration for the atoms α_i for $i < j$. Notice that since $Bel_0(\alpha_k) > Bel_0(\alpha_j)$ for $j < k \le s$, if $\vec{n} \in Y_{\alpha_j}$ then either $n_j = 1$ and each $n_i = 0$ for $i \ne j$, or $n_j = n_{j+1} = ... = n_s = 0$.

Using (7.7) with $\theta = \alpha_j$ we obtain

$$\sum_R w(\bigvee R) = \sum_{\vec{n} \in Y_{\alpha_j}} \sum_{i=1}^s \sum_{\alpha \in T_i} \binom{|T_1|}{n_1} \cdots \binom{|T_s|}{n_s} \frac{n_i}{|T_i|} w(\alpha)$$

$$= \sum_{\substack{\vec{n} \in Y_{\alpha_j} \\ n_j=1}} \{\ \} + \sum_{\substack{\vec{n} \in Y_{\alpha_j} \\ n_j=0}} \{\ \} \tag{7.8}$$

The first of these sums is $\sum_{\alpha \in T_j} w(\alpha)$ whilst, in the second, summation over $i = 1, ..., s$ can be replaced by $i < j$ and hence, since we already have calibration for the α_i with $i < j$, this sum equals

$$\sum_{\substack{\vec{n} \in Y_{\alpha_j} \\ n_j=0}} \sum_{i<j} \binom{|T_1|}{n_1} \cdots \binom{|T_s|}{n_s} n_i Bel_0(\alpha_i)$$

$$= Bel_0(\alpha_j) \sum_{\substack{\vec{n} \in Y_{\alpha_j} \\ n_j=0}} \binom{|T_1|}{n_1} \cdots \binom{|T_s|}{n_s}.$$

On the other hand calibration gives

$$\sum_R w(\bigvee R) = Bel_0(\alpha_j) \sum_{\vec{n} \in Y_{\alpha_j}} \binom{|T_1|}{n_1} \cdots \binom{|T_s|}{n_s}$$

and substituting in (7.8) gives that $\sum_{\alpha \in T_j} w(\alpha)$ equals

$$Bel_0(\alpha_j) \left(\sum_{\vec{n} \in Y_{\alpha_j}} \binom{|T_1|}{n_1} \cdots \binom{|T_s|}{n_s} - \sum_{\substack{\vec{n} \in Y_{\alpha_j} \\ n_j=0}} \binom{|T_1|}{n_1} \cdots \binom{|T_s|}{n_s} \right) = Bel_0(\alpha_j)|T_j|$$

as required. $\square$

Discussion

Suppose $\psi_1, ..., \psi_s$ are exclusive and exhaustive, $K \in CL$, and the constraints

$$Bel(\psi_i) = c_i \qquad i = 1, ..., s$$

are derivable from K, in the sense of theorem 7.1. Define a probability function Bel_0 by

$$Bel_0(\alpha) = \frac{c_i}{|S_{\psi_i}|}$$

where i is such that $\alpha \in S_{\psi_i}$. If Bel_0 satisfies K, then Bel_0 is a calibrated solution of K, by the previous theorem, since it is clearly calibrated with respect to atoms.

Furthermore every calibrated solution arises in this way. For suppose $K \in CL$ has a calibrated solution, Bel_0, say, and let $T_1, ..., T_s$ be as in the above theorem. Then since for $1 \leq i \leq s$ and all $w \in V^L(K)$,

$$w \left(\bigvee T_i \right) = \sum_{\alpha \in T_i} w(\alpha) = |T_i| \, Bel_0(\alpha_i)$$

we see that the constraints

$$Bel \left(\bigvee T_i \right) = |T_i| \, Bel_0(\alpha_i) \qquad i = 1, ..., s$$

are derivable from K, and the $\bigvee T_i$ are exclusive and exhaustive.

We now show that calibration, justified above by appealing to the desirability of accuracy, can also be justified by common sense via the principles of obstinacy and renaming. The following theorem is due to Artingstall and the author, see [53]. Its corollary is stated by Lehner in [44].

Theorem 7.12 *Let $K \in CL$. Then*

(i) *If K has a calibrated solution Bel_0 then $Bel_0 = N(K)$ for any inference process satisfying obstinacy and renaming.*

(ii) *If all inference processes satisfying obstinacy and renaming agree on K then this common value is a calibrated solution of K.*

Corollary 7.13 *If a calibrated solution of $K \in CL$ exists then it is unique.*

Proof of theorem 7.12 (i) Suppose that Bel_0 is a calibrated solution of K and N is a inference process satisfying obstinacy and renaming. Then, by the above discussion, there is a partition $T_1, ..., T_s$ of $\{\alpha_i \mid 1 \leq i \leq J\}$ and $c_1, ..., c_s$ such that

$$Bel(\bigvee T_i) = c_i \qquad i = 1, ..., s$$

are derivable from K, and $Bel_0(\alpha) = \frac{c_i}{|T_i|}$ for $\alpha \in T_i$.

Let K' be the set of constraints

$$\sum_{\alpha \in T_i} Bel(\alpha) = c_i \qquad i = 1, ..., s.$$

Then $K + K'$ is equivalent to K, as K' is derivable from K, so $N(K + K') = N(K)$. Since the atoms can be permuted in each T_i without altering K', renaming gives that $N(K')(\alpha) = N(K')(\alpha')$ whenever α, α' are in the same T_i. Hence $N(K')(\alpha) =$

$\frac{c_i}{|T_i|} = Bel_0(\alpha)$ for each $\alpha \in T_i$ and so $N(K') = Bel_0$. Finally, since Bel_0 satisfies K', by obstinacy,

$$Bel_0 = N(K') = N(K + K') = N(K)$$

as required.

(ii) Let N_m $(m > 0)$ be the inference process which on $K' \in CL$ picks that $\vec{z} \in V^L(K')$ at which the function

$$F(\vec{x}) = \sum_{i \notin I^L(K')} \log(x_i)^{2m+1}$$

is maximal ($z_i = 0$ for $i \in I^L(K')$) where, as usual,

$$I^L(K') = \{j \mid \forall \vec{x} \in V^L(K'), x_j = 0\}.$$

Notice that the maximal point is unique since F is concave. By an earlier observation N_m is obstinate and clearly also satisfies renaming. Furthermore since $\frac{d}{dx} \log(x)^{2m+1} \longrightarrow \infty$ as $x \searrow 0$, a similar proof to that for ME shows N_m to be open-minded.

Now suppose that all the inference processes N_m agree on K, say $N_m(K) = \vec{a} = \langle a_1, a_2, ..., a_J \rangle$, and without loss of generality suppose

$$I^L(K) = \{r+1, r+2, ..., J\},$$

so $a_{r+1} = a_{r+2} = ... = a_J = 0$ and $\vec{a}$ is the maximum point of the function

$$F(\vec{x}) = \sum_{i=1}^{r} \log(x_i)^{2m+1}$$

for $\vec{x} \in V^L(K)$. By open-mindedness $a_1, ..., a_r > 0$. Without loss of generality suppose

$$a_1 < a_2 < ... < a_s$$

are all the distinct a_i for $i = 1, ..., r$ and let

$$Q_i = \{j \mid a_i = a_j\} \text{ for } i = 1, ..., s.$$

Now suppose $\vec{b} \in V^L(K)$. Then for $|\epsilon|$ small enough, $\vec{a} + \epsilon(\vec{b} - \vec{a}) \in V^L(K)$ and

$$F(\vec{a} + \epsilon(\vec{b} - \vec{a})) - F(\vec{a}) = \epsilon(2m+1) \sum_{i=1}^{r} (b_i - a_i) \frac{\log(a_i + \eta\epsilon(b_i - a_i))^{2m}}{a_i + \eta\epsilon(b_i - a_i)}$$

for some $0 < \eta < 1$ by the mean value theorem.

Now if

$$\sum_{i=1}^{r} (b_i - a_i) \frac{\log(a_i)^{2m}}{a_i} \neq 0$$

then by choosing ϵ small enough and of the right sign we could ensure

$$F(\vec{a} + \epsilon(\vec{b} - \vec{a})) - F(\vec{a}) > 0,$$

contradicting the choice of $\vec{a}$. Hence

$$0 = \sum_{i=1}^{r}(b_i - a_i)\frac{\log(a_i)^{2m}}{a_i}$$

$$= \sum_{i=1}^{s}((\sum_{j \in Q_i} b_j) - a_i \mid Q_i \mid)\frac{\log(a_i)^{2m}}{a_i}.$$

Since this holds for all m, dividing by $\log(a_1)^{2m}$ (if $a_1 < 1$) and letting $m \longrightarrow \infty$ shows

$$\sum_{j \in Q_1} b_j = a_1 \mid Q_1 \mid$$

(true even if $a_1 = 1$) and hence, by repeating this trick,

$$\sum_{j \in Q_i} b_j = a_i \mid Q_i \mid \quad for\ i = 1, ..., s.$$

But since $\vec{b} \in V^L(K)$ was arbitrary this says exactly that $\vec{a}$ is a calibrated solution, as required. □

Chapter 8

Belief Revision

Consider again our original example $\mathbb{E}$ where, after reformulating in terms of the expert's belief function, we have obtained a set $\mathbb{K}_0$ of linear constraints on the function Bel. In this context K would normally be referred to as our knowledge base or, as we shall call it, our general knowledge since it refers (in this case) not to beliefs about a particular individual patient but to beliefs about the population of patients as a whole or, equivalently, to beliefs about 'the next patient through the door' who is, as yet, unseen and unknown.

Now suppose this next patient, σ, say, comes through the door and subsequent to the ensuing consultation the medical expert tells us what particular knowledge, K^σ, he has acquired concerning σ. Again, just as in Chapter 1, we shall assume that K^σ can be formulated as a set of linear constraints

$$\sum_{j=1}^{r'} c_{ji} Bel^\sigma(\theta_j) = d_i \quad i = 1, ..., m'$$

where the $c_{ji}, d_i \in \mathbb{R}$, the $\theta_j \in SL$ for the same finite language L as K, Bel^σ is a variable standing for a function from SL to $[0,1]$ and K^σ is satisfied by $Bel_0^\sigma(\theta)$, where $Bel_0^\sigma(\theta)$ is the expert's belief on a scale $[0,1]$ that σ has (or satisfies or exhibits) θ. For example from $\mathbb{E}$, the expert's statement that he is rather confident that σ has either B or F might, with the expert's consent, be formalised as

$$Bel^\sigma(B \vee F) = 0.8.$$

(Constraints involving conditional beliefs $Bel^\sigma(\ | \ )$ do not seem to us very natural in this context so we shall simplify matters by assuming that none appear in K^σ. Alternatively the earlier considerations which eliminated them from K could be used for K^σ to achieve the same end.)

What we would like to know, is how to use the general knowledge K and the special knowledge K^σ to predict the beliefs the expert would give to σ having various conditions, or more generally to ask what relationship could exist between these values and $K + K^\sigma$ for an intelligent agent, although not necessarily human.

In other words our problem is how to assign a value to $Bel^\sigma(\theta)$, for $\theta \in SL$, on the basis of constraints K, K^σ. (Of course when employing our solutions to this problem in a practical expert system we would not expect the expert to be close at hand to provide K^σ – if he was then why bother using the expert system! This problem appears to be avoided in practice by assuming that K^σ, or at least a good approximation to it, can be obtained objectively without the services of the expert, for example by the use of questionnaires. Alternatively one could acknowledge that the experts who gave K and K^σ are not one and the same although that seems to raise further difficulties of knowledge integration which we would prefer not to confront.)

In this chapter we shall consider some suggested solutions to this problem of assigning values to the $Bel^\sigma(\theta)$, usually under some assumptions on the form of K^σ. We shall throughout assume that Bel and Bel^σ are probability functions, that is satisfy (P1–3) . Justifications that, ideally, Bel should be a probability function were given in Chapter 3 and all except the first of these directly carries over to Bel^σ. We shall also make the Watts Assumption as regards both K, the expert's general knowledge, and K^σ, the expert's special knowledge about σ. That is we shall assume that K *is* the expert's general knowledge, so that any general beliefs the expert holds are inferable from K, and similarly that any special beliefs the expert holds about σ are inferable from $K^\sigma + K$. As previously, whilst this is in no sense a necessary assumption for the mathematics, without it (or at least some such assumption) the methods we shall be describing would seem bereft of justification.

The assigning of belief values $Bel^\sigma(\theta)$ on the basis of $K + K^\sigma$ is often referred to as (an example of) belief revision or belief updating for the following reason. Suppose the expert had no knowledge about σ, i.e. $K^\sigma = \emptyset$. Then, in the context of example $\mathbb{E}$, σ would not be distinguishable from 'the next patient through the door' and it would therefore seem, by definition, that Bel_0^σ should be identified with Bel_0 (and in general Bel^σ with Bel). In other words, at this initial level of ignorance concerning σ, Bel_0 itself might justifiably be argued to represent (the expert's) beliefs about θ, etc. However once the expert moves away from this position of ignorance then Bel_0^σ may well have to move away from Bel_0. For example the expert may well assert that symptom D is rather uncommon, say

$$Bel_0(D) = 0.01.$$

So whilst σ was still outside the door she would have $Bel_0^\sigma(D) = 0.01$. However if σ then walks through the door and convinces the expert that she is suffering from symptom D then the expert will revise this to

$$Bel_0^\sigma(D) = 1.0.$$

Notice that there is no sense here in which the earlier beliefs were wrong. (We should point out that the term *belief revision* is used at large in an ostensibly wider context than we are considering here.)

The core of this problem of belief revision lies in the nature of the relationship, if any, between K and K^σ, and in particular between Bel and Bel^σ.

One natural relationship which we might expect of K, K^σ is that if the constraint $Bel(\theta) = 0$ is in K then it should not be the case that $Bel^\sigma(\theta) = a$ is in K^σ for some $a > 0$. That is, it should not be the case that the expert believes it is possible that σ satisfies θ having already asserted the general fact that nothing satisfies θ. Of course this represents an ideal which in reality is sometimes not fulfilled. (Notice however that in such a situation the appearance of σ should cause the honest expert to revise his general knowledge K and raises the interesting question of how this should be carried out.) Nevertheless for this chapter we shall assume that this relationship between K and K^σ does hold, more generally that $K + K^\sigma$ is consistent in the sense of the following definition.

Definition 8.1 $K + K^\sigma$ *is consistent if K and K^σ are separately consistent (i.e. are satisfied by some probability functions Bel, Bel^σ) and whenever $\theta \in SL$ is such that $Bel(\theta) = 0$ for all probability functions Bel satisfying K then $K^\sigma + Bel^\sigma(\theta) = 0$ is consistent.*

This notion of consistency is a natural extension of the relationship mentioned above, namely if K forces $Bel(\theta) = 0$ then $Bel^\sigma(\theta) = 0$ should not be inconsistent with K^σ.

We now look at some popular methods of belief revision or updating.

Bayesian Updating

Apart from $K^\sigma = \emptyset$, possibly the simplest form of K^σ is the single constraint

$$Bel^\sigma(\theta) = 1$$

(or equivalently $Bel^\sigma(\neg\theta) = 0$). As argued in Chapter 1, if in this case K contained the 'rule'

$$Bel(\phi \mid \theta) = a$$

then it would seem that this obliges us to set

$$Bel^\sigma(\phi) = a.$$

This limited method of belief revision is usually referred to as Bayesian updating. In the case where K does not explicitly contain such a rule for ϕ we could argue that we should still set $Bel^\sigma(\phi) = a$ for that a such that $Bel(\phi \mid \theta) = a$ *would* be inferred on the basis of K. In other words, given that we favour using the inference process N, we should, for this K^σ, set

$$Bel^\sigma(\phi) = N(K)(\phi \mid \theta) = \frac{N(K)(\phi \wedge \theta)}{N(K)(\theta)}.$$

We shall refer to this method as Bayesian updating with respect to N. Notice that K^σ is restricted to this special form. (In most texts on belief revision it is assumed that K completely determines Bel. In such cases of course N is irrelevant.)

Proposition 8.2 *Provided $K + (Bel^\sigma(\theta) = 1)$ is consistent and N is open-minded then the Bayesian update with respect to N, $N(K)(\mid \theta)$, is a well defined probability function satisfying $Bel^\sigma(\theta) = 1$.*

Proof For $N(K)(\mid \theta)$ to be well defined it is enough that $N(K)(\theta) \neq 0$. But by the consistency of $K + (Bel^\sigma(\theta) = 1)$, $K + (Bel(\theta) \neq 0)$ must be consistent so $N(K)(\theta) \neq 0$ by open-mindedness. Since $N(K)$ is a probability function, by proposition 2.2 it follows that $N(K)(\mid \theta)$ is a probability function. Finally, $N(K)(\theta \mid \theta) = 1$ is immediate. $\square$

Although we have introduced Bayesian updating for K^σ a single certainty, notice that it can also be applied in the case of

$$K^\sigma = \{Bel^\sigma(\theta_i) = 1 \mid i = 1, ..., m\}$$

when replacing this K^σ by the equivalent single constraint

$$Bel^\sigma(\theta_1 \wedge \ldots \wedge \theta_m) = 1.$$

If we are willing to introduce 'imaginary causes' then Bayesian updating can, in fact, be thought of as the 'most versatile' form of updating, in the sense of the following result due to Diaconis and Zabell [12].

Theorem 8.3 *Suppose Bel_1, Bel_2 are probability functions on SL and are consistent in the above sense (i.e for $\theta \in SL$, if $Bel_1(\theta) = 0$ then $Bel_2(\theta) = 0$). Then there are extensions Bel_1^+, Bel_2^+ of Bel_1, Bel_2 to SL', where L' is L with an additional propositional variable q, such that for $\theta \in SL'$, $Bel_2^+(\theta) = Bel_1^+(\theta \mid q)$.*

Proof Let β be the minimum of the set

$$\left\{ \frac{Bel_1(\alpha)}{Bel_2(\alpha)} \,\middle|\, \alpha \in At^L, \ Bel_2(\alpha) \neq 0 \right\}.$$

By the consistency assumption, $\beta > 0$. Now for $\alpha \in At^L$, define Bel_1^+ on the atoms of $\alpha \wedge q$, $\alpha \wedge \neg q$ of L' by

$$Bel_1^+(\alpha \wedge q) = \beta Bel_2(\alpha)$$

$$Bel_1^+(\alpha \wedge \neg q) = Bel_1(\alpha) - \beta Bel_2(\alpha).$$

By choice of β this latter value is non-negative and

$$Bel_1^+(\alpha) = Bel_1^+(\alpha \wedge q) + Bel_1^+(\alpha \wedge \neg q) = Bel_1(\alpha) \quad \text{for } \alpha \in At^L,$$

$$\sum_{\gamma \in At^{L'}} Bel_1^+(\gamma) = \sum_{\alpha \in At^L} Bel_1^+(\alpha) = 1,$$

so Bel_1^+ extends to a probability function on SL' extending Bel_1. Finally $Bel_1^+(q) = \sum_{\alpha \in At^L} \beta Bel_2(\alpha) = \beta > 0$, and for $\alpha \in At^L$,

$$Bel_1^+(\alpha \mid q) = \frac{Bel_1^+(\alpha \wedge q)}{Bel_1^+(q)} = \frac{\beta Bel_2(\alpha)}{\beta} = Bel_2(\alpha),$$

so putting $Bel_2^+(\theta) = Bel_1^+(\theta \mid q)$ for $\theta \in SL'$ gives the result.   □

Interesting as this result is as a device for deriving a particular answer, it sheds no new light on the question of justification, which we now return to.

Jeffrey's Updating

Despite the minor generalisation referred to above, Bayesian updating is still limited to K^σ being a set of certainties, and in many situations K^σ does not have this form. For instance in our example $\mathbb{E}$ patient σ may claim to have symptom D but the expert may well be less than certain that σ actually has the symptom.

In order to generalise Bayesian updating to the case

$$K^\sigma = \{Bel^\sigma(\theta_i) = \beta_i \mid i = 1, ..., m\}$$

where the β_i are non-zero, $\sum \beta_i = 1$ and the θ_i are exclusive (i.e. $\models \neg(\theta_i \wedge \theta_j)$ for $1 \le i < j \le m$), Jeffrey's rule (see [34]) advocates setting

$$Bel^\sigma(\phi) = \sum_{i=1}^m \beta_i Bel(\phi \mid \theta_i)$$

in the case where the $Bel(\phi \mid \theta_i)$ are determined by K. Notice that this extends Bayesian updating and Bel^σ is indeed a solution of K^σ.

Generalising as above, for such a K^σ and K we shall define Jeffrey's update with respect to an inference process N by

$$\sum_{i=1}^m \beta_i N(K)(\mid \theta_i).$$

As in proposition 8.2 we can easily show that if $K + K^\sigma$ is consistent and N open-minded then this update is a well defined probability function satisfying K^σ.

Whilst this might appear at first sight a rather ad hoc method the following theorem (due to van Fraassen [21]) provides a strong justification for it.

Theorem 8.4 *Suppose that we have a function F such that whenever L is a (finite) language for the propositional calculus and Bel is a probability function on SL and $K^\sigma = \{Bel^\sigma(\theta_i) = \beta_i \mid i = 1, ..., m\}$ is as above, with $Bel(\theta_i) \neq 0$ for $i = 1, ..., m$, then on argument Bel, K^σ, the function F picks a solution Bel^σ to K^σ in such a way that for $\phi \in SL$, $Bel^\sigma(\phi)$ depends only on the values of the $Bel^\sigma(\theta_i)$ given by K^σ,* on the values $Bel(\theta_i)$, $i = 1, ..., m$ and, continuously, on the values $Bel(\phi \wedge \theta_i)$, $i = 1, ..., m$ and is independent of the overlying language L. Then F must be Jeffrey's rule, i.e.

$$Bel^{\sigma}(\phi) = \sum_{i=1}^{m} \beta_i Bel(\phi \mid \theta_i).$$

Remark This result relates to the previous discussions by setting

$$Bel = N(K)$$

for a fixed open-minded language invariant inference process N. It says then that if the value assigned to $Bel^{\sigma}(\phi)$ depends only on the values β_i given by K^{σ} to $Bel^{\sigma}(\theta_i)$ and the values $Bel(\theta_i)$ and, continuously, on the values $Bel(\phi \wedge \theta_i)$, $i = 1, ..., m$ which would have been inferred from K using N (and does not depend on the particular overlying language L) then the value assigned to $Bel^{\sigma}(\phi)$ must be

$$\sum_{i=1}^{m} \beta_i Bel(\phi \mid \theta_i) = \sum_{i=1}^{m} \beta_i N(K)(\phi \mid \theta_i),$$

i.e. exactly that given by Jeffrey's updating. The argument for the limited dependence of $Bel^{\sigma}(\phi)$ seems to be along the lines that there is not obviously anything else on which it should depend. Similar remarks could be applied to the requirement of independence of the overlying language, a requirement which, as we shall see, is crucial for the proof. Finally continuity could be argued for on grounds of robustness although, as is usual in such proofs, it is required simply in order to replace 'rational' by 'real'.

Proof of theorem 8.4

Since the β_i, $Bel(\theta_i)$ will remain fixed throughout this proof we may simplify the notation by writing

$$Bel^{\sigma}(\phi) = F(Bel(\phi \wedge \theta_1), Bel(\phi \wedge \theta_2), ..., Bel(\phi \wedge \theta_m)).$$

By assumption F is continuous in these arguments.

Let ξ_i be the atoms of SL' where $L' \cap L = \emptyset$ and $\mid L' \mid = r$. Extend Bel from SL to $S(L \cup L')$ by

$$Bel(\xi_i \wedge \alpha_j) = 2^{-r} Bel(\alpha_j).$$

Notice that the $\xi_i \wedge \alpha_j$ are the atoms of $S(L \cup L')$ and this does indeed define an extension to a probability function on $S(L \cup L')$.

Then

$$Bel^{\sigma}(\theta_1) = \sum_{j} Bel^{\sigma}(\theta_1 \wedge \xi_j) = \sum_{j} F(Bel(\theta_1 \wedge \xi_j), 0, ..., 0)$$

and $Bel(\theta_1 \wedge \xi_j) = Bel(\xi_j \wedge \bigvee_{\alpha_i \in S_{\theta_1}} \alpha_i) = \sum_{\alpha_i \in S_{\theta_1}} Bel(\xi_j \wedge \alpha_i) = 2^{-r} \cdot Bel(\theta_1)$.
Hence all terms in this first sum are the same and equal to $Bel^\sigma(\theta_1) \cdot 2^{-r}$. Therefore
for $0 \leq s \leq 2^r$,

$$
F(\frac{s}{2^r} Bel(\theta_1), 0, ..., 0) \;=\; F(Bel(\theta_1 \wedge \bigvee_{j=1}^{s} \xi_j), 0, ..., 0)
$$

$$
=\; Bel^\sigma(\theta_1 \wedge \bigvee_{j=1}^{s} \xi_j) = \sum_{j=1}^{s} Bel^\sigma(\theta_1 \wedge \xi_j) = \frac{s}{2^r} Bel^\sigma(\theta_1)
$$

$$
=\; \frac{s}{2^r} \cdot F(Bel(\theta_1), 0, ..., 0).
$$

Therefore by continuity, for $0 \leq \gamma \leq 1$,

$$
F(\gamma Bel(\theta_1), 0, ..., 0) \;=\; \gamma F(Bel(\theta_1), 0, ..., 0)
$$

$$
=\; \gamma Bel^\sigma(\theta_1) = \beta_1 \gamma,
$$

and similarly for $\theta_2, \theta_3, ..., \theta_m$.   Hence, since $\theta_1, ..., \theta_m, \neg(\bigvee_{i=1}^{m} \theta_i)$ are exclusive
and exhaustive (their disjunction is a tautology) and $Bel^\sigma(\neg(\bigvee_{i=1}^{m} \theta_i)) = 1 - \sum_{i=1}^{m} Bel^\sigma(\theta_i) = 0$,

$$
Bel^\sigma(\phi) = \sum_{j=0}^{m} Bel^\sigma(\theta_j \wedge \phi) \;=\; \sum_{j=1}^{m} F(0, ..., 0, Bel(\theta_j \wedge \phi), 0, ..., 0)
$$

$$
=\; \sum_{j=1}^{m} F(0, ..., 0, Bel(\phi \mid \theta_j) Bel(\theta_j), 0, ..., 0)
$$

$$
=\; \sum_{j=1}^{m} \beta_j Bel(\phi \mid \theta_j),
$$

as required.   □
    Unfortunately Jeffrey's updating is not applicable in the, usual, case where the
θ_i are not exclusive. So we finally present a method of updating which extends
Jeffrey's updating and can handle general K^σ.

Minimum Cross Entropy Updating

Given consistent $K + K^\sigma$ and an inference process N we define the *minimum cross
entropy update of* $K + K^\sigma$ *with respect to* N by choosing

$$
\langle Bel^\sigma(\alpha_1), ..., Bel^\sigma(\alpha_J) \rangle
$$

to be that $\vec{x} \in V^L(K^\sigma)$ at which the function

$$I(\vec{x}, N(K)) = \sum_{i=1}^{J} x_i \log \left(\frac{x_i}{N(K)(\alpha_i)} \right) = \sum_{i=1}^{J} (x_i \log(x_i) - x_i \log(N(K)(\alpha_i)))$$

is minimal.

Provided N is open-minded and we agree to take $0 \log(0) = 0$ (which we do throughout) then $I(\vec{x}, N(K))$ (which is variously referred to as the cross entropy or relative Shannon information or Kullback–Leibler divergence from the point $N(K) \in V^L(K)$) is well defined, continuous and (strictly) convex on $V^L(K^\sigma)$, and hence has a unique minimum on there. Indeed as the following proposition shows we can think of this function as a measure of the difference between $\vec{x} \in V^L(K^\sigma)$ and the (chosen) point $N(K) \in V^L(K)$.

Proposition 8.5 *Let* $\vec{\rho^0}, \vec{\rho} \in \mathbb{D}^J$ *be such that if* $\rho_i^0 = 0$ *then* $\rho_i = 0$ *for* $i = 1, \ldots, J$. *Then* $I(\vec{\rho}, \vec{\rho^0}) \geq 0$ *with equality just if* $\vec{\rho} = \vec{\rho^0}$.

Proof By elementary calculus for $x \geq 0$,

$$x \log(x) - x + 1 \geq 0$$

with equality iff $x = 1$. Hence

$$I(\vec{\rho}, \vec{\rho^0}) = \sum \rho_i^0 [\frac{\rho_i}{\rho_i^0} \log(\frac{\rho_i}{\rho_i^0}) - \frac{\rho_i}{\rho_i^0} + 1] \geq 0$$

(even if some $\rho_i^0 = 0$) with equality just if $\frac{\rho_i}{\rho_i^0} = 1$ for all i. $\square$

Notice an immediate consequence of this result is that if $N(K) \in V^L(K^\sigma)$ then $N(K)$ itself is the minimum cross entropy update of $K + K^\sigma$ with respect to N. In particular this occurs if $K^\sigma = \emptyset$ or $K = K^\sigma$ (with Bel in place of Bel^σ of course).

As a more interesting example consider the case where the general knowledge consists of

$$Bel(p) = a, \quad Bel(q \mid p) = b, \quad Bel(q) = c,$$

where $L = \{p, q\}$ and $0 < ab < c < 1 - a + ab$ (thus ensuring consistency), and we learn that the expert's belief in σ exhibiting p is d, i.e. $Bel^\sigma(p) = d$. Then minimum cross entropy updating with respect to ME gives $Bel^\sigma(q) = c + \frac{(b-c)(d-a)}{1-a}$ which is seen to tend to bd as a and c tend to zero.

The following result, due to Williams [70], shows that, with respect to a given open-minded inference process N, minimum cross entropy updating extends Jeffrey's updating, and hence Bayesian updating.

Theorem 8.6 *Suppose that $K + K^\sigma$ is consistent, $K^\sigma = \{Bel^\sigma(\theta_i) = \beta_i \mid i = 1, ..., m\}$ where the θ_i are exclusive, the $\beta_i > 0$, $\sum_{i=1}^m \beta_i = 1$, and N is an open-minded inference process. Then the minimum cross entropy update of $K + K^\sigma$ with respect to N is*

$$\sum_{i=1}^m \beta_i N(K)(\mid \theta_i),$$

i.e it agrees with Jeffrey's updating.

Proof Let $Bel^\sigma \in V^L(K^\sigma)$. Then

$$I(Bel^\sigma, N(K)) \quad = \quad \sum_{i=1}^J Bel^\sigma(\alpha_i) \log\left(\frac{Bel^\sigma(\alpha_i)}{N(K)(\alpha_i)} \right)$$

$$= \quad \sum_{j=1}^m \sum_{\alpha_i \in S_{\theta_j}} Bel^\sigma(\alpha_i) \log\left(\frac{Bel^\sigma(\alpha_i)}{N(K)(\alpha_i)} \right)$$

since $Bel^\sigma(\alpha_i) = 0$ for $\alpha_i \notin \bigcup_{j=1}^m S_{\theta_j}$. This further equals

$$\sum_{j=1}^m \beta_j \left(\sum_{\alpha_i \in S_{\theta_j}} \frac{Bel^\sigma(\alpha_i)}{\beta_j} \left(\log\left(\frac{Bel^\sigma(\alpha_i)}{\beta_j} \right) - \log\left(\frac{N(K)(\alpha_i)}{N(K)(\theta_j)} \right) \right) \right.$$

$$+ \log(\beta_j) - \log(N(K)(\theta_j)))$$

$$= \sum_{j=1}^m \beta_j I(Bel^\sigma(\mid \theta_j), N(K)(\mid \theta_j)) + \text{a term independent of } Bel^\sigma.$$

Since $Bel^\sigma = \sum_{j=1}^m \beta_j N(K)(\mid \theta_j)$ satisfies both K^σ and $Bel^\sigma(\mid \theta_j) = N(K)(\mid \theta_j)$ for $j = 1, ..., m$, it follows from proposition 8.5 that this is the $\vec{x} \in V^L(K^\sigma)$ minimising $I(\vec{x}, N(K))$, as required. □

Justifications for Minimum Cross Entropy Updating

Minimum cross entropy updating is closely related to the maximum entropy inference process, since for $\vec{x} \in \mathbb{D}^J$,

$$I\left(\vec{x}, \left\langle \frac{1}{J}, ..., \frac{1}{J} \right\rangle\right) = \sum_{i=1}^J x_i \log(x_i) + \log(J),$$

so that minimising the cross entropy between $\vec{x}$ and $\left\langle \frac{1}{J}, ..., \frac{1}{J} \right\rangle$ is equivalent to maximising $-\sum x_i \log(x_i)$, the entropy of $\vec{x}$. Hence if $N(K) = \left\langle \frac{1}{J}, ..., \frac{1}{J} \right\rangle$ then the minimum cross entropy update of $K + K^\sigma$ with respect to N is $ME(K^\sigma)$.

Furthermore, Hobson [30] has provided a similar argument to that used in the case of the maximum entropy inference process for justifying

$$\sum_{i=1}^{J} x_i \log(x_i)$$

being the information content of $\vec{x} \in \mathbb{D}^J$ to justify

$$\sum_{i=1}^{J} x_i \log\left(\frac{x_i}{\rho_i}\right)$$

being the additional information content in $\vec{x} \in \mathbb{D}^J$ above that in $\vec{\rho} \in \mathbb{D}^J$. Precisely, let $\bar{I}(x_1, ..., x_n; \rho_1, ..., \rho_n)$ be the 'additional information' content of $\vec{x}$ above that in $\vec{\rho}$ where $\vec{x}, \vec{\rho} \in \mathbb{D}^n$ and $\rho_i \neq 0$ if $x_i \neq 0$. Here we are thinking of $\vec{\rho}$ as representing prior beliefs and $\vec{x}$ a (possible) revised belief in the light of revised constraints. Following the justification given earlier for negative entropy being the unique (up to a positive scalar multiple) measure of information which satisfies some natural requirements we might similarly propose the following natural requirements on $\bar{I}$:

(a) For each n, $\bar{I}(x_1, ..., x_n; x_1^0, ..., x_n^0)$ is continuous (provided $x_i^0 \neq 0$ if $x_i \neq 0$).

(b) For $0 < n \leq n_0$, $\bar{I}(\frac{1}{n}, ..., \frac{1}{n}, 0, ..., 0; \frac{1}{n_0}, ..., \frac{1}{n_0})$ is strictly decreasing in n and increasing in n_0 and is 0 if $n = n_0$.

(c) If $\vec{y}_i, \vec{y}_i^0 \in \mathbb{D}^{m_i}$ for $i = 1, ..., n$, $\vec{x}, \vec{x}^0 \in \mathbb{D}^n$ and $x_i^0 \neq 0$ if $x_i \neq 0$ and $y_{i_j}^0 \neq 0$ if $y_{i_j} \neq 0$, then

$$\bar{I}(x_1 \vec{y}_1, ..., x_n \vec{y}_n; x_1^0 \vec{y}_1^0, ..., x_n^0 \vec{y}_n^0) = \bar{I}(\vec{x}; \vec{x}^0) + \sum_{i=1}^{n} x_i \bar{I}(\vec{y}_i; \vec{y}_i^0).$$

(d) For $\vec{x}, \vec{x}^0 \in \mathbb{D}^n$, with $x_i^0 \neq 0$ if $x_i \neq 0$, and σ a permutation of $\{1, ..., n\}$,

$$\bar{I}(\vec{x}; \vec{x}^0) = \bar{I}(x_{\sigma(1)}, ..., x_{\sigma(n)}; x_{\sigma(1)}^0, ..., x_{\sigma(n)}^0).$$

Of these, (c) is perhaps the most questionable. Its 'justification' is along the same lines as that for the analogous condition for (negative) entropy. Anyhow, conditions (a)–(d) force $\bar{I}(\vec{x}; \vec{\rho})$ to be $c \sum x_i \log\left(\frac{x_i}{\rho_i}\right)$ for some constant c.

The proof of this runs along similar lines to the analogous result for entropy. Namely let

$$A(n, n_0) = \bar{I}(\frac{1}{n}, ..., \frac{1}{n}, 0, ..., 0; \frac{1}{n_0}, ..., \frac{1}{n_0}).$$

Then by using (c) and (d), for $0 < n \leq n_0$, $0 < s \leq s_0$,

$$A(sn, s_0 n_0) = A(s, s_0) + \sum_{i=1}^{s} \frac{1}{s} A(n, n_0) = A(s, s_0) + A(n, n_0).$$

As in the corresponding argument for entropy we can now show that $A(1, n_0) = -c \log(n_0)$ for some constant $c > 0$. For $0 < n < n_0$ and k large let p be such that $2^p \leq \left(\frac{n_0}{n}\right)^k < 2^{p+1}$. Then by (b),

$$A(n^k, 2^p n^k) \leq A(n^k, n_0^k) \leq A(n^k, 2^{p+1} n^k)$$

and by (a) and the above identities,

$$A(n^k, n_0^k) = kA(n, n_0),$$

$$A(n^k, 2^p n^k) = A(1, 2^p) + A(n^k, n^k) = A(1, 2^p) = -pc \log(2)$$

etc. Again by a similar argument to that for entropy these yield

$$A(n, n_0) = -c \log\left(\frac{n}{n_0}\right) \quad \text{for some } c > 0.$$

Now using (c),(d) we obtain for $\sum_{i=1}^{n} r_i = r$, $\sum_{i=1}^{n} r_i^0 = r^0$, and $r_i \leq r_i^0$ for $i = 1, ..., n,$

$$
\begin{aligned}
A(r, r^0) &= \bar{I}\left(\frac{r_1}{r}\left(\frac{1}{r_1}, ..., \frac{1}{r_1}, 0, ..., 0\right), ...; \frac{r_1^0}{r^0}\left(\frac{1}{r_1^0}, ..., \frac{1}{r_1^0}\right), ...\right) \\
&= \bar{I}\left(\frac{r_1}{r}, ..., \frac{r_n}{r}; \frac{r_1^0}{r^0}, ..., \frac{r_n^0}{r^0}\right) + \sum_{i=1}^{n} \frac{r_i}{r} A(r_i, r_i^0).
\end{aligned}
$$

Hence

$$\bar{I}\left(\frac{r_1}{r}, ..., \frac{r_n}{r}; \frac{r_1^0}{r^0}, ..., \frac{r_n^0}{r^0}\right) = -c \log\left(\frac{r}{r^0}\right) + c\sum_{i=1}^{n} \frac{r_i}{r} \log\left(\frac{r_i}{r_i^0}\right) = c\sum_{i=1}^{n} \frac{r_i}{r} \log\left(\frac{r_i}{r_i^0} \cdot \frac{r_0}{r}\right),$$

and the result follows by continuity.

In view of these similar justifications one might feel that it would be perverse, if one was committed to minimum cross entropy updating but used it with respect to an inference process N other than maximum entropy.

We now give a second justification for minimum cross entropy (with respect to ME) which builds on the several justifications for ME already given. In order to introduce this justification consider again our example $\mathbb{E}$ supplemented with knowledge K^σ about patient σ.

On the face of it it appears that Bel_0 and Bel_0^σ refer to different 'sorts' of belief. For it seems reasonable to suppose that Bel_0 is, to a large extent, based on past data, estimates of frequencies of previously seen patients, whilst Bel_0^σ is closer to the idea of betting on a future event and is not obviously any sort of frequency. In order therefore to understand, or at least shed light on, possible modes of belief revision in this context it would seem desirable to consider (various) explanations, or models of the semantic relationship between these two functions Bel_0, Bel_0^σ, that is the relationship between their meanings.

One such explanation is that $Bel_0^\sigma(\theta)$, i.e. 'belief that σ has θ', stands for 'belief that the next patient through the door will have θ, given that she is similar to σ'.

That is we identify $Bel_0^\sigma(\theta)$ with $Bel_0(\theta \mid S)$ where S is the new property of being similar to σ. Then $K + K^\sigma$ would become simply a set of linear constraints on Bel and the problem of belief revision here would be reduced to the problem of selecting Bel to satisfy $K + K^\sigma(S)$, where $K^\sigma(S)$ is K^σ with $Bel^\sigma(\theta)$ replaced throughout by $Bel(\theta \mid S)$ (and multiplying out by $Bel(S)$), or equivalently, to the problem of what inference process N to adopt for generating general knowledge.

Unfortunately $K + K^\sigma(S)$ now omits one important additional belief about σ, namely that 'being similar to σ' is very unlikely. Indeed belief in it should be essentially 'infinitesimal' provided one looks hard enough. This omission can produce somewhat paradoxical results in small examples although in large, real world examples it would have a negligible effect. To correct it we add $Bel(S) = \epsilon$ to $K + K^\sigma(S)$ and define the PV-update of $K + K^\sigma$ with respect to an inference process N by

$$Bel^\sigma(\theta) = \lim_{\epsilon \searrow 0} N(K + K^\sigma(S) + (Bel(S) = \epsilon))(\theta \mid S).$$

For this definition to make sense we need to know that $K + K^\sigma(S) + (Bel(S) = \epsilon)$ is consistent, at least for ϵ small, and then that this limit exists. We shall show in the next theorem that consistency for ϵ small follows from the consistency of $K + K^\sigma$ and that for $N = ME$ this limit always exists and, furthermore, in this case PV-updating agrees with minimum cross entropy updating (with respect to ME). Thus if we accept the earlier arguments for the choice of the maximum entropy inference process and we further accept the reasonableness of identifying $Bel_0^\sigma(\theta)$ with $Bel_0(\theta \mid S)$ then this provides a justification for minimum cross entropy with respect to ME.

Theorem 8.7 *Suppose that $K + K^\sigma$ is consistent. Then*

(i) $K + K^\sigma(S) + (Bel(S) = \epsilon)$ *is consistent for ϵ small, $\epsilon > 0$.*

(ii) *For $\theta \in SL$,* $\lim_{\epsilon \searrow 0} ME(K + K^\sigma(S) + (Bel(S) = \epsilon))(\theta \mid S)$ *exists and equals $Bel^\sigma(\theta)$ for Bel^σ the minimum cross entropy update of $K + K^\sigma$ with respect to ME.*

Proof (i) As usual let $I^L(K) = \{i \mid \forall \vec{x} \in V^L(K), x_i = 0\}$ and for each $i \notin I^L(K)$ pick $\vec{x}^i \in V^L(K)$ such that $x_i^i > 0$. Then for all probability functions Bel satisfying K, $Bel(\bigvee_{i \in I^L(K)} \alpha_i) = 0$ so by the consistency of $K + K^\sigma$ we can pick Bel^σ satisfying K^σ such that $Bel^\sigma(\bigvee_{i \in I^L(K)} \alpha_i) = 0$. Let

$$\vec{u} = (J - \mid I^L(K) \mid)^{-1} \sum_{i \notin I^L(K)} \vec{x}^i \in V^L(K),$$

$$\epsilon_0 = \min\{u_j \mid u_j > 0\}.$$

Then it is easy to see that for $0 < \epsilon \leq \epsilon_0$, $L' = L \cup \{S\}$ the probability function $Bel' : SL' \longrightarrow [0,1]$ satisfies $K + K^\sigma(S) + (Bel(S) = \epsilon)$, where

$$Bel'(\alpha_j \wedge S) \quad = \quad \epsilon Bel^\sigma(\alpha_j),$$

$$Bel'(\alpha_j \wedge \neg S) \quad = \quad u_j - \epsilon Bel^\sigma(\alpha_j), \quad j = 1, ..., J.$$

(ii) Recall that

$$V^L(K) \quad = \quad \{\langle x_1, ..., x_J \rangle \mid \vec{x} A_K = \vec{b}_K, \; x_i \geq 0\}$$

$$V^L(K^\sigma) \quad = \quad \{\langle y_1, ..., y_J \rangle \mid \vec{y} A_{K^\sigma} = \vec{b}_{K^\sigma}, \; y_i \geq 0\}.$$

Then $V^{L'}(K + K^\sigma(S) + (Bel(S) = \epsilon)$ is the set of $\langle x_1, ..., x_J, \; y_1, ..., y_J \rangle$ for which

$$\left. \begin{array}{rcl} (\vec{x} + \vec{y}) A_K & = & \vec{b}_K, \\[2mm] \vec{y} A_{K^\sigma} & = & \epsilon \vec{b}_{K^\sigma}, \\[2mm] x_i, y_i & \geq & 0, \end{array} \right\} \qquad (*)$$

where the x_i correspond to the atoms $\alpha_i \wedge \neg S$ and the y_i to the atoms $\alpha_i \wedge S$.

Let $\vec{\gamma} = ME^L(K)$, let the 2J-vector $\vec{v}(\epsilon), \vec{\delta}(\epsilon) = ME^{L'}(K + K^\sigma(S) + (Bel(S) = \epsilon))$ and let $\vec{\gamma}(\epsilon) = \vec{v}(\epsilon) + \vec{\delta}(\epsilon)$. Clearly since $\sum \delta_i(\epsilon) = \epsilon$, $\lim_{\epsilon \to 0} \vec{\delta}(\epsilon) = \vec{0}$. Also $\lim_{\epsilon \to 0} \vec{\gamma}(\epsilon) = \vec{\gamma}$. To see this, first notice that since ME is open-minded, if $\gamma_j = 0$ then $j \in I^L(K)$ so $\gamma_j(\epsilon) = 0$, since $\vec{\gamma}(\epsilon) \in V^L(K)$, and hence $\delta_j(\epsilon) = 0$. Thus for ϵ sufficiently small

$$\vec{\gamma} - \vec{\delta}(\epsilon), \; \vec{\delta}(\epsilon) \in V^{L'}(K + K^\sigma(S) + (Bel(S) = \epsilon))$$

so

$$E(\vec{\gamma} - \vec{\delta}(\epsilon)) + E(\vec{\delta}(\epsilon)) \leq E(\vec{v}(\epsilon)) + E(\vec{\delta}(\epsilon))$$

where $E(\vec{x}) = -\sum_{i=1}^{J} x_i \log(x_i)$ for $x_i \geq 0$. Hence, since $\vec{\gamma}(\epsilon) \in V^L(K)$,

$$0 \; \leq \; E(\vec{\gamma}) - E(\vec{\gamma}(\epsilon))$$

$$= \; [E(\vec{\gamma}) - E(\vec{\gamma} - \vec{\delta}(\epsilon))] + [E(\vec{\gamma} - \vec{\delta}(\epsilon)) - E(\vec{v}(\epsilon))]$$

$$+ [E(\vec{v}(\epsilon)) - E(\vec{\gamma}(\epsilon))]$$

$$\leq \; [E(\vec{\gamma}) - E(\vec{\gamma} - \vec{\delta}(\epsilon))] + [E(\vec{v}(\epsilon)) - E(\vec{\gamma}(\epsilon))].$$

Hence by uniform continuity of E,

$$\lim_{\epsilon \to 0} E(\vec{\gamma}(\epsilon)) = E(\vec{\gamma}).$$

Furthermore since any cluster point (as $\epsilon \to 0$) of the $\vec{\gamma}(\epsilon)$ must be in the closed set $V(K)$, the concavity of E forces $\lim_{\epsilon \to 0} \vec{\gamma}(\epsilon) = \vec{\gamma}$ as required. Now consider adding the equation

$$\vec{x} + \vec{y} = \vec{\gamma}(\epsilon)$$

to $(*)$. Since this equation is satisfied by $\vec{v}(\epsilon), \vec{\delta}(\epsilon)$ the new system of equations, which is equivalent to

$$\vec{x} = \vec{\gamma}(\epsilon) - \vec{y},$$
$$\vec{y} A_{K^\sigma} = \epsilon \vec{b}_{K^\sigma},$$
$$x_i, y_i \geq 0,$$

has the same maximum entropy solution, viz. $\vec{x} = \vec{v}(\epsilon)$, $\vec{y} = \vec{\delta}(\epsilon)$. Thus $\vec{y} = \vec{\delta}(\epsilon)$ is the solution of

$$\vec{y} A_{K^\sigma} = \epsilon \vec{b}_{K^\sigma}, \quad 0 \leq y_i \leq \gamma_i(\epsilon)$$

which maximises

$$-\sum_{i=1}^{J} (y_i \log(y_i) + (\gamma_i(\epsilon) - y_i) \log(\gamma_i(\epsilon) - y_i)).$$

As remarked above if some $\gamma_i = 0$ then it must be the case that $\gamma_i(\epsilon) = 0$. Thus in the above expression we may drop any summands for which $\gamma_i = 0$. Assuming, for notational convenience, that there are none we may assume $\epsilon < \gamma_k(\epsilon)$ for $1 \leq k \leq J$ and hence the condition $y_i \leq \gamma_i(\epsilon)$ in the above can be dropped since $\vec{y} A_{K^\sigma} = \epsilon \vec{b}_{K^\sigma}$ contains the equation $\sum y_i = \epsilon$.

Now put $\vec{z} = \frac{\vec{y}}{\epsilon}$ so that $\frac{\vec{\delta}(\epsilon)}{\epsilon}$ is the solution of

$$\vec{z} A_{K^\sigma} = \vec{b}_{K^\sigma}, \quad z_i \geq 0,$$

which maximises

$$H(\epsilon, \vec{\gamma}(\epsilon), \vec{z}) = -\sum_{i=1}^{J} (\epsilon z_i \log(\epsilon z_i) + (\gamma_i(\epsilon) - \epsilon z_i) \log(\gamma_i(\epsilon) - \epsilon z_i)).$$

Applying Taylor's theorem to the second terms and using the (given) identities $\sum z_i = \sum \gamma_i(\epsilon) = 1$ we obtain

$$
\begin{aligned}
H(\epsilon, \vec{\gamma}(\epsilon), \vec{z}) = \quad &- \quad \epsilon \log(\epsilon) - \sum \gamma_i(\epsilon) \log(\gamma_i(\epsilon)) + \epsilon \\
&- \quad \epsilon [\sum z_i \log(z_i) - z_i \log \gamma_i(\epsilon)] \\
&- \quad \frac{\epsilon^2}{2} \sum \frac{z_i^2}{\gamma_i(\epsilon) - \eta \epsilon z_i}
\end{aligned}
$$

for some $0 < \eta < 1$. Now let $\vec{\tau}$ be the solution of

$$\vec{z} A_{K^\sigma} = \vec{b}_{K^\sigma}, \quad z_i \geq 0,$$

which minimises

$$I(\vec{z}, \vec{\gamma}) = \sum_{i=1}^J z_i \log \left(\frac{z_i}{\gamma_i} \right).$$

That is, $\vec{\tau}$ is the minimum cross entropy update of $K + K^\sigma$ with respect to ME. To prove the result it is enough to show that

$$\lim_{\epsilon \to 0} \frac{\vec{\delta}(\epsilon)}{\epsilon} = \vec{\tau} \tag{8.1}$$

since then for $\theta \in SL$,

$$\lim_{\epsilon \searrow 0} ME(K + K^\sigma(S) + (Bel(S) = \epsilon))(\theta \mid S)$$

$$= \lim_{\epsilon \searrow 0} \frac{1}{\epsilon} \sum_{\alpha_j \in S_\theta} ME(K + K^\sigma(S) + (Bel(S) = \epsilon))(\alpha_j \wedge S)$$

$$= \lim_{\epsilon \searrow 0} \frac{1}{\epsilon} \sum_{\alpha_j \in S_\theta} \delta_j(\epsilon) = \sum_{\alpha_j \in S_\theta} \tau_j$$

and this last value is precisely the value given to θ by the probability function $\vec{\tau}$.

So it only remains to show (8.1). But by maximality of $\frac{\vec{\delta}(\epsilon)}{\epsilon}$,

$$0 \leq H(\epsilon, \vec{\gamma}(\epsilon), \tfrac{\vec{\delta}(\epsilon)}{\epsilon}) - H(\epsilon, \vec{\gamma}(\epsilon), \vec{\tau})$$

$$\leq -\epsilon[I(\tfrac{\vec{\delta}(\epsilon)}{\epsilon}, \vec{\gamma}(\epsilon)) - I(\vec{\tau}, \vec{\gamma}(\epsilon))] + d\epsilon^2$$

for some constant d since we have dropped those coordinates i for which $\gamma_i = 0$.

Now if the $\frac{\vec{\delta}(\epsilon)}{\epsilon}$ had a cluster point $\vec{\lambda} \neq \vec{\tau}$ as $\epsilon \to 0$ then by choice of $\vec{\tau}$, $I(\vec{\lambda}, \vec{\gamma}) - I(\vec{\tau}, \vec{\gamma}) > c > 0$ for some constant c so for arbitrarily small ϵ,

$$-\epsilon[I(\tfrac{\vec{\delta}(\epsilon)}{\epsilon}, \vec{\gamma}(\epsilon)) - I(\vec{\tau}, \vec{\gamma}(\epsilon))] + d\epsilon^2 \leq -\epsilon c + d\epsilon^2 < 0$$

which is a contradiction. Hence $\frac{\vec{\delta}(\epsilon)}{\epsilon} \longrightarrow \vec{\tau}$ as required.   □

We remark here that, as for ME, PV-updating with respect to CM_∞ and MD is also well defined. What is interesting about these is that they do not extend Bayesian updating, they do not give $N(K)$ in the case $K^\sigma = \emptyset$, nor for $N = MD$ does it give $N(K)$ in the case $K = K^\sigma$. (See [56].)

Chapter 9 ───────────────

Independence

Returning again to example $\mathbb{E}$ and taking belief as probability throughout, we have already noted that, in practice, it would be very exceptional if the set K_0 of knowledge statements determined Bel uniquely, equivalently if $V^L(K)$ was a single point. The reason for this is that if the knowledge statements in K_0 are, as we have implicitly assumed, being stored, and hence are available for collection one at a time in a list, then the number, m, of such constraints will in practice tend to be vastly exceeded by $J(= 2^n)$, the number of atoms in the resulting language, so that the system

$$\vec{x} A_K = \vec{b}_K, \quad \vec{x} \geq 0$$

will typically be under-constrained. An alternative however, which our earlier simple-minded approach ignored, to this pedestrian 'one at a time' picture is that the expert might hold, and provide, whole schemas of constraints at a single go, in much the same way as we might define a set by a condition on its elements rather than listing its elements explicitly. In this fashion it would seem entirely possible that one might elicit from the expert in a realistic time a handful of schemas whose combined effect is to specify so many constraints as to determine uniquely the values of $Bel(\alpha)$ for each of the J atoms α. (Of course in practice this would greatly increase the risk that the knowledge base would become inconsistent.) Notice that if Bel is uniquely determined by the constraints then the Watts Assumption comes for free.

One natural source of such schema is that of *independence* or *conditional independence*. Precisely, in the context of a probability function Bel on SL, $\theta_1, ..., \theta_k \in SL$ are said to be independent if

$$Bel(\theta_1^{\epsilon_1} \wedge ... \wedge \theta_k^{\epsilon_k}) = \prod_{i=1}^{k} Bel(\theta_i^{\epsilon_i})$$

for all $\epsilon_1, ..., \epsilon_k \in \{0,1\}$ where, as usual, $\theta^0 = \neg\theta$, $\theta^1 = \theta$. Notice that for the case $k = 2$ this simplifies to just $Bel(\theta_1 \wedge \theta_2) = Bel(\theta_1) \cdot Bel(\theta_2)$ since this implies $Bel(\theta_1 \wedge \neg\theta_2) = Bel(\theta_1) - Bel(\theta_1 \wedge \theta_2) = Bel(\theta_1)(1 - Bel(\theta_2)) = Bel(\theta_1) \cdot Bel(\neg\theta_2)$

etc. Similarly $\theta_1, ..., \theta_k$ are conditionally independent given $\psi \in SL$, if

$$Bel(\theta_1^{\epsilon_1} \wedge ... \wedge \theta_k^{\epsilon_k} \mid \psi) = \prod_{i=1}^{k} Bel(\theta_i^{\epsilon_i} \mid \psi)$$

for all $\epsilon_1, ..., \epsilon_k \in \{0, 1\}$.

The important point here is that such a statement of independence corresponds to $2^k - 1$ genuine constraints, one for each choice of $\epsilon_1, ..., \epsilon_k \in \{0, 1\}$, less one, since

$$\sum_{\epsilon_1,...,\epsilon_k} Bel(\bigwedge_{i=1}^{k} \theta_i^{\epsilon_i}) = Bel(\bigvee_{\epsilon_1,...,\epsilon_k} \bigwedge_{i=1}^{k} \theta_i^{\epsilon_i}) = 1.$$

Furthermore it has been suggested (see for example Pearl [59]) that experts have an intuitive 'feel' for independence. Certainly we seem to have a nose for causality, or the lack of it. However this latter, which the layman may identify with independence, does not exactly correspond to independence in the above statistical sense. For example the layman may feel that whether or not a person develops lung cancer is independent of whether or not they own a lighter although statistically they are clearly not independent. (See also Tversky and Kahneman [68].)

Nevertheless let us now assume that the expert's assertions of independence can be correctly formulated in this statistical sense. Then this enables us to consider sets K of knowledge statements including not just linear constraints as before but also independence statements. Notice that the constraint equations yielded by such independence statements will not be linear (although in certain favourable circumstances they can be reduced to linear form). Consequently the set $V^L(K)$ need no longer be convex, or even connected, and inference processes with even the bare minimum of what one might think of as desirable properties no longer exist. The following 'dilemma' (see Courtney [8]) illustrates the problem.

An Example

At a certain bottling factory both bottles and caps, in equal numbers, are supplied by two different manufacturers. At the factory bottles from both suppliers are mixed, as are the caps, and bottles and caps are then fed into the bottling machine at separate and independent inputs. Unfortunately bottles and caps from one supplier are fractionally wider than those from the other and at the plant outlet any bottle fitted with a cap from the alternate supplier leaks visibly.

The controller at the end of the production line is aware that the problem is due to the different sizes and from long experience assigns belief value $\frac{3}{8}$ to 'the next bottle off the line will leak'. However what belief should he give to the next bottle being of the wider sort? We would suggest that since there is complete symmetry here between 'wider' and 'narrower' the controller would opt for a belief value $\frac{1}{2}$

that the next bottle was a wider one. However that value is inconsistent with the constraints, assuming belief as probability and independence to be interpreted as above.

To see this let p stand for 'the next bottle is of the wider sort' and q for 'the cap on the next bottle is of the wider sort'. Then the set, K, of constraints is

$$Bel(p) = Bel(q),$$

$$Bel((\neg p \wedge q) \vee (p \wedge \neg q)) = \frac{3}{8},$$

$$Bel(p \wedge q) = Bel(p) \cdot Bel(q),$$

the last arising from the independence of the bottle input and cap input at the plant. The only two probability functions, Bel_1, Bel_2, satisfying K are

$$Bel_1(p \wedge q) = \frac{1}{16}, \quad Bel_1(p \wedge \neg q) = Bel_1(\neg p \wedge q) = \frac{3}{16}, \quad Bel_1(\neg p \wedge \neg q) = \frac{9}{16},$$

$$Bel_2(p \wedge q) = \frac{9}{16}, \quad Bel_2(p \wedge \neg q) = Bel_2(\neg p \wedge q) = \frac{3}{16}, \quad Bel_2(\neg p \wedge \neg q) = \frac{1}{16}.$$

In this case then $V(K)$ consists of just two points and so is not convex, nor even connected. The set of possible values of $Bel(p)$ for $Bel \in V(K)$ is $\{\frac{1}{4}, \frac{3}{4}\}$ and either choice seems irrational on symmetry considerations. On the other hand the 'natural' choice for $Bel(p)$ of $\frac{1}{2}$ does not correspond to any $Bel \in V(K)$.

In practical expert systems allowing independence statements, the problem highlighted in the above example tends not to arise because the independence assumptions, together with the special form of the general, linear, constraints K, usually ensure unique values for $Bel(\theta), Bel(\theta \mid \phi)$ if not for all arguments, at least for those of interest. We shall briefly describe two such approaches because of their importance to the subject.

Prospector Style Independence

In this section we consider an independence assumption which for a special, but rather natural, class of $K \in CL$ determines Bel uniquely.

The idea is as follows. Suppose, just for this section, that $L = \{e_1, ..., e_m, h_1, ..., h_r\}$ and $K \in CL$ is of the form

$$\begin{aligned}
Bel(h_j \mid e_i) &= \beta_{ij}, & i &= 1, ..., m, \ j = 1, ..., r, \\
Bel(e_i) &= \delta_i, & i &= 1, ..., m, \\
Bel(h_k \wedge h_j) &= 0, & 1 &\le j < k \le r, \\
Bel(h_j) &= \gamma_j, & j &= 1, ..., r,
\end{aligned}$$

where $0 < \delta_i < 1$, $\gamma_j > 0$ and $\sum_{j=1}^{r} \gamma_j = 1$. That is, K corresponds to a family of simple rules linking 'evidences' e_i with 'hypotheses' h_j together with base rates for the hypotheses and evidences and the knowledge that the hypotheses are exclusive and exhaustive.

Such a form for K is a rather natural one, at least in a specialised area. For example in a medical situation the h_j might correspond to diseases and the e_i to signs, so in giving K the expert would be asserting that patients have exactly one of these diseases together with how frequent he believed each disease or sign to be and how likely it is that a given sign indicates a particular disease.

Another attractive feature of assuming that the expert's knowledge is of this form (an extension, then, of the Watts Assumption) is that it would be very easy for the expert to confirm the consistency of K, since, as the later considerations will show, K will be consistent just if for each i, $\sum_j \beta_{ij} = 1$ (and $\beta_{ij} \in [0,1]$ of course) and $\delta_i \beta_{ij} \leq \gamma_j$ for each j. (As we shall see in the next chapter however, consistency testing is, apparently, not feasible for *general* sets of linear constraints.)

As we pointed out when discussing our original example $\mathbb{E}$, what we require is some way to predict from K the expert's belief in θ for various $\theta \in SL$. In the situation of K having the above form it has been suggested that one should add to K the additional assumption that the e_i are independent given h_j for $j = 1, ..., r$, i.e.

$$Bel(e_1^{\epsilon_1} \wedge ... \wedge e_m^{\epsilon_m} \mid h_j) = \prod_{i=1}^{m} Bel(e_i^{\epsilon_i} \mid h_j), \qquad (9.1)$$

for $\epsilon_1, ..., \epsilon_m \in \{0, 1\}$, $j = 1, ..., r$.

In practice this assumption, that the e_i are so conditionally independent, can appear entirely justified given that K is supposed to have arisen from a trustworthy expert. For, given some h_j, K seems to provide no *direct* connections between the e_i and hence the expert must view them as 'independent', (otherwise he would have provided some link between them in K!). Interpreting 'independent' in a statistical sense gives (9.1). Indeed in this case we might be tempted to conclude that (9.1) is, unconsciously perhaps, actually part of the expert's knowledge so that adding it to K will still keep the constraints consistent with the expert's actual belief function.

We now show that $K + (9.1)$ has a unique solution Bel. To see this, first notice that since the h_j are exclusive and exhaustive any Bel satisfying $K + (9.1)$ will be uniquely determined by its values on the (exclusive and exhaustive) sentences $h_j \wedge e_1^{\epsilon_1} \wedge ... \wedge e_m^{\epsilon_m}$. But if Bel satisfies $K + (9.1)$ then

$$Bel(h_j \wedge e_1^{\epsilon_1} \wedge ... \wedge e_m^{\epsilon_m}) \;=\; Bel(e_1^{\epsilon_1} \wedge ... \wedge e_m^{\epsilon_m} \mid h_j) \cdot Bel(h_j)$$

$$=\; Bel(h_j) \cdot \prod_{i=1}^{m} Bel(e_i^{\epsilon_i} \mid h_j)$$

$$=\; Bel(h_j)^{1-m} \cdot \prod_{i=1}^{m} Bel(h_j \wedge e_i^{\epsilon_i})$$

and this right hand side is determined by K since

$$Bel(h_j \wedge e_i) \quad = \quad Bel(h_j \mid e_i) \cdot Bel(e_i) \quad = \quad \delta_i \beta_{ij},$$

$$Bel(h_j \wedge \neg e_i) \quad = \quad Bel(h_j) - Bel(h_j \wedge e_i) \quad = \quad \gamma_j - \delta_i \beta_{ij},$$

so *Bel* is uniquely determined.

Conversely suppose we *define Bel* on $h_j \wedge e_1^{\epsilon_1} \wedge \ldots \wedge e_m^{\epsilon_m} \wedge \bigwedge_{k \neq j} \neg h_k$ to be

$$\gamma_j^{1-m} \cdot \prod_{i=1}^{m} (\epsilon_i \delta_i \beta_{ij} + (1 - \epsilon_i)(\gamma_j - \delta_i \beta_{ij}))$$

and to be zero on all atoms not of this form. Then, since $K \in CL$, K is consistent so

$$\gamma_j \quad = \quad Bel(h_j) \geq Bel(h_j \wedge e_i) = Bel(h_j \mid e_i) \cdot Bel(e_i) = \delta_i \beta_{ij},$$

$$\delta_i \quad = \quad Bel(e_i) = \sum_{j=1}^{m} Bel(h_j \wedge e_i) = \sum_{j=1}^{m} \delta_i \beta_{ij},$$

and from this it is easy to check that *Bel* takes non-negative values on atoms, and hence extends to a probability function on SL, which furthermore satisfies all the constraints in $K + (9.1)$.

It is interesting to notice here that this same solution agrees with $ME(K)$ and hence $ME(K)$ satisfies (9.1). The simplest way to see this seems to be to notice that K is equivalent to K', where K' is

$$Bel(h_j \wedge e_i \wedge \bigwedge_{k \neq j} \neg h_k) \quad = \quad \delta_i \beta_{ij}, \qquad i = 1, \ldots, m, \; j = 1, \ldots, r,$$

$$Bel(h_j \wedge \neg e_i \wedge \bigwedge_{k \neq j} \neg h_k) \quad = \quad \gamma_j - \delta_i \beta_{ij}, \quad i = 1, \ldots, m, \; j = 1, \ldots, r,$$

$$Bel(\alpha) \quad = \quad 0 \qquad \text{for any atom } \alpha \text{ not containing} \\ \text{a unique positive occurence of an } h_j,$$

and that, by substituting into the Lagrange multiplier equations for the non-zero atoms, the above solution gives a stationary point for the entropy subject to K'.

In some early expert systems (notably Prospector, an expert system for predicting mineral deposits) a rather stronger version of (9.1) was used with such K (usually as part of a larger knowledge base), namely

$$Bel(e_1^{\epsilon_1} \wedge \ldots \wedge e_m^{\epsilon_m} \mid h_j) \quad = \quad \prod_{i=1}^{m} Bel(e_i^{\epsilon_i} \mid h_j),$$

$$Bel(e_1^{\epsilon_1} \wedge \ldots \wedge e_m^{\epsilon_m} \mid \neg h_j) \quad = \quad \prod_{i=1}^{m} Bel(e_i^{\epsilon_i} \mid \neg h_j),$$

$$(9.2)$$

for $\epsilon_1, ..., \epsilon_m \in \{0, 1\}$, $j = 1, ..., r$.

An advantage of this assumption is that by summing over unspecified $\pm e_i$ (i.e. e_i, $\neg e_i$) and dividing by the corresponding identity for $\neg h_j$ (now sanctioned by (9.2)) we obtain

$$\frac{Bel(h_j \mid e_{i_1}^{\epsilon_1} \wedge ... \wedge e_{i_s}^{\epsilon_s})}{Bel(\neg h_j \mid e_{i_1}^{\epsilon_1} \wedge ... \wedge e_{i_s}^{\epsilon_s})} = \frac{Bel(h_j)}{Bel(\neg h_j)} \cdot \prod_{k=1}^{s} \frac{Bel(e_{i_k}^{\epsilon_k} \mid h_j)}{Bel(e_{i_k}^{\epsilon_k} \mid \neg h_j)}$$

$$= \frac{Bel(\neg h_j)^{s-1}}{Bel(h_j)^{s-1}} \cdot \prod_{k=1}^{s} \frac{Bel(h_j \mid e_{i_k}^{\epsilon_k})}{Bel(\neg h_j \mid e_{i_k}^{\epsilon_k})},$$

which allows rapid and simple calculations and revisions of the conditional odds of hypotheses as more and more evidence becomes available. (Assuming (9.2) has other advantages which are not relevant here, see Heckerman [27].)

Unfortunately, as the next theorem (see R.W. Johnson [35]) shows, (9.2) is only consistent with K in what, in practice, would be very unlikely circumstances. Of course this might have been suspected on the grounds that $K + (9.1)$ already determines Bel uniquely. On the other hand the theorem can seem slightly surprising since one could easily imagine that for most such real K where (9.1) seemed justified, (9.2) would seem equally intuitive. Certainly it is hard to believe that the expert (unless he was an expert on expert systems) would see any significant difference between these two assumptions.

Theorem 9.1 *Let* $L = \{e_1, ..., e_m, h_1, ..., h_r\}$ *with* $m \geq 2, r \geq 3$ *and let* $K \in CL$ *be*

$$Bel(h_j \mid e_i) = \beta_{ij}, \quad i = 1, ..., m, \; j = 1, ..., r,$$

$$Bel(e_i) = \delta_i, \quad\quad i = 1, ..., m,$$

$$Bel(h_k \wedge h_j) = 0, \quad 1 \leq j < k \leq r,$$

$$Bel(h_j) = \gamma_j, \quad\quad j = 1, ..., r,$$

where $0 < \delta_i < 1$, $0 < \gamma_j$ *and* $\sum_{j=1}^{r} \gamma_j = 1$. *Then if* $K + (9.2)$ *is consistent it must be the case that for the (unique) solution to* $K + (9.2)$, *the* e_i *are independent and each* h_j *is independent of all the* e_i *except possibly one.*

Hence for each j there is at most one i for which $Bel(h_j \mid e_i) \neq Bel(h_j)$, equivalently $Bel(h_j \mid \neg e_i) \neq Bel(h_j)$. In other words there is at most one evidence which can give any information at all about the hypothesis h_j. Clearly such a situation, where the 'evidences' scarcely deserve the title, would be very exceptional in an expert system context since one supposes that experts would normally identify evidences which distinguish hypotheses as far as possible.

Proof of theorem 9.1 Assume that $K + (9.2)$ is consistent and Bel is the unique solution. Now notice that by summing over $\pm e_3, \pm e_4, ..., \pm e_m$, (9.2) gives

$$Bel(e_1 \wedge e_2 \wedge \neg h_j) \cdot Bel(\neg h_j) - Bel(e_1 \wedge \neg h_j) \cdot Bel(e_2 \wedge \neg h_j) = 0.$$

Hence

$$
\begin{aligned}
0 &= \sum_{j=1}^{r} (Bel(e_1 \wedge e_2 \wedge \neg h_j) \cdot Bel(\neg h_j) - Bel(e_1 \wedge \neg h_j) \cdot Bel(e_2 \wedge \neg h_j)) \\
&= \sum_{j=1}^{r} \left(\sum_{i,k \neq j} Bel(e_1 \wedge e_2 \wedge h_i) \cdot Bel(h_k) - \sum_{i,k \neq j} Bel(e_1 \wedge h_i) \cdot Bel(e_2 \wedge h_k) \right),
\end{aligned}
$$

since $Bel(e_1 \wedge \neg h_j) = \sum_{i \neq j} Bel(e_1 \wedge h_i)$ *etc.,*

$$= (r-2) \sum_{i,k} (Bel(e_1 \wedge e_2 \wedge h_i) \cdot Bel(h_k) - Bel(e_1 \wedge h_i) \cdot Bel(e_2 \wedge h_k)),$$

since each distinct pair i, k *appears for* $r - 2$ $j's$ *in the previous line whilst for* $i = k$ *the term is zero in any case by (9.1),*

$$= (r-2)(Bel(e_1 \wedge e_2) - Bel(e_1) \cdot Bel(e_2)).$$

Hence e_1, e_2 are independent. Clearly this same argument goes through with e_1, e_2 replaced by $e_{i_1}^{\epsilon_1} \wedge ... \wedge e_{i_s}^{\epsilon_s}, e_{q_1}^{\delta_1} \wedge ... \wedge e_{q_t}^{\delta_t}$ respectively where $s, t > 0$ and $\{i_1, ..., i_s\} \cap \{q_1, ..., q_t\} = \emptyset$ so by repeated application

$$Bel(e_1^{\epsilon_1} \wedge ... \wedge e_m^{\epsilon_m}) = \prod_{i=1}^{m} Bel(e_i^{\epsilon_i}),$$

and the $e_1, ..., e_m$ are independent, as required.

Now suppose that for some j, h_j was not independent of, say, e_1 nor of e_2, so

$$0 \neq (Bel(e_1 \wedge h_j) - Bel(e_1) \cdot Bel(h_j)) \cdot (Bel(e_2 \wedge h_j) - Bel(e_2) \cdot Bel(h_j))$$

$$
\begin{aligned}
= \; & Bel(e_1 \wedge h_j) \cdot Bel(e_2 \wedge h_j) - Bel(e_1) \cdot Bel(h_j) \cdot Bel(e_2 \wedge h_j) \\
& - Bel(e_2) \cdot Bel(h_j) \cdot Bel(e_1 \wedge h_j) + Bel(e_1) \cdot Bel(e_2) \cdot Bel(h_j)^2
\end{aligned}
$$

$$
\begin{aligned}
= \; & Bel(e_1 \wedge e_2 \wedge h_j) \cdot Bel(h_j) \\
& - (Bel(e_1 \wedge e_2 \wedge h_j) \cdot Bel(h_j)^2 + Bel(e_1 \wedge \neg h_j) \cdot Bel(e_2 \wedge h_j) \cdot Bel(h_j)) \\
& - (Bel(e_1 \wedge h_j) \cdot Bel(e_2 \wedge h_j) \cdot Bel(h_j) \\
& + Bel(e_2 \wedge \neg h_j) \cdot Bel(e_1 \wedge h_j) \cdot Bel(h_j)) \\
& + Bel(e_1 \wedge e_2) \cdot Bel(h_j)^2
\end{aligned}
$$

by using (9.1), the independence of e_1, e_2 and the expansion
of $Bel(e_i)$ as the sum of $Bel(e_i \wedge h_j), Bel(e_i \wedge \neg h_j)$,

$$
\begin{aligned}
= \; & Bel(e_1 \wedge e_2 \wedge h_j) \cdot Bel(h_j) \cdot Bel(\neg h_j) - Bel(e_1) \cdot Bel(e_2) \cdot Bel(h_j) \\
& + Bel(e_1 \wedge \neg h_j) \cdot Bel(e_2 \wedge \neg h_j) \cdot Bel(h_j) + Bel(e_1 \wedge e_2) \cdot Bel(h_j)^2
\end{aligned}
$$

by combining the first two terms and then the next three,

$$
\begin{aligned}
= \; & Bel(e_1 \wedge e_2 \wedge h_j) \cdot Bel(h_j) \cdot Bel(\neg h_j) \\
& + Bel(e_1 \wedge e_2 \wedge \neg h_j) \cdot Bel(h_j) \cdot Bel(\neg h_j) \\
& - Bel(e_1 \wedge e_2) \cdot Bel(h_j) \cdot Bel(\neg h_j),
\end{aligned}
$$

by combining the 2nd and 4th terms and using (9.2),

$$= \; 0,$$

contradiction. The theorem follows. Notice that e_1, e_2 could again be replaced by
$e_{i_1}^{\epsilon_1} \wedge \dots \wedge e_{i_s}^{\epsilon_s}$, $e_{q_1}^{\delta_1} \wedge \dots \wedge e_{q_t}^{\delta_t}$ as above so in fact a slightly stronger result holds.   □

Belief Networks

A second, currently popular, approach invoking independence is the assumption
(extending the Watts Assumption) that the expert's knowledge takes the form of a
Belief Network (see for example Pearl [59] – there are a number of similar approaches
in the literature). That is, that there is a directed, acyclic, finite graph $G = \langle V, E \rangle$
whose set of vertices, V, is the set of propositional variables, $\{p_1, p_2, \dots, p_n\} = L$,
say, numbered in such a way that if $\langle p_i, p_j \rangle \in E$ then $i < j$, and the constraint set
K takes the form

$$Bel(p_i \mid p_{i_1}^{\epsilon_1} \wedge \dots \wedge p_{i_{k_i}}^{\epsilon_{k_i}}) = b_{i i_1 \dots i_{k_i}}^{\epsilon_1 \dots \epsilon_{k_i}} \quad (\in [0, 1]),$$

where $i = 1, ..., n$, $\epsilon_1, ..., \epsilon_k \in \{0, 1\}$, and

$$\{p_{i_1}, ..., p_{i_{k_i}}\} = \{q \in V \mid \langle q, p_i \rangle \in E\},$$

together with the independence assumptions that for $i = 1, ..., n$ and $\delta_1, ..., \delta_{i-1} \in \{0, 1\}$,

$$Bel(p_i \mid p_1^{\delta_1} \wedge ... \wedge p_{i-1}^{\delta_{i-1}}) = Bel(p_i \mid p_{i_1}^{\delta_{i_1}} \wedge ... \wedge p_{i_{k_i}}^{\delta_{i_{k_i}}}),$$

where $p_{i_1}, ..., p_{i_{k_i}}$ are as above. (If $\{q \in V \mid \langle q, p_i \rangle \in E\} = \emptyset$ then $Bel(p_i \mid p_{i_1}^{\epsilon_1} \wedge ... \wedge p_{i_{k_i}}^{\epsilon_{k_i}})$ is just taken to be the unconditional belief $Bel(p_i)$.)

The idea behind this assumption is that the directed edges in E represent some sort of direct influence so that the independence assumptions amount to asserting that even from those features p_j which could influence p_i, i.e. from which there is a directed path

$$p_j \longrightarrow p_{r_1} \longrightarrow p_{r_2} \longrightarrow ... \longrightarrow p_{r_t} \longrightarrow p_i$$

in G (so necessarily $j < r_1 < r_2 < ..., r_t < i$), only those which directly influence p_i, i.e. $\{q \mid < q, p_i > \in E\}$, matter, any indirect influence is fully present already in this set.

Notice that for any finite, directed acyclic graph G the vertices can be enumerated in some such way as $p_1, ..., p_n$ to satisfy that if $\langle p_j, p_i \rangle \in E$ then $j < i$. Namely, set p_1 to any tip of G, that is a vertex with no directed edge going to it. Clearly such a vertex must exist, otherwise, starting from any vertex, v_0 say, we could repeatedly go backwards along directed edges

$$v_0 \longleftarrow v_1 \longleftarrow v_2 \longleftarrow ...$$

and hence after $|V| + 1$ steps we must have repeated a vertex and hence have a cycle, contradicting G's being acyclic. Having picked p_1, if we now delete p_1 from G, together with all edges coming out from it, we produce a second, directed acyclic graph G_1 with $|V_1| = |V| - 1$. If we now repeat the process with G_1 and so on until all the vertices are removed then this clearly gives the required enumeration.

A strong argument in favour of the assumption that the expert's knowledge is of this form (if the Watts Assumption is already accepted) is that the expert seems to find it natural and easy to structure the constraints in this way, and generally feels happy with the idea of a blocking set of direct causes which mediate on behalf of indirect causes. (Rather in the style of a management structure where each worker can only directly influence his immediate superiors.)

A second, attractive, feature of such a form for K is that it has exactly one solution, attractive because it neatly avoids the questions of consistency and of what criteria to use to pick a solution. To see that K has a unique solution notice that if *Bel* was a solution then

$$Bel(p_1^{\epsilon_1} \wedge ... \wedge p_n^{\epsilon_n}) = \prod_{i \leq n} Bel(p_i^{\epsilon_i} \mid p_1^{\epsilon_1} \wedge ... \wedge p_{i-1}^{\epsilon_{i-1}})$$

$$= \prod_{i \leq n} Bel(p_i^{\epsilon_i} \mid p_{i_1}^{\epsilon_{i_1}} \wedge ... \wedge p_{i_{k_i}}^{\epsilon_{i_{k_i}}})$$

$$= \prod_{i \leq n} c_{ii_1...i_{k_i}}^{\epsilon_i \epsilon_{i_1}...\epsilon_{i_{k_i}}}$$

where

$$c_{ii_1...i_{k_i}}^{\epsilon_i \epsilon_{i_1}...\epsilon_{i_{k_i}}} = \begin{cases} b_{ii_1...i_{k_i}}^{\epsilon_{i_1}...\epsilon_{i_{k_i}}} & \text{if } \epsilon_i = 1, \\ \\ 1 - b_{ii_1...i_{k_i}}^{\epsilon_{i_1}...\epsilon_{i_{k_i}}} & \text{if } \epsilon_i = 0, \end{cases}$$

this first identity following from the definition of conditional probability (even if the left hand side is zero), the next two using the constraints in K. Hence this is the only possible solution. That the function *Bel* *defined* according to this last identity is a solution to K follows by noticing that

$$Bel(p_i \mid p_{i_1}^{\epsilon_{i_1}} \wedge ... \wedge p_{i_{k_i}}^{\epsilon_{i_{k_i}}}) = \frac{\displaystyle\sum_{\vec{\delta} \in A, \delta_i = 1} Bel(p_1^{\delta_1} \wedge ... \wedge p_n^{\delta_n})}{\displaystyle\sum_{\vec{\delta} \in A} Bel(p_1^{\delta_1} \wedge ... \wedge p_n^{\delta_n})}$$

where $A = \{\vec{\delta} \in \{0,1\}^n \mid \delta_{i_1} = \epsilon_{i_1}, ..., \delta_{i_{k_i}} = \epsilon_{i_{k_i}}\}$

$$= \frac{\displaystyle\sum_{\vec{\delta} \in A, \delta_i = 1} \prod_{j \leq n} c_{jj_1...j_{k_j}}^{\delta_j \delta_{j_1}...\delta_{j_{k_j}}}}{\displaystyle\sum_{\vec{\delta} \in A} \prod_{j \leq n} c_{jj_1...j_{k_j}}^{\delta_j \delta_{j_1}...\delta_{j_{k_j}}}}.$$

Now in this denominator the sum $\sum_{\vec{\delta} \in A}$ can be written as

$$\sum_{\vec{\delta} \in A'} (\prod_{j < n} c_{jj_1...j_{k_j}}^{\delta_j \delta_{j_1}...\delta_{j_{k_j}}})(c_{nn_1...n_{k_n}}^{0\delta_{n_1}...\delta_{n_{k_n}}} + c_{nn_1...n_{k_n}}^{1\delta_{n_1}...\delta_{n_{k_n}}})$$

where $A' = \{\vec{\delta} \in \{0,1\}^{n-1} \mid \delta_{i_1} = \epsilon_{i_1}, ... , \delta_{i_{k_i}} = \epsilon_{i_{k_i}}\}$ and since this second term is 1 we can replace A by A' in the denominator and similarly in the numerator provided $i \neq n$. By repeated use of this trick, starting at n and going down, we can likewise remove each coordinate $j \geq i$ in the denominator and each coordinate $j > i$ in the numerator to give,

$$Bel(p_i \mid p_{i_1}^{\epsilon_{i_1}} \wedge \dots \wedge p_{i_{k_i}}^{\epsilon_{i_{k_i}}}) = \frac{\sum\limits_{\vec{\delta} \in A'', \delta_i = 1} (\prod\limits_{j<i} c_{jj_1 \dots j_{k_j}}^{\delta_j \delta_{j_1} \dots \delta_{j_{k_j}}}) c_{ii_1 \dots i_{k_i}}^{\delta_i \delta_{i_1} \dots \delta_{i_{k_i}}}}{\sum\limits_{\vec{\delta} \in A''} (\prod\limits_{j<i} c_{jj_1 \dots j_{k_j}}^{\delta_j \delta_{j_1} \dots \delta_{j_{k_j}}})},$$

where $A'' = \{\vec{\delta} \in \{0,1\}^i \mid \delta_{i_1} = \epsilon_{i_1}, \dots, \delta_{i_{k_i}} = \epsilon_{i_{k_i}}\}$. However, for $\delta_i = 1$, $c_{ii_1, \dots, i_{k_i}}^{\delta_i \delta_{i_1} \dots \delta_{i_{k_i}}}$
$= b_{ii_1 \dots i_{k_i}}^{\epsilon_{i_1} \dots \epsilon_{i_{k_i}}}$, so cancelling gives the required identity, showing that *Bel* satisfies the linear constraints in K. The same analysis also shows that

$$\sum_{\epsilon_1, \dots, \epsilon_n} Bel(p_1^{\epsilon_1} \wedge \dots \wedge p_n^{\epsilon_n}) = 1,$$

so, since $Bel(p_1^{\epsilon_1} \wedge \dots \wedge p_n^{\epsilon_n}) \geq 0$, *Bel* certainly is a probability function. Furthermore repeating the above procedure for $Bel(p_i \mid p_1^{\epsilon_1} \wedge \dots \wedge p_{i-1}^{\epsilon_{i-1}})$ we would again be able to cancel at exactly the same stage to obtain, again,

$$Bel(p_i \mid p_1^{\epsilon_1} \wedge \dots \wedge p_{i-1}^{\epsilon_{i-1}}) = b_{ii_1 \dots i_{k_i}}^{\epsilon_{i_1} \dots \epsilon_{i_{k_i}}} = Bel(p_i \mid p_{i_1}^{\epsilon_{i_1}} \wedge \dots \wedge p_{i_{k_i}}^{\epsilon_{i_{k_i}}})$$

and hence *Bel* satisfies the independence conditions in K.

Notice that if Bel_0 is *any* belief function on SL then Bel_0 *is* given by a belief network, namely the edges of G are all $\langle p_i, p_j \rangle$ with $1 \leq i < j \leq J$ and the

$$b_{i1 \dots i-1}^{\epsilon_1 \dots \epsilon_{i-1}} = Bel_0(p_i \mid p_1^{\epsilon_1} \wedge \dots \wedge p_{i-1}^{\epsilon_{i-1}})$$

(with the independence now coming for free).

Avoiding as it does any problems of consistency this approach is certainly very attractive as a model of the expert since he also (apparently) has no worries on this score. Also, as we shall see in the next chapter, there are advantages of this model when it comes to the calculation of unconditional beliefs (although not apparently general conditional beliefs).

It is important to appreciate here that the assumption that the expert's knowledge is of this form does not *necessarily* require him to have an unreasonably large mental storage space. For the number of constraints needing to be stored, apart from the direct graph which in practice would be entirely feasible, is

$$\sum_{i=1}^{n} 2^{|\{q \in V \mid \langle q, p_i \rangle \in E\}|}$$

which need not be astronomical provided that the sets of direct influence,

$$\{q \in V \mid \langle q, p_i \rangle \in E\},$$

are small.

The question arises however as to how, in practice, the expert could construct his belief network on the, really, very limited data available to him and why, having done so, his resulting belief function should be a reasonably accurate approximation of nature. Certainly it is our general experience that the expert's freely given knowledge base K omits a large proportion of the constraints which would be required for it to correspond to a belief network. One could, of course, allow here that the expert was being careless and that it is justifiable to directly request him to provide the missing items (asking him at the same time to retract statements not of the required form!). In a sense this is bound to work although if the sets of direct influence are not very small the number of such questions would in reality make this completely infeasible.

In current practice many successful expert systems are based on 'belief networks', where the expert provides the initial directed graph but the conditional probabilities are mainly empirical, and considerable ingenuity has gone into devising efficient algorithms for calculating conditional beliefs for certain limited classes of such belief networks. Indeed there is now a growing interest in the problem of also constructing the network itself from the data, thus effectively removing the contribution of the expert altogether. Since the calculation of (conditional) beliefs from a belief network is now a large subject in its own right and not directly relevant to the aims of this book we shall not pursue it further here except to remark that any successes in the creation of such algorithms could be viewed as support for the view that the expert's beliefs are structured in this way. The reader interested in pursuing this topic is referred to Pearl [58], Hájek et al. [26].

Chapter 10 ─────────────

Computational Feasibility

The material we have developed in the previous chapters could be said to have been justified, in the main, by considerations of common sense or rationality. In view of the fact then that we tend to see ourselves as reasonably efficient uncertain reasoners who, ideally, act rationally and according to common sense, it might be expected, or hoped, that the previous chapters would not have lead us to modes of uncertain reasoning which are practically, i.e. computationally, infeasible. Unfortunately, as we shall now show, this is not in general the case (and so perhaps gives grounds to question 'common sense'). In particular the following practical problems (for each of the frameworks so far introduced) appear to be, in general, beyond the capabilities of computers and hence, presumably, of ourselves:

(i) The problem of checking if a set K of linear constraints is consistent.

(ii) Given consistent K and $\theta \in SL$ the problem of computing an approximation to a value for $Bel(\theta)$ which is consistent with K.

Before giving precise results we recall some definitions from computational complexity theory.

Let X be a set of words (i.e. finite strings of letters) from a finite, non-empty alphabet A. We can identify X with the problem,

$$\text{Given } \sigma \in A^*, \text{ is } \sigma \in X?$$

where A^* is the set of all words from alphabet A.

A problem X is said to be in *polynomial time* (P), written $X \in P$, if there is a deterministic Turing machine M (or similar digital computer, e.g. RAM) and a polynomial $p(x)$ such that on input σ, $\sigma \in A^*$, M halts within $p(|\sigma|)$ steps and accepts just if $\sigma \in X$. ($|\sigma|$ is the length of the word σ.)

It is generally felt that to be feasible, or practically answerable (exactly in all cases), a problem must at least be in P. Thus problems not in P are computationally infeasible, or intractable, according to this view.

X is said to be in *non-deterministic polynomial time* (NP), written $X \in NP$, if there is a non-deterministic Turing machine M and a polynomial $p(x)$ such that for

$\sigma \in A^*$, any computation of M on input σ halts within $p(|\sigma|)$ steps and at least one such computation accepts iff $\sigma \in X$.

Clearly $P \subseteq NP$. As a result of a great deal of research it is conjectured, widely believed and frequently assumed that $P \neq NP$. The quintessential problem in NP is

$$SAT = \{\theta \in SL \mid \theta \text{ satisfiable}\}$$

where, say, L is the infinite language $\{p_i \mid i \in \mathbb{N}\}$ and $\theta \in SL$ is identified with the word from the finite alphabet $\{\wedge, \vee, \neg, (,), 0, 1, p\}$ obtained by replacing each p_i in θ by the word p followed by i in binary. Given a word σ from this alphabet it is easy to check on a deterministic Turing machine in polynomial time if $\sigma \in SL$ so the essentially difficult (i.e. time consuming) part of SAT is to test the satisfiability given that σ is a sentence.

That $SAT \in NP$ can easily be seen by noticing that a non-deterministic Turing machine has, in effect, the ability to make guesses, so to test if $\theta \in SL$ is satisfiable the non-deterministic Turing machine first guesses a valuation V on the propositional variables appearing in θ and then, deterministically and in polynomial time, checks if $V(\theta) = 1$.

By Cook's theorem (see, for example, Hopcroft and Ullman [31], p.325) SAT is a hardest problem in NP in that if $X \in NP$ then $X \leq_P SAT$, that is, there is a function F, computable in polynomial time on a deterministic Turing machine, such that

$$\sigma \in X \Leftrightarrow F(\sigma) \in SAT.$$

Such a hardest problem in NP is said to be NP-complete. By Cook's theorem and transitivity of $\leq_P$, X is NP-complete just if $X \in NP$ and $SAT \leq_P X$.

If X is NP-complete then $P = NP \Leftrightarrow X \in P$. In particular $P \neq NP$ is equivalent to $SAT \notin P$. Hence if we assume $P \neq NP$ and show that X is NP-complete (or simply that $SAT \leq_P X$) then we can conclude that $X \notin P$ and hence accord X the status of being computationally infeasible.

A random Turing machine is a Turing machine which, in certain states, is able to toss a (fixed) die in order to decide what state to move to next (hence it is also a non-deterministic Turing machine). A problem X is said to be in *random polynomial time (RP)*, written $X \in RP$, if there is a random Turing machine M, a polynomial $p(x)$ and $\delta > 0$ such that for input $\sigma \in A^*$, any computation of M on σ halts within $p(|\sigma|)$ steps and

(a) If $\sigma \notin X$ then no computation of M on σ accepts,

(b) If $\sigma \in X$ then the probability that M will accept σ is $\geq \delta$ (i.e. the proportion of accepting computations is $\geq \delta$).

Notice δ can be improved by repeatedly running n times on σ since given $\sigma \in X$ the probability that at least one of these runs accepts is $1 - (1 - \delta)^n$ which tends to 1 as $n \to \infty$.

Clearly $P \subseteq RP \subseteq NP$ and again $RP = NP \Leftrightarrow SAT \in RP$. It is conjectured and widely believed that $RP \neq NP$.

Consistency

The first major computational problem with the frameworks we have set up so far is that of testing the consistency of the set K of linear constraints (a problem we have so far ignored). For suppose K was obtained directly from an expert, as in example E. Then the only obvious justification for believing that K should be consistent with, say, belief as probability, is based on the assumption that the expert's belief function is a probability function and that the expert would not hold an inconsistent knowledge base. However, as almost anyone who attempts to obtain a K in this way discovers, K frequently turns out to be trivially inconsistent with belief as probability (and with the other frameworks we have hitherto considered).

Of course one could attribute this to carelessness, or misunderstanding, or undue haste, on the part of the expert when quantifying his beliefs. Charitably an advocate of, say, belief as probability might feel that allowed sufficient time the expert would 'correctly' express his knowledge in a way consistent with belief as probability. That is, that the expert's 'real K' is consistent. But this seems to presuppose that the expert's beliefs are generated in such a way that K will be guaranteed to be consistent. This can indeed be the case, for example the model of belief given for the first justification of belief as probability in Chapter 3 guarantees that the constraints K derived from this modelling of the expert are consistent with belief as probability, and similarly for the belief networks introduced in the previous chapter.

However if we accept the Watt's Assumption that K *is* the expert's knowledge (or at least a good approximation to it) then what guarantee do we, or the expert, have in general that K is consistent, especially if it has been accumulated from many different sources, and, as is usually the case, does not conform to some special structure such as a belief network?

Unfortunately the general detection of inconsistencies appears to be infeasible, for the frameworks we have introduced so far, as our next few theorems show. These theorems could then be viewed as criticisms of the Watts Assumption or, alternatively, as discouraging omens for would-be builders of large expert systems.

The next theorem has appeared, independently, in several places in the literature so is now best described as folklore.

Theorem 10.1 *Given a set K of linear constraints*

$$\sum_{j=1}^{r} a_{ji} Bel(\theta_j) = b_i \quad i = 1, ..., m$$

where the a_{ji}, $b_i \in \mathbb{Q}$ (= set of rationals), $\theta_j \in SL$, the problem of deciding if K is consistent with Bel being a probability function is NP-complete, and hence infeasible under the assumption $P \neq NP$.

(This is not exactly stated within the above framework since K is not simply a word from some alphabet. Clearly we could have framed it in this way since the coefficients are restricted here to $\mathbb{Q}$. However testing if K has the form of linear constraints is easily seen to be in P so the heart of the problem is the one stated. We shall use this and similar abuses of notation frequently in what follows.)

Proof For $\theta \in SL$,

$$K = \{Bel(\theta) = 1\} \text{ consistent}$$

$$\Rightarrow \quad \text{not } (\vdash \neg\theta), \text{ otherwise } Bel(\theta) = 0$$
$$\text{for all probability functions } Bel, \text{ by proposition 2.1}$$

$$\Rightarrow \quad \theta \text{ satisfiable}$$

$$\Rightarrow \quad V(\theta) = 1 \text{ for some (2-valued) valuation } V$$

$$\Rightarrow \quad \{Bel(\theta) = 1\} \text{ consistent, since such}$$
$$\text{a valuation } V \text{ is a probability function.}$$

So with the above notation if $F(\theta) = \{Bel(\theta) = 1\}$ (with F of a non-sentence being some fixed inconsistent constraint set, say) then

$$\sigma \in SAT \Leftrightarrow F(\sigma) \text{ consistent,}$$

i.e. $SAT \leq_P Consistency$.

It only remains to show $Consistency$ is in NP. Given K a set of constraints (if K was not a set of constraints then detect this deterministically in polynomial time), K is consistent just if $\vec{x}A_K = \vec{b}_K$, $\vec{x} \geq 0$ has a solution, where $\vec{x} = \langle x_1, ...x_J \rangle$. Hence it is enough to test if $\vec{x}A_K = \vec{b}_K$, $\vec{x} \geq 0$ has a solution.

Unfortunately J may be exponential in the length of the input so we cannot (in polynomial time) simply attempt to solve these equalities and inequalities directly. Instead we apply a result from linear programming which says that if A_K has rank t ($\leq m+1 = $ number of columns of A_K) then $\vec{x}A_K = \vec{b}_K$, $\vec{x} \geq 0$ has a solution just if it has a solution with at most t of the x_i non-zero. (To prove this consider a solution $\vec{e}$ with the least number, j say, of non-zero entries. If $j > t$ then the corresponding j rows of A_K are linearly dependent so there is a non-zero $\vec{v}$ with $\vec{v}A_K = \vec{0}$ and $v_i = 0$ when $e_i = 0$. Then $(\vec{e} + \epsilon\vec{v})A_K = \vec{b}_K$ for ϵ small and $\vec{e} + \epsilon\vec{v} \geq 0$. Let $\epsilon > 0$ be maximal such that this is true. Then $\vec{e} + \epsilon\vec{v}$ must have fewer zero coordinates than $\vec{e}$, contradicting the choice of $\vec{e}$.)

The idea then is to guess these $x_{i_1}, ..., x_{i_t}$, guess t linearly independent columns of A_K, say the j_1'th,...,j_t'th columns, and compute the submatrix A of A_K corresponding to these rows and columns using the fact that the p, q'th entry in A_K is

$$\sum_{j=1}^{r} a_{jp} V_q(\theta_j)$$

where V_q is the valuation for which $V_q(\alpha_q) = 1$. (We may assume here that the atoms α_q have been enumerated by

$$\alpha_q = p_1^{\epsilon_1} \wedge p_2^{\epsilon_2} \wedge ... \wedge p_n^{\epsilon_n}$$

where $q = 1 + \sum_{i \leq n} \epsilon_i 2^{i-1}$, $\epsilon_1, ..., \epsilon_n \in \{0, 1\}$, so that V_q can be quickly recovered from q.) By reducing A to row echelon form check that A is non-singular and, if so, compute A^{-1}. Now check that if

$$\langle x_{i_1}, ..., x_{i_t} \rangle = \langle (b_K)_{j_1}, ..., (b_K)_{j_t} \rangle A^{-1}$$

with the remaining $x_i = 0$, then

$$\vec{x} A_K = \vec{b}_K, \quad \vec{x} \geq 0$$

as required. (Notice we only have to compute $t(m+1)$ entries in A_K to confirm this.)

Clearly all this can be carried out in polynomial time (as a function of the input length) and if $\vec{x} A_K = \vec{b}_K$, $\vec{x} \geq 0$ has a solution then there is a sequence of guesses producing a solution. Hence *Consistency* $\in NP$ as required. $\square$

There are various objections one might raise against this result as a criticism of the Watts Assumption (not least of course the equating of practically infeasible with 'not in P', an issue which we will not discuss further here). One immediate objection is that it would appear from this proof that the constraint sets K for which testing consistency is difficult are of the form $\{Bel(\theta) = 1\}$ with θ rather complicated. But 'natural' constraint sets are not of this form, they tend to be sets of constraints of the form $Bel(\theta) = b$ or $Bel(\theta \mid \phi) = c$ with θ, ϕ very simple, for example short conjunctions of literals.

To quash this objection we shall now give an improved version of theorem 10.1 due to Georgakopoulos, Kavvadias and Papadimitriou [25], which shows that we can take K here to be 'very natural'.

Theorem 10.2 *In theorem 10.1 we may restrict K to be of the form*

$$Bel(\theta_i) = b_i, \quad i = 1, ..., m$$

where the $b_i \in \mathbb{Q}$ and the θ_i are conjunctions of at most two literals.

Proof By theorem 10.1 we see that this problem, call it 2-*Consistency*, is in NP. To show that it is NP-complete we show that

$$\text{Chromatic Number} \leq_P 2-\text{Consistency}$$

where *Chromatic Number* is the well known NP-complete problem of deciding if the vertices of a graph $G = \langle V, E \rangle$ can be coloured with k colours so that no two adjacent vertices have the same colour (see Garey, D. Johnson and Stockmeyer [24]). Given k, G let $L = \{p_i^j \mid j = 1, ..., k, \ i \in V\}$ and let

$$K = \begin{cases} Bel(p_i^j) = \frac{1}{k} & \text{for } 1 \leq j \leq k, \ i \in V, \\ Bel(p_i^j \wedge p_i^r) = 0 & \text{for } 1 \leq j < r \leq k, \ i \in V, \\ Bel(p_i^j \wedge p_s^j) = 0 & \text{for } 1 \leq j \leq k, \ \{i, s\} \in E. \end{cases}$$

Then if Bel is a probability function satisfying K, let α be an atom of L such that $Bel(\alpha) > 0$. Define a colouring $C : V \to \{1, ..., k\}$ by $C(i) = j \Leftrightarrow \alpha \models p_i^j$. To see that C is a good colouring notice that C does not give i two distinct colours (since $Bel(p_i^j \wedge p_i^r) = 0$ for $j \neq r$) nor does C give adjacent vertices the same colour (since $Bel(p_i^j \wedge p_s^j) = 0$ for $\{i, s\} \in E$). Also C gives vertex i at least one colour since the constraints in K clearly imply $Bel(\bigvee_{j=1}^k p_i^j) = 1$.

Conversely if C is a k-colouring of G then so is σC where $\sigma \in S_k = $ permutations of $\{1, ..., k\}$. For α an atom of L define

$$Bel(\alpha) = \frac{1}{k!} \cdot |\{\sigma \in S_k \mid \sigma C(i) = j \Leftrightarrow \alpha \models p_i^j \ \forall p_i^j \in L\}|.$$

Then $Bel(p_i^j)$ is the proportion of the colourings in $\{\sigma C \mid \sigma \in S_k\}$ for which vertex i gets colour j and from this it is easy to see that Bel is a probability function satisfying K. The result now follows. □

Theorem 10.2 is also interesting in that it could be easily proved for conjunction of three, rather than two, literals by simply replacing SAT in the proof of theorem 10.1 by the NP-complete problem 3-SAT, the problem of deciding the satisfiability of conjunctions of disjunctions of three (or less) literals. However that refinement cannot get us down to two literals since 2-SAT is actually in P. So in this sense probabilistic satisfaction (i.e. consistency) is harder than simple two-valued satisfaction.

We point out here that theorem 10.2 cannot be improved to the θ_i being single literals since in that case we can simplify further to just propositional variables in which case the set of constraints can clearly only fails to be consistent if it contains $Bel(p) = b$, $Bel(p) = c$ for some $p \in L$ with $b \neq c$ or $b \notin [0, 1]$.

Corollary 10.3 *In theorem 10.1 we may restrict K to be of the form*

$$Bel(\theta_i) = b_i, \quad Bel(\phi_j \mid \psi_j) = 0, \quad i = 1, ..., m, \quad j = 1, ..., q$$

where the θ_i, ϕ_j, ψ_j are propositional variables.

Proof Notice that the K used in the proof of 10.2 is equivalent to

$$Bel(p_i^j) = \tfrac{1}{k} \qquad \text{for } 1 \le j \le k, \; i \in V,$$

$$Bel(p_i^j \mid p_i^r) = 0 \quad \text{for } 1 \le j < r \le k, \; i \in V,$$

$$Bel(p_i^j \mid p_s^j) = 0 \quad \text{for } 1 \le j \le k, \; \{i, s\} \in E.$$

$\square$

Theorem 10.4 *Given a set K of constraints of the form*

$$Bel(\theta_i) = b_i \quad i = 1, ..., m$$

where the $b_i \in \mathbb{Q}$, and the θ_i are conjunctions of at most two literals, the problem of deciding if K is consistent with Bel a DS-belief function is NP-complete, and hence infeasible under the assumption $P \ne NP$.

Proof We proceed as in the proof of theorem 10.2. Firstly if the graph G can be coloured with k colours then there is a probability function, hence a DS-belief function, *Bel* satisfying K, i.e.

$$Bel(p_i^j) = \tfrac{1}{k} \qquad \text{for } 1 \le j \le k, \; i \in V,$$

$$Bel(p_i^j \wedge p_i^r) = 0 \quad \text{for } 1 \le j < r \le k, \; i \in V,$$

$$Bel(p_i^j \wedge p_s^j) = 0 \quad \text{for } 1 \le j \le k, \; \{i, s\} \in E.$$

Conversely suppose that *Bel* is a DS-belief function satisfying K. Let m be the bpa of *Bel* and suppose $m(\bar{\theta}) > 0$. Define a colouring C by

$$C(i) = j \Leftrightarrow \bar{\theta} \le \overline{p_i^j}.$$

Then, as in the proof of theorem 10.2, the constraints K force that no vertex gets more than one colour and adjacent vertices do not get the same colour. To see that every vertex gets at least one colour notice that, since $Bel(p_i^j \wedge p_i^r) = 0$ for

$1 \leq j < r \leq k$, the sets $\{\overline{\phi} > \mathbf{0} \mid \overline{\phi} \leq \overline{p_i^j}\}$, $\{\overline{\phi} > \mathbf{0} \mid \overline{\phi} \leq \overline{p_i^r}\}$ are disjoint for $j \neq r$. Hence if vertex i got no colour then $\overline{\theta} \not\leq p_i^j$ for $1 \leq j \leq k$ so

$$1 = \sum_{j=1}^{k} Bel(p_i^j) = \sum_{j=1}^{k} \left(\sum_{\overline{\phi} \leq p_i^j} m(\overline{\phi}) \right)$$

$$\leq \sum_{\overline{\phi} \neq \overline{\theta}} m(\overline{\phi}),$$

since each $m(\overline{\phi})$ appears at most once in this sum and $m(\overline{\theta})$ does not appear at all. But this last sum is $1 - m(\overline{\theta}) < 1$, giving the required contradiction.

To show that the problem of the consistency of a *general K*,

$$\sum_{j=1}^{r} a_{ji} Bel(\theta_j) = b_i \quad i = 1, ..., m, \quad a_{ji}, b_i \in \mathbb{Q} \text{ etc.}$$

with *Bel* a DS-belief function is in NP we proceed analogously to the proof of theorem 10.1 by guessing (distinct) $H_1, ..., H_t \subseteq At^L$ and values $m(\bigvee H_1), ..., m(\bigvee H_t)$ (with all other bpa values zero) to satisfy the matrix equivalent of K. An added difficulty arises here however in that we require the $|H_i|$ to be bounded by a fixed polynomial of the length of the input (this is needed both in order to make the guesses and to compute the required, small, submatrix).

That this is possible can be seen as follows. Suppose that $G_1, ..., G_t \subseteq At^L$ and $m(\bigvee G_1), ..., m(\bigvee G_t)$ is a solution although possibly not suitably short. Pick $T \subseteq At^L$ such that for $1 \leq i \leq t$, $1 \leq j \leq r$, the $T \cap G_i$ are distinct and non-empty, and if $G_i \not\subseteq S_{\theta_j}$ then $T \cap (S_{\theta_j} - G_i) \neq \emptyset$. Clearly such a T can be found with $|T| \leq t^2 + rt$ and for this T a suitably short solution is given by

$$H_i = T \cap G_i, \quad m'(\bigvee H_i) = m(\bigvee G_i).$$

$\square$

Theorem 10.5 *Given a set K of linear constraints*

$$\sum_{j=1}^{r} a_{ji} Bel(\theta_j) = b_i \quad i = 1, ..., m$$

where the a_{ji}, $b_i \in \mathbb{Q}$, $\theta_j \in SL$, the problem of deciding if K is consistent with Bel satisfying $\mathbf{F}_1$ is NP-complete, and hence infeasible under the assumption $P \neq NP$.

Proof As usual we first give a polynomial time reduction of SAT to this problem of consistency with $\mathbf{F}_1$. Notice that for *Bel* satisfying $\mathbf{F}_1$,

$$Bel(p) \in \{0, 1\} \Leftrightarrow Bel(p \wedge \neg p) = 0$$

and if $Bel(p) \in \{0, 1\}$ for all $p \in L$ then $Bel(\theta) = V(\theta)$ for all $\theta \in SL$, where V is the valuation agreeing with Bel on L. From this it follows that for $\theta \in SL$,

$$\theta \in SAT \quad \Leftrightarrow \quad \text{there is a valuation } V \text{ such that } V(\theta) = 1$$

$$\Leftrightarrow \quad \text{there is a function } Bel \text{ satisfying}$$
$$\mathbf{F}_1 \text{ and } Bel(\theta) = 1 \text{ and } Bel(p \wedge \neg p) = 0$$
$$\text{for each propositional variable } p \text{ occuring in } \theta,$$

$$\Leftrightarrow \quad \{Bel(\theta) = 1, \ Bel(p \wedge \neg p) = 0 \text{ for } p \text{ occuring in } \theta\}$$
$$\text{is consistent with } \mathbf{F}_1.$$

To show that the problem of testing the consistency of K as above with $\mathbf{F}_1$ is in NP notice that we can systematically simplify the expressions in K by guessing min and max values and adding this guess to K. For example, for

$$K = \{Bel(p_1 \wedge (p_2 \vee p_3)) = b\}$$

we could guess that

$$\min\{Bel(p_1), \ Bel(p_2 \vee p_3)\} = Bel(p_1)$$

and replace K by

$$\{Bel(p_1) = b, \ Bel(p_1) \leq Bel(p_2 \vee p_3)\}.$$

Since we only need to introduce one inequality for each occurence of $\wedge, \vee$ in K, we eventually arrive at a set of equations and inequalities in the $Bel(p)$, $p \in L$, of size polynomial in the original K. Furthermore we can now test if this set has a solution, in non-deterministic polynomial time, by essentially the method of the proof of theorem 10.1 (e.g. by replacing an inequality

$$c_0 + \sum_{i=1}^{n} c_i Bel(p_i) \geq 0,$$

by

$$c_0 + \sum_{i=1}^{n} c_i Bel(p_i) = z, \quad z \geq 0$$

etc., where z is a new variable).

Clearly then K is consistent just if some sequence of min and max guesses yields such a set of equations and inequalities in the $Bel(p)$ which has a solution, so that the problem of consistency is in NP as required. $\qquad \square$

By using 3-SAT here in place of SAT we could assume that K has the simple form

$$Bel(\theta_i) = 0 \quad i = 1, ..., m$$

with each θ_i the conjunction of at most three literals.

A similar result to theorem 10.5 holds for $\mathbf{F}_3$, using the fact that for Bel satisfying $\mathbf{F}_3$,

$$Bel(p) \in \{0, 1\} \Leftrightarrow Bel((p \wedge p) \vee (\neg p \wedge \neg p)) = 1.$$

For $\mathbf{F}_2$ the first half of the proof of theorem 10.5 can be adapted, using the fact that for Bel satisfying $\mathbf{F}_2$,

$$Bel(p) \in \{0, 1\} \Leftrightarrow Bel(p \wedge \neg p) = 0,$$

to show that the problem of consistency with $\mathbf{F}_2$ is infeasible assuming $P \neq NP$.

Calculation

We now turn to the problem of computing values for $Bel(\theta)$ consistent with a set of constraints K. We shall prove two main results limiting (apparently) the possibility of doing this feasibly for a range of frameworks. Our first result will require the assumption $P \neq NP$ and the second will require the stronger assumption that $RP \neq NP$. These results are due to Maung and the author [46]. The first applies to inference processes N in the framework of belief as probability.

Theorem 10.6 *Let N be a language invariant inference process satisfying renaming and let $\epsilon > 0$. Then, assuming $P \neq NP$, the problem, given L, $K \in CL$ and $\phi \in SL$, of finding a number ν such that*

$$|N(K)(\phi) - \nu| \leq \frac{1}{2} - \epsilon$$

is computationally infeasible (i.e. not possible on a deterministic Turing machine running in polynomial time).

Thus, in general, it is computationally infeasible to find any non-trivial approximation to $N(K)(\phi)$. Of course if $\epsilon = 0$ we could take $\nu = \frac{1}{2}$ without the need for any computation at all.

Notice that we could drop L from the input by taking it to be the smallest language containing all the propositional variables appearing in K and ϕ.

Proof Suppose on the contrary we had a polynomial time algorithm for approximating $N(K)(\phi)$ for consistent K. We shall show that this implies $SAT \in P$, contradicting $P \neq NP$.

Let $\chi \in SL$. We shall show how to decide if $\chi \in SAT$ in polynomial time. We may assume that each propositional variable p_i, $i = 1, ..., n$ of L appears in

χ, otherwise we can rename the propositional variables, obviously without affecting satisfiability. Fix k such that $2^k > \frac{1}{\epsilon}$ and let $m = n + k$.

For $i < 2^m$, say $i = \sum_{j=1}^{m} \delta_j 2^{j-1}$ in binary, let

$$\eta_i = \bigwedge_{j=1}^{m} p_j^{\delta_j}$$

so the $\overline{\eta_i}$ are precisely the atoms of the Lindenbaum algebra $\overline{SL'}$ where $L' = \{p_1, ..., p_m\}$. Let K consist of the single constraint

$$Bel(\chi \vee \eta_0) = 1.$$

K is consistent since if V is the valuation on L' such that $V(\eta_0) = 1$ then V is a probability function (on SL') satisfying K.

Let $\bigvee_{j \in C} \eta_j$ be the disjunctive normal form logically equivalent to χ where $C \subseteq \{0, 1, ..., 2^m - 1\}$. (If $C = \emptyset$ take the empty disjunction to be just some contradictory sentence in SL'.) Then for Bel a probability function,

$$Bel(\chi \vee \eta_0) = \sum_{j \in C \cup \{0\}} Bel(\eta_j),$$

so K is equivalent to

$$\sum_{j \in C \cup \{0\}} Bel(\eta_j) = 1. \tag{10.1}$$

Now for $i, j \in C \cup \{0\}$, transposing η_i, η_j in (10.1), whilst keeping all the other atoms fixed, clearly does not alter K, so by renaming $N(K)(\eta_i) = N(K)(\eta_j)$. Hence

$$N(K)(\eta_j) = |C \cup \{0\}|^{-1}$$

for $j \in C \cup \{0\}$.

Now consider $N(K)(\chi)$. If χ is satisfiable, say by a valuation V on L, then χ is satisfied by any of the 2^{m-n} valuations on L' which extend V. Each of these valuations is uniquely determined by the atom η_j it satisfies so $|C| \geq 2^{m-n}$. On the other hand if χ is not satisfiable then $|C| = 0$. Hence if $\chi \notin SAT$,

$$N(K)(\chi) = \sum_{j \in C} N(K)(\eta_j) = 0 < \epsilon$$

whilst if $\chi \in SAT$,

$$N(K)(\chi) = \sum_{j \in C} N(K)(\eta_j) = \frac{|C|}{|C \cup \{0\}|} \geq \frac{2^{m-n}}{2^{m-n} + 1} \geq 1 - 2^{-k} > 1 - \epsilon.$$

Hence knowing ν within $\frac{1}{2} - \epsilon$ of $N(K)(\chi)$ tells us $\chi \notin SAT$ if $\nu < \frac{1}{2}$ and $\chi \in SAT$ if $\nu \geq \frac{1}{2}$, and the result follows. $\square$

Notice that this theorem applies to $N = ME$, MD, CM_∞, and also to CM if we allow that the overlying language be also specified in the input (so we can work all along in L' and hence avoid having to assume language invariance).

The infeasibility of obtaining values for $N(K)(\theta)$ might have been suspected when we consider the inference processes we have described. These all 'worked' by first reducing K to a set of equations and inequalities in the exponentially large number J $(= 2^n)$ of variables. Thus any direct calculation would seem to involve all these variables and hence require exponential time. One might therefore conjecture that much better infeasibility results than those above should be possible, namely that any reasonable inference process must use at least exponential time.

Our next theorem will be proved under very weak assumptions on Bel and in consequence can be applied in a wider range of situations. For the purpose of this theorem we shall assume of $Bel : SL \to [0, 1]$ only that

$$(P3) \qquad \text{For } \theta, \phi \in SL \text{ if } \phi \models \theta \text{ then } Bel(\phi) \leq Bel(\theta),$$

i.e. if θ is a logical consequence of ϕ then belief in θ should be at least as high as belief in ϕ.

An immediate consequence of (P3) is that if $\models (\phi \leftrightarrow \theta)$ then $Bel(\theta) = Bel(\phi)$. Clearly (P3) holds for probability functions and DS-belief functions.

In the next theorem, as in theorem 10.6, $L = \{p_1, ..., p_n\}$ is to be thought of as a variable determined by n being minimal such that $K \in CL$.

Theorem 10.7 *Let $\epsilon, \delta > 0$ and assume $RP \neq NP$. Then there is no random Turing machine running in polynomial time which on input $K \in CL$ and $p \in L$ outputs a number ν such that with probability at least $\frac{1}{2} + \delta$,*

$$K + |Bel(p) - \nu| \leq \frac{1}{2} - \epsilon$$

is consistent with Bel satisfying (P3).

Notice again that if $\epsilon = 0$ we could, trivially, find such a ν, namely $\nu = \frac{1}{2}$. Similarly if $\delta = 0$ we could achieve this for $\epsilon \leq \frac{1}{4}$ by putting $\nu = \frac{1}{4}$ with probability $\frac{1}{2}$, $\nu = \frac{3}{4}$ with probability $\frac{1}{2}$.

The importance of this result is that it says that, in general, given $K \in CL$, $p \in L$ it is not feasible – even probabilistically – to calculate any non-trivial approximation to a consistent value for $Bel(p)$ given that Bel satisfies K, even if we weaken the usual requirement that Bel be a probability function, to simply that Bel satisfies just (P3). In particular then, if N is any inference process we cannot, in general, feasibly hope to be able to calculate any non-trivial approximation to $N(K)(\theta)$ even for θ a propositional variable.

Clearly this result is stronger than theorem 10.6 although of course relying on the stronger assumption $RP \neq NP$ (if $P = NP$ then $RP = NP$ since $P \subseteq RP \subseteq NP$).

The proof of theorem 10.7 relies heavily on a result due to Valiant and Vazirani [69], a slightly weakened version of which we present as the next lemma. The first-time reader might prefer to skip the proof of this lemma and proceed directly to the proof of theorem 10.7 in order to first appreciate its significance. Again in this lemma $L = \{p_1, ..., p_n\}$ is to be thought of as variable with n being minimal such that $\chi \in SL$.

Lemma 10.8 *There is a random Turing machine M' running in polynomial time which on input $\chi \in SL$ outputs $\chi' \in SL'$, where $L' = \{p_1, ..., p_{n^2}\}$ such that*

(i) $\chi' \models \chi$

(ii) If χ is satisfiable then with probability at least $\frac{1}{4n}$ there is a unique valuation V on the propositional variables occuring in χ' satisfying χ'.

Proof The first part of the proof consists in obtaining an estimate of a certain probability. Let $\emptyset \neq S \subseteq \{0, 1\}^n$, $\vec{0} = \langle 0, 0, ..., 0 \rangle \notin S$. We are thinking here of S as a set of vectors over $\mathbb{Z}_2$ (so $1 + 1 = 0$).

Let $P_k(S)$ be the probability that for random (with respect to the uniform distribution) $\vec{w}_k, \vec{w}_{k-1}, ..., \vec{w}_2 \in \{0, 1\}^n$, there is some $1 \leq i \leq k$ such that

$$|\{\vec{u} \in S \mid \vec{u}\vec{w}_k^T = \vec{u}\vec{w}_{k-1}^T = ... = \vec{u}\vec{w}_{i+1}^T = 0\}| = 1.$$

Let

$$T_k = \min\{P_k(S) \mid \emptyset \neq S \subseteq \{0, 1\}^n, \vec{0} \notin S, \ Rank(S) \leq k\}.$$

Then $T_1 = 1$ since if $Rank(S) = 1$ then $|S| = 1$. Let $k = Rank(S)$ and let $\{\vec{u}_1, ..., \vec{u}_k\}$ be a maximal linearly independent subset of S. Let A be a non-singular matrix over $\mathbb{Z}_2$ such that $\vec{u}_i A = \vec{e}_i$ for $i = 1, ..., k$ where $\vec{e}_i$ is the vector with 1 in the i'th coordinate and 0 elsewhere. Then for random $\vec{w}_k$,

$$Prob(Rank\{\vec{u} \in S \mid \vec{u}\vec{w}_k^T = 0\} = 0)$$

$$= \ Prob(Rank\{\vec{u} \in S \mid \vec{u}AA^{-1}\vec{w}_k^T = 0\} = 0)$$

$$= \ Prob(Rank\{\vec{u} \in SA \mid \vec{u}A^{-1}\vec{w}_k^T = 0\} = 0)$$

$$= \ Prob(Rank\{\vec{u} \in SA \mid \vec{u}\vec{w}_k^T = 0\} = 0),$$
$$\text{since } A^{-1} \text{ permutes } \{0, 1\}^n,$$

$$\leq \ Prob(\vec{e}_i\vec{w}_k^T = 1 \text{ for } i = 1, ..., k) = \frac{1}{2^k}.$$

Similarly

$$Prob(Rank\{\vec{u} \in S \mid \vec{u}\vec{w}_k^T = 0\} = k)$$

$$= Prob(Rank\{\vec{u} \in SA \mid \vec{u}\vec{w}_k^T = 0\} = k)$$

$$= Prob(\vec{e}_i\vec{w}_k^T = 0 \text{ for } i = 1, ..., k) = \frac{1}{2^k}.$$

Hence for $k \geq 2$, $k = Rank(S)$ and random $\vec{w}_k$,

$$P_k(S) \geq Prob(0 < Rank\{\vec{u} \in S \mid \vec{u}\vec{w}_k^T = 0\} < k) \cdot T_{k-1}$$

$$\geq (1 - \frac{2}{2^k}) \cdot T_{k-1}.$$

Hence $T_2 \geq (1 - \frac{2}{4}) \cdot T_1 = \frac{1}{2}$ and

$$T_k \geq \min\{T_{k-1}, (1 - 2^{1-k}) \cdot T_{k-1}\} \geq \prod_{i=3}^{k}(1 - 2^{1-i}) \cdot T_2$$

$$\geq T_2 \cdot (1 - \sum_{i=3}^{k} 2^{1-i}) \geq \frac{1}{2} \cdot \frac{1}{2} = \frac{1}{4}.$$

We shall shortly use this bound. First however we need to define some sentences. Let χ be as in the statement of the lemma with n maximal such that p_n occurs in χ. We may assume each of $p_1, ..., p_n$ occurs in χ (otherwise rename the variables in χ so that this does hold and revert to the original names at the conclusion of the proof).

In what follows q_i will be additional distinct propositional variables, q_{ij} will stand for p_{in+j}, and the $\vec{w}$ will range over $\{0,1\}^n$. Let $\phi(p_1, ..., p_n, q_1, ..., q_n)$ be $(p_1 \leftrightarrow q_1) \wedge \bigwedge_{j=2}^{n}(q_j \leftrightarrow \neg(q_{j-1} \leftrightarrow p_j))$ where as usual $p \leftrightarrow q$ abbreviates $(p \rightarrow q) \wedge (q \rightarrow p)$ and $p \rightarrow q$ abbreviates $\neg p \vee q$. Then for any valuation V on $\{p_1, ..., p_n, q_1, ..., q_n\}$

$$V(\phi) = 1 \Leftrightarrow \text{ for } 1 \leq j \leq n, \ V(q_j) = \sum_{m \leq j} V(p_m) \mod 2.$$

Thus given a valuation V on $\{p_1, ..., p_n\}$, V has a unique extension V^+ to $\{p_1, ..., p_n, q_1, ..., q_n\}$ with $V^+(\phi(\vec{p}, \vec{q})) = 1$.

Let $\eta(p_1, ..., p_n, w_1, ..., w_n, q_1, ..., q_n)$ be

$$\neg q_n \wedge \phi(p_1^{w_1} \wedge p_1, p_2^{w_2} \wedge p_2, ..., p_n^{w_n} \wedge p_n, q_1, ..., q_n).$$

Then given V a valuation on $\{p_1, ..., p_n\}$ there is at most one extension V^+ of V to $\{p_1, ..., p_n, q_1, ..., q_n\}$ satisfying $\eta(\vec{p}, \vec{w}, \vec{q})$, and such a V^+ exists just if

$$\langle V(p_1), ..., V(p_n)\rangle \cdot \langle w_1, ..., w_n\rangle^T = 0 \mod 2.$$

Let $\langle w_{i1}, w_{i2}, ..., w_{in}\rangle \in \{0, 1\}^n$ for $i = 2, ..., n$ and for $i \le m \le n$ let θ_m be

$$\chi \wedge \bigwedge_{i=2}^{m} \eta(p_1, ..., p_n, w_{i1}, ..., w_{in}, q_{i1}, ..., q_{in}) \quad (= \chi \text{ if } m = 1).$$

Then given V a valuation on $\{p_1, ..., p_n\}$ there is at most one extension V^+ of V to $\{p_1, ..., p_n, q_{21}, ..., q_{2n}, ..., q_{mn}\}$ satisfying θ_m, and such a V^+ exists just if $V(\chi) = 1$ and for $2 \le i \le m$, $\langle V(p_1), ..., V(p_n)\rangle\langle w_{i1}, ..., w_{in}\rangle^T = 0$. Hence, abbreviating $\langle V(p_1), ..., V(p_n)\rangle$ by $V(\vec{p})$,

$$|\{V^+ \mid V^+(\theta_m) = 1\}| = |\{V(\vec{p}) \mid V(\chi) = 1 \text{ and } V(\vec{p})\vec{w}_m^T = ... = V(\vec{p})\vec{w}_2^T = 0\}|.$$

We are now ready to describe M'. Given input $\chi \in SL$ (we assume each of $p_1, ..., p_n$ occurs in χ; if not the required amendments are straightforward) M' first checks if $V(\chi) = 1$ where $V(p_i) = 0$ for $i = 1, ..., n$. If so M' outputs

$$\chi' = \bigwedge_{i=1}^{n^2} \neg p_i.$$

Otherwise M' randomly generates $w_{ij} \in \{0, 1\}$, $1 \le j \le n$, $2 \le i \le n$, randomly picks $1 \le m \le n$ and outputs

$$\chi' = \theta_m \wedge \bigwedge_{i=m+1}^{n} \bigwedge_{j=1}^{n} q_{ij}.$$

Hence, by the estimate for T_n, if χ is satisfiable then with probability at least $\frac{1}{4n}$ there is a unique valuation on $\{p_1, ..., p_n, q_{21}, q_{22}, ..., q_{nn}\}$ satisfying χ', as required.
□

Proof of theorem 10.7 Assume on the contrary that we did have such a random Turing machine M running in polynomial time. We shall show $SAT \in RP$ (and hence the required contradiction) by describing a suitable random algorithm for deciding if $\chi \in SAT$ for $\chi \in SL$. Let M' be the random Turing machine of lemma 10.8.

Now suppose that on input χ, M' has yielded χ' and there is a unique valuation V satisfying χ'. We show how to guess V with a good probability of success. First notice that if $V(p_1) = 1$ then $\chi' \models p_1$ so if Bel is to satisfy $K = \{Bel(\chi') = 1, Bel(\neg \chi') = 0\}$ and (P3) we would have to have $Bel(p_1) = 1$. On the other hand if $V(p_1) = 0$ then $\chi' \models \neg p_1$ so for Bel satisfying K and $(P3)$ we would have to have $Bel(p_1) = 0$ (for if $Bel(p_1) > 0$ then $(P3)$ forces $Bel(\neg \chi') > 0$ since $p_1 \models \neg \chi'$).

Hence we can make a guess, $Z(p_1)$, for $V(p_1)$ by repeatedly running M on K, p_1, nk times (where k is a constant depending on δ) to obtain $\nu_1, ..., \nu_{nk}$ and defining

$$Z(p_1) \;\; = \;\; \begin{cases} 1 & \text{if the majority of the } \nu_i \text{ exceed } \tfrac{1}{2} \\ \\ 0 & \text{otherwise.} \end{cases}$$

Then if $V(p_1) = 1$, $Prob(\nu_i \leq \tfrac{1}{2}) < \tfrac{1}{2} - \delta$ (since with probability at least $\tfrac{1}{2} + \delta$, ν_i is within $\tfrac{1}{2} - \epsilon$ of 1) so, since the probability that $Z(p_1) = 0$ is less than it would be if $Prob(\nu_i \leq \tfrac{1}{2})$ were exactly $\tfrac{1}{2} - \delta$,

$$Prob(Z(p_1) = 0) \;\; \leq \;\; \sum_{\frac{nk}{2} \leq i \leq nk} (\tfrac{1}{2} - \delta)^i (\tfrac{1}{2} + \delta)^{nk-i} \binom{nk}{i}$$

$$\leq \;\; (\tfrac{1}{4} - \delta^2)^{\frac{nk}{2}} \sum_{i=0}^{nk} \binom{nk}{i} = (1 - 4\delta^2)^{\frac{nk}{2}}$$

and $Prob(Z(p_1) = 1) \geq 1 - \beta^{nk}$ where $\beta = \sqrt{1 - 4\delta^2} < 1$. Similarly if $V(p_1) = 0$ then $Prob(\nu_i \geq \tfrac{1}{2}) < \tfrac{1}{2} - \delta$ and again the probability that the majority do not exceed $\tfrac{1}{2}$ is at least $1 - \beta^{nk}$ for this same β. Hence

$$Prob(Z(p_1) = V(p_1)) \geq 1 - \beta^{nk}.$$

Repeating this with each of $p_1, ..., p_n$ in turn we see

$$Prob(Z(p_i) = V(p_i), \; i = 1, ..., n)) \geq (1 - \beta^{nk})^n \geq 1 - n\beta^{nk} > \frac{1}{2}$$

for this suitably large fixed k. Furthermore, by (i) of lemma 10.8, V satisfies χ so, by calculating $Z(\chi)$, we can confirm $\chi \in SAT$ with probability at least $\tfrac{1}{2}$.

Combining this last random algorithm with M' gives a random algorithm which on input χ confirms $\chi \in SAT$ with probability at least $(8n)^{-1}$ if $\chi \in SAT$ whilst clearly never confirming this if $\chi \notin SAT$. Thus repeating this last algorithm $8n$ times on χ will, if $\chi \in SAT$, confirm this with probability at least

$$1 - (1 - \frac{1}{8n})^{8n} \geq 1 - e^{-1}$$

and hence $SAT \in RP$ follows.   □

As with the question of testing consistency there are objections one might raise against this result as a criticism of the Watts Assumption. The most obvious of these is that in practice the expert gives comparatively large sets of rather short, simple constraints, whilst the proof of the above theorem used a very small set of (apparently) very complicated constraints. However this objection can be dismissed by replacing SAT by 3-SAT and observing that if χ is a conjunction of disjunctions of at most three literals then the relevant sentence, χ', may also be taken to be of this form since $q_j \leftrightarrow \neg(q_{j-1} \leftrightarrow (p_j^w \wedge p_j))$ is, by the disjunctive normal form theorem in the language $\{q_{j-1}, q_j, p_j\}$, logically equivalent to a conjunction of disjunctions of at most three literals. For $\chi' = \bigwedge_{s=1}^{k} \phi_{s1} \vee \phi_{s2} \vee \phi_{s3}$ with the ϕ_{si} literals (not necessarily distinct) the same proof goes through with constraint set K' consisting of

$$Bel(\phi_{s1} \vee \phi_{s2} \vee \phi_{s3}) = 1, \quad Bel(\neg\phi_{s1} \wedge \neg\phi_{s2} \wedge \neg\phi_{s3}) = 0, \quad s = 1, ..., k$$

in place of $K = \{Bel(\chi') = 1, \ Bel(\neg\chi') = 0\}$ provided Bel satisfies, in addition to $(P3)$, some conditions, which with $(P3)$, enable us to rebuild K. Sufficient conditions here would be

$(P4)$ If $Bel(\theta) = Bel(\phi) = 1$ then $Bel(\theta \wedge \phi) = 1$,

together with one of

$(P5)$ If $Bel(\theta) = Bel(\phi) = 0$ then $Bel(\theta \vee \phi) = 0$,

$(P6)$ If $Bel(\theta) = 1$ then $Bel(\neg\theta) = 0$.

Clearly then theorem 10.7 holds in this improved form for belief as probability, Dempster–Shafer belief, belief as $\mathbf{F}_1$, $\mathbf{F}_2$, $\mathbf{F}_3$ and belief as possibility.

(We remark here that the constraint set in the proof of theorem 10.6 can similarly be simplified to the form $\{Bel(\phi_{s1} \wedge \phi_{s2} \wedge \phi_{s3}) = 0 \mid s = 1, ..., k\}$ in a slightly enlarged language.)

Belief Networks and Complexity

A second objection that has been raised against the significance of results such as theorem 10.7, as criticisms of the Watts Assumption, is the claim that the expert's set of constraints may be much more structured than those considered in theorem 10.7, or its subsequent simplification. The most popular claim along these lines is that the expert's set of constraints corresponds to a *belief network*, as described in Chapter 9, together with the relevant independence assumptions. That is, there is a directed acyclic graph $G = \langle V, E \rangle$ whose set of vertices V is a set of propositional variables, $\{p_1, ..., p_n\} (= L)$, say, numbered in such a way that if $\langle p_i, p_j \rangle \in E$ then $i < j$ and K takes the form

$$Bel(p_i \mid p_{i_1}^{\epsilon_1} \wedge ... \wedge p_{i_{k_i}}^{\epsilon_{k_i}}) = b_{i \ i_1...i_{k_i}}^{\epsilon_1 \ \epsilon_2...\epsilon_{k_i}} \quad (\in [0, 1])$$

where $i \in \{1, ..., n\}$, $\epsilon_1, ..., \epsilon_{k_i} \in \{0, 1\}$ and

$$\{p_{i_1}, ..., p_{i_{k_i}}\} = \{q \in V \mid \langle q, p_i \rangle \in E\},$$

together with the independence assumptions that for $i \in \{1, ..., n\}$, $\epsilon_1, ..., \epsilon_{i-1} \in \{0, 1\}$,

$$Bel(p_i \mid p_1^{\epsilon_1} \wedge ... \wedge p_{i-1}^{\epsilon_{i-1}}) = Bel(p_i \mid p_{i_1}^{\epsilon_{i_1}} \wedge ... \wedge p_{i_{k_i}}^{\epsilon_{i_{k_i}}}).$$

As proved in Chapter 9 such a set of constraints has a unique solution. Thus the problem of consistency is completely avoided whilst the problem of computing a value of $Bel(\theta)$ consistent with K (and belief as probability) amounts to computing $Bel(\theta)$ for the solution to K.

The following theorem is due to Cooper [7].

Theorem 10.9 *Given a belief network K, G for L and propositional variable $p \in L$ the problem of deciding if $Bel(p) > 0$ (for Bel the probability function determined by this belief network) is NP-complete and hence, assuming $P \neq NP$, infeasible.*

Proof We first show that 3-SAT is reducible to the above problem in polynomial time. So let

$$\chi = \bigwedge_{s=1}^{k} p_{s_1}^{\lambda_{s_1}} \vee p_{s_2}^{\lambda_{s_2}} \vee p_{s_3}^{\lambda_{s_3}},$$

where the $\lambda_{s_i} \in \{0, 1\}$ and, say, $L = \{p_1, ..., p_n\}$. Let $e_1, ..., e_k, q_1, ..., q_k$ be new propositional variables, $L' = L \cup \{e_1, ..., e_k, q_1, ..., q_k\}$ and let G be the directed graph on vertices L' with just the following edges

$$\langle p_i, e_s \rangle \quad \text{if} \quad p_i \in \{p_{s_1}, p_{s_2}, p_{s_3}\},$$

$$\langle e_s, q_s \rangle \quad s = 1, ..., k,$$

$$\langle q_{s-1}, q_s \rangle \quad s = 2, ..., k.$$

Let K consist of

$$Bel(p_i) \qquad = \tfrac{1}{2} \qquad i = 1, ..., n,$$

$$Bel(e_s \mid p_{s_1}^{\nu_1} \wedge p_{s_2}^{\nu_2} \wedge p_{s_3}^{\nu_3}) = \begin{cases} 0 & \text{if all } \nu_i \neq \lambda_{s_i} \\ 1 & \text{otherwise} \end{cases} \quad s = 1, ..., k,$$

$$Bel(q_s \mid e_s^{\nu_1} \wedge q_{s-1}^{\nu_2}) \qquad = \begin{cases} 1 & \text{if } \nu_1 = \nu_2 = 1 \\ 0 & \text{otherwise} \end{cases} \quad s = 1, ..., k,$$

where q_{s-1} is omitted if $s = 1$. Then, together with the independence assumptions, these K, G form a belief network. By the analysis in Chapter 9 if Bel is the solution to these constraints then

$$Bel(q_k) > 0 \Leftrightarrow$$
$$\Leftrightarrow \sum \prod_{s=1}^{k} Bel(q_s^{\epsilon_s} \mid e_s^{\tau_s} \wedge q_{s-1}^{\epsilon_{s-1}}) \prod_{s=1}^{k} Bel(e_s^{\tau_s} \mid p_{s1}^{\delta_{s1}} \wedge p_{s2}^{\delta_{s2}} \wedge p_{s3}^{\delta_{s3}}) \prod_{i=1}^{n} Bel(p_i^{\delta_i}) > 0$$

where this sum is over $\vec{\epsilon}, \vec{\tau}, \vec{\delta} \in \{0, 1\}$ with $\epsilon_k = 1$. But this can be non-zero just if $\epsilon_k = \epsilon_{k-1} = \ldots = \epsilon_1 = \tau_1 = \ldots = \tau_k = 1$ so, since the last term in this product is $2^{-n} \neq 0$,

$$Bel(q_n) > 0 \Leftrightarrow$$

$$\Leftrightarrow \quad \text{for some } \vec{\delta} \in \{0, 1\}^n, \ Bel(e_s \mid p_{s1}^{\delta_{s1}} \wedge p_{s2}^{\delta_{s2}} \wedge p_{s3}^{\delta_{s3}}) > 0 \quad \text{for } s = 1, \ldots, k$$

$$\Leftrightarrow \quad \text{for some } \vec{\delta} \in \{0, 1\}^n, \ \delta_{s_1} = \lambda_{s_1} \text{ or } \delta_{s_2} = \lambda_{s_2} \text{ or } \delta_{s_3} = \lambda_{s_3} \quad \text{for } s = 1, \ldots, k$$

$$\Leftrightarrow \quad \text{for some } \vec{\delta} \in \{0, 1\}^n, \ V(\chi) = 1 \text{ where } V \text{ is the valuation } V(p_i) = \delta_i$$

$$\Leftrightarrow \quad \chi \text{ is satisfiable.}$$

Finally, to show that the problem of deciding if $Bel(p_i) > 0$, for Bel the solution of a belief network K, G, is in NP, notice that, in the notation of Chapter 9, we can verify $Bel(p_j) > 0$ by guessing $\epsilon_1, \ldots, \epsilon_{i-1} \in \{0, 1\}$ and checking that for $i \leq j$ each of

$$c_{i i_1 \ldots i_{k_i}}^{\epsilon_i \epsilon_{i_1} \ldots \epsilon_{i_{k_i}}}$$

is non-zero (where $\epsilon_j = 1$). $\qquad \square$

Theorem 10.9 shows that, assuming $P \neq NP$, we cannot hope, in general, to compute $Bel(\theta)$ *exactly* for Bel satisfying a belief network. However we can probabilistically approximate this value arbitrarily closely as follows:

Given a belief network K, G as in Chapter 9, randomly give values $V(p_i) \in \{0, 1\}$ as follows: having determined $V(p_j)$ for $j < i$, randomly set $V(p_i) = 1$ (and 0 otherwise) with probability

$$b_{i \, i_1 \ldots i_{k_i}}^{V(p_{i_1}) \ldots V(p_{i_{k_i}})}.$$

Then

$$Prob(V(p_i) = 1 \mid V(p_j) = \delta_j, \ 1 \le j < i) =$$

$$= \ Prob(V(p_i) = 1 \mid V(p_{i_j}) = \delta_{i_j}, \ 1 \le j \le k_i)$$

$$= \ b_{i \ i_1 \dots i_{k_i}}^{\delta_{i_1} \dots \delta_{i_{k_i}}}.$$

Hence the probability function *Bel* defined by

$$Bel(p_1^{\epsilon_1} \wedge \dots \wedge p_n^{\epsilon_n}) \ = \ Prob(V(p_i) = \epsilon_i, \ i = 1, \dots, n),$$

$$= \ Prob(V(p_1^{\epsilon_1} \wedge \dots \wedge p_n^{\epsilon_n}) = 1),$$

must be the solution to the belief network and

$$Bel(\theta) = Prob(V(\theta) = 1) = \text{Expected value of } V(\theta).$$

Now repeating the above construction m times to produce $V_1, \dots, V_m$ we have, by elementary statistics,

$$\frac{1}{4m} \ge \frac{Bel(\theta)(1 - Bel(\theta))}{m} = \frac{1}{m} \cdot Var(V_1(\theta)) = Var\left(\sum_{i=1}^{m} \frac{V_i(\theta)}{m}\right)$$

$$\ge Prob\left(\left|\frac{\sum_{i=1}^{m} V_i(\theta)}{m} - Bel(\theta)\right| \ge \epsilon\right) \cdot \epsilon^2$$

for any $\epsilon > 0$ (directly from the definition of variance). Hence given $\epsilon > 0$ for $m \ge \frac{1}{\epsilon^3}$,

$$Prob\left(\left|\frac{\sum_{i=1}^{m} V_i(\theta)}{m} - Bel(\theta)\right| \ge \epsilon\right) \le \frac{\epsilon}{4},$$

the required probabilistic approximation to $Bel(\theta)$. (The bound $\frac{1}{\epsilon^3}$ can be significantly improved but, for completeness, we have settled for it here.)

Whilst the ability to determine, probabilistically, approximations to $Bel(\theta)$ for *Bel* satisfying a belief network is a very significant improvement over the situation for general K (as witnessed by theorem 10.7) the problem of determining *conditional beliefs* still remains infeasible (assuming $RP \ne NP$) as the following theorem shows.

Theorem 10.10 *Let $\epsilon, \delta > 0$ and assume $RP \ne NP$. Then there is no random Turing machine running in polynomial time which on input of a belief network K, G and propositional variables p, q outputs a number ν such that with probability at least $\frac{1}{2} + \delta$,*

$$|Bel(p \mid q) - \nu| \le \frac{1}{2} - \epsilon$$

where Bel is the solution of the belief network. (We count this as vacuously holding if $Bel(q) = 0$.)

Proof The proof is very similar to that of theorem 10.7 and we shall only indicate the new feature. Suppose, on the contrary, such a Turing machine did exist. Let χ' be as in the proof of theorem 10.7. By later remarks we may assume

$$\chi' = \bigwedge_{s=1}^{k} p_{s_1}^{\lambda_{s_1}} \vee p_{s_2}^{\lambda_{s_2}} \vee p_{s_3}^{\lambda_{s_3}}.$$

Let K, G now be as in the proof of theorem 10.9 (with χ' in place of χ). Now suppose that there was a unique valuation, V say, satisfying χ'. Then, as in the proof of theorem 10.9 again, for the solution Bel to K, G we would have $Bel(q_k) > 0$ so $Bel(\ |\ q_k)$ is well defined. Furthermore, directly from the fact that Bel satisfies K, we see that

$$Bel(e_k \wedge q_{k-1} \mid q_k) = \frac{Bel(e_k \wedge q_{k-1} \wedge q_k)}{Bel(e_k \wedge q_{k-1} \wedge q_k) + Bel(\neg(e_k \wedge q_{k-1}) \wedge q_k)} = 1,$$

since $Bel(\neg(e_k \wedge q_{k-1}) \wedge q_k) = 0$, and similarly

$$Bel(e_s \wedge q_{s-1} \mid q_k) = 1 \quad \text{for } s = 1, ..., k,$$

$$Bel(p_{s_1}^{\lambda_{s_1}} \vee p_{s_2}^{\lambda_{s_2}} \vee p_{s_3}^{\lambda_{s_3}} \mid q_k) = 1 \quad \text{for } s = 1, ..., k.$$

Thus $Bel(\chi' \mid q_k) = 1$ and, as in the proof of theorem 10.7, $Bel(p_1 \mid q_k) = 1$ if $V(p_1) = 1$ and 0 otherwise, and the result follows. □

From these results it would seem that the Watts assumption might still be criticised even in the context of the expert's knowledge being in the form of a belief network, since in practice experts appear to experience no 'computational difficulties' when replying to questions about their simple conditional beliefs. Of course it may be that one might put further simplifying conditions on the belief networks in order to facilitate speedy computations of conditional beliefs (indeed an extensive literature already exists, see for example [26], [58], [42]) and so re-instate the Watts Assumption. Such a stand however presumably obliges one to explain how the expert might produce such a belief network from the limited data at his disposal and why nature should allow herself to be accurately modelled in this way.

Chapter 11

Uncertain Reasoning in the Predicate Calculus

The first ten chapters of this book have been built around question Q which in turn was an abstract formalization of the sort of problems arising in examples such as $\mathbb{E}$. In this case question Q was formulated within the propositional calculus. However there are examples of uncertain reasoning where the propositional calculus is too simple to provide a faithful formalization. In such cases it is necessary to use a more expressive logical calculus. In this and the following chapter we shall consider one such extention, uncertain reasoning in the predicate calculus.

To give an example where this seems the most natural logic to use suppose I am running a program which at one point requires my newly acquired computer to randomly pick either zero or one. After running the program ten times I happen to scan through the printout and notice that in fact a zero was chosen each time. What belief should I give to a zero being chosen when I next run the program? What belief should I give to the assertion that I will always get a zero when I run the program (on this computer of course)? Before ever I started I would clearly have been inclined to give the former belief $\frac{1}{2}$ and the latter belief 0. But now, after ten zeros? (Actually this situation did once happen to me, only it was a random number between 0 and 99 which was chosen and it always came out to be 58. So now you know which raffle ticket to choose!)

To formalize this accurately within the propositional calculus seems difficult and problematic at best (although we shall briefly reconsider this point at the end of this chapter). However there is a clear formalization in the predicate calculus. Namely let c_i be a constant symbol standing for the ith run and let P be a unary relation symbol such that $P(c_i)$ is interpreted as 'zero is chosen on the ith run'. Then our knowledge base, K say, consists of

$$Bel(P(c_i)) = 1 \quad i = 1, \ldots, 10$$

and the question is what value should be given to $Bel(P(c_{11}))$? to $Bel(\forall x P(x))$? on the basis of K. Again, as for question Q, the quest is to understand the mechanism and justification by which an intelligent agent might form these beliefs for the purpose of prediction.

Notice that implicit in this example is the assumed existence of an infinite (or at least very large) sequence of possible runs $c_1, c_2, c_3, \ldots$ which fill the universe, or domain, of discourse so that the variable in $\forall x P(x)$ is assumed to range over exactly these c_i, $i \in \mathbb{N}^+$, where $\mathbb{N}^+$ is the set of non-zero natural numbers. These observations motivate the following general formalization.

A Formalization

In order to keep things as simple and elegant as possible we shall work in a language $\mathcal{L}$ for the predicate calculus with just a finite, non-empty, set $P\mathcal{L}$ of relation symbols, constant symbols a_i for $i \in \mathbb{N}$ and no other constant or function symbols. Let $F\mathcal{L}$, $S\mathcal{L}$ denote the set of formulae, sentences of $\mathcal{L}$ respectively. We shall assume some familiarity with the predicate calculus, as might, for example, be found in Mendelson [48]. In particular we shall assume the completeness theorem, i.e. that $\Gamma \vDash \theta$, $\Gamma \vdash \theta$, are equivalent for $\theta \in S\mathcal{L}$, $\Gamma \subseteq S\mathcal{L}$, without further mention.

Within this framework we shall be interested in the following question:

Q' *Given a consistent set K of constraints*

$$\sum_{j=1}^{r} a_{ij} Bel(\theta_j) = b_i, \quad i = 1, \ldots, m$$

with the $\theta_j \in S\mathcal{L}$, $a_{ij}, b_i \in \mathbb{R}$ and $Bel : S\mathcal{L} \to [0, 1]$ what value should be given to $Bel(\theta)$ for $\theta \in S\mathcal{L}$?

Again the word *should* in Q' is to be read as an appeal to find justifications for assigning particular values to $Bel(\theta)$. Similarly *consistent* will mean having a solution, Bel, satisfying whatever additional assumptions are in force at that time.

Within the predicate calculus this question poses far more difficulties than it did for the propositional calculus and we shall, in fact, only consider it in some rather special cases. (Indeed we have already taken a simplifying step by ignoring conditional constraints.)

As for the propositional calculus it would be most exceptional for K to determine $Bel(\theta)$ uniquely for $\theta \in S\mathcal{L}$ so it is necessary to make further assumptions about Bel, etc. One commonly made assumption, which we shall mainly concentrate on in this chapter, is that of identifying belief (values) with probability.

Belief as Probability

We say that $Bel : S\mathcal{L} \to [0, 1]$ is a probability function if for all $\theta, \phi, \exists x \psi(x) \in S\mathcal{L}$,

$(PP1)$ If $\models \theta$ then $Bel(\theta) = 1$.

$(PP2)$ If $\models \neg(\theta \wedge \phi)$ then $Bel(\theta \vee \phi) = Bel(\theta) + Bel(p)$.

$(PP3)$ $Bel(\exists x \psi(x)) = \sup_n Bel\left(\bigvee_{i=0}^n \psi(a_i)\right)$.

$(PP1\text{--}2)$ are direct translations of $(P1\text{--}2)$ into the predicate calculus and ana-logues of propositions 2.1, 2.2 and theorem 2.3 (which we shall still refer to by these names) go through as before. (We shall shortly see that by lemma 11.1, $\models \theta$ could be replaced in $(PP1)$ by 'θ is true in all term structures $M \in TL$', etc.)

Condition $(PP3)$ is sometimes refered to as Gaifman's condition. It in some sense captures the idea that the a_i constitute the whole of the universe. Notice that by $(PP1\text{--}2)$ it is equivalent to

$$Bel(\exists x \psi(x)) = \sum_{i=0}^{\infty} Bel(\psi(a_i) \wedge \bigwedge_{j<i} \neg\psi(a_j))$$

since

$$\sup_n Bel\left(\bigvee_{i=0}^n \psi(a_i)\right) = \sup_n Bel\left(\bigvee_{i=0}^n (\psi(a_i) \wedge \bigwedge_{j<i} \neg\psi(a_j))\right)$$

$$= \sup_n (\sum_{i=0}^n Bel(\psi(a_i) \wedge \bigwedge_{j<i} \neg\psi(a_j))$$

$$= \sum_{i=0}^{\infty} Bel(\psi(a_i) \wedge \bigwedge_{j<i} \neg\psi(a_j)).$$

Gaifman's condition is also rather natural within the following context. Suppose we define for $\theta, \psi \in SL$,

$$\theta \equiv \psi \quad \text{if} \quad \models \theta \leftrightarrow \psi \quad (\text{equivalently} \quad \vdash \theta \leftrightarrow \psi)$$

and

$$\bar{\theta} = \{\phi \in SL \mid \theta \equiv \phi\},$$

$$\overline{SL} = \{\bar{\theta} \mid \theta \in SL\},$$

$$\bar{\theta} \wedge \bar{\psi} = \overline{\theta \wedge \psi}, \quad \bar{\theta} \vee \bar{\psi} = \overline{\theta \vee \psi}, \quad \neg\bar{\theta} = \overline{\neg\theta}, \quad \mathbf{0} = \overline{\theta \wedge \neg\theta}, \quad \mathbf{1} = \overline{\theta \vee \neg\theta}.$$

Then $\wedge$, $\vee$, $\neg$ are well defined operations on $\overline{SL}$ and $\langle \overline{SL}, \wedge, \vee, \neg, \mathbf{0}, \mathbf{1} \rangle$ is a Boolean algebra (exactly analogous to the Lindenbaum algebra of SL from Chapter 4) and we can again define a partial ordering by

$$\bar{\theta} \leq \bar{\psi} \Leftrightarrow \bar{\theta} \wedge \bar{\psi} = \bar{\theta} \Leftrightarrow \bar{\theta} \vee \bar{\psi} = \bar{\psi} \Leftrightarrow \models (\theta \rightarrow \psi).$$

Furthermore, in this algebra,

$$\overline{\exists x \psi(x)} = \bigvee_i \overline{\psi(a_i)} = \bigvee_i \overline{\psi(a_i) \wedge \bigwedge_{j<i} \neg \psi(a_j)}. \qquad (11.1)$$

(Recall, for a Boolean algebra $\mathcal{B}$, $b = \bigvee_{\nu \in C} b_\nu$ means that $b_\nu \leq b$, i.e. $b_\nu = b_\nu \wedge b$, for all $\nu \in C$ and that if $a \in \mathcal{B}$ and $b_\nu \leq a$ for all $\nu \in C$ then $b \leq a$.) To see (11.1) notice that $\models \psi(a_i) \rightarrow \exists x \psi(x)$ so $\overline{\psi(a_i)} \leq \overline{\exists x \psi(x)}$ for all $i \in \mathbb{N}$.

Conversely suppose $\overline{\psi(a_i)} \leq \overline{\eta}$ for all $i \in \mathbb{N}$. Then as above $\vdash \psi(a_i) \rightarrow \eta$. Pick i such that a_i does not appear in η. Then replacing a_i throughout the proof of $\psi(a_i) \rightarrow \eta$ by an unused free variable x yields a proof of $\psi(x) \rightarrow \eta$, and from this it is straightforward to obtain a proof of $\exists x \psi(x) \rightarrow \eta$, so $\overline{\exists x \psi(x)} \leq \overline{\eta}$, as required. The second identity is straightforward to prove.

Now notice that by proposition 2.1, $(PP1\text{-}2)$ imply that if $\models (\theta \leftrightarrow \phi)$ then $Bel(\theta) = Bel(\phi)$. Hence if Bel satisfies $(PP1\text{-}2)$ we can unambiguously define $\overline{Bel} : \overline{S\mathcal{L}} \rightarrow [0,1]$ by

$$\overline{Bel}(\overline{\theta}) = Bel(\theta) \quad \text{for } \theta \in S\mathcal{L}.$$

Furthermore, $(PP1\text{-}2)$ will ensure that $\overline{Bel}$ is a measure on the Boolean algebra $\overline{S\mathcal{L}}$. (Recall that $\mu : \mathcal{B} \rightarrow [0,1]$ is a measure if $\mu(\mathbf{0}) = 0$, $\mu(\mathbf{1}) = 1$ and $\mu(a \vee b) = \mu(a) + \mu(b)$ for $a, b \in \mathcal{B}$, $a \wedge b = \mathbf{0}$. Recall also that μ is countably additive (or a σ-measure) if in addition $\mu(b) = \sum_{i=0}^{\infty} \mu(b_i)$ whenever $b = \bigvee_{i=0}^{\infty} b_i$ in $\mathcal{B}$ with the b_i disjoint, i.e. $b_i \wedge b_j = \mathbf{0}$ for $i \neq j$.) Condition $(PP3)$ is now equivalent to

$$\overline{Bel}\left(\bigvee_i \overline{\psi(a_i) \wedge \bigwedge_{j<i} \neg \psi(a_j)}\right) = \sum_i \overline{Bel}\left(\overline{\psi(a_i) \wedge \bigwedge_{j<i} \neg \psi(a_j)}\right),$$

equivalently

$$\overline{Bel}\left(\bigvee_i \overline{\psi(a_i)}\right) = \sup_n \overline{Bel}\left(\overline{\psi(a_1)} \vee \dots \vee \overline{\psi(a_n)}\right),$$

that is, $\overline{Bel}$ *preserves* the supremum in (11.1).

There is a natural connection between functions Bel satisfying $(PP1\text{-}3)$ and *term structures* for $\mathcal{L}$. Precisely, we call M a term structure for $\mathcal{L}$ if M is a structure for $\mathcal{L}$ with universe (domain) $|M| = \{a_i \mid i \in \mathbb{N}\}$ and each constant symbol a_i of $\mathcal{L}$ is interpreted in M as itself. We use $T\mathcal{L}$ to denote the set of term structures of $\mathcal{L}$.

Given $M \in T\mathcal{L}$, if we define $Bel : S\mathcal{L} \rightarrow \{0,1\}$ (not $[0,1]$, notice!) by

$$Bel(\theta) = \begin{cases} 1 & \text{if } M \models \theta \\ \\ 0 & \text{otherwise} \end{cases}$$

then it is easy to see that *Bel* satisfies (PP1–3). Conversely any $Bel : S\mathcal{L} \to \{0, 1\}$ determines such an $M \in T\mathcal{L}$. Namely put $|M| = \{a_i \mid i \in \mathbb{N}\}$ and define the interpretation of P in M for $P \in P\mathcal{L}$, P j-ary, so that

$$M \models P(a_{i_1}, ..., a_{i_j}) \Leftrightarrow Bel(P(a_{i_1}, ..., a_{i_j})) = 1.$$

Then it is easy to check by induction on the length of $\theta \in S\mathcal{L}$ that

$$M \models \theta \Leftrightarrow Bel(\theta) = 1.$$

The following lemma concerning term structures will be used extensively.

Lemma 11.1 *Let $\Delta \subseteq F\mathcal{L}$ be finite. Then Δ is consistent if and only if Δ is satisfied in some $M \in T\mathcal{L}$.*

Proof If Δ is consistent then by the standard Henkin style proof of the completeness theorem Δ is satisfied in some countably infinite structure N for $\mathcal{L}'$ where $\mathcal{L}'$ is the finite sublanguage of $\mathcal{L}$ with the same relation symbols as $\mathcal{L}$ but with only those constant symbols a_i which actually appear in Δ. Furthermore each such a_i will be interpreted as a distinct element $a_i^{(N)}$ of $|N|$. Now extend N to a structure for $\mathcal{L}$ by interpreting the a_i not appearing in Δ so that the $a_j^{(N)}$ for $j \in \mathbb{N}$ are distinct and enumerate $|N|$. Finally renaming $a_j^{(N)}$ for $j \in \mathbb{N}$ as a_j itself provides an isomorphic copy, M, of N which is a term structure and, since it is isomorphic to N, satisfies Δ.

The converse is, of course, immediate.   □

Henceforth until further notice we shall assume that *Bel* satisfies (PP1-3).

A Representation Theorem

Recall from Chapter 2 that every probability function on $S\mathcal{L}$ is uniquely determined by its values on the atoms of $S\mathcal{L}$. We now show that a similar result (due to Gaifman [23]) holds in our present setup although now we no longer have atoms because of the infinitely many constants in $\mathcal{L}$.

In the following theorem let $QFS\mathcal{L}$ denote the set of quantifier-free sentences of $\mathcal{L}$. The sentences in $QFS\mathcal{L}$ can be thought of as sentences of the propositional language whose propositional variables are the $P(a_{i_1}, ..., a_{i_j})$ where P is a j-ary relation symbol from $P\mathcal{L}$, $j \in \mathbb{N}$, and $i_1, ..., i_j \in \mathbb{N}$.

Theorem 11.2 *Let $\nu : QFS\mathcal{L} \to [0, 1]$ satisfy (PP1–2) for $\theta, \phi \in QFS\mathcal{L}$. Then there exists a unique extension $w : S\mathcal{L} \to [0, 1]$ of ν satisfying (PP1–3). In particular then, if $Bel : S\mathcal{L} \to [0, 1]$ satisfies (PP1–3) then Bel is uniquely determined by its restriction to $QFS\mathcal{L}$.*

For completeness (and because the details will be useful elsewhere) we shall give a full proof, which will require something of a diversion.

To make it easier (we hope) to see what is going on we shall reformulate things slightly (again!). For $\theta \in S\mathcal{L}$ let

$$T(\theta) = \{M \in T\mathcal{L} \mid M \models \theta\},$$

$$R = \{T(\theta) \mid \theta \in QFS\mathcal{L}\} \subseteq \mathcal{P}(T\mathcal{L}) \ (= \text{power set of } T\mathcal{L}).$$

Clearly

$$T(\theta \wedge \phi) = T(\theta) \cap T(\phi),$$

$$T(\theta \vee \phi) = T(\theta) \cup T(\phi),$$

$$T(\neg\theta) = T\mathcal{L} - T(\theta) \quad (\text{written } \neg T(\theta)),$$

$$T(\exists x \psi(x)) = \bigcup_i T(\psi(a_i)).$$

Thus R is closed under intersection, union, complement, so $\langle R, \cap, \cup, \neg, T\mathcal{L}, \emptyset \rangle$ is a Boolean algebra. (Indeed if $G(\bar{\theta}) = T(\theta)$ for $\theta \in S\mathcal{L}$ then the G is well defined and $G : \overline{S\mathcal{L}} \cong \langle \{T(\theta) \mid \theta \in S\mathcal{L}\}, \cap, \cup, \neg, T\mathcal{L}, \emptyset \rangle$.) Now define μ on R by $\mu(T(\theta)) = \nu(\theta)$ for $\theta \in QFS\mathcal{L}$. μ is well defined for if $\nvdash \theta \leftrightarrow \phi$ then one of $\theta \wedge \neg\phi$, $\neg\theta \wedge \phi$, must be consistent and hence $T(\theta \wedge \neg\phi) \neq 0$ or $T(\neg\theta \wedge \phi) \neq 0$ by lemma 11.1. Either way $T(\theta) \neq T(\phi)$. Thus $T(\theta) = T(\phi) \Rightarrow \vdash \theta \leftrightarrow \phi \Rightarrow \nu(\theta) = \nu(\phi)$ as required. It is now easy to check that μ is a measure on R.

Now define an outer measure on $\mathcal{P}(T\mathcal{L})$ by setting

$$\mu^*(X) = \inf\{\sum_{i=1}^{\infty} \mu(C_i) \mid X \subseteq \bigcup_i C_i \ \& \ C_i \in R\},$$

for $X \subseteq T\mathcal{L}$. Notice that since $T\mathcal{L} \in R$, $\mu^*(X) \leq \mu(T\mathcal{L}) = 1$.

Lemma 11.3 *For $X \in R$, $\mu^*(X) = \mu(X)$.*

Proof Clearly since $X \subseteq X$, $\mu^*(X) \leq \mu(X)$. Suppose then that $\mu^*(X) < \mu(X)$, say $C_i \in R$, $X \subseteq \bigcup_i C_i$ and $\sum_i \mu(C_i) < \mu(X)$. Without loss of generality we may assume that the C_i are subsets of X (otherwise replace C_i by $C_i \cap X$) and disjoint (otherwise replace C_i by $C_i - \bigcup_{j<i} C_j$). Let $T(\theta_n) = X - \bigcup_{i=0}^n C_i$, $\theta_n \in QFS\mathcal{L}$. Then θ_n is consistent, since otherwise $\mu(X - \bigcup_{i=0}^n C_i) = \nu(\theta_n) = 0$ so

$$\mu(X) = \mu(X - \bigcup_{i=0}^n C_i) + \mu(X \cap \bigcup_{i=0}^n C_i) = \mu(X \cap \bigcup_{i=0}^n C_i) = \mu(\bigcup_{i=0}^n C_i) = \sum_{i=0}^n \mu(C_i),$$

contradiction. Also $T(\theta_{n+1}) \subseteq T(\theta_n)$, implying, by lemma 11.1, that $\vdash \theta_{n+1} \rightarrow \theta_n$. Hence for each n, $\{\theta_i \mid i \leq n\}$ is consistent and so by compactness $\{\theta_i \mid i \in \mathbb{N}\}$ is consistent. Let $Y \supseteq \{\theta_i \mid i \in \mathbb{N}\}$ be a maximal consistent subset of $QFSL$. Then, clearly, Y determines a unique $M \in TL$ such that for all $\theta \in QFSL$, $M \models \theta \Leftrightarrow \theta \in Y$. In particular $M \models \theta_i$ for $i \in \mathbb{N}$ so $M \in X$ and $M \notin \bigcup_{i=0}^{n} C_i$ for all n. Thus $M \in X - \bigcup_i C_i$, contradicting $X \subseteq \bigcup_i C_i$, as required. $\qquad\square$

(Actually, we have shown rather more here, namely that if $X \subseteq \bigcup_i C_i$ then $X - \bigcup_{i=0}^{n} C_i = \emptyset$ for some n, i.e $X \subseteq \bigcup_{i=0}^{n} C_i$.)

Lemma 11.4 *For disjoint* $X, Y \subseteq TL$, $\mu^*(X \cup Y) \leq \mu^*(X) + \mu^*(Y)$.

Proof Let $\epsilon > 0$ and pick $C_i, D_i \in R$ such that $X \subseteq \bigcup_i C_i$, $Y \subseteq \bigcup_i D_i$ and

$$\sum_i \mu(C_i) < \mu^*(X) + \epsilon, \qquad \sum_i \mu(D_i) < \mu^*(Y) + \epsilon.$$

Then $X \cup Y \subseteq \bigcup_i C_i \cup \bigcup_i D_i$ and

$$\mu^*(X \cup Y) \leq \sum_i \mu(C_i) + \sum_i \mu(D_i) < \mu^*(X) + \epsilon + \mu^*(Y) + \epsilon,$$

so, since ϵ was arbitrary, $\mu^*(X \cup Y) \leq \mu^*(X) + \mu^*(Y)$. $\qquad\square$

Now define $R^+ = \{Y \subseteq TL \mid \text{For all } X \subseteq TL,\ \mu^*(X) \geq \mu^*(X \cup Y) + \mu^*(X \cap \neg Y)\}$. Notice by lemma 11.4 we could replace $\geq$ here by $=$.

Lemma 11.5 $R \subseteq R^+$.

Proof Let $C \in R$, $X \subseteq TL$. Let $\epsilon > 0$ and $D_i \in R$, $X \subseteq \bigcup_i D_i$ such that $\mu(X) + \epsilon > \sum_i \mu(D_i)$. Then $X \cap C \subseteq \bigcup_i(D_i \cap C)$, $X \cap \neg C \subseteq \bigcup_i(D_i \cap \neg C)$ and

$$
\begin{aligned}
\mu^*(X \cap C) + \mu^*(X \cap \neg C) &\leq \sum_i \mu(D_i \cap C) + \sum_i \mu(D_i \cap \neg C) \\
&= \sum_i \mu(D_i) < \mu^*(X) + \epsilon.
\end{aligned}
$$

Hence, since ϵ was arbitrary, $\mu^*(X \cap C) + \mu^*(X \cap \neg C) \geq \mu^*(X)$ as required. $\qquad\square$

Lemma 11.6 R^+ *is closed under complements and finite unions (and hence under finite intersections).*

Proof For complements the result is clear. So suppose $A, B \in R^+$. We wish to show $A \cup B \in R^+$. Let $X \subseteq TL$. Then

$$
\begin{aligned}
\mu^*(X) \ &\geq\ \mu^*(X \cap A) + \mu^*(X \cap \neg A), \qquad \text{since } A \in R^+, \\[4pt]
&\geq\ \mu^*(X \cap A \cap B) + \mu^*(X \cap A \cap \neg B) \\
&\quad + \mu^*(X \cap \neg A \cap B) + \mu^*(X \cap \neg A \cap \neg B), \qquad \text{since } B \in R^+.
\end{aligned}
$$

Now, by lemma 11.4 twice,

$$\mu^*(X \cap (A \cup B)) \ \leq \ \mu^*(X \cap A \cap B) + \mu^*(X \cap ((A \cap \neg B) \cup (\neg A \cap B)))$$

$$\leq \ \mu^*(X \cap A \cap B) + \mu^*(X \cap A \cap \neg B) + \mu^*(X \cap \neg A \cap B),$$

so

$$\mu^*(X) \ \geq \ \mu^*(X \cap (A \cup B)) + \mu^*(X \cap \neg A \cap \neg B)$$

$$= \ \mu^*(X \cap (A \cup B)) + \mu^*(X \cap \neg (A \cup B)),$$

as required.   □

Notice that by the previous two lemmas $\langle R^+, \cap, \cup, \neg, T\mathcal{L}, \emptyset \rangle$ is a Boolean algebra.

Lemma 11.7 R^+ *is closed under countable unions.*

Proof Suppose $A_i \in R^+$ for $i \in \mathbb{N}$. We wish to show $\bigcup_i A_i \in R^+$. We may assume the A_i are disjoint, otherwise replace A_i by $A_i - \bigcup_{j<i} A_j$ ($\in R^+$ by lemma 11.6). Let $X \subseteq T\mathcal{L}$. Then

$$\mu^*(X) \ \geq \ \mu^*(X \cap A_0) + \mu^*(X \cap \neg A_0), \quad \text{since } A_0 \in R^+,$$

$$\geq \ \mu^*(X \cap A_0) + \mu^*(\underbrace{X \cap \neg A_0 \cap A_1}_{X \cap A_1}) + \mu^*(X \cap \neg A_0 \cap \neg A_1),$$

$$\text{since } A_1 \in R^+ \text{ and } A_1 \subseteq \neg A_0.$$

Continuing in this fashion we see that

$$\mu^*(X) \geq \sum_{i=0}^{n} \mu^*(X \cap A_i) + \mu^*(X \cap \bigcap_{i=0}^{n} \neg A_i) \quad \text{for all } n \in \mathbb{N}.$$

Hence

$$\mu^*(X) \geq \sum_{i=0}^{n} \mu^*(X \cap A_i) + \mu^*(X \cap \bigcap_{i=0}^{\infty} \neg A_i) \quad \text{for all } n \in \mathbb{N},$$

since $Y \subseteq Z \Rightarrow \mu^*(Y) \leq \mu^*(Z)$. Thus

$$\mu^*(X) \geq \sum_{i} \mu^*(X \cap A_i) + \mu^*(X \cap \neg \bigcup_{i} A_i) \qquad (11.2)$$

Clearly it is now enough to show that

$$\sum_{i} \mu^*(X \cap A_i) \geq \mu^*(X \cap \bigcup_{i} A_i). \qquad (11.3)$$

To this end let $\epsilon > 0$ and pick for each i, $C_j^i \in R$ such that

$$\sum_j \mu(C_j^i) < \mu^*(X \cap A_i) + \frac{\epsilon}{2^{i+1}} \quad \text{and} \quad X \cap A_i \subseteq \bigcup_j C_j^i.$$

Then $X \cap \bigcup_i A_i \subseteq \bigcup_{i,j} C_j^i$ and

$$\mu^*(X \cap \bigcup_i A_i) \leq \sum_{i,j} \mu(C_j^i) < \sum_i (\mu^*(X \cap A_i) + \frac{\epsilon}{2^{i+1}}) = \sum_i \mu^*(X \cap A_i) + \epsilon.$$

Hence, since ϵ was arbitrary, (11.3) follows as required.   □

Notice that putting $X = \bigcup_i A_i$ gives, by (11.2), (11.3)

Corollary 11.8 *For disjoint $A_i \in R^+$, $i \in \mathbb{N}$,*

$$\mu^*\left(\bigcup_i A_i\right) = \sum_i \mu^*(A_i).$$ □

Now let R^∞ be the smallest subset of $\mathcal{P}(T\mathcal{L})$ extending R and closed under complements and countable unions (and hence under intersections, unions, countable intersections etc.). Precisely

$$R^\infty = \bigcap \{B \mid \quad R \subseteq B \subseteq \mathcal{P}(T\mathcal{L}) \text{ and } B \text{ is closed}$$
$$\text{under countable unions and intersections}\}.$$

Clearly $R \subseteq R^\infty \subseteq R^+$. Define $\mu^\infty : R^\infty \to [0,1]$ by $\mu^\infty(A) = \mu^*(A)$ for $A \in R^\infty$. By lemma 11.3, μ^∞ agrees with μ on R and corollary 11.8 then shows μ^∞ to be a countably additive measure on R^∞. Furthermore μ^∞ is unique in the following sense. Suppose $R' \subseteq \mathcal{P}(T\mathcal{L})$ is closed under complements and countable unions, $R \subseteq R'$ and μ' is a countably additive measure on R' extending μ. Then it is easy to see that

$$\{A \in R^\infty \cap R' \mid \mu^\infty(A) = \mu'(A)\}$$

extends R and is closed under complements and countable unions. Hence, by minimality of R^∞, this set must be R^∞ and hence $\mu^\infty = \mu'$ on $R^\infty \subseteq R'$.

Proof of theorem 11.2 Using the above notation define $w : S\mathcal{L} \to [0,1]$ by $w(\theta) = \mu^\infty(T(\theta))$. Notice that since $T(\exists x \psi(x)) = \bigcup_i T(\psi(a_i))$, $T(\eta \vee \phi) = T(\eta) \cup T(\phi)$ etc., by induction on the length of $\theta \in S\mathcal{L}$, $T(\theta) \in R^\infty$ and μ^∞ is indeed defined on $T(\theta)$. Clearly $w \upharpoonright QFS\mathcal{L} = \nu$.

The required condition $(PP1)$ on w is clear since if $\models \theta$ then $T(\theta) = T\mathcal{L}$ so $w(\theta) = \mu^{\infty}(T\mathcal{L}) = 1$. For $(PP2)$ notice that if $\vdash \neg(\theta \wedge \phi)$ then $T(\theta) \cap T(\phi) = \emptyset$ so

$$
\begin{aligned}
w(\theta \vee \phi) &= \mu^{\infty}(T(\theta \vee \phi)) = \mu^{\infty}(T(\theta) \cup T(\phi)) \\
&= \mu^{\infty}(T(\theta)) + \mu^{\infty}(T(\phi)) = w(\theta) + w(\phi).
\end{aligned}
$$

Finally, for $(PP3)$,

$$
\begin{aligned}
w(\exists x \psi(x)) &= \mu^{\infty}(T(\exists x \psi(x))) \\[2mm]
&= \mu^{\infty}\left(\bigcup_i T(\psi(a_i)) \right) \\[2mm]
&= \mu^{\infty}\left(\bigcup_i \left(T(\psi(a_i)) \cap \bigcap_{j<i} \neg T(\psi(a_j)) \right) \right) \\[2mm]
&= \mu^{\infty}\left(\bigcup_i T\left(\psi(a_i) \wedge \bigwedge_{j<i} \neg\psi(a_j) \right) \right) \\[2mm]
&= \sum_i \mu^{\infty}\left(T\left(\psi(a_i) \wedge \bigwedge_{j<i} \neg\psi(a_j) \right) \right) \\[2mm]
&= \sup_n \left(\sum_{i=0}^{n} \mu^{\infty}\left(T\left(\psi(a_i) \wedge \bigwedge_{j<i} \neg\psi(a_j) \right) \right) \right) \\[2mm]
&= \sup_n \mu^{\infty}\left(T\left(\bigvee_{i=0}^{n} \left(\psi(a_i) \wedge \bigwedge_{j<i} \neg\psi(a_j) \right) \right) \right) \\[2mm]
&= \sup_n \mu^{\infty}\left(T\left(\bigvee_{i=0}^{n} \psi(a_i) \right) \right) = \sup_n w\left(\bigvee_{i=0}^{n} \psi(a_i) \right)
\end{aligned}
$$

as required.

To show the uniqueness we need the following proposition.

Proposition 11.9 *For* $Bel : S\mathcal{L} \to [0,1]$ *satisfying* $(PP1\text{-}3)$ *and* $\psi(x_1, ..., x_k) \in S\mathcal{L}$,

$$
Bel(\exists x_1, ..., x_k \psi(x_1, ..., x_k)) = \sup_n Bel\left(\bigvee_{i_1, ..., i_k \leq n} \psi(a_{i_1}, ..., a_{i_k}) \right).
$$

Proof That the right hand expression cannot exceed the left hand expression follows by proposition 2.1 since

$$\vdash \left[\bigvee_{i_1,\ldots,i_k \leq n} \psi(a_{i_1}, \ldots, a_{i_k}) \rightarrow \exists x_1, \ldots, x_k \psi(x_1, \ldots, x_k) \right].$$

We prove the reverse inequality by induction on k (for all ψ). If $k = 0, 1$ the result is clear so assume the result (for all ψ) for $k - 1$ and let $\epsilon > 0$. Pick n_1 such that

$$Bel(\exists x_1, \ldots, x_k \psi(x_1, \ldots, x_k))$$

$$\leq \epsilon + Bel \left(\bigvee_{i_1,\ldots,i_{k-1} \leq n_1} \exists x_k \psi(a_{i_1}, \ldots, a_{i_{k-1}}, x_k) \right) \tag{11.4}$$

and now pick $n \geq n_1$ such that for each $i_1, \ldots, i_{k-1} \leq n_1$,

$$Bel(\exists x_k \psi(a_{i_1}, \ldots, a_{i_{k-1}}, x_k)) \leq \frac{\epsilon}{n_1^{k-1}} + Bel \left(\bigvee_{i_k \leq n} \psi(a_{i_1}, \ldots, a_{i_k}) \right). \tag{11.5}$$

Now notice that if $\vdash (\theta_i \rightarrow \phi_i)$ for $i = 1, \ldots, m$ then $\vdash (\theta_i \leftrightarrow \theta_i \wedge \phi_i)$ so

$$Bel(\phi_i \wedge \neg\theta_i) = Bel(\phi_i) - Bel(\phi_i \wedge \theta_i) = Bel(\phi_i) - Bel(\theta_i)$$

and

$$Bel \left(\bigvee_i \phi_i \right) \leq Bel \left(\bigvee_i \theta_i \vee \bigvee_i (\phi_i \wedge \neg\theta_i) \right)$$

$$\leq Bel \left(\bigvee_i \theta_i \right) + Bel \left(\bigvee_i (\phi_i \wedge \neg\theta_i) \right)$$

$$\leq Bel \left(\bigvee_i \theta_i \right) + \sum_i (Bel(\phi_i) - Bel(\theta_i)).$$

Applying this and (11.5) we obtain

$$Bel \left(\bigvee_{i_1,\ldots,i_{k-1} \leq n_1} \exists x_k \psi(a_{i_1}, \ldots, a_{i_{k-1}}, x_k) \right)$$

$$\leq Bel \left(\bigvee_{i_1,\ldots,i_{k-1} \leq n_1} \bigvee_{i_k \leq n} \psi(a_{i_1}, \ldots, a_{i_{k-1}}, a_{i_k}) \right) + \epsilon$$

$$\leq Bel \left(\bigvee_{i_1,\ldots,i_k \leq n} \psi(a_{i_1}, \ldots, a_{i_k}) \right) + \epsilon,$$

which with (11.4) and the arbitrariness of ϵ gives the required reverse inequality. $\square$

Using this proposition we can now show the required uniqueness of w. For suppose also that $w' : SL \rightarrow [0,1]$ satisfies $(PP1\text{--}3)$ and $w' \upharpoonright QFSL = \nu$, but $w'(\theta) \neq w(\theta)$ for some $\theta \in SL$. By the prenex normal form theorem (see, e.g., Mendelson [48]) θ is logically equivalent to a sentence in prenex normal form, so by proposition 2.1 we may assume θ is already of this form, say

$$\theta = \exists \vec{x}_1 \forall \vec{x}_2 \exists \vec{x}_3 ... Q\vec{x}_r \phi(\vec{x}_1, \vec{x}_2, ..., \vec{x}_r),$$

where ϕ is quantifier-free, $\vec{x}_1$ has length k and $Q = \exists$ if r is odd, $Q = \forall$ if r is even. (If θ started with a universal quantifier, just replace θ by $\neg \theta$ noticing that, still, $w(\theta) \neq w'(\theta)$.) Further we may assume θ chosen so that r is minimal. Clearly $r > 0$ since w and w' agree on $QFSL$. But then proposition 11.9 yields an immediate contradiction since

$$\bigvee_{i_1,...,i_k \leq n} \forall \vec{x}_2 \exists \vec{x}_3 ... Q\vec{x}_r \phi(a_{i_1}, ..., a_{i_k}, \vec{x}_2, ..., \vec{x}_r)$$

is logically equivalent to a sentence in a prenex normal form with only $r-1$ alternating blocks of quantifiers and hence must get the same value for both w and w'. This finally completes the proof of theorem 11.2. $\square$

The importance of theorem 11.2 is that it shows us that to specify Bel satisfying $(PP1\text{--}3)$ it is enough to specify Bel on $QFSL$ satisfying $(PP1\text{--}2)$. This then puts us in a situation much closer to the propositional calculus except that we now have infinitely many 'propositional variables' $P(a_{i_1}, ..., a_{i_j})$. Indeed we do not need to specify Bel on all of $QFSL$. For, given $n \in \mathbb{N}$, let $\sigma_1^n, ..., \sigma_{k_n}^n$ run through all sentences of the form

$$\bigwedge_{\substack{i_1,...,i_j \leq n \\ P \ j\text{-ary} \\ P \in PL, \ j \in \mathbb{N}}} \pm P(a_{i_1}, ..., a_{i_j}),$$

frequently referred to as *state descriptions*. Let $\theta \in QFSL$ and let n be an upper bound on the i such that a_i occurs in θ. Then we can think of θ as a sentence of the sentential language $\mathcal{L}_n$ which has propositional variables $P(a_{i_1}, ..., a_{i_j})$ for $i_1, ..., i_j \leq n$, $P \in PL$, P j-ary, $j \in \mathbb{N}$. Notice that the σ_j^n are the atoms of $\mathcal{L}_n$, so we have a proof (in both the propositional and predicate calculi) of $\theta \leftrightarrow \bigvee_{j \in S} \sigma_j^n$ for some set $S \subseteq \{1, ..., k_n\}$. Hence $Bel(\theta) = \sum_{j \in S} Bel(\sigma_j^n)$ and it is therefore enough to specify Bel on the σ_j^n and to require (to ensure $(PP1\text{--}2)$) that for each n,

(B1) $Bel(\sigma_i^n) \geq 0$ *and* $\sum_j Bel(\sigma_j^n) = 1,$

(B2) $Bel(\sigma_i^n) = \sum_{\vdash \sigma_j^{n+1} \to \sigma_i^n} Bel(\sigma_j^{n+1}).$

Question Q' Revisited

Question Q' has mainly been considered for the special cases of an empty set of constraints K and of $\mathcal{L}$ containing only unary relation symbols. Notice that when $K = \emptyset$, $Bel(\theta)$ is not determined uniquely unless $\models \theta$ or $\models \neg\theta$. For if $\not\models \theta$, $\not\models \neg\theta$ then, by lemma 11.1, there are $M_1, M_2 \in T\mathcal{L}$ such that $M_1 \models \theta$, $M_2 \models \neg\theta$ and hence, by earlier remarks, there are $Bel_1, Bel_2 : S\mathcal{L} \to \{0,1\}$ satisfying $(PP1\text{--}3)$ and $Bel_1(\theta) = 1$, $Bel_2(\theta) = 0$. Clearly by taking weighted averages of Bel_1, Bel_2 all values between zero and one are also possible.

However, by analogy with the propositional calculus we might hope that some common sense principles (or principles of rational behaviour) might lead to a single value. Unfortunately this hope is still not entirely fulfilled. We shall investigate some such principles in the next chapter. We conclude this chapter by considering a particular, natural, solution in the case $K = \emptyset$ for which we give two (related) justifications based on the 'principle of indifference'.

The Completely Independent Solution

Given $K = \emptyset$ it may seem (at first sight at least) that for $P \in P\mathcal{L}$ we have no reason to assign more or less belief to $P(a_{i_1}, ..., a_{i_j})$ than to $\neg P(a_{i_1}, ..., a_{i_j})$ and furthermore we have no reason to suppose that there is any material connection between distinct $P(a_{i_1}, ..., a_{i_j})$ and $P(a_{s_1}, ..., a_{s_j})$, where $P \in P\mathcal{L}$. Equivalently, in the notation introduced earlier, we have no reason to believe any one σ_i^n more than any other and hence we should set each $Bel(\sigma_i^n)$ the same, i.e. equal to $\frac{1}{k_n}$. Defined in this way, Bel satisfies $(PP1\text{--}2)$ and so extends to $QFS\mathcal{L}$ and hence to $S\mathcal{L}$ so as to satisfy $(PP1\text{--}3)$.

For this belief function Bel consider $Bel(\forall x_1, ..., x_m \theta(\vec{x}))$ where θ is quantifier-free and mentions no a_i nor any 0-ary relation symbols. If $\vdash \forall x_1, ..., x_m \theta(\vec{x})$ then $Bel(\forall x_1, ..., x_m \theta(\vec{x})) = 1$. Suppose then that $\forall x_1, ..., x_m \theta(\vec{x})$ is not a tautology. Let $\gamma_i(x_1, ..., x_m)$, $i \in H$ enumerate all formulae of the form

$$\bigwedge_{\substack{i_1,...,i_j \leq m \\ P \ j\text{-ary} \\ P \in P\mathcal{L}, \ j \in \mathbb{N}^+}} \pm P(x_{i_1}, ..., x_{i_j}).$$

Then for some strict subset J of H (strict since $\forall x_1, ..., x_m \theta(\vec{x})$ is not a tautology),

$$\vdash \theta(\vec{x}) \leftrightarrow \bigvee_{i \in J} \gamma_i(\vec{x}).$$

Clearly for $i_1 < i_2 < ... < i_m < q$ the number of σ_t^q extending $\gamma_i(a_{i_1}, ..., a_{i_m})$ is the same for each i so

$$Bel(\gamma_i(a_{i_1}, ..., a_{i_m})) = \frac{1}{|H|},$$

and for disjoint $\vec{a}^1, ..., \vec{a}^r$,

$$Bel(\gamma_{n_1}(\vec{a}^1) \wedge ... \wedge \gamma_{n_r}(\vec{a}^r)) = \frac{1}{|H|^r}.$$

Hence

$$
\begin{aligned}
Bel(\forall x_1, ..., x_m \theta(\vec{x})) \;\; &\leq \;\; Bel(\theta(\vec{a}^1) \wedge ... \wedge \theta(\vec{a}^r)) \quad \text{by proposition 2.1}\\
&= \;\; \sum\nolimits_{n_1, ..., n_r \in J} Bel(\gamma_{n_1}(\vec{a}^1) \wedge ... \wedge \gamma_{n_r}(\vec{a}^r))\\
&= \;\; \left(\tfrac{|J|}{|H|}\right)^r \longrightarrow 0 \quad as \;\; r \to \infty.
\end{aligned}
$$

We conclude then that such a universal sentence either is a tautology and has belief 1 or it has belief 0. Similarly, by taking negations, an existential sentence (not mentioning a_i or 0-ary relation symbols) has belief value 1 unless it is contradictory, in which case it, of course, has value 0.

We now show that this independent belief function can similarly be derived by considering term structures, i.e. 'possible worlds'. By way of motivation it could be argued that in any real situation there would be only finitely many a_i (although perhaps a very large number). This suggests considering the limiting behaviour of the obvious 'zero-information' belief function on possible worlds with finite domain $\{a_i \mid i \leq n\}$. To this end let $\mathcal{L}^{(n)}$ be $\mathcal{L}$ but with the constant symbols a_i only for $i \leq n$ and $T\mathcal{L}^{(n)}$ the (finite) set of term models for $\mathcal{L}^{(n)}$ with universe $\{a_i \mid i \leq n\}$ (and a_i interpreted as $a_i!$). Define the obviously 'fair' belief function Bel_n on $S\mathcal{L}^{(n)}$ by

$$Bel_n(\theta) = \frac{|\{M \in T\mathcal{L}^{(n)} \mid M \models \theta\}|}{|T\mathcal{L}^{(n)}|}.$$

Set $Bel_\infty(\theta) = \lim_{n \to \infty} Bel_n(\theta)$. (Of course we shall have to check that this limit exists.) The next theorem is due to Fagin [16].

Theorem 11.10 *Bel_∞ is well defined, satisfies (PP1–3) and agrees with the independent solution.*

Proof We first show that Bel_∞ is well defined.

Let $\theta_{n,i}(x_0, ..., x_n)$ for $i < R_n$ range over all formulae of $\mathcal{L}^{(n)}$ of the form

$$\bigwedge_{\substack{i_1,...,i_j \le n \\ P \ j\text{-ary} \\ P \in P\mathcal{L}, \ j \in \mathbb{N}}} \pm P(x_{i_1}, ..., x_{i_j}).$$

Let T be the set of sentences

$$\forall x_0, ..., x_n(\theta_{n,i}(x_0, ..., x_n) \to \exists y \theta_{n+1,j}(x_0, ..., x_n, y)) \tag{11.6}$$

where $n \in \mathbb{N}$, $i < R_n$, $j < R_{n+1}$ and $\theta_{n+1,j}$ is consistent with (i.e. extends) $\theta_{n,i}$. It is easy to see that $T' = T + \theta_{r,q}(a_0, ..., a_r)$ is consistent (simply extend to a model of T by repeatedly adding in the required y). T' is also complete for $\mathcal{L}^{(r)}$. For suppose on the contrary that T' was not complete, i.e. for some $\chi \in S\mathcal{L}^{(r)}$, $T' \nvdash \chi$ and $T' \nvdash \neg\chi$. Then $T + \chi$, $T + \neg\chi$ are both consistent and have countable models M_1, M_2. Enumerate $|M_i|$ as b_j^i, $j \in \mathbb{N}$, where b_j^i is the interpretation of a_j in M_i for $j \le r$, for $i = 1, 2$. We shall construct a binary relation $\sim$ on $M_1 \times M_2$ such that $\sim$ has domain M_1 and range M_2, $b_j^1 \sim b_j^2$ for $j \le r$ and if $P \in P\mathcal{L}$, P j-ary and $c_i^1 \sim c_i^2$ for $i = 1, ..., j$ then

$$M_1 \models P(c_1^1, ..., c_j^1) \Leftrightarrow M_2 \models P(c_1^2, ..., c_j^2).$$

From this it follows by an easy induction on the length of $\theta(x_1, ..., x_n)$, a formula of $\mathcal{L}^{(r)}$, that if $c_i^1 \sim c_i^2$ for $i = 1, ..., n$ then

$$M_1 \models \theta(c_1^1, ..., c_n^1) \Leftrightarrow M_2 \models \theta(c_1^2, ..., c_n^2),$$

giving the required contradiction.

The relation $\sim$ will be formed as the increasing union of finite relations $\sim_m$. First set $\sim_0 = \{\langle b_j^1, b_j^2 \rangle \mid j \le r\}$. Now suppose $\sim_m$ has been found, $\sim_m = \{\langle c_i^1, c_i^2 \rangle \mid i \le n\}$ and for some $i < R_n$,

$$M_1 \models \theta_{n,i}(c_0^1, ..., c_n^1) \quad \text{and} \quad M_2 \models \theta_{n,i}(c_0^2, ..., c_n^2). \tag{11.7}$$

(Notice that this holds when $m = 0$.) Let s be minimal such that either $b_s^1 \notin \{c_i^1 \mid i \le n\}$ or $b_s^2 \notin \{c_i^2 \mid i \le n\}$ (if neither just put $\sim_{m+1} = \sim_m$), say it is the former (the case for the latter is analogous). Put $c_{n+1}^1 = b_s^1$ and let j be such that

$$M_1 \models \theta_{n+1,j}(c_0^1, ..., c_{n+1}^1).$$

Then by (11.7) $\theta_{n+1,j}$ extends $\theta_{n,i}$ so by (11.7) and the fact that (11.6) holds in M_2,

$$M_2 \models \exists y \theta_{n+1,j}(c_0^2, ..., c_n^2, y).$$

Picking such a y gives the required c_{n+1}^2 and the inductive hypothesis now holds for $\sim_{m+1} = \{\langle c_i^1, c_i^2 \rangle \mid i \leq n+1\}$, as required.

Now suppose $\lambda \in SL^{(r)}$ and fix $\theta_{r,q} = \theta_{r,q}(a_0, ..., a_r)$. Without loss of generality suppose $T + \theta_{r,q} \vdash \lambda$. Then $\chi_1, ..., \chi_s \models \theta_{r,q} \to \lambda$ for some $\chi_1, ..., \chi_s \in T$.

Now let $n, m \in \mathbb{N}$, $m \geq n$. Since Bel_m clearly satisfies $(PP1\text{--}3)$ for $SL^{(n)}$, for $\forall \vec{x}(\theta_{n,i}(\vec{x}) \to \exists y \theta_{n+1,j}(\vec{x}, y))$ an axiom of T,

$$Bel_m \left(\forall \vec{x}(\theta_{n,i}(\vec{x}) \to \exists y \theta_{n+1,j}(\vec{x}, y)) \right)$$

$$= 1 - Bel_m \left(\exists \vec{x}(\theta_{n,i}(\vec{x}) \wedge \forall y \neg \theta_{n+1,j}(\vec{x}, y)) \right)$$

$$\geq 1 - (m+1)^{n+1} \max Bel_m \left(\forall y \neg \theta_{n+1,j}(a_{i_0}, ..., a_{i_n}, y) \right)$$

where the maximum is taken over $\vec{a}$ for which $\theta_{n,i}(\vec{a})$ is consistent, $\vec{a} \in \{a_0, ..., a_m\}^{n+1}$. But

$$Bel_m \left(\forall y \neg \theta_{n+1,j}(a_{i_0}, ..., a_{i_n}, y) \right) =$$

$$= \text{proportion of } M \in T\mathcal{L}^{(m)} \text{ in which no } y \text{ satisfies } \theta_{n+1,j}(a_{i_0}, ..., a_{i_n}, y),$$

$$\leq \prod_{\substack{s \leq m \\ s \notin \{i_0, ..., i_n\}}} (\text{proportion in which } \neg\theta_{n+1,j}(a_{i_0}, ..., a_{i_n}, a_s) \text{ holds})$$

$$\leq (1 - 2^{-k})^{m-n} \quad \text{where } k \text{ is the number of conjuncts in } \theta_{n+1,j}.$$

Hence for each $\chi \in T$ there are n, $\delta > 0$ such that for $m \geq n$

$$Bel_m(\chi) \geq 1 - (m+1)^{n+1}(1-\delta)^{m-n}.$$

Thus $\lim_{m \to \infty} Bel_m(\chi) = 1$. Let

$$\begin{aligned}
S &= \{q < R_r \mid \theta_{r,q}(a_0, ..., a_r) + T \vdash \lambda\}, \\
\psi &= \bigvee_{q \in S} \theta_{r,q}(a_0, ..., a_r), \\
\psi' &= \bigvee_{q \notin S} \theta_{r,q}(a_0, ..., a_r).
\end{aligned}$$

Then $T_0 \vdash \psi \to \lambda$ and $T_0 \vdash \psi' \to \neg\lambda$, since T' is complete, for some finite $T_0 \subset T$. Hence, for m sufficiently large,

$$Bel_m(\psi \to \lambda), \ Bel_m(\psi' \to \neg\lambda) \geq Bel_m(\bigwedge T_0) \geq 1 - \sum_{\chi \in T_0} Bel_m(\neg\chi)$$

so $Bel_m(\psi \to \lambda)$, $Bel_m(\psi' \to \neg\lambda) \to 1$ as $m \to \infty$. Thus

$$
\begin{aligned}
Bel_m(\lambda) &= Bel_m(\lambda \wedge \psi) + Bel_m(\lambda \wedge \psi') \\
&= Bel_m(\psi) - Bel_m(\psi \wedge \neg\lambda) + Bel_m(\lambda \wedge \psi') \\
&= Bel_m(\psi) - (1 - Bel_m(\psi \to \lambda)) + (1 - Bel_m(\psi' \to \neg\lambda)).
\end{aligned}
$$

So $\lim_{m \to \infty} Bel_m(\lambda) = \lim_{m \to \infty} Bel_m(\psi) = \frac{|S|}{R_r}$ since clearly the $\theta_{r,q}(a_0, ..., a_r)$ are all satisfied by the same proportion of $M \in T\mathcal{L}^{(m)}$ (i.e. $\frac{1}{R_r}$) independent of m. We have shown that Bel_∞ is well defined. Furthermore $(PP1\text{-}2)$ follow for Bel_∞ immediately from the corresponding properties for the Bel_m. To show $(PP3)$ for Bel_∞ assume $\lambda = \exists x \phi(x)$ and carry over the above notation. For $q \in S$ let S_q be the set of those $q' < R_{r+1}$ for which $\theta_{r+1,q'}$ extends $\theta_{r,q}$ and

$$\theta_{r+1,q'}(a_0, ..., a_{r+1}) + T \vdash \phi(a_{r+1}). \tag{11.8}$$

If $S_q = \emptyset$ then, by the completeness result, whenever $\theta_{r+1,q'}$ extends $\theta_{r,q}$,

$$\theta_{r+1,q'}(a_0, ..., a_{r+1}) + T \vdash \neg\phi(a_{r+1}).$$

But then by taking the disjunction of these $\theta_{r+1,q'}$,

$$\theta_{r,q}(a_0, ..., a_r) + T \vdash \neg\phi(a_{r+1}),$$

so, since a_{r+1} does not appear on the left hand side,

$$\theta_{r,q}(a_0, ..., a_r) + T \vdash \neg\exists y \phi(y)$$

contradicting $q \in S$.

So pick $q' \in S_q$. Let $\epsilon > 0$ and fix $r < t < m$, t large. Then

$$
\frac{Bel_m\left(\bigvee_{r < i \le t} \theta_{r+1,q'}(a_0, ..., a_r, a_i) \right)}{Bel_m(\theta_{r,q}(a_0, ..., a_r))} =
$$

$$
\begin{aligned}
&= \text{The proportion of those } M \in T\mathcal{L}^{(m)} \text{ satisfying} \\
&\quad \theta_{r,q}(a_0, ..., a_r) \text{ which satisfy at least one of} \\
&\quad \text{the } \theta_{r+1,q'}(a_0, ..., a_r, a_i) \text{ for } r < i \le t
\end{aligned}
$$

$$
\begin{aligned}
&\ge\ 1 - (1 - 2^{-B})^{t-r} \quad \text{where } B \text{ is the number of} \\
&\qquad \text{conjuncts in } \theta_{r+1,q'}
\end{aligned}
$$

$$\ge\ 1 - \epsilon \quad \text{for } t \text{ sufficiently large.}$$

Now let Φ be a finite subset of T such that (11.8) holds with Φ in place of T for each such q, q'. Then, for large m,

$$Bel_m(\exists x \phi(x)) \geq Bel_m(\bigvee_{i \leq t} \phi(a_i))$$

$$\geq \sum_{q \in S} Bel_m(\Phi \wedge \bigvee_{r < i \leq t} \theta_{r+1,q'}(a_0, ..., a_r, a_i)), \quad by \ (11.8),$$

$$\geq \sum_{q \in S} \left[Bel_m(\bigvee_{r < i \leq t} \theta_{r+1,q'}(a_0, ..., a_r, a_i)) - Bel_m(\neg\Phi) \right]$$

$$\geq \sum_{q \in S} [Bel_m(\theta_{r,q}(a_0, ..., a_r)) \cdot (1 - \epsilon) - Bel_m(\neg\Phi)]$$

$$\geq Bel_m(\bigvee_{q \in S} \theta_{r,q}(a_0, ..., a_r)) \cdot (1 - \epsilon) - R_r \cdot Bel_m(\neg\Phi).$$

Taking the limit as $m \to \infty$ gives (recalling the result for λ),

$$Bel_\infty(\exists x \phi(x)) \geq Bel_\infty(\bigvee_{i \leq t} \phi(a_i)) \geq Bel_\infty(\exists x \phi(x)) \cdot (1 - \epsilon).$$

Condition $(PP3)$ now follows since ϵ can be made arbitrarily small by enlarging t.

Finally Bel_∞ clearly agrees with the independent solution on the σ_m^n and hence, by theorem 11.2, agrees everywhere. $\qquad\square$

Chapter 12 ————————————

Principles of Predicate Uncertain Reasoning

The results at the end of the previous chapter, especially the model provided by Fagin's theorem 11.10, seem to provide strong evidence in favour of the completely independent solution when $K = \emptyset$.

However, closer inspection seems to show this solution to be apparently at odds with common sense. For suppose, having settled for this independent belief function Bel, we then observe $P(a_0), ..., P(a_n)$ to be true. Then according to Bayesian updating we would assign updated belief

$$Bel(P(a_{n+1}) \mid P(a_0), ..., P(a_n))$$

to $P(a_{n+1})$. But for this independent solution this value is still $\frac{1}{2}$. This flies in the face of common sense which would dictate that, certainly for large n, one's belief in $P(a_{n+1})$ should be enhanced by receiving the evidence of $P(a_1), ..., P(a_n)$.

A second criticism is that this belief function gives all non-tautological universal sentences value 0. However in practice we might feel that universal sentences do sometimes hold and hence that it is being 'unfair' in dismissing them so. Again however there is a problem of how much weight should be given to a non-tautological universal if not zero.

Both of these criticisms suggest that in our 'common sense' view not all possible structures/worlds should carry the same weight, i.e. that some structures are a priori more likely than others. The difficulty is of course to explain and quantify this asymmetry.

In this chapter we shall consider some principles, mainly due to Carnap (see [3], [4], [5], [6]) aimed at justifying other solutions. However the conclusions seem far less satisfying than for the propositional case and the underlying problem of uncertain reasoning in the predicate calculus, at least from a probabilistic viewpoint, seems as deep and tantalizing as ever.

Carnap's Principles

In [4], [6] (pp.974–976), Carnap suggests a number of further assumptions on Bel, beyond simply $(PP1$–$3)$, based on principles of 'common sense'. Several of these concern symmetry and it is one of these which we shall consider first.

Let τ be a permutation of $\mathbb{N}$ and for $\theta \in SL$ let θ^τ, etc., be the result of simultaneously replacing each a_i in θ, etc., by $a_{\tau(i)}$. The following principle (and its later variants) should be viewed in the context of question Q'. (More exactly we should formulate them as desiderata of an inference process, much as we did for the propositional calculus. However there seems little reason for developing all the further notation this would require and we shall trust instead that the reader can appreciate the principles in this more informal setting.)

First Symmetry Principle $(SP1)$ If $K = K^\tau$ then $Bel(\theta) = Bel(\theta^\tau)$.

In this principle we can restrict θ to be quantifier-free or even of the form σ_i^n. This is a consequence of the following lemma.

Lemma 12.1 *Let τ be a permutation of $\mathbb{N}$ and suppose that $Bel(\theta) = Bel(\theta^\tau)$ for all $\phi \in QFSL$. Then $Bel(\theta) = Bel(\theta^\tau)$ for all $\theta \in SL$.*

Proof Suppose on the contrary that this failed for some θ. By proposition 2.1(c) and the prenex normal form theorem we may assume that this θ is in prenex normal form, say,

$$\theta = Q_1\vec{x}_1 Q_2\vec{x}_2 ... Q_r\vec{x}_r \phi(\vec{x}_1 ... \vec{x}_r),$$

with ϕ quantifier-free and $Q_1, Q_2, ..., Q_r$ alternating between $\exists$ and $\forall$. We may further assume that $Q_1 = \exists$ (otherwise replace θ by $\neg\theta$) and that r is minimal with the property that $Bel(\theta) \neq Bel(\theta^\tau)$ for some such θ. Notice that $r > 0$ since $Bel(\theta) = Bel(\theta^\tau)$ for $\theta \in QFSL$.

Then by proposition 11.9, if $\vec{x}_1$ has length k,

$$Bel(\theta) = \sup_n Bel\left(\bigvee_{i_1,...,i_k \leq n} Q_2\vec{x}_2 ... Q_r\vec{x}_r \phi(a_{i_1}, ..., a_{i_k}, \vec{x}_2, ..., \vec{x}_r)\right)$$

$$= \sup_n Bel\left(\bigvee_{i_1,...,i_k \leq n} Q_2\vec{x}_2 ... Q_r\vec{x}_r \phi^\tau(a_{\tau(i_1)}, ..., a_{\tau(i_k)}, \vec{x}_2, ..., \vec{x}_r)\right)$$

by minimality of r since this disjunction is logically equivalent to a sentence in prenex normal form with just $r - 1$ alternating blocks of quantifiers,

$$\leq \sup_n Bel\left(\bigvee_{j_1,...,j_k \leq t_n} Q_2\vec{x}_2 ... Q_r\vec{x}_r \phi^\tau(a_{j_1}, ..., a_{j_k}, \vec{x}_2, ..., \vec{x}_r)\right)$$

where $t_n = \max\{\tau(0), \tau(1), ..., \tau(n)\}$

$$\leq \; \sup_m Bel \left(\bigvee_{j_1,...,j_k \leq m} Q_2 \vec{x}_2 ... Q_r \vec{x}_r \phi^\tau (a_{j_1}, ..., a_{j_k}, \vec{x}_2, ..., \vec{x}_r) \right)$$

$$= \; Bel(\theta^\tau)$$

$$\leq \; \sup_m Bel \left(\bigvee_{i_1,...,i_k \leq s_m} Q_2 \vec{x}_2 ... Q_r \vec{x}_r \phi^\tau (a_{\tau(i_1)}, ..., a_{\tau(i_k)}, \vec{x}_2, ..., \vec{x}_r) \right)$$

where $s_m = \max\{\tau^{-1}(0), ..., \tau^{-1}(m)\}$

$$= \; \sup_m Bel \left(\bigvee_{i_1,...,i_k \leq m} Q_2 \vec{x}_2 ... Q_r \vec{x}_r \phi(a_{i_1}, ..., a_{i_k}, \vec{x}_2, ..., \vec{x}_r) \right)$$

$$\leq \; Bel(\theta),$$

giving the required contradiction. $\square$

Corollary 12.2 *Let τ be a permutation of $\mathbb{N}$ and suppose that $Bel(\sigma_i^n) = Bel((\sigma_n^i)^\tau)$ for $n \in \mathbb{N}$, $i = 1, ..., k_n$. Then $Bel(\theta) = Bel(\theta^\tau)$ for all $\theta \in S\mathcal{L}$.*

Proof For $\theta \in QFS\mathcal{L}$, θ is logically equivalent to $\bigvee_{j \in S} \sigma_j^n$ for some $S \subseteq \{1, ..., k_n\}$ and $n \in \mathbb{N}$ so

$$Bel(\theta) = \sum_{j \in S} Bel(\sigma_j^n) = \sum_{j \in S} Bel((\sigma_j^n)^\tau) = Bel(\theta^\tau).$$

The result for $\theta \in S\mathcal{L}$ now follows by the lemma. $\square$

We now give a result (due to Gaifman [23] for $K = \emptyset$), which shows that $(SP1)$ is consistent.

Theorem 12.3 *If K (as in Q') is consistent and $K = K^\tau$ for τ a permutation of $\mathbb{N}$ then there is a function $Bel : S\mathcal{L} \to [0,1]$ satisfying (PP1-3) and K and $Bel(\theta) = Bel(\theta^\tau)$ for all $\theta \in S\mathcal{L}$.*

Proof Roughly the idea of the proof is to pick Bel satisfying K and then define Bel^0 so as to satisfy the requirements of the theorem, by

$$Bel^0(\theta) = \text{the average of } \{Bel(\theta^\tau) \mid K = K^\tau\}.$$

Unfortunately since there may be infinitely many such τ we need to use a rather sophisticated 'weighted average'. So with this in mind let

$$\mathbb{N}^{<\mathbb{N}} = \{\pi \mid dom(\pi) \text{ is a finite subset of } \mathbb{N}, \; \pi : dom(\pi) \to \mathbb{N}\}.$$

For $\pi \in \mathbb{N}^{<\mathbb{N}}$ let $h_\pi = \prod_{m \in dom(\pi)} 2^{-1-\pi(m)}$. Notice that for fixed finite $S \subseteq S' \subseteq \mathbb{N}$, $\tau \in \mathbb{N}^{<\mathbb{N}}$ with $dom(\tau) = S$,

$$\sum_{\pi: S \to \mathbb{N}} h_\pi = \prod_{j \in S} \left(\sum_{i=0}^{\infty} 2^{-i-1} \right) = 1,$$

$$\sum_{\substack{\pi: S' \to \mathbb{N} \\ \tau \subseteq \pi}} h_\pi = h_\tau.$$

Now let *Bel* satisfy K and, initially, for simplicity, suppose $K = \emptyset$. For $\theta \in S\mathcal{L}$ let all the a_i mentioned in θ be amongst $\{a_i \mid i \in S\}$ and set

$$Bel^0(\theta) = \sum_{\pi: S \to \mathbb{N}} h_\pi Bel(\theta^\pi)$$

where θ^π is the result of simultaneously replacing each a_i in θ by $a_{\pi(i)}$. By the second identity above this definition is independent of the particular S chosen. We show that Bel^0 satisfies $(PP1\text{--}3)$ and $Bel^0(\theta) = Bel^0(\theta^\tau)$ for any permutation τ of $\mathbb{N}$. That Bel^0 satisfies $(PP1\text{--}2)$ follows directly from the corresponding properties for *Bel* since if $\vdash \theta$ then $\vdash \theta^\pi$ and $(\theta \vee \phi)^\pi = \theta^\pi \vee \phi^\pi$ etc. (Recall that any 'covering' S gives the same answer.) To show $(PP3)$ we consider, for clarity, the special case of $\exists x \psi(a_0, x)$ where a_0 is the only constant symbol appearing in ψ, the full result then being an easy generalization. Let $\epsilon > 0$. Then,

$$Bel^0(\exists x \psi(a_0, x)) = \sum_{\pi_0: \{0\} \to \mathbb{N}} h_{\pi_0} Bel(\exists x \psi(a_{\pi_0(0)}, x))$$

$$\leq \sum_{\substack{\pi_0: \{0\} \to \mathbb{N} \\ \pi_0 \in Q}} h_{\pi_0} Bel(\psi(a_{\pi_0(0)}, a_{j_1}) \vee \ldots \vee \psi(a_{\pi_0(0)}, a_{j_k})) + \epsilon$$

for some finite Q and $j_1 < \ldots < j_k$. Letting $Rg(\pi)$ denote the range of π for $\pi \in \mathbb{N}^{<\mathbb{N}}$, pick r so large that

$$\sum_{\substack{\pi: \{1,\ldots,r\} \to \mathbb{N} \\ \{j_1,\ldots,j_k\} \not\subseteq Rg(\pi)}} h_\pi \leq \sum_{s=1}^{k} \sum_{\substack{\pi: \{1,\ldots,r\} \to \mathbb{N} \\ j_s \notin Rg(\pi)}} h_\pi \leq k \left(1 - \frac{1}{2^{j_k+1}} \right)^r < \epsilon. \qquad (12.1)$$

Then, by $(PP1\text{--}2)$,

$$Bel^0(\exists x \psi(a_0, x))$$

$$\geq Bel^0(\psi(a_0, a_1) \vee \ldots \vee \psi(a_0, a_r))$$

$$= \sum_{\substack{\pi_0:\{0\}\to N \\ \pi:\{1,\ldots,r\}\to N}} h_{\pi_0} \cdot h_\pi Bel(\psi(a_{\pi_0(0)}, a_{\pi(1)}) \vee \ldots \vee \psi(a_{\pi_0(0)}, a_{\pi(r)}))$$

$$\geq \sum_{\substack{\pi_0 \in Q \\ \pi:\{1,\ldots,r\}\to N \\ \{j_1,\ldots,j_k\}\subseteq Rg(\pi)}} h_{\pi_0} \cdot h_\pi Bel(\psi(a_{\pi_0(0)}, a_{j_1}) \vee \ldots \vee \psi(a_{\pi_0(0)}, a_{j_k}))$$

$$\geq \sum_{\pi_0 \in Q} h_{\pi_0}(1-\epsilon) Bel(\psi(a_{\pi_0(0)}, a_{j_1}) \vee \ldots \vee \psi(a_{\pi_0(0)}, a_{j_k})) \quad \textit{by } (12.1)$$

$$\geq (1-\epsilon)(Bel^0(\exists x \psi(a_0, x)) - \epsilon).$$

Hence, since ϵ was arbitrary,

$$Bel^0(\exists x \psi(a_0, x)) = \sup_n Bel^0(\psi(a_0, a_1) \vee \ldots \vee \psi(a_0, a_n)),$$

as required.

Finally for τ a permutation of N, define $\pi\tau$ for $\pi \in N^{<N}$ to have domain

$$\{\tau^{-1}(m) \mid m \in dom(\pi)\}$$

and $\pi\tau(\tau^{-1}(m)) = \pi(m)$ for $m \in dom(\pi)$. Then $h_{\pi\tau} = h_\pi$ and if S is a finite subset of N such that $i \in S$ for every constant symbol a_i appearing in θ^τ then

$$Bel^0(\theta^\tau) = \sum_{\pi:S\to N} h_\pi Bel(\theta^{\pi\tau})$$

$$= \sum_{\pi\tau^{-1}: S\to N} h_{\pi\tau^{-1}} Bel(\theta^\pi) = \sum_{\pi: \tau^{-1}S\to N} h_\pi Bel(\theta^\pi) = Bel^0(\theta),$$

since if a_i appears in θ then $\tau(i) \in S$ so $i \in \tau^{-1}S$.

To handle the case $K \neq \emptyset$ let $b = \{i \mid a_i \text{ appears in } K\}$ and let

$$H = \{\pi \in N^{<N} \mid \pi \text{ is } 1-1, \, b = dom(\pi) \text{ and } K^\pi = K\}.$$

(Notice that if $\pi \in H$ then π is a permutation of b.) Now set

$$Bel^0(\theta) = \frac{\displaystyle\sum_{\substack{\pi: S\cup b\to N \\ \pi\restriction b \in H}} h_\pi Bel(\theta^\pi)}{\displaystyle\sum_{\pi \in H} h_\pi},$$

where S is such that $i \in S$ for every a_i in θ. Then the same arguments as before go through, but replacing arbitrary $\pi: S \to N$ by $\pi: S\cup b \to N$ with $\pi \restriction b \in H$, to show that Bel^0 satisfies $(PP1\text{--}3)$ and $Bel^0(\theta) = Bel^0(\theta^\tau)$ whenever $K = K^\tau$. To show that Bel^0 satisfies K, notice that since Bel satisfies K, if the equation

$$\sum \alpha_{ij} Bel(\theta_j) = \beta_i$$

is in K and $\pi \in H$ then

$$\sum \alpha_{ij} Bel(\theta_j^\pi) = \beta_i$$

is also in K, and so satisfied by Bel. It now follows easily that

$$\sum \alpha_{ij} Bel^0(\theta_j) = \frac{\sum_{\pi \in H} \sum \alpha_{ij} Bel(\theta_j^\pi) h_\pi}{\sum_{\pi \in H} h_\pi} = \frac{\sum_{\pi \in H} \beta_i h_\pi}{\sum_{\pi \in H} h_\pi} = \beta_i,$$

as required. $\qquad\square$

The above proof also works if we replace $K = K^\tau$ by K *and* K^τ *equivalent* (in the sense that they have the same solutions), although the elements of H now need not necessarily be permutations of b and in showing that $Bel^0(\theta^\tau) = Bel^0(\theta)$ whenever K is equivalent to K^τ we take the summation over those $\pi : S \cup b \cup \tau(b) \to \mathbb{N}$ for which K and K^τ are equivalent.

As we mentioned earlier, the simple-minded idea of defining $Bel^0(\theta)$ to be the average of the $Bel(\theta^\tau)$ for τ such that $K = K^\tau$ does not work because there may be infinitely many such τ. Such a simple-minded proof would however go through for permutations of the (finitely many) k-ary relation symbols in $\mathcal{L}$ and also for transpositions of $P, \neg P$ for $P \in P\mathcal{L}$. Thus we could obtain similar results to theorem 12.3 for each of the following symmetry assumptions.

Second Symmetry Principle $(SP2)$ If $K = K^\pi$ then $Bel(\theta) = Bel(\theta^\pi)$ where π is a permutation of the k-ary relation symbols in $\mathcal{L}$ (for each k) and is extended to $S\mathcal{L}$ in the obvious way.

Third Symmetry Principle $(SP3)$ If $K = K^\pi$ then $Bel(\theta) = Bel(\theta^\pi)$ where π transposes $P, \neg P$ for some $P \in P\mathcal{L}$ and is extended to $S\mathcal{L}$ in the obvious way.

Again we get equivalent principles if we restrict θ to $QFS\mathcal{L}$ or even to θ of the form σ_i^n.

The Unary Case

In view of the inherent difficulties in question Q' and because there seems little gain in doing otherwise, we shall, until further notice, restrict ourselves to the simple case of $K = \emptyset$ and $\mathcal{L}$ having a single unary relation symbol P. Thus by earlier remarks it is enough to limit ourselves to asking what value we should give to $Bel(\bigwedge_{j=0}^n P^{\epsilon_j}(a_j))$ on the basis of no evidence (i.e. $K = \emptyset$). We furthermore shall henceforth assume that *Bel* satisfies $(PP1\text{–}3)$ and $(SP1)$ so that $Bel(\bigwedge_{j=0}^{n-1} P^{\epsilon_j}(a_j))$ is simply a function of $|\{j \mid j < n \text{ and } \epsilon_j = 0\}|$ and n, say

$$Bel(\bigwedge_{j=0}^{n-1} P^{\epsilon_j}(a_j)) = C_{r,m}$$

where $|\{j \mid j < n \text{ and } \epsilon_j = 0\}| = m$, $r = n - m$. Let

$$P_{r,m} = Bel\left(\bigvee\{\bigwedge_{j=0}^{n-1} P^{\epsilon_j}(a_j) \mid |\{j < n \mid \epsilon_j = 0\}| = m\}\right)$$

$$= \text{Probability that } P \text{ holds of exactly } r \text{ of } a_0, ..., a_{n-1}$$

$$= \binom{n}{r} C_{r,m} \quad \text{where } n = m + r.$$

Since *Bel* satisfies $(PP1\text{–}3)$ and $(SP1)$ it is easy to see that the $C_{r,m}$ and $P_{r,m}$ satisfy the following identities:

(i)
$$\sum_{i=0}^{n} \binom{n}{i} C_{i,n-i} = \sum_{i=0}^{n} P_{i,n-i} = 1,$$

(ii)
$$C_{0,0} = 1,$$

(iii)
$$C_{r+1,m} + C_{r,m+1} = C_{r,m}.$$

Diagramatically we have

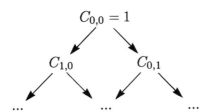

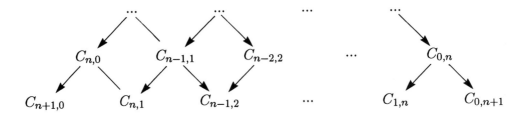

where each parent equals the sum of its children.

Conversely notice that for this language the σ_i^{n-1} are precisely the $\bigwedge_{i=0}^{n-1} P^{\epsilon_i}(a_i)$ so that given such a diagram, by corollary 12.2 and the remarks following theorem 11.2, we can define Bel satisfying $(PP1\text{–}3)$ and $(SP1)$ by setting

$$Bel \left(\bigwedge_{i=0}^{n-1} P^{\epsilon_i}(a_i) \right) = C_{r,m},$$

where $m = |\{i < n \mid \epsilon_i = 0\}|$, and clearly this is the diagram for this Bel.

Suppose $C_{r,m} = 0$ with $r > 0$. Then $0 = C_{r,m+1} = C_{r,m+2} = \ldots$ so $C_{r-1,m} = C_{r-1,m+1} = C_{r-1,m+2} = \ldots$ and by (i) either $r - 1 = 0$ or $C_{r-1,m} = 0$. From this observation it is clear that if some $C_{r,m}$ with $r, m > 0$ is zero then all such $C_{r,m}$ are zero and

$$C_{1,0} = C_{2,0} = C_{3,0} = \ldots, \qquad C_{0,1} = C_{0,2} = C_{0,3} = \ldots .$$

According to (a special case of) de Finetti's celebrated representation theorem on exchangeable measures, see [29], the general solution here is given by

$$C_{r,m} = \int x^r (1 - x)^m \mu(dx)$$

where μ is a measure on $[0, 1]$. Since this result itself is not needed in what follows we shall omit it, prefering instead to provide direct, elementary proofs of those corollaries of this result (see Fine [18]) which are directly relevant.

If, in addition to $(PP1\text{–}3)$ and $(SP1)$ Bel also satisfies $(SP3)$ then $C_{r,m} = C_{m,r}$ and $P_{r,m} = P_{m,r}$ (and μ in de Finetti's theorem may be taken symmetric).

Another principle suggested by Carnap [6] (pp. 974–976) was, roughly, that one's belief in a future event should be an increasing (not necessarily strictly) function of the proportion of times that event has occured in the past. Precisely, for $\mathcal{L}$ as above:

Principle of Instantial Relevance (PIR)

$$Bel \left(P^{\epsilon}(a_{i_{n+1}}) \mid P^{\epsilon}(a_{i_n}) \wedge \bigwedge_{j<n} P^{\epsilon_j}(a_{i_j}) \right) \geq Bel \left(P^{\epsilon}(a_{i_{n+1}}) \mid \bigwedge_{j<n} P^{\epsilon_j}(a_{i_j}) \right)$$

where the i_j, $j = 0, \ldots, n+1$, are distinct.

We shall only consider this principle in the case when the $C_{r,m}$ are all non-zero. Notice that in this case if Bel also satisfies $(SP1)$ then PIR is equivalent to

$$Bel \left(P^{\epsilon}(a_{n+1}) \mid P^{\epsilon}(a_n) \wedge \bigwedge_{j<n} P^{\epsilon_j}(a_j) \right) \geq Bel \left(P^{\epsilon}(a_n) \mid \bigwedge_{j<n} P^{\epsilon_j}(a_j) \right),$$

equivalently

$$C_{m_1+2,m_2} \cdot C_{m_1,m_2} \geq (C_{m_1+1,m_2})^2 \quad \text{and} \quad C_{m_1,m_2+2} \cdot C_{m_1,m_2} \geq (C_{m_1,m_2+1})^2.$$

We now show a rather surprising connection between PIR and the symmetry principle $(SP1)$.

Theorem 12.4 *If Bel satisfies $(SP1)$ then*

$$C_{r+2,m} \cdot C_{r,m} \geq (C_{r+1,m})^2 \quad \text{and} \quad C_{r,m+2} \cdot C_{r,m} \geq (C_{r,m+1})^2.$$

In particular if all the $C_{r,m}$ are non-zero then PIR holds.

Before proving this theorem we derive a lemma.

Lemma 12.5 *Assume $(SP1)$ and let the $C_{r,m}$ be as above. Then for $n \geq m = m_1 + m_2$,*

$$C_{m_1,m_2} = \sum_{m_1 \leq n_1 \leq n - m_2} \binom{n-m}{n_1 - m_1} C_{n_1,n_2},$$

where $n_2 = n - n_1$.

Proof

$$C_{m_1,m_2} = Bel\left(\bigwedge_{i=0}^{m_1-1} P(a_i) \wedge \bigwedge_{i=m_1}^{m-1} \neg P(a_i) \right)$$

$$= \sum_{\epsilon_1,\dots,\epsilon_{n-m}} Bel\left(\bigwedge_{i=0}^{m_1-1} P(a_i) \wedge \bigwedge_{i=m_1}^{m-1} \neg P(a_i) \wedge \bigwedge_{i=1}^{n-m} P^{\epsilon_i}(a_{m+i-1}) \right)$$

$$= \sum_{m_1 \leq n_1 \leq n - m_2} \binom{n-m}{n_1 - m_1} C_{n_1,n_2}$$

since there are $\binom{n-m}{n_1-m_1}$ ways in which exactly $n_1 - m_1$ of the $\epsilon_1, \dots, \epsilon_{n-m}$ are 1. $\square$

Proof of theorem 12.4 Using the notation in the lemma let

$$q(n_1, n_2) = \binom{n-m}{n_1 - m_1} C_{n_1,n_2},$$

where we are thinking of m_1, m_2 as fixed and n_1, n_2, n as variable. Notice that by the lemma

$$C_{m_1,m_2} = \sum_{m_1 \leq n_1 \leq n - m_2} q(n_1, n_2) \leq 1,$$

$$C_{m_1+1,m_2} = \sum_{m_1+1 \leq n_1 \leq n - m_2} \binom{n - (m+1)}{n_1 - (m_1 + 1)} C_{n_1,n_2}$$

$$= \sum_{m_1+1\leq n_1\leq n-m_2} \left(\frac{n_1 - m_1}{n - m}\right) q(n_1, n_2) = \sum_{m_1\leq n_1\leq n-m_2} \left(\frac{n_1 - m_1}{n - m}\right) q(n_1, n_2),$$

$$C_{m_1+2,m_2} = \sum_{m_1\leq n_1\leq n-m_2} \frac{(n_1 - m_1)(n_1 - m_1 - 1)}{(n - m)(n - m - 1)} q(n_1, n_2).$$

Applying the Schwarz Inequality, $\sum a_i^2 \cdot \sum b_i^2 \geq (\sum a_i b_i)^2$, with

$$a_i = \sqrt{q(n_1, n_2)}, \quad b_i = \sqrt{\frac{(n_1 - m_1)(n_1 - m_1 - 1)}{(n - m)(n - m - 1)}} \cdot \sqrt{q(n_1, n_2)},$$

gives

$$C_{m_1+2,m_2} \cdot C_{m_1,m_2} \geq \left(\sum_{m_1\leq n_1\leq n-m_2} q(n_1, n_2) \cdot \sqrt{\frac{(n_1 - m_1)(n_1 - m_1 - 1)}{(n - m)(n - m - 1)}}\right)^2$$

so in order to show that $C_{m_1+2,m_2} \cdot C_{m_1,m_2} \geq (C_{m_1+1,m_2})^2$ it suffices to show that

$$\lim_{n\to\infty} \sum_{m_1\leq n_1\leq n-m_2} q(n_1, n_2) \cdot \left(\frac{n_1 - m_1}{n - m} - \sqrt{\frac{(n_1 - m_1)(n_1 - m_1 - 1)}{(n - m)(n - m - 1)}}\right) = 0.$$

Since for fixed $k > m_1$ this limit is zero if we restrict the summation to $m_1 \leq n_1 < k$, it is sufficient to show that by picking k large enough,

$$\sum_{k\leq n_1\leq n-m_2} q(n_1, n_2) \cdot \left(\frac{n_1 - m_1}{n - m} - \sqrt{\frac{(n_1 - m_1)(n_1 - m_1 - 1)}{(n - m)(n - m - 1)}}\right)$$

can be made arbitrarily small (for large n). But using the fact that

$$\sum_{m_1\leq n_1\leq n-m_2} q(n_1, n_2) \leq 1$$

and that

$$0 \leq \frac{n_1 - m_1}{n - m} - \sqrt{\frac{(n_1 - m_1)(n_1 - m_1 - 1)}{(n - m)(n - m - 1)}} = \frac{n_1 - m_1}{n - m}\left(1 - \sqrt{\frac{(n - m)(n_1 - m_1 - 1)}{(n_1 - m_1)(n - m - 1)}}\right)$$

$$\leq 1 - \sqrt{\frac{(n - m)}{(n - m - 1)} \cdot \frac{(k - m_1 - 1)}{(k - m_1)}} \quad \text{for } k \leq n_1 \leq n - m_2$$

we see that this does indeed hold for sufficiently large k and n (depending on k). Replacing P by $\neg P$ throughout gives the required second inequality. $\square$

It should be clear that this proof carries over to a much more general situation. For suppose for the moment we relax our assumption that $\mathcal{L}$ consists of just a unary predicate and let $\theta(x)$ be a formula of $\mathcal{L}$ which does not mention any of the a_i. Then repeating the proof of theorem 12.4 with θ in place of P shows that for Bel satisfying $(PP1\text{--}3)$ and $(SP1)$ (with $K = \emptyset$), and $i_0, ..., i_{n+1}$ distinct,

$$Bel\left(\theta(a_{i_{n+1}}) \wedge \theta(a_{i_n}) \wedge \bigwedge_{j<n} \theta^{\epsilon_j}(a_{i_j})\right) \cdot Bel\left(\bigwedge_{j<n} \theta^{\epsilon_j}(a_{i_j})\right) \geq$$

$$\geq \left(Bel\left(\theta(a_{i_n}) \wedge \bigwedge_{j<n} \theta^{\epsilon_j}(a_{i_j})\right)\right)^2.$$

We shall use this generalisation later in justifying yet another symmetry principle.

For the present however we return to the case of $\mathcal{L}$ consisting of just a single unary predicate and prove another welcome, although perhaps unexpected, consequence of $(PP1\text{--}3)$ and $(SP1)$.

Theorem 12.6 *Suppose that $(SP1)$ holds for Bel. Then*

(i) $C_{r+1,m} \cdot C_{r,m+1} \geq C_{r,m} \cdot C_{r+1,m+1}$,

(ii) $C_{r+2,m} \cdot C_{r,m+1} \geq C_{r+1,m} \cdot C_{r+1,m+1}$,

(iii)   *If $r + m = s + t$ and $r \geq s$ then $C_{r+1,m} \cdot C_{s,t} \geq C_{s+1,t} \cdot C_{r,m}$.*

In particular if all the $C_{r,m}$ are non-zero and $n = r + m$ then

(i)' $Bel(P(a_n) \mid \bigwedge_{i=0}^{r-1} P(a_i) \wedge \bigwedge_{i=r}^{n-1} \neg P(a_i))$

$$\geq Bel(P(a_{n+1}) \mid \bigwedge_{i=0}^{r-1} P(a_i) \wedge \bigwedge_{i=r}^{n} \neg P(a_i)),$$

(ii)' $Bel(P(a_{n+1}) \mid P(a_n) \wedge \bigwedge_{i=0}^{r-1} P(a_i) \wedge \bigwedge_{i=r}^{n-1} \neg P(a_i))$

$$\geq Bel(P(a_{n+1}) \mid \neg P(a_n) \wedge \bigwedge_{i=0}^{r-1} P(a_i) \wedge \bigwedge_{i=r}^{n-1} \neg P(a_i)),$$

(iii)' $Bel(P^{\epsilon}(a_n) \mid \bigwedge_{j<n} P^{\epsilon_j}(a_j)) \geq Bel(P^{\epsilon}(a_n) \mid \bigwedge_{j<n} P^{\delta_j}(a_j))$

whenever $|\{j \mid \epsilon = \epsilon_j\}| \geq |\{j \mid \epsilon = \delta_j\}|$.

Proof First note that under the assumption that the $C_{r,m}$ are non-zero, by propositions 2.1, 2.2 and PIR,

$$
Bel\left(P(a_n)\,\middle|\,\bigwedge_{i=0}^{r-1} P(a_i) \wedge \bigwedge_{i=r}^{n-1} \neg P(a_i)\right)
$$

$$
= \; 1 - Bel\left(\neg P(a_n)\,\middle|\,\bigwedge_{i=0}^{r-1} P(a_i) \wedge \bigwedge_{i=r}^{n-1} \neg P(a_i)\right)
$$

$$
\geq \; 1 - Bel\left(\neg P(a_{n+1})\,\middle|\,\bigwedge_{i=0}^{r-1} P(a_i) \wedge \bigwedge_{i=r}^{n} \neg P(a_i)\right)
$$

$$
= \; Bel\left(P(a_{n+1})\,\middle|\,\bigwedge_{i=0}^{r-1} P(a_i) \wedge \bigwedge_{i=r}^{n} \neg P(a_i)\right),
$$

giving $(i)'$. Using PIR and $(i)'$ now gives $(ii)'$ and repeated use of $(ii)'$ and $(SP1)$ gives $(iii)'$.

Parts (i)–(iii) are proved similarly by replacing

$$
Bel\left(P(a_n)\,\middle|\,\bigwedge_{i=0}^{r-1} P(a_i) \wedge \bigwedge_{i=r}^{n-1} \neg P(a_i)\right)
$$

by $\frac{C_{r+1,m}}{C_{r,m}}$ etc. and multiplying through by the denominators, noting that in the final inequality either the terms common to both sides are non-zero and can be cancelled or the right hand side of the inequality must also be zero. □

Again, as for theorem 12.4, this result straightforwardly extends to a general language with $\theta(x)$ in place of $P(x)$.

These last two theorems have shown that the rather natural principle $(SP1)$ together with the entirely reasonable requirement that the $C_{r,m}$ are non-zero (about which we shall have more to say later) forces Bel to have some very attractive, and perhaps unexpected, properties. Clearly from de Finetti's theorem it follows that there are many such probability functions Bel. We now present one such family of functions which have enjoyed considerable attention.

Carnap's Continuum of Inductive Methods

In the case of PL having the single unary relation symbol P, W.E. Johnson (see [36]) and later, independently, Carnap (see [3], [4]) suggested taking the solution Bel to $K = \emptyset$ to be given by

$$
Bel\left(\bigwedge_{j=0}^{r-1} P(a_{i_j}) \wedge \bigwedge_{j=r}^{n-1} \neg P(a_{i_j})\right) = C_{r,m} = \frac{\prod_{i=0}^{r-1}(i+\frac{\lambda}{2})\,\prod_{i=0}^{m-1}(i+\frac{\lambda}{2})}{\prod_{i=0}^{n-1}(i+\lambda)},
$$

equivalently,

$$Bel\left(P(a_{i_n}) \mid \bigwedge_{j=0}^{r-1} P(a_{i_j}) \wedge \bigwedge_{j=r}^{n-1} \neg P(a_{i_j})\right) = \frac{r + \frac{\lambda}{2}}{n + \lambda},$$

where $n = m + r$, $i_0, ..., i_n$ are distinct and λ is a parameter (hence the 'continuum'), $0 \leq \lambda \leq \infty$. (Actually the values $\lambda = \infty, \lambda = 0$, where $\frac{0}{2} = \frac{1}{2}$, are usually omitted from this scale, although their inclusion tidies things up rather pleasantly.) As a point of interest, in the case $PL = \{P_1, ..., P_s\}$ with the P_i unary, Carnap proposed combining such belief functions, Bel_i for SL_i where $PL_i = \{P_i\}$, as above by treating the SL_i as statistically independent, i.e. for $\theta_i \in SL_i$, $Bel(\theta_1 \wedge ... \wedge \theta_s) = \prod_{i=1}^{s} Bel_i(\theta_i)$.

The case $\lambda = \infty$ here gives

$$Bel\left(\bigwedge_{j=0}^{r-1} P(a_{i_j}) \wedge \bigwedge_{j=r}^{n-1} \neg P(a_{i_j})\right) = 2^{-n},$$

and hence equals the completely independent solution. Notice that by earlier remarks this choice of $C_{r,m}$ gives that Bel satisfies $(SP1)$ and $(SP3)$.

Concerning the value of λ it is in a sense a measure of the 'believer's' unwillingness to be swayed away from his initial assumption that P and $\neg P$ are equally likely. This assumption, which is presumably based on some sort of symmetry, could be modelled by the agent imagining that he has already seen some previous λ a's of which exactly $\frac{\lambda}{2}$ satisfied P. From this viewpoint it would seem then common sense that if, in a further n real a's, P (say) had been satisfied r times then the belief that the next a would satisfy P should be

$$\frac{\text{Number of real and imagined } a\text{'s satisfying } P}{\text{Number of real and imagined } a\text{'s}} = \frac{r + \frac{\lambda}{2}}{n + \lambda}.$$

Clearly then large λ correspond to a strong initial commitment to P and $\neg P$ being equally likely. In particular $\lambda = \infty$ corresponds to an unshakable faith in this and gives us again the independent solution. Expressed in this way it seems that the choice of λ is in practice to be determined by general contingent knowledge about the world. Whether purely logical considerations could be brought to bear to determine λ in the absence of such knowledge remains problematic.

We now give two 'justifications' for this suggested solution, which is now commonly refered to as Carnap's continuum of inductive methods.

First Justification

W.E. Johnson in [36], and independently, some twenty years later, Carnap in [4], gave an argument that, for a suitable language $\mathcal{L}$ and assuming $(SP1)$ and a rather dubious principle (*SP4*), *Bel* is the only sensible solution for $K = \emptyset$. (Actually in our situation of $\mathcal{L} = \{P\}$ the assumption is equivalent to (*SP3*) but unfortunately in this case this assumption is insufficient, as later examples will show.)

We now give a version of their derivation. Suppose, just for this derivation, that $PL = \{P_1, ..., P_s\}$ with the P_i unary but now with $s > 1$. Let $Q_i(x)$, $0 < i \leq 2^s$ run through all state descriptions for x, that is all sentences of the form

$$\bigwedge_{j=1}^{s} P_j^{\epsilon_j}(x).$$

In this context W.E. Johnson and Carnap suggested the following principle, often refered to today as Johnson's sufficientness principle.

Fourth Symmetry Principle (SP4) $Bel\left(Q_i(a_n) \mid \bigwedge_{j=0}^{n-1} Q_{i_j}(a_j)\right)$ is a function only of n and $|\{j < n \mid i_j = i\}|$.

As we shall see from our next lemma (*SP4*) implies (*SP2–3*) and indeed is equivalent to (*SP3*) in the case $s = 1$. However for $s > 1$ it seems to be open to criticism. For example for $s = 2$ it implies that

$$Bel(P_1(a_1) \wedge P_2(a_1) \mid P_1(a_0) \wedge \neg P_2(a_0)) = Bel(P_1(a_1) \wedge P_2(a_1) \mid \neg P_1(a_0) \wedge \neg P_2(a_0)).$$

However on one side the evidence, $P_1(a_0) \wedge \neg P_2(a_0)$, 'half supports' $P_1(a_1) \wedge P_2(a_1)$, whereas on the other the evidence, $\neg P_1(a_0) \wedge \neg P_2(a_0)$, gives 'no support at all' to $P_1(a_1) \wedge P_2(a_1)$. (Actually, as Miller [49] points out, this criticism is itself open to question. Nevertheless it still seems strong enough to put a serious dent in (*SP4*).) We shall shortly show that Carnap's continuum is, for $s > 1$, a consequence of (*SP4*). Firstly however we shall derive a lemma.

Lemma 12.7 (*SP4*) *implies that for* π *a permutation of* $\{1, ..., 2^s\}$,

$$Bel\left(\bigwedge_{j \leq k} Q_{i_j}(a_j)\right) = Bel\left(\bigwedge_{j \leq k} Q_{\pi(i_j)}(a_j)\right).$$

Proof We show the lemma by induction on k. Using (*SP4*) let

$$Bel\left(Q_i(a_n) \mid \bigwedge_{j < n} Q_{i_j}(a_j)\right) = g(n, m),$$

where $m = |\{j < n \mid i_j = i\}|$. For $k = 0$ both sides equal $g(0,0)$. Assume the result for $k - 1$. Then

$$Bel\left(\bigwedge_{j \leq k} Q_{i_j}(a_j)\right) = Bel\left(Q_{i_k}(a_k) \mid \bigwedge_{j < k} Q_{i_j}(a_j)\right) \cdot Bel\left(\bigwedge_{j < k} Q_{i_j}(a_j)\right)$$

$$= \quad g(n, |\{j < k \mid i_j = i_k\}|) \cdot Bel\left(\bigwedge_{j<k} Q_{\pi(i_j)}(a_j)\right)$$

$$= \quad g(n, |\{j < k \mid \pi(i_j) = \pi(i_k)\}|) \cdot Bel\left(\bigwedge_{j<k} Q_{\pi(i_j)}(a_j)\right)$$

$$= \quad Bel\left(\bigwedge_{j\leq k} Q_{\pi(i_j)}(a_j)\right)$$

as required. $\square$

Notice that if $g(n, m) = 0$ for some n, m then,

$$Bel\left(\bigwedge_{i=0}^{m} Q_1(a_i) \wedge \bigwedge_{i=m+1}^{n} Q_{j_i}(a_i)\right) = 0$$

for $j_{m+1}, ..., j_n \neq 1$. Hence

$$Bel\left(\bigwedge_{i=0}^{m} Q_1(a_i) \wedge \bigwedge_{i=m+1}^{n} \neg Q_1(a_i)\right) = 0$$

and by a straightforward adaptation of an earlier proof for the $C_{r,m}$ (where P replaced Q_1) we see that

$$Bel\left(Q_1(a_0) \wedge \bigwedge_{i=1}^{n-m} \neg Q_1(a_i)\right) = 0.$$

By lemma 12.7 it now follows that

$$Bel\left(\bigwedge_{j\leq k} Q_{i_j}(a_j)\right) = 0$$

whenever the i_j are not equal and hence that

$$Bel\left(\bigwedge_{j\leq k} Q_i(a_j)\right) = \frac{1}{2^s} \quad \text{for } i = 1, ..., 2^s$$

with all other state descriptions of $a_0, ..., a_k$ getting value zero.

In such a case it is hard to imagine that Bel is a particularly sensible solution since it jumps to the certain conclusion $Q_j(a_i)$ for all i on the basis of the single observation that Q_j holds of a_0.

Theorem 12.8 *For $s > 1$, Bel satisfying $(SP1)$, $(SP4)$ and g defined as above*

$$g(n, m) = \frac{m + \frac{\lambda}{2^s}}{n + \lambda} \quad \text{for some } 0 \leq \lambda \leq \infty.$$

(Take $g(n, m) = \frac{1}{2^s}$ for $\lambda = \infty$ and $g(0, 0) = \frac{1}{2^s}$ for $\lambda = 0$.)

Proof By the above discussion it is enough to consider only the case when $g(n, m) > 0$ for all $n \geq m$. First notice that

$$1 = Bel\left(\bigvee_{j=1}^{2^s} Q_j(a_0)\right) = \sum_{j=1}^{2^s} Bel(Q_j(a_0)), \quad \text{since the } Q_j \text{ are disjoint,}$$

$$= 2^s g(0, 0),$$

so $g(0, 0) = 2^{-s}$. Now let $t + r + q = n$ and

$$\theta = \bigwedge_{j=0}^{t-1} Q_1(a_j) \wedge \bigwedge_{j=t}^{t+r-1} Q_2(a_j) \wedge \bigwedge_{j=t+r}^{n-1} Q_3(a_j).$$

(It is here that we need $s > 1$ to ensure the existence of Q_3.) Notice that $Bel(\theta) \neq 0$, since, as in the example above, $Bel(\theta)$ can be written as a product of conditionals each of which is non-zero by the assumption, $g(n, m) > 0$ for all $n \geq m$. Then

$$1 = Bel\left(\bigvee_{j=1}^{2^s} Q_j(a_n) \,\middle|\, \theta\right)$$

$$= Bel(Q_1(a_n) \mid \theta) + Bel(Q_2(a_n) \mid \theta)$$

$$+ Bel(Q_3(a_n) \mid \theta) + \sum_{j=4}^{2^s} Bel(Q_j(a_n) \mid \theta)$$

$$= g(n, t) + g(n, r) + g(n, q) + (2^s - 3)g(n, 0). \tag{12.2}$$

Also

$$Bel(Q_1(a_{n+1}) \mid Q_2(a_n) \wedge \theta) \cdot Bel(Q_2(a_n) \mid \theta) =$$

$$= Bel(Q_1(a_{n+1}) \wedge Q_2(a_n) \mid \theta)$$

$$= Bel(Q_2(a_n) \mid Q_1(a_{n+1}) \wedge \theta) \cdot Bel(Q_1(a_{n+1}) \mid \theta).$$

By $(SP1)$ a_n, a_{n+1} can be transposed in this last expression giving

$$g(n+1, t) \cdot g(n, r) = g(n+1, r) \cdot g(n, t). \tag{12.3}$$

Putting $n = 1 = t$, $r = q = 0$ in (12.2) gives

$$1 = g(1, 1) + (2^s - 1)g(1, 0). \tag{12.4}$$

By the discussion following the proof of theorem 12.4 (with $\theta = Q_1$), $g(1, 1) \geq g(1, 0)$ and by assumption $g(1, 0) > 0$, so $1 > g(1, 1) \geq \frac{1}{2^s}$. Hence for some $0 < \lambda \leq \infty$, $g(1, 1) = \frac{1 + \frac{\lambda}{2^s}}{1 + \lambda}$ and substituting in (12.4) gives $g(1, 0) = \frac{\frac{\lambda}{2^s}}{1 + \lambda}$. Thus we have the theorem for $n \leq 1$ (and $\lambda = \frac{1 - g(1,1)}{g(1,1) - \frac{1}{2^s}}$).

Now assume $g(n, r) = \frac{r + \frac{\lambda}{2^s}}{n + \lambda}$ for $0 \leq r \leq n$. By (12.3) for $r \leq n$ ($t = 0$) we see that

$$g(n+1, 0) \cdot (r + \frac{\lambda}{2^s}) = g(n+1, r) \cdot \frac{\lambda}{2^s}$$

so $g(n+1, r) = (r + \frac{\lambda}{2^s}) \cdot c$ for some constant c. Substituting in (12.2) with $n+1$ in place of n and $0 < q < n$ shows that $c = (n + 1 + \lambda)^{-1}$. Also by (12.2) with $n + 1$ in place of n, $r = n + 1$ gives

$$1 = g(n+1, n+1) + (2^s - 1)g(n+1, 0)$$

and hence $g(n+1, n+1) = 1 - \frac{(2^s - 1)\frac{\lambda}{2^s}}{n + 1 + \lambda} = \frac{n + 1 + \frac{\lambda}{2^s}}{n + 1 + \lambda}$ completing the proof. $\quad\square$

Corollary 12.9 *Under the assumptions of theorem 12.8,*

$$Bel\left(\bigwedge_{j=0}^{n} Q_{i_j}(a_j)\right) = \frac{\prod_{r=1}^{2^s} \prod_{t=0}^{n_r - 1}(t + \frac{\lambda}{2^s})}{\prod_{t=0}^{n}(t + \lambda)}$$

where $n_r = |\{j \leq n \mid i_j = r\}|$.

Proof Notice that $Bel\left(\bigwedge_{j=0}^{n} Q_{i_j}(a_j)\right) = \prod_{j=0}^{n} Bel\left(Q_{i_j}(a_j) \mid \bigwedge_{m=0}^{j-1} Q_{i_m}(a_m)\right)$ and now plug in the values for the right hand side given by the theorem. $\quad\square$

Notice that for the case $s = 1$ this gives the values $C_{r,m}$ as above. However the derivation of corollary (12.9) requires $s > 1$ in which case the assumption $(SP4)$ is perhaps questionable.

Second Justification

Our second justification is rather statistical in nature and in this case applies directly when $P\mathcal{L} = \{P\}$, P unary.

Imagine that before receiving any information concerning the truth or falsity of the $P(a_i)$ I felt that the events '$P(a_i)$' were independent and all of the same (subjective) probability, p_0 say. However having no prior information about p_0 I felt that any value for it between 0 and 1 was equally likely; more formally, I was assuming a uniform probability density function $f_0(p) = 1$ on the possible values of p_0.

Suppose that now I learn that $P(a_i)$ holds for some r particular values of $i < n$ and fails for the remaining $n - r = m$ values; without loss of generality (as it turns out) say I learn $P(a_0), ..., P(a_{r-1}), \neg P(a_r), ..., \neg P(a_{n-1})$. Then using the continuous version of Bayesian updating I would update f_0 to the new probability density function,

$$f(p) = \lim_{\delta p \searrow 0} \frac{1}{\delta p} \cdot Prob\left(p_0 \in [p, p + \delta p] \,\middle|\, \bigwedge_{i=0}^{r-1} P(a_i) \wedge \bigwedge_{i=r}^{n-1} \neg P(a_i)\right)$$

$$= \lim_{\delta p \searrow 0} \frac{1}{\delta p} \cdot \frac{Prob\left(\bigwedge_{i=0}^{r-1} P(a_i) \wedge \bigwedge_{i=r}^{n-1} \neg P(a_i) \wedge p_0 \in [p, p + \delta p]\right)}{Prob\left(\bigwedge_{i=0}^{r-1} P(a_i) \wedge \bigwedge_{i=r}^{n-1} \neg P(a_i)\right)}$$

$$= \lim_{\delta p \searrow 0} \frac{1}{\delta p} \cdot \frac{\int_p^{p + \delta p} p_0^r (1 - p_0)^m dp_0}{\int_0^1 p_0^r (1 - p_0)^m dp_0} = p^r (1 - p)^m \frac{(m + r + 1)!}{r! m!}.$$

Using this updated probability density function now gives a (subjective) probability for $P(a_n)$ of

$$\frac{(m + r + 1)!}{r! m!} \cdot \int_0^1 p^{r+1}(1 - p)^m dp = \frac{r + 1}{n + 2},$$

which is exactly the value given by Carnap's continuum (if we identify *Bel* with *Prob*) in the case where the parameter $\lambda = 2$.

This then corresponds to the informal justification given earlier in the case where we 'imagine' two previous observations, $P(a_{-1})$ and $\neg P(a_{-2})$ say.

Of course putting this in the original context of attempting to predict the expert's beliefs it is hard to credit a human expert being unconsciously capable of mentally deriving such a formula in this or the previous justification. However as we also remarked earlier we are interested in the possibilities for intelligent uncertain reasoning and certainly it seems possible that *some* intelligent agent could act in this way. (This same point could be made on various occasions in this book.)

At the same time the reader might well ask why we do not pursue this line further and perhaps consider more sophisticated statistical inference procedures. Well, we acknowledge this point but if we were to attempt this path we believe that this book, in so far as it addresses the question of predicting an intelligent agent, would move on to ever thinner ice. Just assuming belief to be probability is, as Chapter 10 seems to indicate, already a grand idealization so we shall resist the temptation to develop the statistical arguments beyond this simple justification at this time.

Whilst Carnap's continuum does, for $\lambda < \infty$, remove the objection to the independent solution that updating has no effect it still suffers from the criticism of giving non-tautological universal sentences value 0, unless $\lambda = 0$. This, in fact, is a special case of a rather more general result which we now prove for the language with $P = \{P_1, ..., P_s\}$, P_i unary etc. as above.

Theorem 12.10 *Suppose that Bel satisfies* $(SP1)$, $(SP3)$, *and*

$$\sum_n Bel\left(Q_1(a_n) \,\middle|\, \bigwedge_{i=0}^{n-1} \neg Q_1(a_i) \right) = \infty.$$

Then for any non-tautological sentence $\forall \vec{x} \theta(\vec{x})$ *with* θ *quantifier-free and not involving any* a_i, *$Bel(\forall \vec{x} \theta(\vec{x})) = 0$. (Notice that the assumption holds for Carnap's continuum when* $0 < \lambda \leq \infty$.)

Proof Suppose $\forall x_1, ..., x_n \theta(x_1, ..., x_n)$ is not a tautology, where θ is quantifier-free and does not mention any a_i. Then, since each state description $\bigwedge_{i=1}^n Q_{j_i}(x_i)$ implies $\theta(\vec{x})$, or $\neg\theta(\vec{x})$, and since $\theta(\vec{x})$ is not a tautology, there must be some such state description logically implying $\neg\theta(\vec{x})$, equivalently $\theta(x_1, ..., x_n) \rightarrow \neg\bigwedge_{i=1}^n Q_{j_i}(x_i)$. Hence, by repeated use of proposition 2.1,

$$Bel(\forall \vec{x} \theta(\vec{x})) \;\leq\; Bel\left(\bigwedge_{i_1,...,i_n \leq t} \theta(a_{i_1}, ..., a_{i_n}) \right)$$

$$\leq\; Bel\left(\bigwedge_{i_1,...,i_n \leq t} \neg(Q_{j_1}(a_{i_1}) \wedge ... \wedge Q_{j_n}(a_{i_n})) \right)$$

$$=\; Bel\left(\bigwedge_{i_1 \leq t} \neg Q_{j_1}(a_{i_1}) \vee ... \vee \bigwedge_{i_n \leq t} \neg Q_{j_n}(a_{i_n}) \right)$$

$$\leq\; \sum_{k=1}^n Bel\left(\bigwedge_{i_k \leq t} \neg Q_{j_k}(a_{i_k}) \right), \qquad \text{by proposition 2.1}$$

$$=\; nBel\left(\bigwedge_{i \leq t} \neg Q_1(a_i) \right) \qquad \text{by } (SP3)$$

$$\leq\; nBel\left(\neg Q_1(a_t) \,\middle|\, \bigwedge_{i < t} \neg Q_1(a_i) \right) \cdot Bel\left(\bigwedge_{i < t} \neg Q_1(a_i) \right)$$

$$=\; n\left(1 - Bel\left(Q_1(a_t) \,\middle|\, \bigwedge_{i < t} \neg Q_1(a_i) \right) \right) \cdot Bel\left(\bigwedge_{i < t} \neg Q_1(a_i) \right)$$

$$= n \prod_{0 < j \le t} \left(1 - Bel\left(Q_1(a_j) \middle| \bigwedge_{i<j} \neg Q_1(a_i) \right) \right) \longrightarrow 0 \quad \text{as } t \to \infty$$

by the assumption that $\sum_t Bel\left(Q_1(a_t) \middle| \bigwedge_{i<t} \neg Q_1(a_i) \right) = \infty$.

$\square$

Notice that if, instead, $\forall \vec{x} \theta(\vec{x})$ did mention some $a_0, ..., a_k$, let

$$\vdash \theta(\vec{x}) \leftrightarrow \bigvee_{1 \le i_0,...,i_k \le 2^s} \left[\bigwedge_{j \le k} Q_{i_j}(a_j) \wedge \bigvee_{\langle m_1,...,m_n \rangle \in R_{i_0,...,i_k}} (Q_{m_1}(x_1) \wedge ... \wedge Q_{m_n}(x_n)) \right].$$

Then if $R_{i_0,...,i_k} = \{1, ..., 2^s\}$,

$$\vdash \theta(\vec{x}) \wedge \bigwedge_{j \le k} Q_{i_j}(a_j) \leftrightarrow \bigwedge_{j \le k} Q_{i_j}(a_j)$$

whilst if $R_{i_0,...,i_k} \subset \{1, ..., 2^s\}$ then, as above,

$$Bel\left(\forall \vec{x} \theta(\vec{x}) \wedge \bigwedge_{j \le k} Q_{i_j}(a_j) \right) = 0.$$

Hence

$$Bel(\forall \vec{x} \theta(\vec{x})) = Bel\left(\bigvee \bigwedge_{j \le k} Q_{i_j}(a_j) \right) = \sum Bel\left(\bigwedge_{j \le k} Q_{i_j}(a_j) \right)$$

where the disjunction/sum is over those $i_0, ..., i_k$ for which $R_{i_0,...,i_k} = \{1, ..., 2^s\}$.

Notice also that this result does not use $s > 1$, it holds equally well for the special case $PL = \{P\}$ which we have been mainly considering.

We now turn to another approach to picking a solution Bel for $K = \emptyset$, $PL = \{P\}$ which aims at understanding (well, at least giving a consistent explanation of) the relationship between $P(a_i)$ and $P(a_j)$.

Solutions via Propositional Inference Processes

In this section we again suppose that $PL = \{P\}$ with P unary. If we were to accept that there was no connection between the $P(a_i)$ then we could treat them all as distinct propositional variables. Thus we could take an inference process N on the CL_n which satisfies the principles of language invariance and renaming and define $Bel(\theta) = N(\emptyset)(\theta)$ for $\theta \in SL_n$. (Recall from the previous chapter that L_n is the propositional language which has propositional variables $P(a_{i_1}), ..., a_{i_j})$ for $i_1, ..., i_j \le n$, $P \in PL$, P j-ary, $j \in \mathbb{N}$.)

Then since $QFS\mathcal{L} = \bigcup_n S\mathcal{L}_n$, *Bel* would be defined on $QFS\mathcal{L}$ (and hence extend to $S\mathcal{L}$) and the principles assumed of N would ensure that $(SP1)$, $(SP3)$ hold for *Bel*. Clearly in this case we obtain again the independent solution, which, as mentioned earlier, fails to take account of the relationship between $P(a_i)$ and $P(a_j)$. However we might inject this relationship (if only we understood it well enough!) into the situation by replacing $\emptyset$ by some set $K_\mathcal{L}$ which does capture it.

There are various candidates for $K_\mathcal{L}$ of which we shall mention just one. As motivation consider again the example at the start of the previous chapter concerning my program running on an unfamiliar computer which gave 0 as a random choice from $\{0, 1\}$ on each of the first ten runs. A natural explanation of this phenomenon is that there are some, possibly unknown, factors, Q_r say, which are causing a surfeit of zeros to be chosen. Indeed in this case I might conjecture the computer is not working correctly or (more likely) my program contains an error. There is not then a direct relationship between $P(a_i)$, $P(a_j)$ for $i \neq j$, it is rather that both are caused, or probably caused, by the same unknown factors Q_r.

In the simple case of $K = \emptyset$, $P\mathcal{L} = \{P\}$ (i.e. $s = 1$) then, a 'natural' candidate for $K_\mathcal{L}$ is

$$Bel(P(a_i) \mid Q_k) = \beta_k \quad \text{for } i \in \mathbb{N}, \ k \in E, \quad (0 \leq \beta_k \leq 1)$$

$$Bel(Q_k) = \lambda_k \qquad \text{for } k \in E, \qquad (0 \leq \lambda_k \leq 1)$$

$$Bel(Q_k \wedge Q_t) = 0 \qquad \text{for } k, t \in E, \qquad \left(\sum \lambda_k \leq 1\right)$$

where the Q_k for $k \in E$ are 'explanations' of $P(a_i)$ being unduly frequent if $\beta_k > \frac{1}{2}$, scarce if $\beta_k < \frac{1}{2}$, and these explanations are disjoint (i.e. we do not countenance multiple simultaneous explanations). Unfortunately $K_\mathcal{L}$ is infinite, making direct application of an inference process inappropriate. However in the case of the maximum entropy inference process, ME, it is straightforward to show, using the principles of language invariance, relativisation and independence, that for $\theta \in QFS\mathcal{L}$, $\lim_{n \to \infty} ME(K_\mathcal{L}^n)(\theta)$ exists and yields a probability function *Bel* satisfying $K_\mathcal{L}$, where $K_\mathcal{L}^n$ is $K_\mathcal{L}$ restricted to those $P(a_i)$, Q_k with $i, k \leq n$. (Indeed if E is finite then $Bel(\theta) = ME(K_\mathcal{L}^n(\theta))$ eventually.) In particular then for this solution *Bel*,

$$Bel\left(\bigwedge_{i=0}^{r-1} P(a_i) \wedge \bigwedge_{i=r}^{n-1} \neg P(a_i)\right) = \frac{1}{2^n}(1 - \sum_{k \in E} \lambda_k) + \sum_{k \in E} \lambda_k(\beta_k^r(1 - \beta_k)^m + (1 - \beta_k)^r \beta_k^m),$$

and *Bel* satisfies $(SP1)$, $(SP3)$.

In this example the β_k, λ_k are parameters. By varying these parameters one can arrange the value of $\lim_{n \to \infty} Bel\left(P(a_n) \mid \bigwedge_{i=0}^{n-1} P(a_i)\right)$ to be anywhere between

$\frac{1}{2}$ and 1, and similarly $Bel(\forall x P(x))$ to be non-zero (but only if some $\beta_k = 1$). Furthermore it seems quite reasonable to suppose that, in the case of my surprising program, some such explanations Q_k, together with the β_k, λ_k, do exist. However their choice, just as for Carnap's λ, seems to require going beyond purely logical considerations to one's personal general knowledge about the particular example. What the parameters should be in a situation where absolutely nothing is known a priori is problematic.

On a more optimistic note this example, with its emphasis on attempting to explain the relationship between the $P(a_i)$, does illustrate an attractive general approach to the problem of uncertain reasoning in the predicate calculus.

To put the conclusions of this chapter and the previous one into perspective we note that as far as uncertain reasoning is concerned we have only really considered the very simple case where $K = \emptyset$ and $P\mathcal{L}$ contains only unary predicates (often only one). Even in this case our conclusions leave a lot to be desired. Clearly this is an area where much still needs to be understood.

Glossary

$\mathbb{E}$ 1

$\mathbb{K}_0$ 1

L 4, 6, 9

SL 4

$\mathbb{R}$ 5

K_0 6

$Bel(\ )$ 6

$Bel(\ |\ )$ 6

Q 6, 14-15

K 6, 9

$(P1)$ 7

$(P2)$ 7

$(DS1)$ 8

$(DS2)$ 8

$(DS3)$ 8

$|S|$ 8

$\equiv$ 8, 34, 162

$F_\wedge$ 8, 52

$F_\vee$ 8, 52

$F_|$ 8, 52

$F_\neg$ 8, 52

$p_1, ..., p_n$ 9

V 10

$p_i^{\epsilon_i}$ 13

$\alpha_1, ..., \alpha_J, \alpha$ 13, 14

J 13

S_ϕ 13

At^L 13

$\mathbb{D}^L$ 13

A_K 14

$\vec{b}_K$ 14

$V^L(K)$ 15

V_x 18

$(Co1)$ 24

$(Co2)$ 24

$(Co3)$ 24

$(Co4)$ 24

$(Co5)$ 24

$\mathbb{N}$ 26

(DS) 34

m 34

$\overline{SL}$ 34

$\overline{\theta}$ 34, 162

$\overline{\theta} \wedge \overline{\phi}$ 34, 162

$\overline{\theta} \vee \overline{\phi}$ 34, 162

$\neg\overline{\theta}$ 34, 162

$\mathbf{1}$ 34, 162

$\mathbf{0}$ 34, 162

$\overline{\theta} \leq \overline{\phi}$ 35, 162

bpa   35

Bel^m 35

$Pl(\theta)$ 38

$W(Bel)$ 40

$\oplus$ 42

$Bel(\theta||\phi)$ 44

$F_\rightarrow$ 52

$F_\leftrightarrow$ 52

$(\mathbf{F_1})$ 52

$(\mathbf{F_2})$ 53

$(\mathbf{F_3})$ 53

$(N1)$ 54

$(N2)$ 54

$(N3)$ 54

$(C1)$ 55

$(C2)$ 55

$(C3)$ 55

$(C4)$ 55

$(N4)$ 58

$(D1)$ 60

$(D2)$ 60

$(D3)$ 60
$(D4)$ 60
$(Po1)$ 62
$(Po2)$ 62
$(Po3)$ 62
C^L 63
CL 68
CM^L 69-70
CM_∞^L 73-74
$I^L(K)$ 74
CM_∞ 75
MD^L 76
ME^L 76
$\upharpoonright$ 77
ME 79
MD 79
$K_1|K_2$ 83
$\mathbb{I}$ 83
$\vdash_\mathbb{I}$ 85
$\triangle$ 91
$\hat{A}_K$ 92
$E(\vec{x})$ 101
$Bel^\sigma(\ )$ 112
K^σ 112
$I(\vec{x},\vec{y})$ 119
$\pm$ 132
P 139
$|\sigma|$ 139
NP 139
$P \neq NP$ 140
SAT 140
$\leq_P$ 140
RP 140
$RP \neq NP$ 141
$\mathbb{Q}$ 141

$\mathcal{S}_k$ 144
$3\text{--}SAT$ 144
$2\text{--}SAT$ 144
$(P3)$ 150
$\mathbb{Z}_2$ 151
$\mathbb{N}^+$ 161
$\mathcal{L}$ 161
$P\mathcal{L}$ 161
a_i 161
$F\mathcal{L}$ 161
$S\mathcal{L}$ 161
Q' 161
$(PP1)$ 162
$(PP2)$ 162
$(PP3)$ 162
$\overline{S\mathcal{L}}$ 162
$\overline{Bel}$ 163
$|M|$ 163
$T\mathcal{L}$ 163
$QFS\mathcal{L}$ 164
$\mathcal{P}(T\mathcal{L})$ 165
σ_i^n 171
$\mathcal{L}_n$ 171
$(B1)$ 172
$(B2)$ 172
$\mathcal{L}^{(n)}$ 173
$T\mathcal{L}^{(n)}$ 173
R_n 174
$(SP1)$ 179
$\mathbb{N}^{<\mathbb{N}}$ 180
$(SP2)$ 183
$(SP3)$ 183
PIR 186
$(SP4)$ 191

References

[1] J. Aczel, *Lectures on functional equations and their applications*, Academic Press, Mathematics in Science and Engineering, 1966, Vol.19, pp.319–324.

[2] R.E. Bellman and M. Giertz, *On the analytic formalism of the theory of fuzzy sets*, Inform. Sci., 1973, Vol.5, pp.149–157.

[3] R. Carnap, *Logical foundations of probability*, Routledge & Kegan Paul Ltd., 1951.

[4] R. Carnap, *The continuum of inductive methods*, University of Chicago Press, 1952.

[5] R. Carnap and R.C. Jeffrey, eds., *Studies in inductive logic and probability*, University of California Press, 1971.

[6] R. Carnap, *Replies and systematic expositions*, in: The Philosophy of Rudolf Carnap, ed. P.A.Schilpp, La Salle, Illinois, Open Court, 1963.

[7] G.F. Cooper, *The computational complexity of probabilistic inference using Bayesian belief networks*, Artificial Intelligence, 1990, Vol.42, pp.393–405.

[8] P. Courtney, *Doctoral thesis*, Manchester University, Manchester, U.K., 1992.

[9] R.T. Cox, *Probability, frequency and reasonable expectation*, American Journal of Physics, 1946, Vol.14, No.1, pp.1-13.

[10] E.Ya. Dantsin and V.Ya. Kreinovich, *Probabilistic inference in prediction systems*, Soviet Math.Dokl., Vol.40, No.1, pp.8–12 (1990).

[11] A.P. Dempster, *A generalization of Bayesian inference*, Journal of the Royal Statistical Society, Series B, 1968, Vol.30, pp.205–247.

[12] P. Diaconis and S. Zabell, *Updating subjective probability*, Journal of the American Statistical Association, 1982, Vol.77, pp.822-830.

[13] H.G. Eggleston, *Convexity*, Cambridge Tracts in Mathematics and Mathematical Physics No.47, Cambridge University Press, 1969.

[14] R. Fagin and J. Halpern, *A new approach to updating beliefs*, in: Uncertainty in artificial intelligence: Vol.VI, eds. P.P. Bonissone, M. Henrion, L.N. Kanal and J.F. Lemmer, 1991 Elsevier Science Publishers, pp.347–374.

[15] R. Fagin, J. Halpern and N. Megiddo, *A logic for reasoning about probabilities*, Proceedings of the 3rd IEEE symposium on Logic in Computer Science, 1988, pp.277–291.

[16] R. Fagin, *Probabilities on finite models*, Journal of Symbolic Logic, Vol.41, No1, 1976, pp.50–58.

[17] R. Fagin and J.Y. Halpern, *Uncertainty, belief and probability*, in the Eleventh International Joint Conference on Artificial Intelligence (IJCAI-89), 1989, pp.1161–1167.

[18] T.L. Fine, *Theories of probability*, Academic Press, New York, 1973.

[19] B. de Finetti, *Sul significato soggetivo della probabilità*, Fundamenta Mathematicae, 1931, Vol.17, pp.298–329.

[20] B. de Finetti, *La prévision: ses lois logiques, ses sources subjectives*, Annales de l'Institute Henri Poincaré, 1937, Vol.7, pp.1–68.

[21] B.C. van Fraassen, *A demonstration of the Jeffrey conditionalization rule*, Erkenntnis, 1986, Vol.24, pp.17–24.

[22] L.W. Fung and K.S. Fu, *An axiomatic approach to rational decision-making in a fuzzy environment*, in: Fuzzy sets and their applications to cognitive and decission processes, eds. L.A. Zadeh, K.S. Fu, K. Tanaka, M. Shimura, Acadamic Press, New York, 1975, pp.227–256.

[23] H. Gaifman, *Concerning measures in first order calculi*, Israel Journal of Mathematics, 1964, Vol.2, pp.1–18.

[24] M. Garey, D. Johnson and L. Stockmeyer, *Some simplified NP-complete problems*, Theoretical Computer Science, 1976, Vol.1, pp.237–267.

[25] G. Georgakopoulos, D. Kavvadias and C. Papadimitriou, *Probabilistic satisfiability*, Journal of Complexity, 1988, Vol.4, pp.1–11.

[26] P. Hájek, T. Havránek and R. Jiroušek, *Uncertain information processing in information systems*, Boca Raton, CRC Press, 1992.

[27] D. Heckerman, *Probabilistic interpretation for MYCIN's certainty factors*, in: Uncertainty in artificial intelligence, eds. L.N. Kanal & J.F. Lemmer, North Holland, Amsterdam, 1986, pp.167–195.

[28] H.M. Hersch and A. Caramazza, *A fuzzy-set approach to modifiers and vagueness in natural languages*. J.Exp.Psychol.: General, 1976, Vol.105, pp.254–276.

[29] E. Hewit and L.J. Savage, *Symmetric measures on cartesian products*, Transaction of the American Mathematical Society, 1955, Vol.8, pp.484-489.

[30] A. Hobson, *Concepts in statistical mechanics*, Gordon & Breach, 1971.

[31] J.E. Hopcroft and J.D. Ullman, *Introduction to automata theory, languages and computation*, Addison-Wesley, 1979.

[32] P. Horwich, *Probability and evidence*, Cambridge University Press, 1982.

[33] E.T. Jaynes, *The well-posed problem*, Foundations of Physics, 1973, Vol.3, pp.477–492.

[34] R.C. Jeffrey, *The logic of decision*, Gordon & Breach Inc., New York, 1965.

[35] R.W. Johnson, *Independence and Bayesian updating methods*, in: Uncertainty in artificial intelligence, eds. L.N.Kanal & J.F.Lemmer, North Holland, Amsterdam, 1986, pp.197–201.

[36] W.E. Johnson, *Probability: The deductive and inductive problems*, Mind, 1932, Vol.49, pp.409–423.

[37] J.G. Kemeny, *Fair bets and inductive probabilities*, Journal of Symbolic Logic, 1955, Vol.20, pp.1–28.

[38] G.J. Klir and T.A. Folger, *Fuzzy sets, uncertainty and information*, Prentice-Hall, Englewood Cliffs, New Jersey, 1988.

[39] V.Ya. Kozlenko, V.Ya. Kreinovich and M.G. Mirimanishvili, *The optimal method of describing the expert information*, in: Applied Problems in System Analysis, Proceedings Georgian Polytechnic Institute, 1988, No.8, pp.64–67.

[40] V.Ya. Kreinovich and A.M. Lokshin, *On the foundations of fuzzy formalism: Explaining formulas for union, intersection, negation, normalization and modifiers*, Technical Report UTEP-CS-90-28, University of Texas at El Paso Computer Science Departement, 1990.

[41] H.E. Kyburg, *Bayesian and non-Bayesian evidential updating*, Artificial Intelligence, 1987, Vol31, pp.271–293.

[42] S.L. Lauritzen and D.J. Spiegelhalter, *Local computations with probabilities on graphical structures and their application to expert systems*, Journal of the Royal Statistical Society B, 1988, 50(2), pp.157–224.

[43] J. Lawry and G.M. Wilmers, *An axiomatic approach to systems of prior distributions in inexact reasoning*, to appear in: Knowledge representation and reasoning under uncertainty, eds. M. Masuch and L. Polos, Lecture Notes in Computer Science, Berlin 1994.

[44] P. Lehner, *Probabilities and reasoning about probabilities*, International Journal of Approximate Reasoning, 1991, Vol.5, No.1, pp.27–43.

[45] I. Maung, *Doctoral thesis*, Manchester University, Manchester, U.K., 1992.

[46] I. Maung and J.B. Paris, *A note on the infeasibility of some inference processes*, International Journal of Intelligent Systems, 1990, Vol.5, No.5, pp.595–604.

[47] W. McLewin, *Linear programming and applications: A course text*, Input-Output Publishing Company, London, 1982.

[48] E. Mendelson, *Introduction to mathematical logic*, Wadsworth Inc., 1987.

[49] D. Miller, *Popper's qualitative theory of versimilitude*, British Journal for the Philosophy of Science, 1974, Vol.25, pp.166–177.

[50] R.E. Neapolitanos, *Probabilistic reasoning in expert systems: theory and algorithms*, Wiley, New York, 1990.

[51] G.C. Oden, *Integration of fuzzy logical information*, Journal of Experimental Psychol.: Hum. Percept. Perform., 1977, Vol.3, No.4, pp.565–575.

[52] N.R. Pal, J.C. Bezdek and R. Hemasinha, *Uncertainty measures for evidential reasoning I: A review*, International Journal of Approximate Reasoning, 1992, Vol.7, pp.165–183.

[53] J.B. Paris and A. Vencovská, *Principles of uncertain reasoning*, Proceedings of the ICCS-91, San Sebastian, Spain.

[54] J.B. Paris and A. Vencovská, *Proof theory for inexact reasoning*, submitted for publication.

[55] J. Paris and A. Vencovská, *A note on the inevitability of maximum entropy*, International Journal of Approximate Reasoning, 1990, Vol.4, No.3, pp.183–224.

[56] J.B. Paris and A. Vencovská, *A method for updating that justifies minimum cross entropy*, International Journal of Approximate Reasoning, 1992, Vol.7, pp.1–8.

[57] J.B. Paris and A. Vencovská, *On the applicability of maximum entropy to inexact reasoning*, International Journal of Approximate Reasoning, 1989, Vol.3, No.1, pp.1–34.

[58] J. Pearl, *Probabilistic reasoning in intelligent systems: Networks of plausible inference*, San Mateo, Morgan Kaufmann, 1988.

[59] J. Pearl, *Fusion, propagation and structuring in belief networks*, Artificial Intelligence, 1986, Vol.29, pp.241–288.

[60] A. Perez, *The maximum entropy principle and the barycentre approach in knowledge integration*, Proceedings of the Third Joint Soviet–Swedish International Workshop on Information Theory, Sochi, USSR, 1987.

[61] F.P. Ramsey, *The foundations of mathematics and other logical essays*, London, 1931.

[62] A.J. Sanford and S.C. Garrod, *Understanding written language*, Wiley, 1981.

[63] G. Shafer, *A mathematical theory of evidence*, Princeton University Press, 1976.

[64] C.E. Shannon and W. Weaver, *The mathematical theory of communication*, University of Illinois Press, Urbana, Illinois, 1964.

[65] A. Shimony, *Coherence and the axioms of confirmation*, Journal of Symbolic Logic, 1955, Vol.20, pp.263–273.

[66] P. Suppes, *Probabilistic inference and the concept of total evidence*, in: Aspects of inductive logic, eds. J. Hintikka and P. Suppes, North-Holland, Amsterdam, 1966, pp.49–65.

[67] E. Trillas, *Sobre functiones de negacion en la teoria de conjunctos difusos*, Stochastica, 1979, Vol.3, No.1, pp.47–59.

[68] A. Tversky and D. Kahneman, *Judgement under uncertainty: Heuristics and biases*, Science, 1974, No.185, pp.1124–1131.

[69] L.G. Valiant and V.V. Vazirani, *NP is as easy as detecting unique solutions*, Theoretical Computer Science, 1986, Vol.47, pp.85–93.

[70] P.M. Williams, *Bayesian conditionalisation and the principle of minimum information*, British Journal for the Philosophy of Science, 1980, Vol.31, pp.131–144.

Index

accuracy 4, 104-105
Aczel, J. 25
affine set 66
approximation 158
atomicity principle 102-104
atoms 13-14
Artingstall, C. 109

basic probability assignement 35
    consonant 63
    vacuous 80
barycentre inference process 75
Bayesian updating 114-116, 119, 126,
    178, 195
belief 4-5
    as probability 17-33, 161-172
    as possibility 62
    conditional 4, 101, 158-159
    independent sources of 42
    consonant 63
    Shafer–Dempster 34-51, 79
    truth-functional 52-65, 80
    updating 113
belief functions 4
    conditional 4
    Dempster–Shafer 7-8, 34-51, 79, 82,
      145-146, 150
      conditional 42-48
    truth–functional 8, 52-65
belief network 134-138, 141, 155-159
belief revision 112-126
belief updating 112-126
belief values 4
    fair 20-23
Bellman, R.E. 56
Bertrand's paradox 71-72

betting 20
Blaschke metric 91,
Blaschke topology 92, 94
Boltzmann, L. 78
Boolean algebra 162-163, 165, 167
Brandeis dice problem 72-74

calibration 105-111
Carnap, R. 178, 185, 189-191, 199
Carnap's principles 178-197
Carnap's continuum of inductive
    methods 189-194, 195
causality 128
centre of mass inference process 69-70,
    72-75, 87, 89, 95, 98, 101, 150
    continuity 92
    equivalence 87
    independence 101
    language invariance 73
    obstinacy 99
    open mindedness 95
    relativization 100
    renaming 98
certainty factors 5
closed set 66
common sense 66, 67, 102, 104, 139,
    178
    principles 69, 82, 178
completely independent solution
    172-177, 178, 196
completeness theorem 161, 164
computational complexity 139-159
computational feasibility 4, 104,
    139-159
conditional
    beliefs 4, 101, 158-159

belief function 4
    Dempster–Shafer 42-48, 145
    constraints 8-9, 48, 112
    independence 127-128
    possibility 65
    odds 132
    probability 7, 11-12, 17-18, 101,
        112, 114
confidence coefficients 5
consistency 4, 66, 68, 82
    of a set of formulae in predicate
        calculus 164
    of a set of constraints 6, 161
        problem of checking 130, 139,
        141-148, 156
    of $K + K^\sigma$ 114
Consistency (problem) 142, 143
consonant
    basic probability assignement 63
continuity of an inference process
    89-94
Courtney, P. 90, 92, 128
convexity of V^L 66
Cook's theorem 140
Cooper, G.F. 156
countably additive measure 163
Cox, R.T. 24
Cox's theorem 24-32
cross entropy 118-126

de Finetti, B. 19
de Finetti's representation theorem
    185
Dempster, A.P. 34, 40
Dempster–Shafer belief functions 7-8,
    34-51, 79, 82, 145-146, 150
    conditional 42-48
    relation to probability 36-38, 39-42
    representation for 39
Dempster's rule of combination 42-44
Diaconis, P. 115
diagram of *Bel* 184-185

Dirichlet priors 73
disjoint (elements of a Boolean alg.)
    163
Dutch Book 20

Eggleston, H.G. 91
entropy 76-79, 121
equivalence principle 82-83, 87, 102
equivalence
    of sets of constraints 8-9, 82-83, 183
    logical 8
exclusive (formulae) 7
exhaustive set of formulae 118
expert system 1-2, 138
expert's knowledge 1, 67
    general 1, 113
    special 113

Fagin, R. 44, 48, 84, 173
Fagin's theorem 178
fairness 20-23
feasibility 4, 104, 139-159
Fine, T.L. 185
first symmetry principle 179
focal elements 63
Folger, T.A. 63
fourth symmetry principle 191
Fu, K.S. 56
Fung, L.W. 56
fuzzy logic 8, 52-62

Gaifman, H. 180
Gaifman's condition 162
Garey, M. 144
Georgakopoulos, G. 143
Giertz, M. 56
Gordon's theorem 85
graph
    directed, acyclic, finite 134

Hájek, P. 138
Halpern, J. 44, 48, 84
Heckerman, D. 132

Henkin style proof 164
Hobson, A. 121
Hopcroft, J.E. 140
Horwich, P. 105

imaginary causes 115
independence 127-138
    statistical 101, 128
    conditional 127
    principle 102, 198
    Prospector style 129-134
independent evidence 43
independent sources of belief 42
indifference principle 70-71, 96, 98-99,
        172
    weak 99
infeasibility 139-159
inference process 66-81, 82, 109, 179
    barycentre 75
    centre of mass 69-70, 72-75, 87, 89,
        95, 98, 101, 150
        continuity 92
        equivalence 87
        independence 101
        language invariance 73
        obstinacy 99
        open-mindedness 95
        relativization 100
        renaming 98
    for Dempster–Shafer belief 79-80
    language invariant 73-76, 148
    limit centre of mass 73-75, 87, 89,
        91, 95, 98, 101, 126, 150
        continuity 91
        equivalence 87
        independence 101
        language invariance 74-75
        obstinacy 99
        open-mindedness 95
        relativization 100
        renaming 98

maximum entropy 76, 78-79, 87, 91,
        95, 98, 101, 102, 120-126, 131,
        150, 198
        continuity 91
        equivalence 87
        independence 101
        language invariance 76, 79
        obstinacy 99
        open-mindedness 95
        relativization 100
        renaming 98
    minimum distance 76, 87, 89, 91,
        95, 98, 101, 126, 150
        continuity 91
        equivalence 87
        independence 101
        language invariance 76, 79
        obstinacy 99
        open-mindedness 95
        relativization 100
        renaming 98
    open-minded 95, 115, 120, 124
    for possibility 81
    statistical 69
    for truth-functional belief 80-81
information measure 76-78, 121-122
inner measure 48-50
instantial relevance principle 185
intractability 139-159
irrelevant information
    principle 87-89, 102

Jaffray, J.Y. 44
Jaynes, E.T. 72
Jeffrey's rule 116
Jeffrey's updating 116-118, 119
Johnson, D. 144
Johnson, R.W. 132
Johnson's sufficientness principle 191
Johnson, W.E. 190, 191

Kahneman, D. 128

Kavvadias, D. 143
Kemeny, J.G. 19
Klir, G.J. 63
knowledge base 1, 67, 68, 113
Kreinovich, V.Ya. 58
Kullback–Leibler divergence 119
Kyburg, H.E. 40

Lagrange multiplier equations 131
language invariance 73-76, 89, 96, 148,
        150, 197, 198
    centre of mass inference process 73
    limit centre of mass inference
        process 74-75
    maximum entropy inference process
        76, 79
    minimum distance inference process
        76, 79
Laplace's principle 70
Lehner, P. 105, 106, 109
limit centre of mass inference process
        73-75, 87, 89, 91, 95, 98, 101,
        126, 150
    continuity 91
    equivalence 87
    independence 101
    language invariance 74-75
    obstinacy 99
    open-mindedness 95
    relativization 100
    renaming 98
Lindenbaum algebra 34, 149, 162
linear programming 142
logical equivalence 8

Maung, I. 81, 91, 148
maximum entropy inference process
        76, 78-79, 87, 91, 95, 98, 101,
        102, 120-126, 131, 150, 198
    continuity 91
    equivalence 87
    independence 101

language invariance 76, 79
obstinacy 99
open-mindedness 95
relativization 100
renaming 98
measure 19, 48, 163, 165
    countably additive 163
    inner 48-50
    of information 76-78, 121-122
    of non-specificity 80
    outer 50-51, 165
    σ-measure 163
Mendelson, E. 161, 171
Megiddo, N. 84
Miller, D. 98, 191
minimum cross entropy updating
        118-126
    justification for 120-126
minimum distance inference process
        76, 87, 89, 91, 95, 98, 101, 126,
        150
    continuity 91
    equivalence 87
    independence 101
    language invariance 76, 79
    obstinacy 99
    open-mindedness 95
    relativization 100
    renaming 98

necessity 63
non-deterministic polynomial time
        (problem) 139
non-deterministic Turing machine 140
nonspecificity 80
    measures 80
NP 139
NP-complete problem 140, 141, 145,
        146, 156

obstinacy principle 99, 102, 109
odds

conditional 132
open-mindedness principle 95, 102
open-minded inference process 95, 115,
120, 124
outer measure 50-51, 165

P 139
$P \neq NP$ 37, 145, 146, 148, 156, 157
Papadimitriou, C. 143
Pearl, J. 128, 134, 138
plausibility 38, 43, 63-64
polynomial time (problem) 139
possibility 62-65, 81
conditional 65
possible structures 178
possible worlds 19,, 48, 67, 70, 173, 178
predicate calculus 160, 161
principle
Laplace's 70
equivalence 82-83, 87, 102
independence 102, 198
indifference 70-71, 96, 98-99, 172
weak 99
instantial relevance 185
irrelevant information 87-89, 102
language invariance 73-76, 89, 96,
148, 150, 197, 198
obstinacy 99, 102, 109
open-mindedness 95, 102
relativization 100, 102, 198
renaming 71, 95-98, 102, 109, 148,
197
weak 97
symmetry
first 179
second 183
third 183
fourth 191
principles 82-111, 178-199
Carnap's 178-197
common sense 69, 82, 178
probabilistic approximation 158

probability 10-33
as willingness to bet 19-23
conditional 7, 11-12, 17-18, 101,
112, 114
density function 195
functions
real 69
representation for 13-14, 164-172
sets of 40-41
of learning the truth of ϕ 37
propositional calculus 4, 9, 13
propositional language 4, 5, 9
proof theory for uncertain reasoning
83-87
Prospector 129, 131
style independence 129
problem
2-*Consistency* 143-144
2-*SAT* 144
3-*SAT* 144, 148, 155, 156
Chromatic Number 144
computationally infeasible 139-140,
148, 156, 158
Consistency 142, 143
intractable 139
non-deterministic polynomial time
139
NP-complete 140, 141, 145, 146,
156
of computing an approximation to
Bel 139, 148-159
of consistency testing 139, 141-148,
156
polynomial time 139
random polynomial time 140
SAT 140,142, 144, 146-148, 153-154
PV-updating 123-126

question Q 6, 9, 14-15, 51, 61, 67, 68,
78, 160
question Q' 161, 172, 179, 183

Ramsey, F.P. 19

random polynomial time (problem)
        140
random Turing machine 140, 150, 158
rationality 20, 82, 102, 104
renaming principle 71, 95-98, 102, 109,
        148, 197
    weak 97
relativization principle 100, 102, 198
representation for probability
        functions 13-14, 164-172
    representation of DS-belief
        functions 39
RP 140, 150, 153, 154
RP ≠ *NP* 141, 150, 158

satisfiability 140
scaling 58-59
second symmetry principle 183
Shafer, G. 34
Shannon, G.E. 77
Shannon measure of uncertainty 76-78
    relative 119, 120-126
Shimony, A. 19
state descriptions 171
statistical
    independence 101, 128
    methods of inference 69
Stockmeyer, L. 144
Suppes, P. 12
symmetry (principles)
    first 179
    second 183
    third 183
    fourth 191

T-conorm 60
term structure 162-164, 172
third symmetry principle 183
T-norm 55
Trillas, E. 55
truth values 4-5
truth-functional belief 8, 52-65
    inference processes for 80
Tversky, A. 128

Ullman, J.D. 140
updating
    Bayesian 114-116, 119, 126, 178,
        195
    Jeffrey's 116-118, 119
    minimum cross entropy 118-126
    PV-updating 123-126
urn model 18, 37

Valiant, L.G. 151
valuation 10, 18, 52
van Fraassen, B.C. 116
Vazirani, V.V. 151
Vencovská, A. 74, 102

Watts Assumption 67, 68, 82, 105,
        113, 127, 130, 134, 135, 141, 143,
        154, 155, 159
weak principle of indifference 99
weak renaming principle 97
Weaver, W. 77
Williams, P.M. 119

Zabell, S. 115